Good
Old Days
Good
Old Ways

GOOD OLD DAYS, GOOD OLD WAYS
First edition 1999
Published by Reader's Digest (Australia) Pty Limited, 26–32 Waterloo Street, Surry Hills, NSW 2010
Copyright © 1999 Reader's Digest (Australia) Pty Ltd
Copyright © 1999 Reader's Digest (New Zealand) Ltd
Copyright © 1999 Reader's Digest Association Far East Ltd
Philippines copyright © 1999 Reader's Digest Far East Ltd

National Library of Australia Cataloguing-in-Publication data:

Good old days, good old ways: wisdom of the past for the needs of today.

Includes index.
ISBN 0 86449 377 0.

1. Home economics. 2. Gardening. 3. Games. 4. Beauty, Personal. I. Reader's Digest (Australia). II. Title.

640

Colour separations by Rainbow Graphics Arts Co. Ltd, Hong Kong
Printed and bound by Dai Nippon Printing Company (HK) Ltd, Hong Kong

READER'S DIGEST

Good Old Days Good Old Ways

WISDOM OF THE PAST FOR THE NEEDS OF TODAY

Reader's Digest • Sydney • Auckland

Project Editor
Janet Healey

Assistant Editor
Catherine Magoffin

Designer
Robyn Latimer

Contributors

Consultants
Roy Edwards, Kim Fletcher, Les Miller,
Andree Movsessian, Maurice Saxby

Writers/Researchers
Maggie Aldhamland, Wendy Blaxland,
Janet Healey, Margaret McPhee,
Judith Simpson, Beverley Weynton

Picture Researcher
Joanna Collard

Photographers
John Hollingshead, John Paul Urizar

Stylists
Barbara Beckett, Louise Owens

Illustrator
Janet Jones

Indexer
Barbara Crighton

Proofreader
Laraine Newberry

Production Controller
Bruce Holden

Reader's Digest General Books

Editorial Director
Carol Natsis

Art Director
Phillip Bush

Managing Editor
Averil Moffat

About this book

S ince about 1950, lifestyles in the industrialised world have changed dramatically. Not only has the pace of living increased, but technological advances have meant that more and more aspects of daily life have become mechanised. Clean, temperature-controlled electric and gas cooking and heating have replaced wood and coal firing; washing machines, clothes dryers, dishwashers and vacuum cleaners have done away with much of the hard labour that was once associated with domestic chores; and faxes, the internet and jet travel have revolutionised the way we spend our leisure time. Most importantly, perhaps, innovations in communications and transportation have altered the very structure of society; we are now more mobile, but we no longer live in small, community-based groups but as individuals who are often isolated from our fellows.

We are all caught up in this flurry of development, but in embracing technological change we risk losing a great treasure: the sense of continuity and the satisfaction of tasks completed by our own hand. Past generations inherited and handed down household skills and techniques and used precious leisure time for creative pursuits or for cementing friendships and social relationships.

The writers of *Good Old Days, Good Old Ways* have delved into forgotten corners of libraries and dusty attics to rediscover some of these time-tested, economical and environmentally friendly practices. The book is a storehouse of wisdom from the past about organising your kitchen; cooking for your family and friends; keeping your house clean and tidy; carrying out simple home maintenance; caring for clothes and household linen; looking after your garden; staying healthy and treating common ailments at home; making your own beauty products; teaching children life skills through play; and spending your leisure time creatively. There are also illustrated step-by-step instructions for simple but useful skills such as sharpening a chisel and making a kite, all drawn from sources published between 1850 and 1950.

In addition, on every page you'll find reproductions of photographs, engravings and advertisements that will bring those half-remembered days vividly to mind, as well as evocative quotations from magazines, novels, memoirs, poems and rhymes that will shed light on life as it was in those earlier times. And finally, interspersed in the text are intriguing snippets of historical information about the people, the discoveries and the inventions that profoundly influenced everyday life in the hundred years from 1850 to 1950, such as Michael Faraday's discovery of electromagnetic induction, which made possible the harnessing of electrical power.

We at Reader's Digest are confident that you will derive as much information, pleasure and sheer fun from reading this book as we have acquired in making it.

The editors

Contents

THE HEART OF THE HOME

The ideal kitchen 12
Equipping your kitchen 14
My keen knife 16
Tinker, tailor 18
Good old wood 19
Whose turn is it? 20
In place and at hand 23
Cookers and coolers 24
A pinch of this 26
Waste not 28
Shoo fly 30
Blooming lovely 32
Safety in the kitchen 34

EAT, DRINK AND BE MERRY

Clues for home cooks 38
Feed the man meat 41
Season to taste 46
A pretty kettle of fish 48
Delicacies from Down Under 52
Nature's nourishment .54
The staff of life 59
Cooks and books 64
Eat up your vegies 66
Pickles and preserves .68
What's for afters? 70
The cup that cheers 71

NEAT AS A NEW PIN

Paint, polish and wallpaper 76
Hanging on the wall 82
A touch of class 84
Light and shade 86
Mopping up 88
Colour your world 90
Heaven scent 93
Window dressing 94
Full many a flower 97
Fun with flowers 98
All that glitters 100
Feeding the furniture 102
Splish, splash! 105
Keeping an orderly house 106
The versatile veranda 112

ON THE HOME FRONT

Surveying your castle 116
Jewels of tools 118
A place for everything 120
Piping sweetly 122
Let there be light 124
Open, sesame! 125
Look out below 126
Around and above us 128
Clues with glue 130
As good as new 132
Reflections 137
Don't let the bugs bite 138
Cosy and warm 140
A room with a view 142
Lay them straight 145
A roof over our heads 146
Outside the house 147

SOAPSUDS AND STITCHES

Pre-wash rituals 150
A stitch in time 152
Out, damned spot! 154
Rub-a-dub-dub 156
Sunshine and breezes 160
The smoothing iron 162
A glorious washing day 164
Ring up the curtain! 166
Cleaning without water 168
In store and transit 170
Colour changes 172
Making over and making do 175
New lease of life 178
Patchwork pieces 180
Hand and foot 182
Hat tricks 184

HOW DOES YOUR GARDEN GROW?

Planning your old-world garden 188
Tools of the trade 190
The good earth 191
The everyday miracle 192
In the beginning 194
The water of life 198
Friends and foes 199
Designing women 202
Animals in the garden 204
Warmth and shelter 205
The kindly fruits of the earth 207
Harvest home 209
Making the most of your garden 210
Birds in the high hall-garden 214
Indoor gardens 216
Enclosures 219
Lawns and pathways 222
Completing the picture 224

SOVEREIGN REMEDIES

Health and long life 228
Cool, clear water 232
Good old ways with common ills 234
Nature's remedies 240
Colds and flu 246
Life savers 248
I'm not hungry 250
Home nursing 252
Looking after the little ones 256
When new ways are better 260

SHE WALKS IN BEAUTY

The basics of beauty 264
Facing the world 266
Gilding the lily 272
A pair of sparkling eyes 274
Smiling through 277
The crowning glory 279
Hairstyles in history 284
The body beautiful.......................286
Rubbed the right way 292
Perfect presentation 294

CHILD'S PLAY

BC – before computers 298
Come out to play 300
Knucklebones 305
Blowing in the wind 306
For a rainy day 308
Hanky panky 314
Deal them out 316
String and things 318
A good read 320
Tricks of the trade 322
Party time! 325

FUN AND GAMES

Stepping out 330
Picnic frolics 333
Tell me a story 335
Your move 336
Let's party! 338
Cross the gypsy's palm 343
Beside the seaside 344
Going to the fair 346
Most sincerely yours 348
On the air 350
Playing the game 352
Happy travelling 353
Under canvas 355
Merry Christmas! 358

INDEX 360

ACKNOWLEDGMENTS 367

The heart

of the home

TIME-TESTED WAYS TO MAKE YOUR
KITCHEN A PLEASANT PLACE TO WORK

The ideal kitchen

FORETHOUGHT IS THE KEY TO SUCCESS — AND
NOWHERE IS THIS MORE IMPORTANT THAN IN
PLANNING YOUR KITCHEN.

We have come a long way from the huge, gloomy kitchens of
the Victorian era, which used to be separate from the rest of
the house in case they caught fire, and from the resolutely
bright kitchens of the 1950s. But the principles of working
in an organised and cheerful environment have not changed.

WHERE SHOULD THE KITCHEN BE? Mrs Isabella Beeton, whose
books on cookery and domestic economy have initiated
generations of Englishwomen into the mysteries of running a
home, described the kitchen as 'the great laboratory of every
household.' These days, decisions about the size and position
of rooms in a building are usually left to the architect or the
builder, and few home owners have any say in the matter.

However, if you do get the chance to voice your opinion, Mrs
Beeton's guiding principles represent the accumulated wisdom of
many years. She advocated: 'convenience of distribution in its parts,
with largeness and dimension; excellence of light, height of ceiling
and good ventilation; easiness of access, without passing through the
house; plenty of fuel and water which, with the scullery, pantry and
storeroom, should be so near it as to offer the smallest possible trouble
in reaching them.'

ORGANISING THE KITCHEN Arrange your kitchen so that everything
is within easy reach, without too much stooping or stretching.

Working space Your main kitchen working areas — the stove, the
sink and the work bench — must be as close together as possible. They
should provide an uninterrupted surface, and the space encompassed
by them should not have to carry any through traffic.

Storage The general principle is to keep things as close as possible to
where they will be used, and to store things that you use all the time
in convenient places. Carry built-in cupboards right up to the ceiling
to provide extra storage space and prevent dirt accumulating on top.

Some foodstuffs require special storage: for instance, keep root
vegetables in the dark, store bread in a cool place, and — in cool
climate areas — do not store eggs near strong-smelling items.

TIME AND MOTION TIPS *Within the Home*, published in 1924, informed
readers that 'the first consideration in arranging kitchen equipment is
to save steps and labour. The kitchen should be clean, odourless and
attractive.' A couple of labour-saving tips from the past will make
your kitchen tasks easier.

*The 19th century kitchen was
kept separate from the rest of the
house, and in the larger houses
was the servants' domain.*

A KITCHEN SCENE
'He kissed the maid in the kitchen, and
seemed upon the whole a most loving,
kissing, kind-hearted gentleman.'
– LETTERS TO THE REV. J. NEWTON,
WILLIAM COWPER (1731–1800)

One is to use a wheeled trolley to take crockery, cutlery and serving dishes to and from the table. This saves endless trips and conserves your time and energy. A trolley can also provide useful temporary bench space in the kitchen.

Another is to keep a comfortable stool in the kitchen, and work seated whenever you can to save your legs and back.

DECOR Modern kitchens tend to be smaller than those of earlier days, and the time-honoured rule that a small or dark room needs a light colour scheme is particularly applicable.

Colour schemes For a kitchen with a cool outlook, *The Happy Home*, published in the 1950s, suggested cream picked out with signal red, or light beige and forest green. If your kitchen has a warm outlook, try a blend of white or silver-grey and steel blue. Use washable paint.

Floor coverings The ideal floor covering for a kitchen should be unaffected by grease, easily cleaned, warm, quiet and easy on the feet. Fruit juices and other foods should not leave permanent stains. It should also be resilient to minimise breakages.

On cement or tile floors, use rubber mats in front of the sink, stove and working benches to protect washers-up and cooks from sore feet.

LIGHT AND AIR Good lighting is important if you want to work easily in your kitchen, and to keep it cheerful too. If you can, have two or three windows in two walls in your kitchen and a glass pane in the kitchen door. Hang mirrors in dark corners to reflect the light and increase the apparent space. It is essential that the main working areas – the stove, sink and bench – be well lit.

The kitchen should be as airy as possible; make sure windows can be opened at both the bottom and the top. In a single-storey house a skylight is a plus for both lighting and ventilation.

Condensation is a common problem, even in well ventilated kitchens, but our grandmothers had some effective ways of dealing with it. If your kitchen walls run with moisture, wipe them with a lambswool polisher dipped in hot water and a little cloudy ammonia; for walls that are not badly marked with steam, omit the ammonia. Prevent condensation on glass by rubbing it with a cloth dipped in a mixture of equal parts of glycerine and methylated spirits.

CLEANING THE KITCHEN Because of what goes on in kitchens, they need constant cleaning. Keep the kitchen clean and neat, and it will be cheerful to work in, and easier too.

The weekly clean A typical cleaning routine from the early 1900s, modified here for a modern kitchen, lists these tasks for a weekly kitchen turn-out:
- Sweep the ceiling, walls and floor.
- Scrub the draining board and sink and clean and deodorise the drain with a solution of hot water and washing soda.
- Wipe down all surfaces.
- Wash the windows.
- Clean and polish the floor.

Oil and grease collect on the surface of the stove every time you cook a meal, making regular cleaning essential.

Equipping your kitchen

KITCHEN TASKS DO NOT CHANGE, BUT THE EQUIPMENT AVAILABLE TO PERFORM THEM HAS DEVELOPED DRAMATICALLY IN THE PAST HUNDRED YEARS.

Mrs Beeton's famous *Book of Cookery and Household Management*, published in 1861, included in its list of important equipment a toasting fork, a bottle jack, a candle box, a cinder-sifter, four iron stewpans, a dripping pan, two fish kettles, a pepper box, a pair of bellows and three jelly moulds. Fifty years later, a typical list of essential kitchen equipment published in a home management handbook included a rolling pin (glass if possible), an egg whisk, a meat safe and meat cover, a millet broom, a hair broom, a Turk's head broom, a polishing mop and vacuum cleaner or carpet sweeper, and a scrubbing brush and kneeling pad, as well as soup plates, dinner plates, dessert plates, bread and butter plates, sauce boats and jam dishes, egg spoons and a mustard pot – and noted that 'this provides for bare necessities'!

The amount of equipment you need will depend on your living space, your lifestyle and your budget – but remember that it is perfectly possible to cook delicious family meals and to entertain in style with the bare minimum of equipment, provided you buy sensibly in the first place.

TRADITIONAL EQUIPMENT FOR A MODERN KITCHEN Nowadays a microwave oven and a dishwasher are likely to take priority over three different brooms, but there are some kitchen items that are as useful now as they have been for decades. Electric kettles have been on the market since 1923, pop-up toasters since 1927 and electric food processors since 1936.

As well as these not-so-modern automated aids, your kitchen should contain a basic inventory of traditional equipment, such as mixing bowls, wooden spoons, a rolling pin, a potato masher, an egg beater, a flour sieve, a colander, a rubber spatula and a set of kitchen knives – the best you can afford.

Measuring devices Measuring jugs, cups and spoons and a reliable set of kitchen scales take the guesswork out of cooking. The old advice was to use metal measuring containers for hot liquids and glass containers for other ingredients, but modern heatproof glass will withstand most hot liquids except boiling fat or oil. Glass has the further advantage of being see-through, permitting accurate measurement by eye.

Graters Properly designed graters will grate your ingredients without grating your fingers. Regardless of its shape, make sure your grater is of metal strong enough to keep it rigid at all times. If you are

The range of kitchen utensils is enormous and every cook has a favourite, but most could hardly be considered essential.

a keen cook, you may want to provide yourself with a large grater for cheese and vegetables and a small one for lemon and orange zest and spices such as nutmeg.

CLEANING EQUIPMENT Kitchen floors need frequent and thorough cleaning. The best tools are still an old-fashioned broom, brush and dustpan for dry fragments and a floor mop and bucket for liquid spills. For benches, have cloths that can be disinfected by boiling or bleaching. For washing up you will need dish cloths, a dish mop and a pot scrubber.

Tea towels Pure linen tea towels or glass towels are the best buy. It is false economy to buy cheap tea towels – there is nothing more frustrating than trying to dry glass with a cloth that will not absorb moisture, or one that deposits lint on the glass.

Hand towels If you use a roller towel for drying your hands in the kitchen, Turkish towelling is a good choice because it will stand up to hard wear and washing.

SERVING EQUIPMENT From time to time in the past, tableware has become very elaborate in design and consequently hard to clean, but both taste and common sense tend to ensure that simple, easy-care designs will always reassert their popularity.

China and glass Choose a simple pattern and a practical design: for instance, make sure that the cups sit steadily in their saucers and that the handles are easy for a normal hand to grasp. Serving dishes should not have awkward knobs and handles. Jugs and carafes should be easy to lift and manipulate, with lips that pour well.

Coffee pots and teapots Make sure they have handles that do not become too hot to hold, spouts that pour properly and do not dribble, and smooth inner surfaces that are easy to clean. Keep coffee pots and teapots scrupulously clean; coffee and tea can leave deposits of oil or tannin that will contaminate the next brew that you make.

'LABOUR-SAVING' GADGETS According to Mrs C. S. Peel, 'The greatest labour-saving Apparatus which we possess is the brain; it has not been worn out by too much use' (*The Labour-Saving House*, published in 1917). This advice is as sensible now as it was 80 years ago; give some thought to what equipment you really need in the kitchen, bearing in mind the space constraints in a modern kitchen and the time constraints of modern life.

A lemon squeezer of maple and porcelain

Getting rid of useless gadgets From time to time, everybody buys kitchen gadgets that are never used and that merely occupy valuable space and collect grime. Take the time to make a clean sweep of everything that is cluttering up your kitchen. Get out all your kitchen gadgets and get rid of anything that you never use or that is broken or duplicated. Have the strength of mind not to hang onto something 'in case it comes in useful'. Well placed hooks and shelving will keep your kitchen benches clear and let you put your essential gadgets where you can easily reach them.

An old-fashioned dustpan is still indispensable for sweeping up dry spillages and any breakages.

WHAT AM I?
What is as round as a dishpan,
   as deep as a tub,
And still the ocean cannot fill it up?
[Answer: A sieve]

My keen knife

'THERE IS NO GREATER SOURCE OF KITCHEN
SATISFACTION THAN A GOOD KNIFE — AND
NO GREATER SOURCE OF ANNOYANCE
THAN A POOR ONE.'

So wrote H. Bennett in *More for Your Money*, published in
1937. Knives have existed ever since humans needed to first
kill then carve up their prey, but even as late as medieval times
most men owned only one knife, which hung at their belt,
ready to cut throats or carve meat. Only the wealthy could
afford special knives for table use. Forks arrived much
later in history, being in general use in Europe in the
17th century, but even after they caught on, many people
continued to use a combination of their fingers and an all-purpose knife
to eat their food. A knife and fork made a prestigious wedding present
for a bride, who would wear them on her belt in a decorated sheath.

*The Victorians were prolific
inventors of household gadgets.
This knife-cleaning machine
solved the problem of washing
ivory-handled knives.*

CHOOSING YOUR KNIVES Sharp-edged, well made knives make every
kitchen job much easier. The quality of a knife depends on the quality
and temper of the steel, the shape of the blade, the quality of the
handle, and the way the blade and handle are joined.

Don't economise on knives; buy the best you can afford, making sure
that the handle is durable and firmly attached to the shank of the
blade. A handle shaped to fit your hand is best. The shank of the blade
should extend the full length of the handle, and should be secured
with large, firm rivets. Do not buy cheap knives with shanks that
taper to a point and are anchored to the handle with a brad or a metal
collar; the handle will work loose and the knife will be difficult to use.

KNIVES FOR ALL REASONS Different kitchen knives are designed for
different purposes, and using the right knife will lead to quicker and
better work. The number of knives you need will depend on how
much cooking you do and at what level. For most people, the
following set of knives will meet all needs.

Cook's knife The most versatile and indispensable of kitchen knives —
if you can afford only one good kitchen knife, make it a cook's knife.
It should have a 20-cm blade that tapers to a point, and can be used
to cut and chop just about every foodstuff, from raw meat to herbs.
Choose a good carbon steel blade with a handle roomy enough to
prevent your fingers being cramped.

Paring knife A small, pointed knife with a 10-cm blade, used to peel
and slice vegetables and fruits. Some types of paring knives have
serrated edges, which are particularly useful for slicing fruit.

Bread knife A long-bladed knife (26 cm) with a serrated or saw edge.
Bread knives with scalloped edges will not cut as well. The blade of a
bread knife should be stiff rather than flexible.

Words of Wisdom

Ross Campbell, a well loved
Australian humorous writer,
pinpointed the importance of
knives in domestic life:

'Women often become very fond
of knives. I don't mean women
of the Carmen type, who carry a
stiletto in their garter to use on
erring boyfriends. I mean
women who use knives for
peeling potatoes and other
kitchen tasks …

Most women love only one
knife at a time. My wife has
been devoted for years to a small
one, nothing much to look at,
which she calls "my knife". If
one of the children takes her
knife to sharpen coloured pencils
and doesn't bring it back, there
is a fuss. She feels as lost without
her knife as Wyatt Earp when he
has mislaid his gun or Robin
Hood during an arrow shortage.'

— *THE AUSTRALIAN WOMEN'S WEEKLY*
(1959)

Carving knife A well tempered carbon steel knife with a narrow, flexible blade about 20 cm long.
Palette knife This knife is not used for cutting, but has a flexible blade for lifting and turning food and scraping out mixing bowls.
Kitchen shears A useful accessory for jointing chickens, ducks and rabbits, and for preparing fish. Some types of poultry shears can be dismantled for easier cleaning and sharpening.

CARING FOR KNIVES Keep your kitchen knives sharp; they will be easier to use and also less dangerous, since you do not need to exert so much pressure when cutting. Give them a few strokes with a steel or a sharpening stone before and after use – yes, every time! – and have them professionally sharpened at regular intervals.

Avoid patent knife sharpeners with two sets of concentric steel discs; they will ruin your knives.

Wash kitchen knives individually by hand, using cold or lukewarm water, dry them thoroughly and store them in a wooden knife block or with the blades sheathed. Never heat a knife blade in a flame, since this will destroy the temper of the steel.

Rusty knives Soak rusty knives in raw linseed oil for a few hours and you will be able to wipe off the rust and polish the knives with emery paper. Rub the rusty steel in one direction with emery paper sprinkled with paraffin, and finish with an old cloth.

Stained blades Clean stained knife blades with emery paper rubbed with a slice of raw potato.

Stained knife handles Old-fashioned ivory handles can be restored by rubbing them with salt moistened with lemon juice.

EMERGENCY CORKSCREWS If you have mislaid the corkscrew, stick two forks vertically into the cork on opposite sides of it, not too near the edge. Run the blade of a stout knife through the prongs of the forks and twist as you would an ordinary corkscrew. Another emergency method is to tie a string to an ordinary large screw and screw it well into the cork; provided the cork is sound, a steady, gentle pull on the string should dislodge all but the most stubborn cork.

A set of high quality kitchen knives is a keen cook's pride, to be tended lovingly and sharpened regularly.

Tinker, tailor

IF YOU ARE LUCKY, YOU MAY HAVE INHERITED SOME OF THOSE DEEP, ROUND-BELLIED COOKING POTS THAT GRACED THE KITCHENS OF OLD.

Even so, from time to time you will need to buy new cooking utensils, whether you are setting up house, buying a wedding present or replenishing your own stock of cookware.

TIPS FOR CHOOSING COOKWARE The pots you buy will have to last for a long while; choose carefully and make sure you select pots and pans with guarantees, so that if they are faulty they can be replaced.
• Pots should be of good quality, but not necessarily heavy; a fairly lightweight pan is suited to oven-top gas cooking.
• Pots should be well balanced, with no tendency to tip.
• Lids should fit tightly or cooking efficiency will be lowered.
• Handles should not conduct heat, and should be designed so that the pot can be comfortably and safely moved about.
• Straight-sided pans with flat bottoms that completely cover the heating unit are the most economical, as they use less fuel.

WHICH MATERIAL? There will always be controversy about the best material for pots and pans. All materials have their advantages.

Aluminium is light and conducts heat well, but thin aluminium pans will quickly lose their shape, burn food, and waste fuel because they do not retain heat.

Iron is durable, conducts heat well and is easy to clean. But iron pots need a breaking-in period, are heavy and will rust if they are not kept dry and greased. Heat new cast-iron cookware gradually the first time it is used to prevent warping and cracking. You should baptise a new ironware frying pan by boiling vinegar in it and then rinsing it thoroughly.

Enamelware absorbs heat rapidly but does not conduct it evenly, so food may burn before it is thoroughly cooked. Make sure the base is heavy enough so that the utensil will not warp and crack the enamel coating.

Glass, earthenware and stoneware oven dishes conduct heat slowly but evenly. They can be taken straight from the oven to the table, and are easy to clean. But sudden temperature changes may cause them to crack.

"MY VIMMY"

Precious iron and enamelware pots deserve to be looked after. When commercial cleaning products first became available, the claims were both many and miraculous.

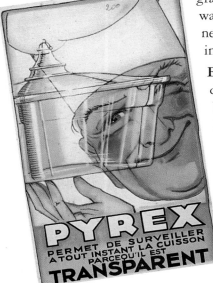

PYREX
PERMET DE SURVEILLER A TOUT INSTANT LA CUISSON PARCEQU'IL EST
TRANSPARENT

Taking Care of the Pence

To clean burnt aluminium saucepans, rub them with rotten apples and then use a scouring powder.

Good old wood

THE UNASSUMING WOODEN
SPOON AND BOARD ARE
THE KEEN COOK'S SILENT BUT
FAITHFUL ACCOMPLICES.

There is nothing like the feel of a wooden spoon that has stirred its way through years of good food, or the worn but welcoming smoothness of a pastry board that has helped you to satisfy healthy appetites for decades. And wood has practical advantages too: it is hard-wearing, easy to handle and care for and inexpensive to replace.

WOODEN SPOONS Wooden spoons are indispensable in the kitchen; they are quiet to use, comfortable to handle, easy to clean, and do not scratch enamel or fragile nonstick surfaces.

They are versatile too: you can use the same wooden spoon for everything from scrambled eggs to jam making. However, do keep one wooden spoon just for curry, because the flavours penetrate the wood and will migrate to everything else the spoon touches.

Slotted wooden cake spoons are best for beating cake mixtures, because they incorporate more air into the mixture.

WOODEN BOARDS Kitchen boards should consist of one piece and, for ease of working and cleaning, should be smooth and free from flaws.

Pastry boards should be big enough to take fairly large sheets of pastry. Treat them with care; scraping them with a knife or scrubbing them with abrasives will roughen the surface and spoil your pastry. To save scrubbing, rub a pastry board with a crust of fresh bread to remove the dough and grease and leave the board clean and dry.

Chopping boards are smaller, thicker and heavier than pastry boards. Wash cutting boards after use to prevent stains and odours from clinging to them. Very bad marks can be removed by scrubbing with a scrubbing brush sprinkled with a little powdered eggshell.

ROLLING PINS Hardwoods are best for rolling pins, which should be heavy and smooth. Rolling pins are available in different lengths.

LOOKING AFTER WOODEN KITCHENWARE Wood will serve you well if you follow these few simple rules.

Hard brushes and abrasive cleaners will tear the fibres of wood and take out the softer parts, and abrasive cleaners and scrubbing across the grain will cut the fibres. Scrub wood in cold or lukewarm water with a soft brush; hot water softens and swells the fibres.

Wood warps if it is exposed to a hot fire, or even strong sunlight, and also if it is left wet for any length of time. After washing wood, wipe it and let it dry in an airy place.

The kitchen dresser arrived in the 18th century with the advent of cheap wooden tableware. Before that time, kitchen utensils were stored in separate repositories.

Hard-wearing, resilient wood has been used to make all manner of kitchen implements. This early 19th century bowl and roller set was designed for crushing oats.

Whose turn is it?

REMEMBER THE SECRETS SHARED OVER SOAPSUDS
AND TEA TOWELS, AND THE GOOD FEELING WHEN
THE PILES OF DISHES HAD BEEN VANQUISHED?

Constant hot water, modern detergents and dishwashers have taken much of the hard work out of washing up, but there are still items such as silver and heirloom china that must be washed by hand with special care. In the days of large households, dishwashing was a fine art, and we can still learn from those days and share the labour and the confidences with a family member or a friend.

MATERIALS Like any job that has to be tackled over and over again, washing up is easier if you have the right materials. Make sure you start with a clean sink and plugs that fit firmly into the drain and will not be dislodged by cutlery.

Water Our grandmothers did not have unlimited supplies of hot water, so they would scrape and rinse dishes before washing up to avoid having to keep heating fresh water. Follow their example and save both water and power.

Cleaning agents Modern detergents are easier to wash up with than soap, but because they are liquid it is very easy to use too much. Whichever cleaning agent you use, follow the example of the past and be economical – you will save money and help to protect the environment.

Rubber gloves Keep a pair of rubber gloves for washing up only. When the rubber starts to wear and crack, replace them; they can still do duty protecting your hands while you clean the silver. Wash greasy rubber gloves while they are still on your hands with warm soapy water and then rinse them in clean cold water.

Dishcloths, dish mops and sponges Have separate dishcloths for greasy pans, greasy dishes, and nongreasy plates, and boil them regularly. If you use a dish mop, wash it well in hot soapy lather, rinse it thoroughly and wring it out. Shake out the head and stand the mop head up in an empty jar to dry.

To refresh kitchen sponges, dissolve a large handful of salt and a tablespoon of washing soda in a litre of warm water and immerse the sponges in the solution. Rinse them in several changes of cold water.

METHOD A systematic approach makes any task easier, and washing up is no exception. Collect everything together at the end of the bench nearest the kitchen sink. Put away leftovers and scrape and rinse the plates. Arrange china neatly into piles and put all the cutlery together.

Washing dishes can be a dreary task if you tackle it alone. Chatting with a friend while you share the work makes the experience more enjoyable.

Cutlery is quite easy to clean but silver tends to stain. A little salt rubbed on the discoloured area should remove the blemish.

Wash the cleanest items first – the order will usually be glasses, then dishes, then cutlery, and finally pots and pans. A folded towel in the bottom of the sink or washbasin is good insurance against breakages when washing your best china and crystal.

GLASS Waterford crystal or Woolworths special, glass dresses up a table and makes the simplest meal into a treat. But glass must be glittering with cleanliness; the tiniest touch of grease will show up as an ugly smear.

Tumblers and wine glasses A dish mop is the best tool for washing drinking glasses; it reaches to the bottom of the glass, cleans lipstick and grease from the rims and minimises the risk of breakages. After washing, rinse glasses thoroughly in hot water to remove detergent, upend them on a folded tea towel to dry, and polish with a glass cloth.

Decanters Wine always throws a slight deposit that is liable to stain the insides of decanters where a mop or bottle brush can't reach. To clean a decanter, try this trick from the good old days. Put in a tablespoon of baking soda and crushed eggshells, fill the decanter with warm water and soak it. Rinse the decanter well after cleaning.

PLATES AND DISHES Most plates and dishes nowadays are fairly sturdy; simply wash them in hot water and detergent, making sure you clean the undersides as well as the tops, rinse in hot water and leave them to drain.

Fine china Don't put fine china into very hot water, because it is apt to crack and break. Try this old method of washing china: put it into a large saucepan with several sheets of newspaper between each piece, fill the saucepan with cold water and bring it slowly to the boil. After a few minutes, take the pan away from the heat and leave the china in the water until it is cold.

Milk jugs Milk rapidly becomes rancid and the taste and odour are hard to get rid of. Rinse milk jugs well in cold water, then steep them in very hot soapy water, and lastly rinse in cold water.

Stained dishes Remove tea and coffee stains from cups and mugs by rubbing them with kitchen salt while the china is still wet. When dishes become discoloured from being placed in the oven, rub them with scouring powder and then wash them as usual.

THE FIRST DISHWASHERS
These helpful additions to any kitchen were invented in the middle of the 19th century. The 'Polliwashup' of the 1920s asked the housewife to add water from a boiling kettle, use a tablet of soap to make a lather, and turn a handle six times in each direction. Clothes washers were sometimes offered with wire baskets for dishes (presumably the dishes were not washed at the same time as the linen!). The simplest aid to washing up was described in *Home and Garden* in 1923 as 'Overcoming the Drudgery of the Dishcloth', and consisted of a short length of hose attached to the hot tap with a spray nozzle at the end.

The Way We Were

'When a maid appears with a valued teacup in one hand and handle in the other, and announces, "It just came off in me hand, Mum," nine times out of ten she tells the truth, having held the cup by the handle when wiping, not knowing that it gives a peculiar twist which will, if the grasp be strong and unyielding, literally twist the handle off. Servants should be guided in dish-wiping as well as dish-washing.'

– *Good Housekeeping* (1913)

CUTLERY An old-fashioned but effective cutlery cleaner is sand; place the cutlery on a damp cloth and rub it well with the sand. Rinse, making sure all traces of sand are removed; pay particular attention to the tines of the forks.

Never leave cutlery with ivory, wooden, horn, bone or composition handles lying in water. Wash the blades in hot water, but keep it away from the handles as much as possible.

Silver Wash table silver as soon as possible after use, because some foods leave stains that are hard to remove and will corrode the silver if left. When you are drying silver make sure your cloth is completely dry; a damp cloth will leave smears and marks.

There are many silver-cleaning techniques from the days when most households had at least some silver or silver plate. One of the easiest ways to clean silver cutlery is to dissolve a little ammonia and soap in very hot water, soak the cutlery in the solution for a few minutes, and then dry and polish it with a soft cloth.

POTS AND PANS Fill pots and pans with hot water to soak as soon as they are empty. Wash greasy and burnt pans with a solution of washing soda and hot water. Soak rice, potato and porridge pots in cold water; clean and dry them as soon as possible. Rub grease from pots and pans with newspaper, or add a bit of oatmeal to absorb it.

Burnt pots and dishes To clean a badly burnt saucepan, pour in a little olive oil, heat it gently and let it stand for an hour or two. Pour off the oil, saving it for the next burnt pot, and clean the saucepan as usual; you will generally find that the stain has disappeared.

Clean burnt-on food from a pie dish by dipping it in very hot water and then quickly turning it upside down onto a perfectly flat surface to trap the steam, which will loosen the burnt material.

Tinware Tin is an ideal material for baking trays and cake tins, but looking after it needs some care. Tinware that is crusted with biscuit or cake mixture will last much longer if you fill it with cold water, add washing soda and let it stand on a warm stove until the crust is loosened and can be easily removed.

To clean tinware, scrape it with an old knife, soak it in cold water, scrub it with sand, rinse it in hot water, and dry it thoroughly — preferably in a warm oven. Tinware should be boiled occasionally.

Ironware and enamelware Do not put ironware and enamelware away until it is completely dry, and store it with the lid off in a warm dry place. To clean an enamel pan, boil a handful of barley in it. Bleach discoloration from enamelware with a mixture of coarse salt and vinegar. Soak an enamel baking dish that looks hopelessly burnt and blackened in a mixture of water and strong soap powder, then pour off the mixture and rub it with a soft cloth; you should find that all the stain has gone.

Teapots and coffee pots To prevent mustiness, store tea and coffee pots with their lids off and put a lump of sugar in a metal teapot.

Scald an enamel coffee pot thoroughly after each use, and give it a regular clean with hot soapy water, rinsing well.

DOLLY MOP

Useful, attractive and easy to make, this dolly mop makes a charming and inexpensive kitchen gift. It is adapted from a reader's contribution to *The Australian Woman's Mirror* (1926).

You will need a wooden spoon and a dish mop of approximately the same length, some kitchen string, thick watercolour paints, an art paintbrush, a tea towel, a duster, a dishcloth and about a metre of ribbon.

Place the bowl of the spoon against the head of the mop with the rounded side facing outwards. Tie them together with generous lengths of kitchen string just below the bowl and at their lower ends. Push the mop strings aside and paint a face on the bowl of the spoon.

Pin the tea towel round the spoon and mop to make a dress, then add the duster for an apron and the dishcloth for a shawl. Then write the following rhyme on a pretty card:

You stir your porridge with
* my face,*
And with my apron dust the place.
Wash up the dishes with
* my shawl,*
'Tis strongly made and not
* too small.*
My skirt you see is not a hobble –
'Twill dry your glass without
* much trouble.*
But if you want a mop instead
You'll find it in my woollen head.
Although my hair has turned
* quite white,*
I'll work for you both day
* and night!*

Hang the card round the doll's neck with a length of the ribbon, and tie the rest of the ribbon round her neck.

In place and at hand

THE STORAGE PROBLEM IS FREQUENTLY AT ITS MOST CRITICAL IN THE KITCHEN.

Few other rooms in the house are the scene of so much regular activity and are repositories for so many objects. You can work much more quickly and effectively when everything has its own place and you know exactly where to put your hand on what you need.

CREATING SPACE There are all sorts of tricks you can use to maximise working and storage space in your kitchen.

A tray drawer A tray drawer hinged to the leg of a table or bench will keep small gadgets handy but out of sight. It is easy to make – see the column on the right.

Wall hooks Make S-bend hooks with light-gauge galvanised fencing wire and suspend them from a short length of electric wiring screwed into the wall. They are very handy for hanging saucepans and larger utensils. If you are hanging up an eggbeater or anything else that is difficult to clean, slip a small bag over it to keep it free from dust.

Cupboard doors Attach small racks to the insides of cupboard doors to hold odds and ends like herbs and spices.

STORING EQUIPMENT A rule of thumb that our practical grandmothers followed was to make sure that items in constant demand were kept in the most accessible places.

Tableware Stack plates and saucers that are in everyday use in piles of no more than six. Shallow shelves for plates and narrow shelves for glasses simplify storage and minimise breakages and chips. Hang cups by their handles from cuphooks – but not immediately above piles of plates, where they may be knocked off and broken.

Cutlery Keep cutlery in special racks or in a baize-lined basket or drawer divided into compartments to avoid scratching silver and mislaying small items.

SHELVING The more shelving you have in the kitchen the better, both for safer stacking and for easier access. If the shelving in your cupboards is inadequate, you can make movable shelves using boards supported on bricks or wooden uprights.

Temporary shelves On high days and holidays, or whenever you are catering for large numbers, your storage and working space will need to expand. Convert the space beneath a table or bench into a storage area by adding a couple of shelves below the working surface. Nail two small battens to each table leg to make supports for shelves that you can remove when they are no longer required.

MAKING A TRAY DRAWER
A swing-out drawer is invaluable for storing small gadgets like tin openers, bottle openers and potato peelers. You need a bench or table with free space beneath it, a wooden cutlery tray (from hardware stores), a hinge, a wooden cupboard knob and some elementary woodworking skill.

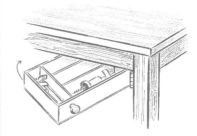

Attach one leaf of the hinge to the back of the cutlery drawer at the corner and the other leaf to the inner side of the table leg. Screw the cupboard knob to the side of the cutlery drawer and use it to move the drawer in and out.

Cutlery canteens and plate racks are convenient ways to store matching sets of tableware.

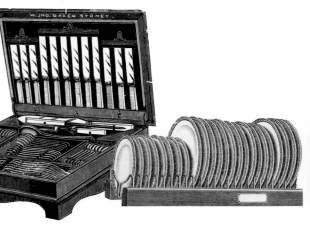

COOKERS AND COOLERS

The way in which food is heated and cooled has undergone dramatic changes since our grandparents' time. In 1850, cooking involved using solid fuels such as wood and coal, but by 1950 these had been replaced by gas and electricity in many households.

The roaring wood or coal fire, tended throughout the day to heat water and cook the next meal, dominated the 19th century kitchen. Although gas had been developed for cooking as early as 1826, it was expensive and popularly believed to taint food, and it made little progress as a cooking fuel until the end of the century, when increased supply made it more affordable. Electric stoves were slow to take off in Australia, as only a small number of houses were wired for electricity at the beginning of the 20th century.

Keeping food fresh had always been a problem in hot climates. Food safes and ice chests were the only cooling systems available until refrigeration was developed early in the 20th century.

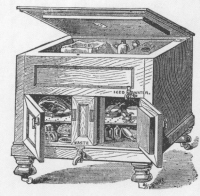

COOL AS A CUCUMBER

Ice was used to preserve food from very early on. The ice safe, with its drip tap, was a kitchen feature in our grandparents' day.

LAUGHING GAS

The Kooka stove, with its distinctive trademark, was once synonymous with gas cooking in Australia. Manufactured in Sydney, Kooka stoves were produced in large numbers by the Metters company.

COOKING WITH GAS

The convenience of the gas cooker is illustrated by this domestic scene, in which dad arrives home to a cooked dinner. Gas was piped into Australian homes from the beginning of the 20th century, making the gas stove the most affordable and efficient method of cooking.

THE HOME FRIDGE

Refrigeration was invented early in the 19th century, but it was not until 1922 that gas-powered domestic refrigerators arrived. This 1930s model included a surprising number of modern features and came with a temperature control dial.

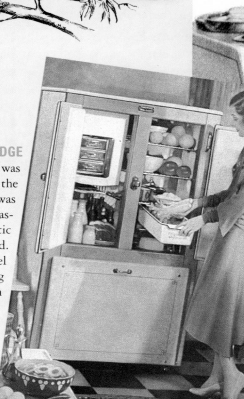

A MEATY PROBLEM

In Australia, flies and heat were a major food storage problem before refrigeration, especially for fresh meat. Coolers like this 1920s drip safe kept insect life away and circulated water-cooled air.

OUTBACK REFRIGERATION

The Coolgardie safe, invented by miners for use in the hot Western Australian goldfields, used the principle of water evaporation to keep food fresh.

MAKING A COOLGARDIE SAFE

The Coolgardie safe is an extremely efficient cooler, and it is quite easy to improvise one.

1. Rest the legs of a table in tin cans filled with water to deter insects. Place a tray on the table and a stool on top.

2. Fill the tray with water and cover the stool with a piece of hessian – the hem should rest in the water. Place a bowl of water on the seat of the stool and hang strips of hessian from the bowl over the sides. Use the rungs of the stool as supports for trays of food.

THE ELECTRIC REVOLUTION

As early as the 1890s there were a number of electric hotplates, frying pans and saucepans on the market. But cooks found them hard to use, and often forgot to turn switches on and off. By the 1920s, electric cookers had improved considerably and the arrival of cheap electrical power in the suburbs saw them enjoy a surge in popularity.

A pinch of this

TRYING OUT OLD RECIPES IS FUN, BUT FOR SOME OF THEM YOU NEED TO UNDERSTAND THE RECIPE CONVENTIONS OF EARLIER DAYS.

Cooks in those days relied largely on inherited skill and long practice to get their quantities and proportions right and assumed that their readers would have the same skills and experience, so that many of their recipes are somewhat approximate. They also used a range of weights and measures, from vague pinches and handfuls to very precise apothecaries' measures.

IMPERIAL MEASUREMENTS The imperial system of weights and measures is based on the weight of an average grain of wheat – in metric measurement, a tiny 0.0648 grams, not measurable with ordinary domestic equipment. Dry ingredients are given in ounces and pounds: for cooking purposes, an ounce is equivalent to 30 grams and 16 ounces (rounded up to 500 grams) make a pound. Liquid ingredients are given in fluid ounces and pints: a fluid ounce is 30 millilitres, and 20 fluid ounces make a pint (600 millilitres).

The following conversion tips may help you to interpret recipes from the good old days.

Dry ingredients
- A rounded tablespoon of salt weighs 1 ounce.
- A heaped tablespoon of flour weighs 1 ounce.
- A cup of rice weighs half a pound.

Liquid ingredients
- Sixty drops equal 1 teaspoon.
- Two teaspoons make 1 dessertspoon.
- Two dessertspoons or 4 teaspoons make 1 tablespoon.
- Four tablespoons make 2 fluid ounces.
- Sixteen tablespoons make 1 cup.
- One cup equals half a pint.
- Eight to ten standard eggs weigh 1 pound.

MEASURING BY VOLUME Many recipes used cup or spoon measurements for all types of ingredients, and this is often easier than weighing out the ingredients on kitchen scales. Remember, however, that 'cup' and 'spoon' are specific culinary measures; equip your kitchen with a set of metric measuring cups and spoons.

Dry ingredients Unless your recipe specifies otherwise, always sift flour, sugar and spices before you measure them. Sifting livens and loosens powdered substances until they almost double in bulk.

WEIGHING BEAM
If you need to improvise kitchen scales, you can make a rough balance with a length of plywood and a piece of curtain dowel.

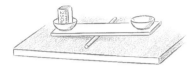

1. Screw the plywood to the dowel across the exact centre of the plywood and glue or screw identical sturdy plastic dishes to each end of the ply. Place a counterweight – something that is the exact weight you wish to measure – in one dish.

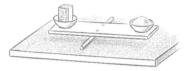

2. Add the item to be weighed to the other dish until the beam is perfectly level.

Spoons designed for the table vary in size; it pays to use measuring spoons to gauge quantities.

Many old recipes specify measurements as 'rounded', 'heaped' or 'level'. For a rounded measure, fill the container and then shake it slightly until the contents are rounded on top. A heaped measure is all that the container will hold without spilling. A level measure is a heaped measure levelled off with the back of a knife. In today's metric measures, however, all spoon and cup measures are level.

Liquid ingredients Make sure the measuring container is full to the brim. To judge quantities of liquid in a glass measuring jug, make sure your eye is level with the marks on the jug.

Solid fats can be awkward to measure in bulk. A neat tip from the old days is to use the principle of displacement: for instance, to measure half a cup of butter, half fill a cup measure with cold water and then add butter until the cup is full. This method has the added advantage of avoiding waste.

Modern kitchen shops stock a large range of measuring cups, spoon and jugs to help you to achieve the right proportions of the various ingredients.

Waste not

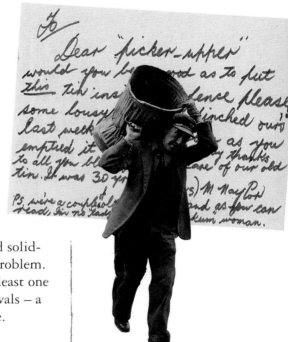

RECYCLING IS NOT A NEW CONCEPT —
OUR FOREBEARS REUSED EVERYTHING,
FROM EGGSHELLS TO PAPER BAGS.

Anything that could not go into the garden as
compost or mulch would be burned and the
heat used to warm the house, heat the water or
cook the meals. But when packaging became
'disposable' and gas and electric stoves replaced open fires and solid-
fuel ranges, or 'kitcheners', getting rid of rubbish became a problem.
By the 1930s, most people in developed countries needed at least one
garbage bin, which was emptied at more or less regular intervals — a
rare instance of a domestic chore being taken out of the home.

PLASTIC Plastic is choking our waterways and covering our planet
with indestructible rubbish. Do what our grandparents did — although
they did it because they had no choice: shop with a basket or fabric
bag. Or use and reuse a cardboard box for your groceries. Patronise
shops that don't thrust everything automatically into plastic bags and
that provide cardboard cartons for their customers.

PAPER AND CARDBOARD Use paper printed on only one side for lists
and *aides memoires*, or as scribbling paper for children. Large cardboard
boxes make great cubby houses or knockabout toys for children.

Cardboard makes good mulch for the garden; put plenty of dry plant
material or compost on top of it until it is well soaked with water.
Worms particularly love corrugated cardboard. Wetted paper will also
make a good mulch if it is weighted down. It will retain moisture and
encourage earthworm activity around trees.

Use egg cartons as seed propagation trays. When the seedlings are
ready to transplant, cut out the individual cups, cut out the bottom
and plant the whole cup, which will eventually
rot. This prevents transplant shock.

METAL Paint large fruit juice tins and use
them as containers for plants or to hold
kitchen stores. A large tin can with the top
cut out and holes punched in the bottom
makes an effective improvised watering can.

You can crush and bury steel cans — they
will eventually break down in the soil and
release their essential elements. They benefit
fruit trees especially. Bury used steel wool in
the garden, particularly under hydrangeas;
the blue flowers will become more vivid,
and the pink ones will turn mauve.

*Garbage collection has undergone
dramatic changes in recent years
with the separation of recyclable
waste but the friendly note to the
garbage collector and the kerbside
Christmas present are traditions
that still endure.*

GLASS Glass jars make perfect storage containers for anything from leftovers to buttons and screws. Make sure they are well washed and completely dry before you store anything in them. In the garden, upend glass jars over young seedlings to form miniature greenhouses that will concentrate moisture and protect the plants from cold.

Pretty or unusually shaped glass jars add that extra touch to homemade spreads and preserves that you want to sell at the local fete or give away to friends.

COMPOST AND PLANT FOODS Much of the food waste produced in the kitchen can be used either on the compost heap or directly on the garden. Cover your kitchen compost bucket, and keep it small so that the scraps do not have time to decompose in the kitchen.

Kitchen scraps Look on scraps as food for plants, rather than as rubbish. Some food scraps can be used directly on the garden.
Banana peel Bananas are a rich source of potassium, phosphorus and nitrogen. Banana peel will give your staghorn ferns a lift if you tuck them in among the leaves. Cut up bananas that are bruised or too ripe to use and dig them into the soil around your gardenias and hoyas.
Eggshells Crush and scatter eggshell on the garden around lime-loving plants, but do not use them under acid-loving plants such as azaleas.

Compost enrichers Add tea leaves, which have a high nitrogen content, phosphorus and potash, and hair clippings. Coffee grounds are valuable in compost because they are high in proteins and oils, but do not add them directly to the soil.

Extend your compost with paper; it works best if it is torn up. Cardboard can be composted too, at the bottom of the heap or packed around the sides of the bin. You can also use sawdust, but make sure it has not come from treated wood, which may contain toxic substances.

Cooking oil and fat and fish and meat scraps are organic and can therefore be composted, but as they decompose they attract flies, so cover the compost with soil or underfelt. For meat scraps, the temperature in the centre of the heap needs to be quite high. Make a hole in the centre of the heap and put the meat scraps in, then cover it with sawdust or grass clippings. The heat should kill any maggots and the covering will deter flies.

Compost problems Kitchen wastes do not have enough carbon to fuel the composting process, so add materials that contain carbon, such as shredded paper and grass clippings. Otherwise it will smell offensive and attract pests.

The presence of ants and caterpillars means that the compost is too dry – sprinkle it with a little water. Maggots and cockroaches mean that there is food for them and the temperature is low enough for them to flourish. Mice or rats in your compost mean that proteins are not being broken down. For all these problems, add grass clippings to raise the internal temperature of the compost heap.

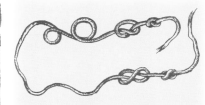

The Way We Were

At one time people hoarded bits of string, to be produced when needed or used for playing cat's cradle or practising knots:

'"String?" said Mr Puffett. "If it's string you're looking for, I reckon you've come to the right place for it. When I sees a bit o' string, my lord, I picks it up and puts it away, 'andy when wanted." He pulled up his sweaters with a grunt and began to produce rolls of string from his pockets as a conjurer produces coloured paper. "There's all sorts 'ere, you can take your choice … safe bind, safe find, I says …".'

– *Busman's Honeymoon*,
Dorothy L. Sayers (1937)

Turning material regularly in the compost heap improves aeration, which speeds up the rate at which waste breaks down.

Shoo fly

WHEN IT COMES TO HOUSEHOLD PESTS, PREVENTION
IS A GREAT DEAL BETTER THAN CURE.

Ants and cockroaches gather where there are food scraps. Take
precautionary measures in your kitchen: make sure that food is kept
covered, crumbs are swept up and spills cleaned up promptly.
Cockroaches love darkness and warmth, so clean out cupboards and
other likely haunts for pests regularly. Watch closely for the first signs
of an infestation, and take steps at once to prevent it from spreading.

HERBAL DETERRENTS One of the oldest remedies against many kinds
of pests is mint; mint leaves used to be scattered in church pews and
around the great communal halls of castles to repel vermin, since mice
and rats hate the smell. Lavender is another weapon against many
insect pests. As well as putting lavender bags in wardrobes and clothes
drawers, try keeping a bunch of lavender in the kitchen.

INSECTICIDES Commercial insecticides have had a bad press in the
recent past. In the first half of the 20th century, DDT was a widely
used insecticide, and it was many years before scientists discovered
that its toxic effects were spreading through the food chain to all
living things. In most countries, DDT is now banned.

However, commercial insecticides, if properly used, are safer than
they once were, and they can be an option for bad pest infestations. If
you decide to use a commercial insecticide, read the manufacturer's
instructions and cautionary notes carefully and follow them faithfully.
Keep such products away from food, children and pets, and also from
soft furnishings, since some of them are harmful to fabrics.

ANTS The only way to really get rid of ants is to find their nest and
destroy it by pouring boiling water into it. As a stopgap measure,
pour boiling water on individual groups of ants.

ANTS have been used to cure all
sorts of ills. An old Scotch recipe for
deafness called for ants' eggs mixed
with the juice of onions to be dropped
into the ear. Gout and rheumatism
were to be cured with spirits of ants,
made by mixing 10 parts of fresh
bruised ants into 15 parts each of
alcohol and water. In the 16th century
winged ants were a favourite
ingredient in love philtres, dropped
surreptitiously into wine or the
intended beloved's food. It was said to
have 'a wonderful effect in arousing
the tender passion, even with the
coldest heart.'

The Way We Were

An unorthodox way to get rid of cockroaches in the northern
hemisphere was to use hedgehogs, in whose diet they featured:

'It is within my personal knowledge that a certain large hotel in
London was cleared of cockroaches by four hedgehogs; previous
to the "appointment" to the job a professional beetle-destroyer
had been employed, at a wage of fifty two pounds per annum, to
exterminate the cockroaches, a task which it was either beyond
his resources, or outside his intentions, to achieve during four
years of work.'

HOUSEHOLD PESTS AND HOUSEHOLD REMEDIES, W. R BOELTER (1909)

Ants love sweet things, so make sure that sweet foods are well covered and that no sugar has been spilt. You can borrow a technique from the old days and use the sweet tooth of the ants to trap them: coat the inside of a glass jar with treacle and leave it near the ant run. When the ants are stuck in the treacle, rinse them away.

To get rid of ants in pot plants, try dissolving a piece of camphor the size of a hazelnut in 2 litres of hot water, allow it to cool, and use the solution on the plants.

COCKROACHES In temperate to warm climates, old buildings – especially houses with basement kitchens – are often invaded by cockroaches, no matter how careful you are about cleanliness. They like warmth and darkness, so they congregate in kitchens, particularly near the stove. They are attracted by all kinds of foods, and they will also attack shoes and leather garments.

Cockroaches are tough and fertile and notoriously hard to eradicate. They will eat practically anything, they are very resistant to poisons, and their eggs are hard to destroy because they are very well protected inside specially hardened egg cases, usually hidden in crevices.

Pyrethrum extract To guard against infestations of cockroaches, block cracks with papier maché, wood filler or plaster. Spray pyrethrum extract liberally around the joins between the skirting board and the floor, and anywhere else that you suspect the cockroaches emerge from.

Commercial methods Cockroaches continually clean themselves, so poisoned powders and baits will kill adult insects, but you must be very careful to keep poisons away from children and pets. Fumigation will get rid of the nymph cockroaches – the immature forms – but often it simply drives them out to someone else's kitchen, only to return to yours as soon as the poison has dissipated.

Traps Our grandparents devised various ways of trapping cockroaches by enticing them into baited containers that they could not get out of. Such traps are worth trying if you have only a few cockroaches, but the effect will be negligible in a serious infestation. One old method is to put some treacle in a glazed or enamelled basin and rest pieces of wood between the edge of the basin and the surrounding floor. The cockroaches will climb into the treacle and get stuck.

FLIES Flies lay their eggs where food is easily available for the maggots when they hatch, such as in rubbish or manure. The eggs hatch in less than a day, and the adult fly develops in eight to nine days.

Flies are always with us, and nothing will get rid of them completely. However, scrupulous cleanliness can help a great deal. Cover all food, keep household rubbish in covered containers, and make sure your store cupboard is always shut.

Flies will keep away from the kitchen if it is filled with the wonderful smell of peppermint. Place a few drops of peppermint oil in a jug of water and put it in a corner of the kitchen.

'For a hygienic home' … a 1928 Italian advertisement sings the praises of an American pesticide, claiming that it will exterminate 'flies, mosquitoes, fleas, bedbugs, lice, cockroaches and ants'.

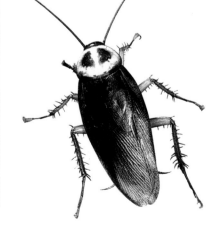

Cockroaches are nocturnal, so it is best to carry out eradication treatments at night when the roaches emerge from their nests.

Blooming lovely

IN THE GOOD OLD DAYS, THE HERB
GARDEN AND THE VEGETABLE PATCH
WERE EXTENSIONS OF THE KITCHEN.

Many of us still have a kitchen that opens directly into a garden, and can grow our own fresh herbs and vegetables as country folk have been doing for generations. Even in a small inner-city garden it is possible to find room to grow herbs and the smaller vegetables in pots or small soil beds. Those who live in flats or apartments are more restricted. They cannot simply step out of the kitchen door for a handful of fresh mint or a bundle of tender carrots. The solution to this is to bring the garden into the kitchen by growing culinary plants in window boxes and plant pots.

HERBS You can grow many herbs from seed, and good flower shops often stock sets of seeds, potting mixture and charming little pots that will sit comfortably on the windowsill of even the smallest kitchen. Or you can do as our grandparents did and take cuttings of your favourite herbs to raise in the kitchen.

To strike a cutting, select a supple nonflowering twig of a healthy plant and pull it gently away, retaining a heel of bark from the parent stem. Take off the lower leaves and push the cutting firmly into fine earth in a flowerpot. Water the pot well, place a glass jar over it to keep the moisture in and encourage germination, and put it in a shaded place where you can keep an eye on it. When new growth appears, the roots have developed and you can move the cutting to a lighter position. Plant it out into a larger pot when it is established.

Fresh herbs Fresh herbs are a delight in the kitchen, not only for cooking but for their subtle colours and scents, which help to make the kitchen a pleasant place to be. Use herbs fresh whenever you can, but also make the most of your herbs by drying them.

Dried herbs Gather herbs for drying when they are just beginning to blossom. If you are drying herbs grown out of doors, pick them after the morning sun has driven off the dew. Dry herbs quickly, and store them as soon as they are completely dry – otherwise they may start to reabsorb moisture. Herbs like sage, rosemary and thyme have tough leaves and dry easily because they have little moisture content, but more succulent plants such as basil, borage and comfrey take longer.

You can suspend herbs in loose bunches in a shaded place in the kitchen, away from direct sunlight, and enjoy their perfume as they dry. In cold or wet conditions, spread them on a baking tray and dry them in the oven when it is cooling down after a cooking session.

Herbs are dry if they rustle like tissue paper when you shake them gently. Put them in airtight containers, remembering to label them – one dried herb looks much like another. If you use glass containers,

Words of Wisdom
In 1869, Catherine E. Beecher and Harriet Beecher Stowe (above), who became famous as the author of *Uncle Tom's Cabin*, gave this advice in their book *The American Woman's Home*:

'If parents wish their daughters to grow up with good domestic habits, they should have, as one means of securing this result, a neat and cheerful kitchen … It should always, if possible, be entirely above ground and well lighted. It should have a large sink, and a drain running underground so that everything can be kept sweet and clean. If flowers and shrubs be cultivated around the kitchen door and windows, and the yard near them be well turfed, it will add much to the kitchen's agreeable appearance.'

– QUOTED IN HELEN LYION ADAMSON, *GRANDMOTHER'S HOUSEHOLD HINTS* (1963)

store them in the dark; the herbs will deteriorate if they are exposed to light. After several days, check glass containers: if there is any trace of moisture on the glass, take the herbs out and dry them for longer.

SCENTED WAYS The odours of fresh baking and roasting are irresistible, but cooking smells can linger and become stale and distasteful. Your rows of fragrant herbs on the windowsill will help to keep your kitchen fresh and sweet. Candles permeated with herbal essences are another time-tested way of sweetening the atmosphere.

Herb candles Candles dipped in herb-scented wax are simple and inexpensive to make. You will need 50 grams of a dried herb, a packet of paraffin-wax candles, 350 grams of paraffin wax and 35 grams of stearin (both from craft shops). Use any herb that takes your fancy; one of the most fragrant is dried rosemary. Melt the paraffin wax in a double boiler over simmering water and add the dried herbs, stirring constantly to distribute the herbs evenly. Then melt the stearin in another double boiler and add this to the wax. Holding a candle by the wick, dip it carefully into the wax mixture for about five seconds, then remove the candle and let it dry for a minute. Repeat the procedure until the candle has a thick coating of herb wax.

A sunny window is the perfect place to grow small plants such as herbs.

Herbs grown and dried in the kitchen can be used to make sweet-smelling candles.

Safety in the kitchen

THE KITCHEN CAN BE A DANGEROUS PLACE,
ESPECIALLY WHEN SMALL CHILDREN ARE MEMBERS
OF THE HOUSEHOLD.

In earlier times, kitchens were full of hazards such as open fires
and coal gas cookers. Life is safer today, with electricity and
natural gas, but exposed heating elements, hot fats and boiling
water, broken glass, carelessness with knives and incorrect
storage of poisons are common causes of kitchen accidents. Less
obvious but equally perilous are badly maintained electrical
equipment, slippery floors, and poor lighting and ventilation.

Inspect and repair your kitchen furniture and machines regularly;
and make a habit of storing all poisons, including cleaning agents, in a
locked cupboard.

PREVENTING BURNS AND SCALDS Make sure that open fires and solid
fuel stoves have adequate fire guards. Control switches for heating
appliances, stoves and all electrical equipment should be out of the
reach of children.

A tablecloth was regarded as essential for even the simplest meal in
the old days; families with crawling babies or toddlers were advised to
use small tablecloths that did not overhang the table or to secure the
cloth in some way so that children could not pull it off the table and
bring down hot dishes with it. These days the best advice is to
dispense with tablecloths altogether, at least while children are small.

Keep all hot liquids out of reach of children, and turn the spouts of
kettles and teapots and the handles of saucepans to the back of the
stove so that children cannot accidentally pull them onto themselves.

BROKEN GLASS AND CHINA With all the care in the world, glass and
china sometimes get broken. Use wet blotting paper or newspaper to
pick up fragments of broken glass or china. Ban bare feet in the
kitchen, just in case a sharp sliver is lurking on the floor.

Reducing breakages Make sure your china and glass are of good
quality, and keep them on shelves that are easy to get at. If you have a
stone or quarry tiled floor, follow your grandmother's example and put
down rugs in the working areas.

China and glassware are most vulnerable to breakage when they are
not properly stacked, either before or after they have been washed.
Stack stemmed glasses bottom side up, and never put tumblers inside
each other because they often break as they are being separated.

SHARP OBJECTS Sharp knives, skewers and many other kitchen
implements are essential but dangerous. Do not leave sharp objects
lying about. Keep kitchen knives in a knife block or in sheaths, never
in a drawer with unprotected blades. Drive the tips of skewers into

*A French promotional postcard
of 1928 made the questionable
claim that 'there's no need to
worry about fire' if you have
the four-leaf clover brand of
aluminium saucepan with an
insulated handle.*

The Way We Were

Life was more perilous in the
old days, as these late 19th
century 'Cautions for the
Prevention of Accidents'
demonstrate:

'Never sleep anywhere near
charcoal; if drowsy at any work
where charcoal fires are used,
take the fresh air.

Be wary of children, whether
they are up or in bed; and
particularly when they are near
the fire, an element with which
they are very apt to amuse
themselves.

Never quit a room leaving
the poker in the fire.'

– ENQUIRE WITHIN (1880)

wine corks for safe storage in a drawer or a tall jar. Keep can openers, potato peelers and so on in their own drawer or compartment.

Children and knives If a baby catches hold of a sharp object, do not try to pull it away – the baby may instinctively hold on tighter and be cut. Instead, hold the baby's empty hand and offer a favourite toy or something pretty or nice to eat, so that the child will drop the sharp object in order to pick up the other.

FLOORS AND FLOOR COVERINGS Slippery floors are a hazard anywhere, but particularly in the kitchen. Leave the areas under rugs unpolished and make sure your rugs have a nonslip backing. Floor coverings that are frayed or curled at the edges increase the risk of people tripping and falling; if the rugs cannot be mended effectively, replace them.

Wipe up spills as quickly as possible, making sure you do it thoroughly and do not simply spread the spill over a wider area.

Preventing spills An apron with a wide ruffle or a gaping pocket at the bottom that stands out enough to catch crumbs or drops will help to prevent messes on the floor. As a bonus, it will also protect your clothing and make the task of cleaning the kitchen floor easier.

Use both hands to lift heavy saucepans and dishes – large saucepans should have double handles for this purpose.

KITCHEN FIRES Outbreaks of fire in the kitchen are less common than they were in the days when open fires were the norm, but fire is still a risk. Make sure that every member of the household knows how to call the fire brigade. Keep a fire extinguisher in your kitchen for electrical fires; make sure that it is working, and that everyone knows how to use it. Use a fire blanket to smother larger fires.

THE FIRST FIRE EXTINGUISHER
A machine that used compressed air to deliver water under high pressure was invented in England in 1816. A more portable French model of about 50 years later employed a combination of sodium bicarbonate and sulphuric acid to develop the water pressure. Later models used no water: a foam extinguisher developed in Russia in 1904 generated a foam that smothered oil and petrol flames, and an American model of 1909 vaporised carbon tetrachloride with pressurised carbon dioxide to emit a heavy nonflammable gas that starved the flames of oxygen.

But domestic extinguishers were not common, even when homes were more at risk than they are now from open fires and soot-choked chimneys; most householders made do with buckets of sand.

Appliances Examine gas and electrical appliances regularly for faults, and have any defects repaired by a professional.

Oil-based fires If oil or cooking fat overheats and catches fire, turn off the heat, throw flour or sand over the flames and put a lid over the pan. *Caution*: Never use water on an oil-based fire – it will merely spread the flames.

Naked flames Be careful with naked flames such as matches and candles. Add 30 grams of alum to the last rinsing water for curtains and children's clothes to fireproof them. Never hang clothes or curtains where they can come into contact with naked flames.

LIGHTING No one can work for long under poor lighting without feeling tired and having strained eyes. Position lights in the kitchen so that the light from them shines onto the work bench and the task you are doing. Do not hang lights in the kitchen too low; they add to the heat and can be a source of discomfort.

Choose a light fitting for the kitchen that is easy to clean and that allows you to replace bulbs easily. Clean kitchen light fittings regularly – they soon collect a film of dirt that blocks the light.

Eat, Drink

and be

Merry

SIMPLE TIPS, TECHNIQUES AND
RECIPES TO REMIND YOU OF DAYS PAST

Clues for home cooks

PREPARING DELICIOUS HOME-COOKED MEALS
FOR FAMILY AND FRIENDS IS ONE OF THE MOST
SATISFYING OF DOMESTIC EMPLOYMENTS.

In days of old, housewives spent a large part of each
day on cooking and its associated tasks – planning
menus, shopping, preparation, cleaning up. Modern
technology has eliminated much of the hard work:
refrigeration keeps foods fresh for days instead of
hours; food processors and blenders, and new
ways of processing and marketing foods, mean
that we no longer need to spend laborious
hours of preparation in the kitchen; and
modern stoves allow easy and almost instant temperature control. But
the principles of good home cookery have not changed over the years,
and the rules that our grandmothers used still apply.

*Goodness knows what she's
making but – like all good cooks
– she has the ingredients and
equipment to hand!*

USING RECIPES The word *recipe* is Latin for
'take'. Its modern meaning is derived from
medieval pharmaceutical prescriptions, which
often began with such alarming instructions
as: 'Take horse dunge and putt to it so much
Ale as will make it like hasty puding …'
According to the 19th century French
gastronome Jean-Anthelme Brillat-
Savarin, 'The discovery of a new dish does
more for the happiness of mankind than the discovery of
a star', but very few recipes are really new. In the old days family
recipes, or 'receipts', were often jealously guarded and passed down
from mother to daughter under seal of strict secrecy – but the 'secret'
was usually nothing more than the inclusion of an unusual ingredient
in a standard recipe.

Successful cookery is not so much a matter of following recipes
slavishly as of interpreting them and introducing your own variations.
Experiment with recipes. Who knows? You may discover a new dish
and thus add to 'the happiness of mankind'!

This goes with that … Some foods and flavours complement each
other perfectly, either as textures or as taste sensations. A topping of
crisp breadcrumbs adds contrast to vegetables or fish baked in a
creamy sauce. Celery contributes a subtle peppery flavour to virtually
any casserole recipe. Tomatoes and basil not only grow happily
together but make ideal salad partners with a little extra virgin olive
oil and a sprinkling of freshly ground black pepper. And mustard
enhances the flavour of cheese, as in the old supper favourite Welsh
rarebit – cheese melted in beer, thickened with a little cornflour,
seasoned with mustard and black pepper and grilled on toast.

*Good home cooking involves
learning a few simple techniques,
such as adding liquid to a flour
and butter roux to make a
smooth, lump-free sauce.*

New recipes Finding – or inventing – a new recipe can be an exciting experience, but there is a golden rule of cookery: never try out a new recipe on dinner guests unless you know them very well indeed. Test it first on the family. This is not just a matter of whether the recipe works and tastes all right; you also need to find out exactly how much preparation and cooking time to allow, and whether there are any techniques that you need to perfect.

PLANNING At one time it was customary to plan menus a full week ahead, and many old cookery books included sample weekly menus for households of varying degrees of affluence and for various times of the year, based on seasonal availability of foods. With today's more flexible lifestyle, we do not need or want to be so rigid, but planning menus in advance avoids waste, thus saving time and money, and ensures that you provide a balanced diet.

Menus Plan menus so as to provide the right proportions of all the major food groups – meat and fish, dairy products and eggs, cereals and grains, and fruits and vegetables. Modern nutritionists

recommend a diet that includes small amounts of fat and sugar, moderate amounts of meat, fish and dairy foods, and large amounts of cereals, fruits and vegetables.

Timing is important: design menus so that you do not find yourself frantically finishing off several complicated dishes at the last minute. For example, if the main dish is a soufflé, which must be rushed to the table the minute it is cooked, make sure that you cook simple accompaniments such as steamed vegetables that can be prepared a little in advance and left to take care of themselves.

Eating is about enjoyment as well as nourishment. Keep the tastes of your consumers in mind: there is no point in serving spinach or rice pudding every week because 'it's good for you' if no one will eat it. As early as 1920, C. Frederick's *Scientific Management in the Home* advised: '... if certain kinds of meals are preferred other than the conventional ones, let the homemaker follow these ...'

GOING TO MARKET Buying food used to be a daily task, and shopping was a social occasion when people would meet friends and exchange local gossip. The housewife, or in well-to-do households a trusted servant, would sally forth in the morning armed with a shopping basket and a list of what was required for the day's meals. Good shoppers would establish amicable relations with the various suppliers – the butcher, the fishmonger, the baker, the grocer and the greengrocer – to ensure that their purchases were of the finest quality.

Nowadays a weekly food shopping trip is all that most of us have time for. But it still pays to plan your shopping time carefully and take the trouble to find the most reliable local suppliers.

Before you shop, make a list, not forgetting to check the store cupboard in case you need to replenish your stock of items that you do not need to buy every week, such as flour, sugar, salt, tea and canned goods. Stick to your list; do not yield to the temptation to buy

Words of Wisdom

Mrs Isabella Beeton took managing a household seriously and taught women to value their work:

'As with the commander of an army, or the leader of any enterprise, so it is with the mistress of any house. Her spirit will be seen through the whole establishment; and in just proportion as she performs her duties intelligently and thoroughly, so will her domestics follow her path. Of all those acquirements, which more particularly belong to the feminine character, there are none which take the higher rank in our estimation than such as enter into a knowledge of household duties; for on those are perpetually dependent the happiness, comfort and well-being of a family.'

– *150 Years of Cookery and Household Management*, Graham Nown (1986)

'bargain offers' unless you know you will use them. Some wise advice from the past is never to shop for food when you are hungry – if you do, you will almost certainly make some unwise purchases.

COOKING EFFICIENTLY Before you start to cook, make sure you have enough working space and set out all the ingredients and implements you will need. Work systematically, doing everything possible in advance so that you leave yourself enough time for tricky or last-minute operations. A good rule is to rinse or wash up dishes as you go, even if your resolution falters as matters speed up towards the end.

Oven temperature Many old recipes specify oven temperatures in terms such as 'hot' or 'moderate', because the writers were not using thermostatically controlled ovens. A widely used test of oven heat in the old days was the writing paper test, and it can still be useful today if you are cooking in a new or unfamiliar oven. Put a sheet of white writing paper in the preheated oven for two minutes:
• if it catches fire, the oven is too hot;
• if it turns dark brown, the oven is 'very hot';
• if it turns light brown, the oven is 'hot';
• if it turns yellow, the oven is 'moderate';
• if it turns pale yellow, the oven is 'low'.
Modern ovens are thermostatically controlled and calibrated in degrees Celsius. But temperature control varies from oven to oven – a reading of 250°C may be 'hot' in one oven but 'very hot' in another. The only infallible guide is experience with your own oven. As a rough guide:
• 250°C is 'very hot';
• 220°C is 'hot';
• 190°C is 'moderate';
• 130°C is 'low'.

SETTING THE TABLE In the good old days, every meal was an occasion. The whole family was expected to be present, and no one was permitted to leave the table until everybody had finished eating. In many households each meal had its own crockery, cutlery, tablecloth and table napkins.

Times have changed, but it is pleasant every so often to evoke the elegance of the past at a meal with family or friends. The room should be comfortably warm, softly lit and well ventilated. The tablecloth should be large enough to cover the table entirely and hang about halfway to the floor all around. A 'silencer' – a piece of felt or an old tablecloth tied to the legs of the table with tapes – protects the table from heat and spills, muffles noise and gives the upper cloth a smooth appearance. Damask or linen table napkins add a final touch of class. Cutlery, glass and crockery should be sparkling clean, and salt cellars and pepper pots should be well filled, and within easy reach. Flowers and candles make attractive centrepieces, but do not use tall arrangements that will hide diners from each other and impede conversation.

A TABLE FOR TWO
Then on my sleeve you lay your
    brilliant hand
And lead me to the lighted table land.
All things expect you: walls and
    ceiling swim
In mellower light; the chairs stand
    straight and trim;
The tables dressed with snow behold
    you come;
The mouth of every crystal glass
    is dumb;
The knives and forks in silver
    order shine
And grace descends upon the food
    and wine.
– 'THE DINNER', A.D. HOPE (1907–)

SETTING THE TABLE

Allow enough space at each table setting for diners to sit in comfort, without having to jam their elbows into their sides.

Feed the man meat

HUMANS HAVE EVOLVED AS MEAT EATERS, AND
IN MANY PARTS OF THE WORLD MEAT IS AN
INDISPENSABLE SOURCE OF PROTEIN.

Meat is the muscle tissue of animals. It consists of fibres held together
by connective tissue called collagen. Cooking is a way of predigesting
meat, since heat converts the collagen into gelatine and the meat
becomes tender and chewable. The parts of the animal that get least
exercise yield the tender cuts that are used for roasting and grilling at
high temperatures. The toughest parts are minced to break up the
fibres and collagen before cooking, and those in between are cooked
slowly in liquid to dissolve the collagen.

Our careful grandmothers made it their business to know how to
buy good meat and get the best nutritional value from their purchases.

BUYING MEAT AND POULTRY Look for these characteristics.
Beef should be bright to dark red, finely fibred and flecked with fat
('marbled') in the thicker bits. The fat should be firm and yellowish-
white; it should not be sticky to the touch.
Lamb should be fairly light red and fine-grained and the fat should be
white and firm and evenly distributed over the flesh.
Pork should be quite pale and fine-grained, with translucent white fat.
Chicken should be almost white and very fine-grained. Flex the end
of the breastbone to test whether a chicken is suitable for roasting: if
it bends easily, the bird is young and tender and can be roasted, but
if it is rigid the chicken will have to be casseroled.

STORING MEAT Store meat on a plate in the refrigerator, covered
loosely with greaseproof paper. Never store meat wrapped in plastic;
it will rapidly develop an unpleasantly slimy surface. Large cuts, such
as roasts, will keep longer than small ones – about four days. Chops
and steak will keep for three days, diced meats for two, and minced
meat and sausages should be cooked within 24 hours of purchase.

Take meat out of the refrigerator and allow it to reach room
temperature before cooking it.

ROAST MEATS One of the great traditions of British cooking is
the Sunday roast, which was always eaten in the middle of the
day. In Australia in the 1940s, it was the custom in church-going
families to start the roast and its accompanying roast vegetables
before leaving for the 11 o'clock service, and children were told
that the angels would cook the Sunday dinner while they were at
church. On returning, the only remaining tasks were to cook any
boiled or steamed vegetables and make the gravy.

Roasting is more effective with large joints of meat than small
ones, and in the old days even quite small households would cook

*As our grandmothers knew very
well, the best way to ensure that
you buy good meat is to cultivate
a good butcher.*

*Intensive farming has made
chicken and turkey much more
available and affordable than
they once were, but turkey is still
the traditional Christmas roast.*

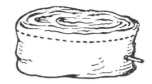

a huge joint on Sunday. The leftovers were made into sandwiches, chopped up for curry and minced to make cottage pie.

Lamb was for years the favoured roasting meat in Australia and New Zealand, because the first white settlers found sheep easy to raise. New Zealanders ate so much lamb that they coined comic names for it, such as Colonial Goose.

Principles of roasting Roasting is the earliest and simplest way of cooking meat. Before kitchens were routinely equipped with enclosed ovens, meat was roasted by fastening it onto a rotating spit in front of an open fire. The radiant heat shrank the meat fibres and forced the juices to the surface, where they dried into a delicious crust.

To roast meat in the good old way, put a baking dish with a little dripping in it on the lower oven rack and heat the oven to very hot. Rub the fatty surfaces of the joint with salt and pepper and sprinkle on any herbs that you may want to use. Put the meat on the upper oven rack, fatty side up; the meat juices and the melted fat will drip down into the baking tray. After 20 minutes turn the oven down to moderate and put any vegetables that you want to roast with the meat into the baking dish.

For many people, 'the roast beef of old England' symbolises all that is best of British cookery. This quaint engraving of a rolled roast is from a 1908 edition of Mrs. Beeton's Cookery Book. The dotted line around the roast illustrates the direction in which to carve the joint.

Shepherd's pie, with its golden crust of mashed potato permeated underneath with tasty meat juices, is an all-time favourite with children and adults alike.

Cooking time varies with the age and shape of the joint and with the degree of doneness required. As a rough guide, allow 40 minutes per kilogram to begin with and then test by piercing the meat with a fine skewer. If the juice runs red, the meat is underdone, or rare; if pink, it is medium done; if clear, it is well done. When the meat is done to your liking, take it from the oven and let it stand for 15–20 minutes. The fibres will relax and the joint will be tender and juicy.

Accompaniments to roasts Roast potatoes are good with any roast meat. Peel one medium-sized potato per person, cut in half and boil for 5 minutes. Drain and dry, score with a fork, put into the baking tray and spoon the fat and meat juices over.

Other traditional accompaniments to various roast meats are:
Beef Brussels sprouts; gravy, made by cooking a little flour in the meat juices and working in 1 cup of stock; grated horseradish; Yorkshire pudding (see page 61).

Lamb Fresh green peas; mint sauce, made by infusing chopped mint in cider vinegar.

Pork Baked onions; apple sauce, made by stewing apples and onions together and beating in some butter.

Chicken and turkey Bacon, laid across the breast of the bird for the last 20 minutes of cooking; bread sauce, made by simmering an onion studded with cloves in milk and then removing the onion and cooking white bread to a mush in the flavoured milk.

GRILLED MEATS AND FRIED MEATS Grilling is a form of roasting. In the old days grilling was done on a gridiron on top of the stove, but modern stoves have enclosed grillers with the heat radiating downwards. The heat must be intense to dry off the meat juices quickly, and the timing is very important. For steak or chops of a standard thickness, allow 4 minutes per side.

Frying is an alternative method of cooking small pieces of tender meat by exposing it to very hot fat. In these health-conscious days, most people shallow-fry meats in oil or polyunsaturated margarine rather than deep-frying in dripping, as was the custom in the old days.

Lamb's fry Australians and New Zealanders cook the liver of the lamb by slicing it thinly, dredging it in flour and frying it quickly for a minute or two – it becomes leathery if it is cooked for any longer.

MINCED MEATS In the good old days, every kitchen was equipped with a mincer, which was clamped onto a bench or table top and used to grind up leftover roast meat or fresh meat that was too tough to be tenderised by cooking. The meals that could be made with mince were many, and all were economical and nourishing.

Shepherd's pie In a large frying pan, heat 2 tablespoons of dripping or oil and brown 1 kg of minced lamb and a medium brown onion, peeled and chopped. Keep turning the meat until it has changed colour, and then stir in 2 cups of meat stock and 1 tablespoon of Worcestershire sauce. Cook at simmering point for about 30 minutes, stirring frequently to break up the mince.

Words of Wisdom

'Butchers, usually, are very pleasant people, in spite of having at some time in their lives deliberately chosen to be butchers. They will assist your efforts to economize with amazing benevolence, and will agree with you that a piece of "lean end" or flank, stripped of its cartilage and fat and put once though the grinder, is as good meat as anybody could ask for.'

– *How to Cook a Wolf*,
M.F.K. Fisher (1943)

Before food processors, a mincer was an essential kitchen tool. Pictured here is Spong's Patent British Mincer, advertised by Harrods of London in 1895.

The Way We Were

Bacon was a staple food for the British working classes in the old days:

'He got his breakfast, made the tea, packed the bottom of the doors with rugs to shut out the draught, piled a big fire, and sat down to an hour of joy. He toasted his bacon on a fork and caught the drops of fat on his bread; then he put the rasher on his thick slice of bread, and cut off chunks with a clasp-knife, poured his tea into his saucer, and was happy.'

– SONS AND LOVERS, D.H.LAWRENCE (1913)

In the meantime, peel 4 large potatoes and boil them in salted water. Drain and mash them thoroughly with a little butter or margarine. Put the mince into a shallow ovenproof dish and smooth the mashed potato over it with the back of a fork so as to leave the marks of the tines. Bake in a hot oven until the potato topping is golden.

When made with minced beef, this recipe created what was more commonly known as cottage pie; today the names are interchangeable.

Oxford sausages Sausages can be a meal in themselves or an accompaniment to other meats. With modern food processors it is easy to make your own sausage meat from this 19th century recipe.

You will need 300 grams each of pork (fat and lean but without skin), lean veal and beef suet, 150 grams of breadcrumbs, the rind of ½ a lemon, ½ a teaspoon of pepper, 1 teaspoon of salt, and ¼ of a teaspoon each of savory, nutmeg, marjoram and sage. Mince the pork, veal and suet together and mix in all the other ingredients. Make the mixture into flat cakes, dredge in flour and gently fry them.

STEWED MEATS Stewing is cooking gently in water or stock, with various vegetables, herbs and spices added for extra flavour. Old cookery books sometimes call this method boiling, but the liquid should never get beyond simmering point; if it boils fiercely the meat will be tough and fibrous. Casseroling, pot-roasting and cooking meat in pies and puddings are all stewing methods.

Stewing is economical because it uses the cheaper cuts, and easy because the timing is not critical. Stews and casseroles benefit from being cooked the day before eating and heated up again the following day, which gives the various flavours the chance to intermingle.

Irish stew In its classic form this dish is simply mutton, onions, potatoes, water and salt and pepper. Some versions add carrots and celery, and sometimes pearl barley is included to make a heartier dish.

For each person, you need 2 lamb neck chops, 1 large potato, 1 medium-sized onion and 1 cup of water. Trim the chops but leave a little fat on them, as part of the pleasure of this dish is the way in which the potatoes absorb the juices and melted fat. Peel and slice the vegetables about 1 cm thick.

Put the ingredients in alternating layers in a heavy casserole dish, sprinkling each layer with salt and pepper and finishing off with a

Taking Care of the Pence

Economise by saving bacon fat to use as dripping or for frying eggs. Trim the rinds and fat from the bacon and melt the fat over a very low heat. Discard the rinds when all the fat is melted.

In England during World War II, fats were very scarce and bread and dripping – a thick piece of bread lightly spread with bacon fat or dripping from the roasting pan and sprinkled with salt – was a treat to be prized.

neat layer of potato. Pour in the water, cover and cook in a moderate to low oven for about 4 hours, checking every so often to make sure that there is still plenty of liquid. Serve with a dark green vegetable such as spinach or broccoli.

Pot roast This is a cold-climate dish in which a whole piece of beef is cooked with stock and root vegetables. Brown a 1 kg piece of beef on all sides to seal in the juices; this is called searing. Put the meat in a heavy casserole and surround it with onions, potatoes and turnips, peeled and cut to the same size. Add salt, pepper, and water or stock to halfway up the sides of the casserole. Cover and cook on top of the stove over a low heat for about an hour. The meat will be meltingly tender and the vegetables permeated with lots of delicious juices.

CURED MEATS Salting and smoking meats was essential in the days before refrigeration, in order to preserve the parts of the slaughtered beast that would not be cooked immediately. Few people today would bother to cure meats at home, but butchers and delicatessens stock a variety of cured meats.

Bacon, which pork that has been salted and smoked, is a perennial favourite with a variety of uses. Bacon bones add flavour to pea and lentil soups and grilled or fried rashers of bacon are excellent with eggs cooked in virtually any style.

Concentrated meat extracts such as Oxo have been around for many years. They are useful for boosting the flavour of stocks, soups, gravies and casseroles.

Boiled beef and carrots This makes a good occasional change from fresh meats. The meat is cured in brine, which changes its colour; instead of the dark red of fresh beef, it is paler and brighter.

Cover a 1 kg piece of corned silverside with water in a heavy saucepan and add 2 large carrots and 1 large onion, peeled and roughly chopped, 1 tablespoon of brown sugar, 1 tablespoon vinegar, 1 bay leaf, 1 teaspoon of black peppercorns and 2 or 3 cloves. Bring to the boil and simmer gently for about 1 hour.

Just before the meat is done, cook some fresh carrots; those in the pot with the meat will be very salty and soft, and must be discarded. A good accompaniment is parsley sauce (see page 49). The sauce with its predominance of fresh parsley has a slight sweetness that counteracts the saltiness of the corned beef.

MEAT STOCKS In the kitchens of the past, a large stockpot stood at the back of the stove, and bones, meat scraps and vegetables were thrown in and kept simmering for hours, or even days. It is still economical and rewarding to make your own stock for soups and gravies.

Before the days of kitchen benchtops, a large table was the principal kitchen working space.

Put bones and meat scraps, including the giblets if you are making chicken stock, into a large saucepan, cover them with water and add chopped carrots and onions, fresh herbs tied together with string, and some black peppercorns. Bring the mixture to simmering point; a fine scum will form on the surface. Skim this off with a spoon, and keep doing so until the scum ceases to form.

After several hours, strain the stock through a fine sieve. Discard the scraps, let the liquid cool completely, and skim the congealed fat from the surface. The stock can be boiled up again and reduced for a more intense flavour and easier storage.

SEASON TO TASTE

The spice routes of the 18th and 19th centuries, when fast clipper ships would ferry exotic herbs and spices as well as tea and coffee from India, were the descendants of a very long tradition of trading in herbs and spices. According to Roman historians Herodotus and Pliny, spice caravans were making their laborious journey to Egypt from a collecting point in southern Arabia as early as 2000 years before Christ. The city of Alexandria was a centre of the spice trade long before it grew to fame as a centre of intellectual activity, and in the 15th and 16th centuries Portuguese and Spanish high-masted sailing ships called caravels carried this precious cargo northward. The Vikings, who were great sea travellers, traded in spices, not always legally, through contacts that they had established in the Middle East.

One advantage of herbs and spices as ship's cargo was that they were light and compact, so the trading ships could make extra profits by taking on an additional cargo of salt, which they could offload en route.

... TO MAKE YOU CRY

An engraving from 1843 shows a woman pounding horseradish roots in a huge mortar and pestle. The fresh root of horseradish is traditionally served with roast beef. Rarely for a temperate-zone plant, horseradish root is extremely pungent.

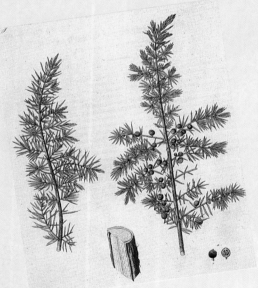

A VERSATILE HERB

The juniper plant has a long and honourable history; among other things, it rates a mention in the Old Testament *Book of Kings* as one of the fragrant timbers used to build King Solomon's temple.

In cookery, juniper berries are used to flavour game stuffings and casseroles, but their most famous gustatory use is as the principal flavouring agent in gin. Juniper berries also have medicinal uses.

A coloured drawing from 1813 (left) shows the wood, the berries and the appearance of the plant before and after bearing.

POUNDING IT OUT

A mortar and pestle, made of hardwood, stone or thick ceramics, is an age-old way of pulverising herbs and spices. Many cooks still prefer to grind spices in this way instead of using an electric grinder. The mortar is a bowl with a curved inner surface, and the pestle is a club-shaped rod.

A STAR AMONG SPICES

In its natural state, star anise is one of the prettiest of spices. Oil from the seeds is used instead of aniseed (from a related plant) for flavouring, and the pulverised seeds are widely used in Oriental cookery.

MAKING A SPICE RACK

With just a little expertise, you can make yourself a spice rack that will be just right for your kitchen and for the containers that you prefer to use. Use hardboard for the backboard, dressed timber for the ends and shelves, and screen moulding to hold the jars in place. Sand the rack and paint it to suit your kitchen.

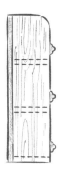

Cut the rack ends and the shelves to fit your jars, allowing enough room for easy removal and replacement of the jars. Round off the rack ends, glue or tack the shelves and the ends to the backboard, and then glue or tack the screen moulding across the front.

SALT, MUSTARD, VINEGAR, PEPPER

The Victorians and the Edwardians used containers called cruets for table condiments. Children turned the four ingredients into a rhythmic list and developed it into a skipping game.

WATCH OUT FOR FINGERS!

Some spices are impossible to pulverise in a mortar and pestle, so people have come up with various mechanical devices to do the job. Most of them, like this early Australian nutmeg grater, need care if grated fingers are to be avoided.

AN AROMATIC OPTION

Nowadays we buy and store herbs and spices in glass jars, but before glass became a cheap and widely available storage choice, wooden containers were the best way of storing herbs and spices. They were often made of timber that was itself highly scented, and the scents of the wood and the stored herbs and spices would blend into a delicious fragrance that perfumed the whole store cupboard. Shown on the right is an early Australian example of a spice box designed with separate compartments and a sliding lid like that of a modern pencil box.

A pretty kettle of fish

FISH IS 'A GOOD, HONEST, WHOLESOME, HUNGRY
BREAKFAST,' WROTE ISAAK WALTON (1593–1683).

In the days when Christian religious observances were quite strict, it
was forbidden to eat meat on Fridays. Fish was an obvious substitute,
and people came up with many ways to cook it.

BUYING AND STORING FISH Fish begins to lose flavour and texture as
soon as it is taken from the water, so it is important to buy and eat fish
as fresh as possible. Whole fish should have bright, protruding eyes
and smooth, springy skin with no hint of stickiness. Filleted fish
should be firm-fleshed and not running with moisture. Store fresh fish
for no more than a day, loosely covered with foil in the refrigerator.

COOKING FISH For cooking purposes, fish fall into two categories,
'oily' and 'white'. Oily fish, such as mackerel, salmon and tuna, have a
higher fat content and tend to have darker flesh. They are best cooked
by grilling or baking. White fish, such as flathead and ocean perch, are
suitable for frying, boiling and steaming.

FRESH FISH The great advantage of fresh fish for the busy cook is that
it is so quick to prepare and cook. Fish is cooked when the flesh,
which is slightly opalescent when raw, becomes opaque. This takes
only a few moments. On the other hand, timing is important; cooked
for too long, the flesh will be dry and flavourless.

Fish and chips Fish fried in batter with chips is one of life's culinary
delights. Use fillets of white fish such as flathead or whiting.

For a light, crisp batter, you will need 2 eggs, 4 tablespoons of plain
flour, about 150 ml of milk and 1 tablespoon of olive oil. Separate the
eggs and sift the flour into a basin. Beat in about three quarters of the
milk, working slowly to avoid lumps. Beat in the egg yolks and the
oil, and then add the rest of the milk. Let the mixture stand for an
hour. Just before you are ready to coat the fish, whisk the egg whites
to a stiff froth and fold them into the batter mixture.

Heat a good depth of cooking oil in a frying pan.
Dredge the fillets of fish in flour, draw them through
the batter until they are well coated and drop them
into the hot oil. Cook for about 5 minutes and serve
immediately with hot chips and wedges of lemon.

Baked fish In the old days fish was generally baked
whole, sometimes stuffed, but this recipe works for
fish fillets as well, as it includes butter. It is good
with both oily and white fish.

Place the fish in a baking dish and squeeze lemon
juice over it, then sprinkle it with ½ a teaspoon of
salt and some chopped parsley, dot with butter and

*Fish knives and forks used to be
an indispensable household item.
They were always made of silver
or silver plate, because steel
cutlery was thought to spoil the
taste of the fish.*

*In English coastal villages, when
the fishing boats came in, the
local fish shop would put up a
sign: 'FRYING TONIGHT'.*

cover it with buttered foil. You can add shallots and thyme to the baking dish for extra flavour. Bake the fish in a moderate oven for 20–30 minutes (10–15 minutes for fillets), depending on the size and thickness of the pieces.

Serve baked fish with parsley sauce. Steep a whole peeled onion in 1 cup of milk over a low heat. Blend 2 teaspoons of cornflour to a paste with a little milk, mix in the onion-flavoured milk and stir over a moderate heat until the mixture thickens. Enrich the sauce with a knob of butter, season with salt and freshly ground black pepper and stir in a good handful of chopped parsley.

Fish cakes Any type of fish can be used, including smoked and canned fish. Canned fish must be drained for making fish cakes.

You will need 2 cups of mashed potato, 2 cups of fish, a pinch of mixed herbs, salt and pepper, flour, frying batter and oil for frying. (Follow the batter recipe for fish and chips on the facing page.)

Mix the fish, potatoes, herbs, salt and pepper thoroughly together. Divide the mixture into six parts and shape each into a round, flat cake. Dip them in flour, then in the frying batter and deep-fry in the oil until they are a rich golden colour.

SMOKED FISH Oily fish are smoked to preserve them. The most famous of all is the Scottish finnan haddie, smoked haddock. The haddock is split and flattened, and turns golden when it is smoked. Smoked cod can be cooked the same way – grilled with butter, poached in water, or milk, or baked with butter and a little water.

Freshly caught fish, their silvery scales glistening as they catch the light, are some of nature's most beautiful treasures.

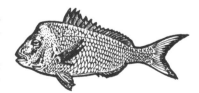

A FISHING SONG
You shall have a fishie
In a little dishie,
You shall have a fishie
When the boat comes in.

– TRADITIONAL

49

Kedgeree Kedgeree is a legacy of the British occupation of India. As made in India, kedgeree consists of rice boiled with onions, pulses, eggs and seasonings. The British version leaves out the pulses and incorporates fish – usually smoked cod or smoked haddock, although it can be made with any fish, cooked or uncooked.

You will need 250 grams of smoked cod or haddock, 1 cup of white rice, 4 eggs, salt and chopped parsley. Poach the fish for about 7 minutes. Drain and flake the fish, reserving the cooking liquor. Cook the rice for 15 minutes in the fish liquor, with added water if necessary; add salt, depending on how salty the fish liquor is. Rinse the rice and let it drain thoroughly. Hard-boil the eggs, shell them and chop them up. Mix all the ingredients evenly together, pile into a serving dish and sprinkle with chopped parsley.

Some kedgeree recipes include a little curry powder and crumbled hard-boiled egg sprinkled over the dish with the parsley.

CANNED FISH Like smoking, canning is a good method of preserving oily fish but not white fish. The canning process slightly lightens the colour and softens the texture of the fish.

Tuna mornay Known in some countries as tunny, tuna is a game fish that can weigh as much as half a tonne. Canned tuna enjoys the company of cheese, and *mornay* means cooked with cheese.

You will need 1 large tin of tuna in brine, the juice of 1 lemon, ground black pepper, 1 tablespoon of margarine, 1 medium onion, 1 tablespoon of flour, 1 cup of milk and ½ a cup of grated cheese.

Drain the tuna, flake it into an ovenproof dish and season with the lemon juice and black pepper. Melt the margarine over a low heat and soften the chopped onion in it. Work the flour into the margarine and cook for a few minutes. Off the heat, work the milk into the flour until the mixture is quite thin, add the grated cheese, return to a medium heat and stir until the sauce thickens.

Pour the cheese sauce over the tuna and agitate a little with a fork so that the sauce penetrates right into the layer of tuna flakes. Bake in a moderate oven until the top is well browned – even burnt in places.

Salmon mousse For this dish, use the best brand of canned red salmon you can find – salmon from Scotland or Canada is the best.

You will need 1 medium-sized tin of salmon, 1 sachet of gelatine, 2 cups of hot water, the juice of 1 lemon, 2 hard-boiled eggs, pepper and salt. Break up the salmon, including the bones and the canning liquor. Melt the gelatine in the hot water and stir in the lemon juice, the pepper and the salt. Add the salmon and mix in thoroughly.

Wet a mousse mould, lay slices of hard-boiled egg around the bottom, pour the salmon mixture over and leave to set. Turn out carefully and serve decorated with lemon wedges and parsley.

Mix in a small quantity of mayonnaise for a richer, creamier mousse.

Devilled herrings Herrings are an excellent canning fish. Try this Australian recipe from the early 1900s.

A professional fisherman basks in the glory of a successful night out in the boat.

A poached whole salmon garlanded and crowned with prawns attains the status of a work of art in this gorgeous illustration from an 1890s cookery book.

You will need 1 small onion, 1 tablespoon of butter, 1 heaped tablespoon of flour, ½ a teaspoon of prepared mustard, ½ a teaspoon of curry powder, a pinch of cayenne, Worcestershire sauce, 1 small can of herrings in brine, 300 ml of milk, breadcrumbs and grated cheese.

Chop the onion and soften it in the melted butter over a low heat. Mix in the flour, mustard, curry powder, cayenne and Worcestershire sauce. Add the milk slowly, working it in a little at a time, and stir over a low heat until the sauce thickens.

Drain, skin, bone and flake the herrings and stir them into the sauce. Put the mixture in a pie dish, sprinkle it with breadcrumbs and grated cheese and dab some butter over the top. Bake in a very hot oven until the top is browned; this last step can be done under the griller, but be careful handling the hot dish.

OYSTERS 'He was a bold man that first eat an oyster,' said Jonathan Swift, author of *Gulliver's Travels*. Bold he may have been, but he did the world a favour when he discovered how delectable these ocean dwelling molluscs can be.

Angels on horseback The origin of their name is a mystery, but these little savouries have graced elegant gatherings for decades.

For four 'angels' you will need 1 slice of bread, lemon juice, 4 shelled oysters and 2 rashers of bacon. Remove the crusts and cut the bread into four; fry in bacon fat. Dip each oyster in lemon juice, wrap in ½ a rasher of bacon and grill quickly – the oysters should be scarcely cooked. Serve immediately on the fried bread.

Oyster steak Australians took this lavish dish to their hearts in the affluent sixties and seventies, when it was known as carpetbag steak. Restaurants specialising in it called it Surf and Turf.

For each person you will need a piece of very tender steak, cut about 5 cm thick, a few raw shelled oysters, cayenne and lemon juice. Dip the oysters in the lemon juice and sprinkle them with a little cayenne. Make a slit in the steak and stuff in as many oysters as you can. Close the slit with a small skewer. Grill for 10–20 minutes, depending on whether the steak is to be rare, medium or well done.

In the early 1900s Worcestershire sauce was heavily promoted as a universal flavouring agent for savoury dishes.

The Way We Were

A true passion for oysters knows no limits:

'I kept him company as far as the third dozen, after which I let him go on alone. He went up to thirty-two dozen, taking more than an hour over the task, for the servant was not very skilful at opening them.

Meanwhile, I was inactive, and as that is a distressing condition to be in at the table, I stopped my guest when he was still in full career. "My dear fellow," I said, "it is not your fate to eat your bellyful of oysters today; let us have dinner."

We dined: and he acquitted himself with the vigour and appetite of a man who had been fasting.'

– *The Physiology of Taste*, Brillat-Savarin (1755–1826)

Delicacies from Down Under

LONG BEFORE A DISTINCTIVE LOCAL CUISINE
EMERGED, AUSTRALASIAN CHEFS WERE MAKING
THEIR CONTRIBUTION TO THE ART OF COOKERY.

The cookery skills brought by the first white settlers were firmly in
the English tradition. Meat and vegetables and floury puddings were
the staple foods, and they were needed to provide the energy for the
often backbreaking work of taming the land. Paradoxically, though,
it was in delicate confectionary that Australia first made its mark on
international cuisine, with dishes such as peach Melba and pavlova.

LAMINGTONS If Australia has a national dish, it is the lamington,
named for Baron Lamington, Governor of Queensland from 1895 to
1901. In the old days women would gather to make dozens of
lamingtons to raise money for community causes, and 'lamington
drives' are still a uniquely Australian fund raiser.

You need 4 eggs, 2 cups of caster sugar, 2 teaspoons of vanilla
essence, 1 cup of self-raising flour, 60 grams of butter, 3 cups of icing
sugar, 2 cups of cocoa, 2 cup of boiling water, and desiccated coconut.

Line two 20 cm square cake tins with buttered greaseproof paper
and preheat the oven to moderate. Beat the eggs, caster sugar and
vanilla together until the mixture is thick and creamy. Fold in the
sifted flour and add the butter, melted and cooled. Turn the mixture
into the tins and bake for 25 minutes. Cool and cut into squares.

Mix together the icing sugar, cocoa, water and vanilla and stir over
hot water until smooth. Keeping the bowl over the hot water, dip the
cake squares into the chocolate mixture and roll quickly in coconut.

PAVLOVA Western Australian chef Bert Sachse named the 'pav' after
Anna Pavlova, the great Russian ballerina of the early 20th century.
You will need 4 egg whites, 2 cups of caster
sugar, 3 teaspoon of cornflour, 1 teaspoon of
vinegar, 1 teaspoon of vanilla essence, and
whipped cream and fresh fruit for
the topping.

Heat the oven to moderate and
spread a sheet of rice paper on
a baking tray. Whisk the egg
whites and salt to a stiff froth and
beat in the sugar a little at a time.
Fold in the cornflour, vinegar and
vanilla, turn the mixture onto

*Adventurous Australians have
always experimented with
cooking and eating native
animals. This menu, recorded
in 1895, is from a gold-mining
settlement in Queensland.*

the rice paper and mould it into a shallow flan shape. Reduce the oven heat to low and cook the pavlova for 75 minutes. Turn off the heat and leave the pavlova to cool.

Fill the hollow with whipped cream and decorate with fresh fruit – strawberries, passionfruit and kiwifruit are popular choices.

ANZAC BISCUITS These crisp, easy and economical biscuits take their name from the Anzacs – the Australian and New Zealand Army Corps – who fought in World War I. Eggs were scarce, and the recipe needs none. Anzacs keep well, and mothers, sisters, sweethearts and wives would send them to their menfolk in the war zones.

To make Anzac biscuits, you will need 1 cup of rolled oats, 1 cup of coconut, 1 cup of flour, 1 cup of sugar, 125 grams of butter, 1 tablespoon of golden syrup, 2 tablespoons of boiling water and 1 teaspoon of bicarbonate of soda.

Preheat the oven to fairly low and grease several baking trays. Mix the rolled oats, coconut, flour and sugar well together. Melt the butter and syrup, add the boiling water and bicarbonate of soda and mix into the blended dry ingredients. Drop teaspoons of the mixture onto the baking trays, leaving enough room between for the biscuits to spread. Cook the biscuits for about 20 minutes. Leave them on the baking trays for 5 minutes to firm, and then cool completely on wire racks. Store in an airtight tin.

PEACH MELBA In its original form, peach Melba was a swan modelled from ice with peaches and vanilla ice cream nestling between its wings and a topping of spun sugar. It was inspired by Dame Nellie Melba's singing in Wagner's opera *Lohengrin*, which features a swan. Later, the swan disappeared and a raspberry purée replaced the spun sugar.

You will need vanilla-flavoured sugar syrup, and for each person 1 peach, 1 scoop of vanilla ice cream and a generous helping of puréed raspberries. Poach the peaches in the syrup until just tender, remove, drain, peel and chill. Put the peaches into individual glass dishes, cover them with ice cream and pour the raspberry purée over.

WHITEBAIT FRITTERS Whitebait are baby sprats and herrings, called 'fry', and they are eaten whole. They grow well in cool waters, such as those off New Zealand, and whitebait fritters are a New Zealand favourite.

You will need 250 grams of New Zealand whitebait, flour to dust, salt and freshly ground pepper, 2 eggs and vegetable oil – peanut oil for preference – for frying.

Put the whitebait into a bag with the flour, salt and pepper and shake to coat the fish. Beat the eggs and add the floured whitebait. Pour a thin coating of oil into a frying pan, heat the oil, and drop in dollops of the whitebait mixture. Fry on each side for about 2 minutes, or until the fritters are crisp and golden. Garnish with chopped parsley and lemon wedges.

'HAPPY LITTLE VEGEMITES'
In 1923, Melbournian Fred Walker had the idea of developing a yeast extract that would rival the similar English product, Marmite. It did not sell well under the brand name Vegemite, so he renamed it Parwill, with the marketing slogan 'If Marmite, Parwill!!' Not surprisingly, this terrible pun failed to boost sales, so Vegemite it became again, this time with market success. The recipe remains a trade secret.

The salty black spread was so addictive that it became a compulsory inclusion in 'mercy parcels' dispatched to Australians overseas suffering from withdrawal symptoms . Vegemite is now American-owned and is retailed overseas, but many Australians still lament the foreign ownership of a uniquely Australian icon.

The French chef Auguste Escoffier created peach Melba in honour of Dame Nellie Melba, the internationally renowned Australian singer.

Nature's nourishment

WHEN MEAT AND FISH WERE THE WEALTHY PERSON'S
DIET, EGGS AND DAIRY FOODS PROVIDED SUSTENANCE
TO MANY, BOTH IN CITIES AND ON THE FARMS.

Over the years, creative cooks have devised endless ways to use eggs,
cheese, butter and milk. From the humble boiled egg to the
sophisticated cheese soufflé, eggs and dairy foods have been used alone
or together to supplement meat and fish or to substitute for them.

EGGS Both the yolks and the whites of eggs contain a great deal
of protein, and the yolks also have a high fat content. The yolk is
enclosed in a membrane, which is stronger when the egg is fresh and
therefore less likely to break. For this reasons, recipes that require the
whites to be separated from the yolks and whisked should be made
with fresh eggs, because any trace of fat in the whites inhibits the tiny
bubbles from forming.

Storing eggs Our grandparents used various substances to seal eggs
for storage, but refrigerators and modern egg farming practices have
made this unnecessary. In fact, eggs will keep for quite a long time.
Check the packing date and buy the freshest eggs you can find. Store
them in the refrigerator in their carton or in a covered egg rack,
because eggshells are permeable and strong flavours of other foods,
such as onions, may contaminate the eggs.

Cooking eggs Eggs are best used at room temperature, so take out
the number you need in advance. Boiled eggs are less likely to crack if
they are not put into boiling water straight from the refrigerator, and
egg whites are easier to whisk to a froth when they are slightly warm.

   Both the whites and the yolks of eggs coagulate when they are
heated, and it is this that makes eggs so useful for thickening sauces.
But it also means that timing is crucial for egg dishes that contain no
flour, since even a few seconds too long can harden the eggs into a
rubbery consistency. When cooking whole eggs, allow a little longer
for large ones. Newlaid eggs need a little longer than older ones.

MILK AND CREAM Milk and its by-products – cream, butter and
cheese – are rich in protein and fat. They have myriad uses in cooking,
usually in combination with other foods.

Storing milk Fresh milk quickly goes sour, and in the old days fresh
milk was taken straight from the cow every day and stored in the
coolest place available. On farms, making butter and cheese so as not
to waste precious milk were routine tasks. Even with pasteurisation,
homogenisation and refrigeration, milk does not keep well. Never
leave milk out, especially in a warm climate. Milk that has started to
sour tastes unpleasant but it is not unsafe to consume; you can use it
for making scones, pikelets or batter.

*Metal labels like these were a
feature of many dairies in the old
days. Prices changed constantly,
and would be added by hand.*

BUTTER AND CHEESE Cheese is a solid milk protein called casein, produced by the action on milk of a curdling agent called rennet, an enzyme from the stomach lining of a young calf.

Storing butter and cheese Salted butter keeps better than unsalted, but many people prefer the taste of unsalted butter. Keep butter covered in the refrigerator.

Invest in a cheese dish – a platter with a domed lid; it will keep cheese fresh for weeks.

PLAIN EGGS Eggs eaten with nothing except a little seasoning have a subtle flavour that is all their own. Boiling, poaching and frying are ways of cooking whole eggs that have never disappeared from favour. For a yolk that is still liquid, cook eggs for 3 minutes; for a slightly firmer yolk, cook for 5 minutes.

• Check the shells of eggs that are to be boiled for signs of cracking and put aside any that look vulnerable. Turn the water down to simmer temperature before immersing the eggs and lower the eggs in gently with a spoon.

• Lightly grease a poaching pan to stop the eggs from sticking, and add a dash of cider vinegar to the poaching water. The vinegar stops the egg white from disintegrating; it also adds a distinctive taste.

• Lard and dripping are the best fats for frying eggs; cooking oil will do, but margarine is not suitable because it contains colourings, preservatives and stabilisers that burn and cause the eggs to stick.

Fried eggs are shown here advertising an oil stove that was said to yield up to 19 hours of cooking from 1 gallon (4.5 litres) of fuel.

Eggs are the sole nourishment of many living creatures before they are born, and milk their only food for some time after birth.

Baked eggs This is a method of cooking whole eggs that is less common now than it was when solid fuel stoves ensured a hot oven all day long.

Heat a shallow ovenproof dish in a moderately hot oven and then take it out and glaze it with butter or margarine. (Don't heat the fat in the oven, as it may burn.) Break 2 eggs per person into the dish and put a pat of butter on each egg. Bake in a hottish oven for about 15 minutes; when the eggs are cooked the tops should be opaque and firmly set but the underneath should wobble slightly if you shake the dish. An extra touch is to shake a little grated cheese over the eggs before baking them.

An early ice cream churn (above) and food mixer (right) relied on person power to agitate the paddles.

OMELETTES There are three types of omelette: the basic French omelette; the frothy omelette, which is Scandinavian; and the Spanish omelette. Omelettes must be served immediately they are cooked.

French omelette For one person, you will need 3 eggs, salt and pepper and a little butter, and an omelette pan about 15 cm in diameter. (The size is important, as the depth of egg in the pan must be exactly right.) Heat the pan, meanwhile beating the seasoned eggs lightly in a bowl. When the pan is very hot, sizzle a nut of butter in it; the butter should turn golden brown. Swirl the melted butter around the pan and pour in the beaten eggs. Quickly push the mixture in from the side with a spatula so that liquid egg flows down to replace the cooked bottom layers. Continue until the top is set; this should take about a minute. Tilt the pan, roll the omelette up with a fork and tip it onto a warmed plate.

Frothy omelette Whisk 2 or 3 eggs into a thick pale golden froth. Heat and butter the pan as for a French omelette, pour the eggs in and lower the heat a little. When the top of the whisked egg mixture is set, fold the omelette in half – it will probably squidge out at the side, but you can half-turn it to seal the gap. Cook it for a little longer; it will puff up as the air bubbles in the whisked egg expand.

Spanish omelette This omelette is denser in texture than the other two. The English used to call it a hodge-podge, and it is a good way to use up leftovers. Chop up cooked vegetables, meat or fish very small, mix them into beaten eggs, and cook the whole thing like a thick pancake in butter or cooking oil. Fold it over if it is not too thick, or turn it to cook the other side.

Taking Care of the Pence

Scrambled eggs can be eked out by using fewer eggs and adding a little milk, or even water, to the mixture. You need to be more careful with the cooking though: watch the pan closely and snatch it from the heat the moment the mixture is cooked.

SCRAMBLED EGGS Allow 2 eggs per person and beat them until the yolks and the whites are thoroughly blended. Add a little salt and pepper. Over a low heat, glaze a heavy-based saucepan with butter or margarine, swirling it around to coat the bottom and part of the sides.

Pour in the egg mixture and stir continuously with a wooden spoon over a low heat. Keep the wooden spoon in contact with the bottom of the saucepan to lift the flakes of egg mixture as they coagulate and allow the uncooked mixture to sink to the bottom. Take the pan off the heat while there is still some free liquid, as the eggs will continue to cook for a little while in the retained heat of the mixture. Serve scrambled eggs on crisp buttered toast.

The Way We Were

'The dairy was certainly worth looking at. It was a scene to sicken for with a sort of calenture in hot and dusty streets – such coolness, such purity, such fresh fragrance of new-pressed cheese, of firm butter, of wooden vessels perpetually bathed in pure water; such soft colouring of red earthenware and creamy surfaces, brown wood and polished tin, grey limestone and rich orange-red rust on the iron weights and hooks and hinges. But one gets only a confused notion of these details when they surround a distractingly pretty girl of seventeen, standing on little pattens and rounding her dimpled arm to lift a pound of butter out of the scale.'

– *Adam Bede*, George Eliot (1859)

SOUFFLES A thick sauce is incorporated into stiffly beaten egg whites and the mixture is cooked in a very hot oven for 20–25 minutes. The soufflé will puff up to three or four times its uncooked volume, and will have an attractive cratered crust.

Vanilla soufflé You will need 30 grams of butter or margarine, 30 grams of plain flour, 150 ml of milk, a vanilla pod, 30 grams of caster sugar and 6 eggs.

Simmer the vanilla pod in the milk for about 10 minutes. Melt the fat in a saucepan, stir in the flour and cook gently for a few minutes. Over a medium heat, work in the milk to make a thick sauce. Stir in the sugar. Separate the eggs and beat four of the yolks into the mixture one at a time; cool the sauce before you do this, or the yolks will coagulate and go lumpy.

Now comes the tricky part. Make sure everybody is ready to eat: the diners must wait for the soufflé, not the soufflé for the diners.

Heat the oven to very hot and butter and flour a 14 cm soufflé dish. Beat the 6 egg whites into a stiff froth with a whisk or an egg-beater; electric beaters produce bubbles of egg white that are too small, resulting in a tougher, less puffy soufflé. Fold the soufflé base into the egg whites very quickly and gently with a rubber spatula to make a creamy froth. Pour the mixture into the soufflé dish and put it in the oven immediately.

Do not open the oven for at least 15 minutes – a breath of cold air can ruin a soufflé. Then inspect the soufflé cautiously until you are sure it has risen properly. Serve immediately.

Cheese soufflé Use the same quantities of butter, flour, milk and eggs as for a vanilla soufflé, and add 60 grams of mixed grated cheddar and parmesan cheese to the sauce after you have incorporated the milk, with a few grinds of black pepper and a pinch or two of salt.

MAYONNAISE Mayonnaise is a blend of oil and lemon juice held together with egg yolk and mustard. You will need 2 egg yolks – use those left over from making a soufflé – a little salt, dry mustard, 30 ml of lemon juice and 180 ml of extra virgin olive oil.

Beat the salt and ½ a teaspoon of mustard into the egg yolks and then stir in the lemon juice. Beat the oil into the mixture literally drop by drop, as slowly as possible. In the old days this was very hard

MAKING A SOUFFLE COLLAR

For a soufflé that will stand up proudly out of its dish, make a paper collar.

1. Lightly butter a piece of greaseproof paper long enough to wrap around the dish with a little overlap. Tie the greaseproof paper around the dish before you pour in the soufflé mixture.

2. When you take the soufflé out of the oven, take the collar off and you will find that the soufflé will have risen above the sides of the dish in an impressive crusty dome.

work, as the beating was done with a fork, but today hand-held electric beaters make it much easier.

CUSTARDS It is easy to make your own custard, and once you have done it you will never buy commercial varieties again. Both these custards can be flavoured with vanilla or your favourite liqueur.

Pouring custard This recipe makes an excellent custard that won't separate, because the cornflour ensures that the mixture binds properly. Mix 30 grams each of cornflour and caster sugar into a thick paste with 3 egg yolks. Thin this paste with a little milk and add it to 600 ml of milk in a saucepan. Heat gently, stirring all the time, until the custard thickens to a pouring consistency.

Baked custard This custard has no flour to bind it. First warm 600 ml of milk with 30 grams of sugar until the sugar is dissolved (do ot overheat). Beat 4 egg yolks together, add the sweetened milk, pour the mixture into an ovenproof bowl and stand in a larger ovenproof bowl of water. Cook in a low oven until the custard is set and slightly browned on top – 90 minutes to 2 hours.

SWEET TREATS Hundreds of cakes and desserts rely on eggs or milk or both. Here are two old-time favourites.

Bread and butter pudding This classic but economical dish is delicious hot or cold.

You will need 4 slices of white bread, dried fruits such as sultanas, candied cherries and candied peel, 2 eggs, 300 ml of milk and 30 grams of caster sugar. Butter the bread and cut the slices in half diagonally, leaving the crusts on. Arrange them with the corners pointing upwards in a deep ovenproof dish and sprinkle them with the dried fruits and candied peel. Whisk the eggs, milk and sugar together and pour the mixture over the bread and fruit. Bake in a low oven for about an hour, or until the crusts are golden and crisp.

Raisin bread makes an excellent bread and butter pudding, but you will need to add some extra dried fruits. For a special tang, add a little nutmeg and cinnamon to the egg and milk mixture.

Meringues Make these baked shells of icing sugar and egg white when you have egg whites left over from custards. Beat 2 egg whites into a stiff froth and then gradually beat in 4 rounded tablespoons of sifted icing sugar. The mixture will look like thick, stiff cream. Place small dollops from a forcing bag or straight from a spoon on a greased baking tray. Cook in a very low oven for 2 hours.

To make meringues Chantilly, join the bases of two meringues with whipped cream, place them in cupcake papers and pipe extra cream around the join to decorate.

WHAT AM I?
A box without hinges, lock or lid,
Yet golden treasure within is hid.

[ANSWER: AN EGG]

The staff of life

BEFORE HUMANS DEVELOPED TOOLS FOR HUNTING AND KILLING ANIMALS, THEY LIVED LARGELY ON PLANT FOODS, ESPECIALLY GRAINS AND CEREALS.

Cereals and grains are our most important source of nutrition. Even dedicated meat eaters are dependent on cereal products, since the animals they eat feed on grains and cereals and convert them into the animal protein that constitutes meat. Cereals are the basis of innumerable breads, pastries, cakes and puddings.

The odour of home-baked bread is the essence of nostalgia: some estate agents today advise vendors to bake bread so that buyers will be seduced by the fragrance wafting through the house.

BREAD Whether the house-selling strategy works or not, making your own bread is fun. It is time-consuming, but much of the time is taken up while the bread dough is rising, or 'proving', and you can go away and do something else while you wait.

Basically, bread is a mixture of flour, water, sugar, salt, and a raising agent such as yeast. The ingredients are mixed into a stiff dough, which you then pummel, or 'knead', strenuously with your fists and fingers until the texture is smooth and springy, which means that the gluten in the flour has developed and is ready to hold the shape of the finished loaf. The yeast feeds on the sugar and flour, producing a gas that permeates the dough and causes it to rise.

Fresh yeast looks rather like putty and is available from bakers, or use dried yeast, following the instructions on the packet.

Basic white bread For two loaves, you will need 1 kg of plain flour, 600 ml of water and 1 tablespoon each of salt, white sugar and brewer's yeast. Heat the water to comfortably hot and dissolve the salt and sugar in it. Cream the yeast with a little of the liquid and mix it with the main liquid.

Make a well in the centre of the flour and pour in the liquid. Mix into a fairly stiff dough and knead well for about 5 minutes. Put the dough into a clean greased bowl, cover with a tea towel and leave in a warm place to rise – about 2 hours.

Divide the risen dough in half; it will collapse, but will rise again with the second proving. Mould each half into a loaf shape, put into greased loaf tins and leave to rise for about 30 minutes. Bake in a very hot oven for about 40 minutes.

Kiwi bread In July 1980 there was a baker's strike in Sydney and people dredged their memories and swamped the airways with ways of making bread at home. Kiwi bread was one of these.

Mix together 3 cups of wholemeal self-raising flour, 1 teaspoon of salt, 3 teaspoons of honey and 1 can of beer. Bake in a greased tin in a hot oven for about 40 minutes.

For those who have tried it, the satisfaction gained from baking your own bread at home is said to be boundless ... and the pleasure it will bring to your family is purely an extra reward!

BATTER DISHES Batter is a runny mixture of eggs, flour and milk that is fried into pancakes, baked into batter puddings or used to coat pieces of meat, fish or fruit, which are then deep-fried.

The formula for making batter is 1 egg, 3 tablespoons of plain flour and 150 ml of milk; slightly sour milk makes a good batter. Sift the flour into a bowl and break the egg into the centre. With a fork, gradually whisk the egg into the flour to produce a stiff mixture. When all the flour is incorporated, beat in the milk until you have a thin, runny mixture that is completely free from lumps. Stand the batter in a cool place for about an hour before using it.

Lemon pancakes In a frying pan, melt just enough butter or margarine to coat the bottom of the pan. When it is smoking, pour in a pool of batter and tilt the pan so that its base is covered with a thin layer of batter. Shake the pan over a moderate heat until the pancake starts to slide about. Turn the pancake to cook the other side, and slide it onto a hot plate. Pour lemon juice over, sprinkle with caster sugar and roll up. The whole process should take only 2 or 3 minutes.

Making breads and pastries needs practice, but it is well worth spending the time to learn.

A sifter with a handle is a useful piece of equipment and makes less mess than a sieve.

Yorkshire pudding In Helene Hanff's charming book *84 Charing Cross Road*, an English woman tells her American correspondent how to cook this famous batter pudding to accompany roast beef:

'When you put your roast in the oven, put in an extra pan to heat. Half an hour before your roast is done, pour a bit of the roast grease into the baking pan, just enough to cover the bottom will do. The pan must be very hot. Now pour the batter in and the roast and pudding will be ready at the same time … a good Yorkshire pudding will puff up very high and brown and crisp and when you cut into it you will find that it is hollow inside.'

PASTRY Pastry is a combination of flour, fat and liquid to make a crisp crust for pies and tarts. The easiest pastry to make at home is short pastry, which is used for tarts, flans and sausage rolls.

You will need 250 grams of self-raising flour, 125 grams of butter or cooking margarine and about 120 ml of very cold water. Cut the butter into small pieces and rub it into the flour with your fingertips, lifting the mixture to incorporate as much air as possible; this is what will make the pastry light. Stop when the mixture starts to look like fine breadcrumbs; if you keep going the fat will melt, the mixture will start to coalesce and the pastry will be ruined.

Add the water and mix it in to form a fairly soft dough. Knead the dough gently for a minute or two to form an elastic ball, then wrap it in foil and put it in the refrigerator for 30 minutes.

Treacle tart Line a flan dish with short pastry rolled to about 6 mm thick. Trim the edges neatly and save the trimmings. Sprinkle about 30 grams of fine white breadcrumbs into the bottom of the lined flan dish and pour golden syrup generously over them. Cut the pastry trimmings into narrow strips, twist them and arrange across the tart in a lattice pattern. Bake in a hot oven for about 30 minutes. Allow to cool a little before serving – the treacle will be very hot.

Sausage rolls Skin some pork sausages, keeping their shape, and roll out short pastry to about 5 mm thick. Enclose the sausage meat in the pastry, following the steps in the right-hand column. Put into a hot oven. After 20 minutes, turn the oven to moderate so that the heat will cook the sausage filling right through without burning the pastry.

CAKES AND BISCUITS In the good old days, cakes and biscuits – plain for the family, fancy for visitors – were an essential part of the afternoon tea ritual.

Plain cake This is the basis for numerous classic cake recipes. You will need 250 grams each of butter and caster sugar, 3 eggs, 500 grams of self-raising flour and about 150 ml of milk.

Cream the sugar and butter together and gradually add the beaten eggs, making sure that each addition is throughly incorporated before you add the next bit. Slowly fold in the sifted flour and then enough milk to make a very thick batter. Pour this into a greased and lined cake tin and bake for an hour in a moderate oven.

Add crystallised cherries to the batter for cherry cake, grated orange zest for orange cake, or caraway seeds for seed cake.

MAKING SAUSAGE ROLLS
Home made sausage rolls will win you fans whenever finger food is on the menu.

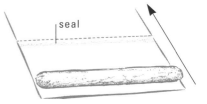

1. Roll out the pastry, trim the edges square and lay the skinned sausages end to end. Roll the pastry over the sausage meat and seal with beaten egg. Cut at the seal and repeat.

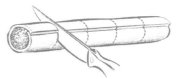

2. With a sharp knife, cut the long roll into 5 cm lengths.

3. Place the rolls on a baking tray, score them several times and glaze with beaten egg.

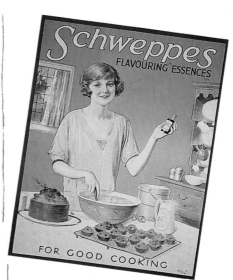

Commercial flavouring essences, introduced in the early 1900s, made cake baking an easier task.

The Way We Were

'Mr Moscrop had a wooden spade with an enormously long handle. With this he could reach right to the back of the oven. Sliding the blade under the loaves, he began to draw them out and put them on the two long deal tables. Some were for Mr Moscrop's shop and delivery round. Others had been baked for customers who made up their own dough at home. Fanciful people pricked their initials into the top of the dough. Others wrote their names on pieces of paper and skewered them onto the loaves with matchsticks. These pieces of paper were now brown and brittle and would fall to bits if you touched them.'

– MY SON, MY SON, HOWARD SPRING (1938)

Ginger snaps These biscuity cylinders filled with whipped cream make a spectacular addition to a tea table. Make snaps on the day you want to eat them: they do not keep.

You will need 2 heaped tablespoons of self-raising flour, ½ a teaspoon of ground ginger, 2 tablespoons each of golden syrup and butter, 3 rounded tablespoons of sugar, and a piece of well oiled thick dowelling about 20 cm long.

Combine the flour and ginger and add all the other ingredients to make a firm dough. Shape the dough into a roll and divide the dough into 16 equal-sized pieces. Put them on greased baking trays, about 10 cm apart and flatten them to the size of a 50 cent piece. Cook in a moderate oven for about 20 minutes When they are ready they will be flat and bubbling and quite dark in colour.

Take the snaps from the oven, wait about a minute and try rolling one around the dowelling. If it disintegrates, let the rest of the snaps cool for a little longer before rolling. When cool and firm, fill with whipped cream; add a little sugar and brandy to the whipped cream to make the ginger snaps into brandy snaps.

Devil's food cake This chocolate treat never loses its popularity. Join the layers with cream and sprinkle the top with grated chocolate.

You need ¾ of a cup of butter or cooking margarine, a scant 2 cups of brown sugar, 3 eggs, ¾ of a cup of water, 90 grams of bitter chocolate, 2¼ cups of self-raising flour, 2 teaspoons of baking powder, ¾ of a teaspoon of salt, and ¾ of a cup of sour milk flavoured with vanilla essence.

Beat the sugar and the softened butter until you have a thick cream, and slowly add the beaten eggs. Boil the water and melt the chocolate in it over a low heat. Add the chocolate to the egg mixture when cool, blending thoroughly. Sift the flour, combine it with the rest of the dry ingredients and sift three more times.

Before fast foods, cooking for a party was very labour-intensive. If dad could be persuaded to lend a hand, it was twice as much fun and half as much work.

Beating well, alternately add the flour and the milk to the chocolate mixture. Grease and line three shallow pans and pour in the mixture. Bake in a moderate oven for 25–30 minutes.

DESSERTS Life in the old days was more strenuous than it is now, and many desserts were substantial concoctions and tended to be quite sweet to give people the energy they needed for their daily work.

Old-fashioned rice pudding This version of rice pudding is made with uncooked rice. The texture is quite firm; use more milk if you prefer a creamier pudding.

You will need 3 cups of milk, a strip of lemon rind, 3 teaspoons of butter, 3 rounded tablespoons of sugar and 1 cup of white rice.

Warm the milk and lemon rind over a low heat. Add the butter and sugar and stir until the sugar has melted. Add the rice, stir and heat the mixture to just below simmering point. Pour into an ovenproof dish, sprinkle with nutmeg and bake in a low oven for 4 hours.

Jam roly poly Made with suet pastry, this was an old-time nursery favourite. It could be either steamed or baked. It was served with custard, and the jam would ooze into the custard in streaks of colour.

You will need 250 grams of self-raising flour, 125 grams of shredded suet (from good supermarkets), water and jam.

Thoroughly mix together the flour and suet and add water to make a fairly soft dough. Flour the pastry board well and roll out the dough, keeping the sides as straight as possible, to make a thickish sheet. Spread the dough with jam and roll it up from the shorter edge.

To bake a jam roly poly, put it into a greased baking tin and cook it in a medium oven for about an hour. When it is done, the top should be an attractive golden-brown.

To steam the roly poly, wrap the roll of dough in a well floured pudding cloth and tie up the ends firmly; alternatively, enclose it completely in foil. Place it in the top compartment of a large double boiler and keep the water bubbling in the bottom compartment for about 2 hours.

PORRIDGE Oats is one of the healthiest and most nourishing of cereals, as our grandmothers knew very well.

The following is an authentic Scottish recipe for breakfast porridge. You will need 2 cups of water, 1 cup of pinmeal (very finely ground) oats and ½ a teaspoon of salt. (Porridge tastes insipid without salt, even if you have a sweet tooth.)

Boil the water and salt and gradually add the oats; sprinkle in rather than pouring it, because it has a tendency to form lumps. Cook the porridge for about 20 minutes, stirring frequently.

Porridge is generally eaten with milk or cream, but tastes vary from region to region where other flavourings are concerned. In the northern parts of Britain, for example, porridge is often eaten with salt and pepper; in the south, people prefer brown sugar or treacle.

ROLLING PINS

'Wooden rolling pins found in many nineteenth-century households were usually made of sycamore, which does not colour or flavour food. Some were ridged to crush oatmeal and salt. Although more expensive, porcelain rolling pins were also common. They could be filled with water to provide extra weight and keep the pastry cool whilst rolling. Nailsea glass rolling pins were very popular. Hot, molten glass was rolled in coloured enamel chips, reheated and then reblown to create marvellous coloured patterns. Made near English ports, they were often given as "love tokens" by departing mariners. Many held salt and were hung by the fire so that the salt kept dry.'

– *FORGOTTEN HOUSEHOLD CRAFTS*, JOHN SEYMOUR (1987)

In the old days, the kitchen was a natural cooking school, and 'licking the spoon' was one of the perks of helping mummy.

Cooks and Books

The cookery books that fill so many shelves in modern bookshops and make so much money for publishers are a relatively recent development. Until about the middle of the 20th century, books about food and cooking were not highly illustrated and were meant to be read for pleasure, not simply plundered for recipes or admired for their stunning photography.

Some modern food writers and publishers have continued this tradition: the great *Larousse Gastronomique* is still with us, and is constantly updated; American writer Waverley Root has given us a magnificent volume called simply *Food*; and the Frenchman Maguelonne Toussaint-Samat a fascinating and scholarly book called *History of Food*. These are books about more than cookery; they are about eating as a sensual and intellectual experience.

THE FIRST FOODIE?

Jean Anthelme Brillat-Savarin was a French lawyer, musician and gastronome. In 1825, at the age of 70, he published an extraordinary meditation on food, *La Physiologie du goût* ('The Physiology of Taste'), a title later brilliantly translated into English as 'The Philosopher in the Kitchen.'

AN AUSSIE KITCHEN

Mrs Isabella Mary Beeton published her *Book of Cookery and Household Management* in 1861. Since then it has never been out of print, and the 1891 edition featured an engraving of an Australian kitchen (below). Mrs Beeton died at 29 after giving birth to her fourth son.

USING LOCAL PRODUCE

The *English and Australian Cookery Book* was written by 'an Australian aristologist' and published in 1864. It was subtitled *Cookery for the Many, as well as for the 'Upper Ten Thousand'*. The frontispiece consisted of a heraldic shield showing the six Australian colonies, superimposed upon the Australian coat of arms.

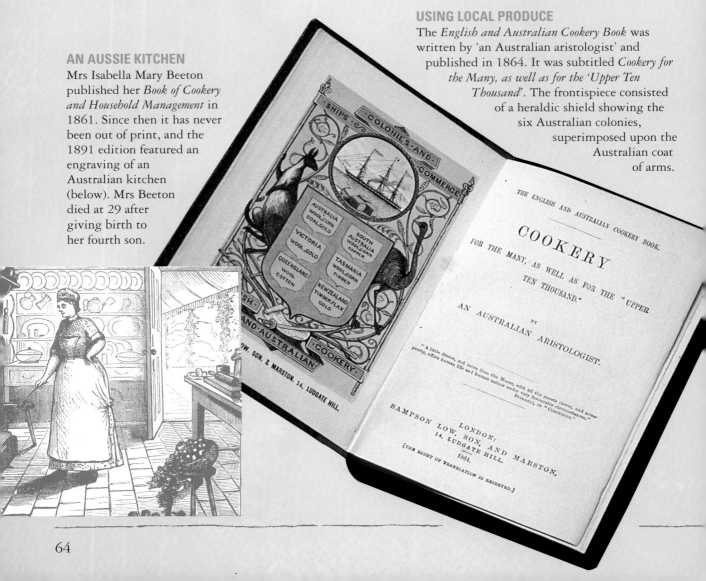

THE ENGLISH AND AUSTRALIAN COOKERY BOOK.

COOKERY

FOR THE MANY, AS WELL AS FOR THE "UPPER TEN THOUSAND."

BY AN AUSTRALIAN ARISTOLOGIST.

LONDON:
SAMPSON LOW, SON, AND MARSTON,
14, LUDGATE HILL.
1864.
[THE RIGHT OF TRANSLATION IS RESERVED.]

AN AUSTRALIAN COOK

In the late 1890s Mrs Hannah Maclurcan, who had been running clubs and hotels in Queensland and New South Wales since she was 17, published *Mrs Maclurcan's Cookery Book: A Collection of Practical Recipes Specially Suitable for Australia*. The charming photograph on the right was first given to the world in *The Story of the Wentworth Hotel*, by Charles Maclurcan.

NATIVE TUCKER

'Most people, even Australians, are prejudiced against the wallaby,' wrote Mrs Maclurcan, and went on to point out that wallaby can be prepared in the same way as the English cook hare.

DINING EDWARDIAN STYLE

An illustration from the 1907 edition of Mrs Beeton's classic work on cookery and household management shows how seriously the Edwardians took their formal dining. The geometric creases in the tablecloth are completely characteristic of the time.

DESIGNER ICE CREAM

W.H Auden said of American food writer M.F.K. (Mary Frances Kennedy) Fisher: 'I do not know of anyone in the United States today who writes better prose.' *Diplomate au Kirsch*, an ice cream made with 3 cups of whipped cream, macaroons, candied fruit and kirsch, is one of the old recipes she shared with her readers. Make it in a modern ice cream machine or – better – in an old-fashioned wooden churn packed with ice and rock salt.

1. Pour the ice cream mixture into the inner drum.

2. Pack ice and salt into the space between the inner and the outer containers and insert the wooden paddle and the handle.

3. Turn the handle constantly until the ice cream is ready – a tedious but rewarding task.

Eat up your vegies

THE HOME COOKS OF THE PAST DEVISED HUNDREDS OF WAYS OF MAKING TASTY DISHES WITH VEGETABLES.

Thrifty housewives made cuts of meat go further with vegetable soups for starters and imaginative vegetable accompaniments to main meals, as well as the occasional vegetarian main meal.

SOUP, BEAUTIFUL SOUP Soup is ridiculously easy to make, and you can use almost any vegetable or combination of vegetables.

Leek and potato soup To serve four, you need 2 tablespoons of butter or polyunsaturated margarine, 3 leeks, 3 large potatoes, salt and pepper.

Cut off the dark parts of the leeks and boil them in about 1 litre of water for 15 minutes to make a stock. Slice the white parts thinly, peel the potatoes and chop them into fairly small pieces. Melt the fat in a large saucepan, add the vegetables, cover and cook over a low heat until the leeks have softened.

Strain the stock and add it to the vegetables. Bring the mixture to the boil, reduce to a simmer and cook until the vegetables are tender. Break up the potatoes with a potato masher and season to taste.

You can use onions instead of leeks; meat stock instead of vegetable stock; or half stock and half milk for a richer soup.

Onion soup For four people, you need 4 medium-sized brown onions, 1 litre of chicken stock, salt and pepper, 4 slices of white bread and 60 grams of grated cheese. Peel the onions and slice them very finely, and cook them in the stock until they are very soft – about 20 minutes. Add salt and pepper to taste.

Toast the bread, ladle the soup into flame-proof bowls, place a slice of toast on top of each and sprinkle with the grated cheese. Put the bowls under a hot griller until the cheese is melted.

Scotch broth The thrifty Scots made this hearty soup to sustain them against the long hard winters. The stock was made with a sheep's head; this was served as a meat course on one day, and the soup was eaten the following day.

The essential ingredients are mutton stock, cooked barley, and leeks or onions. Carrots, turnips and peas are also traditional inclusions. Chop the vegetables into small pieces, add

An elderly man proudly displays his 1942 prize-winning crop of vegies. During and after World War II, vegetable growing was a valuable contribution to dwindling food supplies, and governments urged as many people as possible to grow their own.

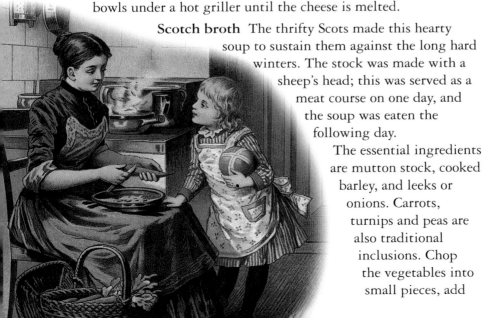

them to the stock with the barley, and cook until the vegetables are tender. If you are including fresh peas, add them for the last five minutes of the cooking time.

MAIN DISHES In the old days vegetables tended to be regarded chiefly as accompaniments to meat dishes, but there were several well loved vegetable dishes that appeared regularly on our grandmothers' tables.

Cauliflower cheese To serve four people, you will need 1 medium-sized cauliflower, 1 tablespoon of butter or margarine, 1 tablespoon of plain flour, 1 cup of milk, 100 grams of grated cheese, salt, pepper and breadcrumbs. Break the cauliflower into florets and boil for about 5 minutes in a cup of salted water; do not let it become soft, as it will cook further when it is baked with the cheese sauce. Drain it, reserving the cooking liquid, and put it into a baking dish.

Melt the fat in a saucepan, work in the flour and cook gently for 5 minutes. Gradually add the cauliflower water, working it in to make a smooth mixture. Bring to the boil and slowly add milk until you have a sauce of a pouring consistency. Stir in half of the grated cheese and add pepper to taste. Pour the sauce over the cooked cauliflower, sprinkle the top with the breadcrumbs and the rest of the grated cheese, and bake in a hot oven until the topping is crisp and golden.

Half a teaspoon of dry mustard and ½ a teaspoon of nutmeg added to the sauce will enhance the flavour of this dish. You can also mix chopped fried bacon with the cauliflower.

Vegetable pie Use fresh vegetables in season – a good combination is 1 large brown onion, 1 large carrot, 2 stalks of celery, 1 medium-sized turnip and 1 cup of peas. Some recipes include 1 tablespoon of sago.

Peel the vegetables and chop them into small pieces. Cook them, and the sago if desired, in a very small amount of boiling water until tender – about 10–15 minutes. Pile the vegetables into a pie dish, sprinkle them with salt and pepper to taste, and cover with a sheet of short pastry (see page 61). Bake in a moderate oven for about half an hour, or until the pastry is well risen and golden.

For a tasty variation, flavour the pastry with herbs or grated cheese. Or, if you do not want to make pastry, cover the pie with mashed potato and sprinkle the top with grated cheese.

Jacket potatoes Topped with butter and chives or melted cheese, a potato baked in its jacket can be a meal in itself. Choose large, old potatoes, which our grandmothers described as floury potatoes. They should be roughly the same size so that they will all be cooked at the same time.

You will need 1 potato for each person. Wash the potatoes and pierce the skins several times with a fork to prevent them from bursting. Rub the skins with butter or margarine or coat them with cooking oil. Bake them for about an hour in a hot oven. Squeeze them to test whether they are cooked – they should feel soft.

To serve, make a cross-shaped cut in the top of each potato, fold back the flaps and insert a knob of butter. Provide extra butter and chopped chives, grated cheese, crispy crumbled bacon, or anything else your imagination suggests.

Words of Wisdom

'All round are signs of it, everywhere, little trickles of snobbish judgment, always changing, ever present. In France old Crainquebille sold leeks from a cart, leeks called "the asparagus of the poor". Now asparagus sells for the asking, almost, in California markets, and broccoli, that strong age-old green, leaps from its lowly pot to the *Ritz*'s copper saucepan. Who determines, and for what strange reasons, the social status of a vegetable?'

– *Serve it Forth*, M.F.K. Fisher (1941)

Long before electrically powered food processors, there were various mechanical devices for making food preparation easier. This vegetable chopper dates from the 19th century.

Pickles and preserves

FRESH FRUITS AND VEGETABLES USED
TO BE AVAILABLE ONLY IN SEASON.

Most fruits and vegetables are now available year round,
but many are still seasonal, and they are tastier and more
nutritious when they have been recently harvested. Pickle
and preserve bumper crops as our mothers and grandmothers did.

Jars for pickles and preserves must be scrupulously clean and dry.
Boil them for 10 minutes and drain and dry them thoroughly.

PICKLED ONIONS The ploughman's lunch dates from the days when
agricultural workers would take a packed lunch, which traditionally
included picked onions. This old recipe does not require any
application of heat and the pickled onions will be crisp and crunchy.

*The pride and joy of an old-time
pantry was an array of gleaming
jars of pickles and preserves that
would meet the family's needs for
fruits and vegetables during the
barren winter months.*

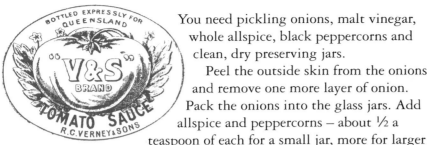

You need pickling onions, malt vinegar, whole allspice, black peppercorns and clean, dry preserving jars.

Peel the outside skin from the onions and remove one more layer of onion. Pack the onions into the glass jars. Add allspice and peppercorns – about ½ a teaspoon of each for a small jar, more for larger jars. Cover the onions with vinegar, seal the jars and put them in a dry place. They will be ready to eat in about a fortnight and will keep for around six months.

Other spices that can be used in the pickling mixture are ginger, cayenne, nutmeg, cloves and mace. Experiment with small quantities and various combinations until you find the one that pleases you best.

ITALIAN TOMATO SAUCE This basic pasta sauce needs only very ripe tomatoes, fresh basil leaves and preserving jars. The longer the sauce is left sealed and stored, the more flavoursome it will become.

Put the tomatoes into boiling water until the skins start to split. Remove them from the pot and when they are cool enough to handle, peel the skins away. Purée the tomato pulp: in the old days this was done by hand, but electric blenders have made the task much easier.

Put 2 or 3 fresh basil leaves into the bottom of each jar, fill the jars with the tomato purée, place more basil leaves on top and seal the jars. The basil acts as a preservative as well as a flavouring. Place the bottles of sauce upright in a large pot, fill the pot with water and bring slowly to the boil. Turn off the heat and remove the bottles when cool.

QUINCE JELLY This old recipe is time-consuming but is said to be unfailing. The quinces should not be too ripe.

Wipe and chop 2 kg of quinces, including the peels and cores, and put them in a jar with 600 ml of water. Seal the jar, stand it in a large saucepan of water and boil, renewing the water as required, until the quinces are soft and pulpy; this can take hours. Strain the pulp through muslin (see right-hand column), measure it, and allow 500 grams of sugar to 600 ml of juice.

Boil the juice and at the same time spread the sugar in a baking dish. Heat the sugar in the oven, turning it frequently to prevent burning. After the juice has boiled for 20 minutes, add the hot sugar and boil for a few minutes. The mixture should jellify quite quickly.

MARMALADE For marmalade, chunks or fine slices of fruit are suspended in a clear jelly. Citrus fruits are perfect for marmalade.

Peel 8 oranges and 2 lemons and slice the peels very thinly. Cover them with water, cook for 5 minutes, drain and repeat twice. Chop up the flesh of the fruits, discarding the pith and the seeds, and add the cooked peels. Then add three times the volume of water and let the mixture stand overnight.

Cook the mixture for 40 minutes, then add about 7 cups of sugar and boil the syrup rapidly until it passes the 'wrinkle test' (see *Words of Wisdom*, right-hand column).

IMPROVISING A JELLY BAG
To make a clear jelly, allow the fruit pulp to strain through muslin or cheesecloth. Do not try to speed up the process by pushing the pulp through.

Method 1 Upend a kitchen stool, put a large bowl on the seat, and tie the cheesecloth securely to the legs of the stool.

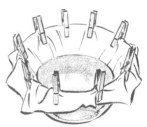

Method 2 Peg the cheesecloth firmly around the rim of a large, deep bowl.

Words of Wisdom

The wrinkle-on-a-plate test appears in many old cookery books as an infallible way of testing whether jams and jellies are cooked. Take the jam mixture from the heat, pour a little onto a cold plate and put it in a cool place for a few minutes. Tilt the plate: if wrinkles appear on the surface of the jam, it is ready.

What's for afters?

OUR GRANDMOTHERS KNEW THE DIETARY VALUE OF
FRESH FRUITS, AND MANY OF THEIR DESSERTS WERE
BASED ON FRUITS IN SEASON.

*Fruit jellies in decorative moulds
are a long-time favourite light
dessert, especially useful for
tempting the appetites of sick
people and 'picky eaters'. Use
commercial jelly crystals and
boost the flavour and the
nutritional value with fresh
or canned fruits.*

Apples were a great standby for family meals, being available for
most of the year and easy to make into simple, nourishing dishes
such as apple crumble and baked apples. And for the more elaborate
meals that were served to dinner guests, a fruit fool based on
seasonal fruits was a quick, delicious and impressive choice.

APPLE DESSERTS In the old days there was a marked distinction
between eating apples and cooking apples. With the breeding of
new varieties this distinction has become blurred, but for these old-
fashioned recipes it is still best to use the cooking varieties: in
Australia the Granny Smith is the most popular cooking apple.

Baked apples Choose large green cooking apples of the same size,
one for each diner. Core them, but not right through; leave a small
'plug' of flesh at the stem end so that the stuffing won't fall out.
Stand them on a greased baking dish and fill the cored centres with
a mixture of sultanas, candied peel, brown sugar, lemon zest and
cinnamon. Put a dollop of butter on top of the stuffing and bake the
apples for about an hour in a moderate oven.

Apple crumble is really an easy version of apple pie. Make the
crumble topping first, because the apple will discolour very quickly
once it is cut. You do not need to add water: the apples will release
ample moisture as they stew gently under the crumble topping.

You will need 1 cup of plain flour, ⅓ of a cup of butter, 4 large
apples and ⅓ of a cup of sugar. Rub the butter into the flour until the
mixture resembles fine breadcrumbs. Peel and core the apples and slice
them thinly into a deep pie dish. Sprinkle them with the sugar, spread
the crumble mixture over them and bake in a moderate oven until the
topping is crisp and golden-brown – about 40 minutes. For extra
flavour, add the juice of half a lemon to the apples and sprinkle the
topping with a mixture of cinnamon, nutmeg and brown sugar.

FRUIT FOOLS The name 'fool' probably comes from the French *fouler*,
'to press', as the fresh or cooked fruit is pressed through a sieve to
make a purée, which is then mixed with cream and sugar.

Raspberry fool You will need 2 punnets of fresh raspberries, some
caster sugar and 300 ml of fresh cream. Put three quarters of the
raspberries into a bowl and sugar them to taste. Push the rest of the
raspberries through a sieve and add sugar to taste. Whip the cream
until it is smooth and quite thick and then stir in the raspberry purée.
Gently fold in the sugared raspberries. Spoon the fool into individual
glass dishes and chill before serving.

THE APPLE IN HISTORY
The apple is the prototype of fruits.
In the Christian story Adam and Eve
were tempted by an apple, and in early
days the term apple was applied to an
amazing variety of vegetables and
fruits. This is reflected in many
languages: the French call potatoes
pommes de terre ('earth apples');
the Italian for tomato is *pomodoro*
('golden apple'); and pomegranate
literally means 'seedy apple'.

The cup that cheers

ALL LIVING THINGS NEED WATER TO STAY ALIVE, BUT FLAVOURED DRINKS — HOT, COLD AND ALCOHOLIC — SUSTAIN THE SPIRIT AS WELL.

In the good old days there were social rituals for consuming various drinks. Early morning tea restored water lost during the night. Morning coffee and afternoon tea sustained flagging energies. After school or at the end of the working day, a cool fresh lemonade revived the spirits. In the evening, a dry martini in summer or a glass of mulled wine in the winter in the company of friends was convivial and relaxing. A mug of cocoa or hot milk and honey just before bed promoted restful sleep.

TEA It has been estimated that, worldwide, 14 000 cups of tea are consumed every second. This may be no more than a wild guess, but it is certain that tea is one of the most popular drinks in the world.

Making tea Tea quickly becomes stale, so buy small quantities and keep it in an airtight container. The good old wisdom is that brown earthenware pots make the best tea.

Fill the kettle with fresh cold water, bring it almost to the boil and half fill the teapot to warm it. While the water is coming to a rapid boil, empty the teapot, put in a heaped teaspoon of tea leaves per person and 'one for the pot' and pour on the boiling water. Allow the tea to stand, or 'draw', for three minutes and then pour it into the cups through a strainer. Pour off all the tea at once; if it is allowed to brew for more than about eight minutes, it develops a metallic, 'stewed' taste from the tannin it contains.

Traditionally, teas from India and Ceylon are served with milk and China tea with a slice of lemon. Both can be drunk with no additions. Purists shudder at the idea of adding sugar.

COFFEE Coffee reached the Western world in 1683, when the invading Turkish army retreated from the Siege of Vienna. They left behind some sacks of coffee beans, and the Viennese coffee house tradition was established. In 1689 Edward Lloyd opened a coffee house in London and developed a system of insurance for coffee cargoes; this was the origin of Lloyds of London, the insurance firm.

Making coffee The golden rule for making coffee is that it should be strong: as early as 1861, Mrs Beeton noted that 'the greatest and most common fault in English coffee is the too small quantity of the ingredient.' She advised using 1 tablespoon of coffee to 150 ml of water per cup.

Relaxing between domestic tasks with a refreshing cup of tea kept our grandmothers going through the long, demanding days.

Versions of this simple mechanical coffee grinder from the late 19th century are still available today, and are ideal for grinding small quantities of coffee beans.

Buy coffee in small quantities, store it in an airtight container, and preferably grind it freshly just before use. Every coffee lover has a preferred blend and method, but most experts recommend filtering, in which a muslin or paper filter is supported over the coffee pot and boiling water poured slowly over the coffee. Filtering is the best way of producing a clear, aromatic brew without the bitterness that comes from boiling or steeping.

Serving coffee In continental Europe, where coffee first became popular in the Western world, it was and is customary at breakfast to drink *café au lait* – strong coffee served in a large bowl with a generous addition of hot milk – and at other times *café noir* – strong black coffee served in a tiny cup called a demitasse.

COCOA Cocoa powder is extracted from the seeds of the cacao tree, which grows in the West Indies and South America. Originally cocoa was known as the food of the gods, and the Mayas used cocoa beans as currency.

To make hot cocoa, mix 1 teaspoon of cocoa and 2 teaspoons of sugar to a smooth paste with a little hot water. Heat 250 ml of milk, pour it over the cocoa paste and then pour the mixture back into the saucepan and heat to almost boiling. Drink as it is, or sprinkle ground nutmeg or cinnamon over the top.

Old-fashioned dark cocoa made up with full cream milk gives you the option of sweetening to suit your own taste.

COOL DRINKS Homemade soft drinks have a tang and freshness that no commercial product can match, and they have the added advantages that you know exactly what is in them and can control the degree of sweetness.

Lemonade A simple old-time recipe for lemonade is to take 1 lemon, 2 lumps of sugar and 1 cup of water for each person. Over a jug, rub the sugar lumps over the skins of the lemons so that the aromatic oil is absorbed. Squeeze the lemons, strain out the pips and add the lemon juice to the sugar lumps in the jug. Heat the water and pour it over, stir until the sugar is dissolved and allow to cool. Serve chilled with a sprig of mint.

A recipe from the 1930s for 'perfect lemonade' is a little more complicated and unusual. Peel the zest from 6 lemons. Add the juice of 12 lemons and 500 grams of sugar. Pour over 2 litres of boiling water and stir until the sugar is dissolved. Boil 1 litre of milk and add it to the lemon mixture. Let it stand overnight and then strain it through muslin.

The Sunbeam Mixmaster, first marketed in 1936, took the hard labour out of juicing citrus fruits.

Ginger beer Ginger beer is a traditional favourite, and ginger has long been known as a prophylactic against colds and flu. Old recipes tend to specify enormous quantities, but this easy version from colonial Australia is manageable in a modern kitchen.

In an earthenware bowl, mix together 500 grams of sugar, 30 grams of fresh ginger, crushed slightly, and a sliced lemon. Pour on 5 litres of boiling water and stir until the sugar is dissolved. Let the mixture cool to lukewarm, and then stir in 1 tablespoon of brewer's yeast. Cover the mixture and let it stand for 24 hours. Strain and bottle the mixture, filling the bottles only as far as the base of the neck to allow for fermentation. Cork or cap the bottles firmly and store in a cool place for two days before drinking.

Iced tea and coffee These make a refreshing change from sweet cold drinks, and are a good use for leftover tea or coffee. Pour the cold liquid over 2 ice cubes. For iced tea, add a squeeze of lemon juice or a slice of lemon. For iced coffee, add cold milk and a scoop of vanilla or coffee ice cream to a small cup of strong black coffee in a tall glass. Whipped cream is an indulgent but delicious topping.

ALCOHOLIC DRINKS Our forefathers devised any number of ways of using alcoholic liquors as the basis of mixed drinks.

Mulled wine has been around since at least medieval times. It is a good way to use red wine that is not quite drinkable by itself, and mulled wine on a winter evening is a great comforter.

You will need 600 ml of port or claret, 1 cup of water, some sugar, cloves, grated nutmeg and a cinnamon stick. Boil the spices in the water to extract the flavour – about 15 minutes – then add the wine, and sugar to taste; claret needs more sugar than port, and individual tastes may require more or less sugar. Heat the mixture, but do not let it boil or all the alcohol will be driven off. Strain the mixture to remove the spices and serve in front of an open fire.

Buttered rum punch is another cold-weather drink. Pour a measure of rum into a mug, add 1 teaspoon of golden syrup, top with boiling water and stir. Add a little butter and a sprinkling of cinnamon.

Athelbrose is a Scottish concoction. The name means 'a noble brew', and it packs quite a punch. To make it, pour 250 ml each of Scotch whisky and French brandy over a honeycomb in a glass jar. Let it stand for four days, strain and drink.

Eggnog is a mixture of beaten egg, sugar, spirits and cream that is eaten with a spoon rather than drunk. For one serving, beat together 1 egg yolk and 2 teaspoons of caster sugar until smooth and thick. Beat in a generous tot of brandy, whisky or rum and about twice the amount of cream. Whip the egg white to a froth, fold into the mixture and serve with a sprinkling of cinnamon.

Mixed drinks did not become popular until well into the 20th century, even though cocktails *(coquetels)* had originated in France as early as the end of the 18th century. Mixing additives with spirits was one unforeseen result of the Prohibition movement in America: some illegally distilled alcohol was so terrible that it was necessary to mask the taste in order to drink it. Here, however, are two mixed drinks that have withstood the test of time.
Martini Mix 3 parts of gin with 1 part of French vermouth over crushed ice; strain into conical stemmed glasses and garnish with lemon peel, a green olive or a cocktail onion.
Old fashioned Soak a lump of sugar with angostura bitters and place it in the bottom of a small tumbler. Add ice cubes and a generous tot of scotch, bourbon or rye whisky. Garnish with any combination of maraschino cherries, orange slices, lemon slices and pineapple chunks.

IN PRAISE OF WINE
O, for a draught of vintage! that hath been
Cool'd a long age in the deep-delved earth,
Tasting of Flora and the country green,
Dance, and Provençal song, and sunburnt mirth!
O for a beaker full of the warm South,
Full of the true, the blushful Hippocrene,
With beaded bubbles winking at the brim,
And purple-stained mouth …
– 'ODE TO A NIGHTINGALE',
JOHN KEATS (1795–1821)

Mixed drink glasses come in all shapes and sizes, from the classic conical martini glass to tall glasses for longer drinks.

Neat as a

Neat as a

new pin

KEEPING YOUR HOME SPICK AND SPAN
THE WAY GRANDMA USED TO DO

Paint, polish and wallpaper

By the Stone Age, people were already ornamenting the walls of their caves with paintings of the world around them.

Later, walls were clad with tapestries, rugs or panelling. By 1850, wallpaper was all the rage; paint and whitewash were also used, but it was not until the 1940s that paint began to outstrip wallpaper in popularity.

Keeping interior walls and woodwork clean and fresh has always been an important task for homemakers. Our houseproud grandmothers believed that cleanliness is next to godliness, and they kept their homes pristine without the aid of expensive proprietary products or labour-saving devices. Try some of their methods and save money.

CLEANING PAINTED WALLS Work from the bottom upwards to prevent 'runs' that will leave permanent stains. Wet the wall with water and an old paintbrush. While the surface is wet, apply a solution of 100 grams of washing soda to 4 litres of water – an inexpensive cleaning agent with a mild action that will not damage the paint. Rub the surface briskly, and then rinse off the solution with fresh water and wipe dry with a soft towel.

Grease and smoke stains mark paintwork quite badly because of their acid content. Use a stronger washing soda solution, repeating the application over badly marked areas.

Paste cleaner Ceilings and large areas of wall are awkward to clean because of the risk of spotting or damage to lower portions of the room. A paste cleaner may be the answer. Mix 500 grams of plain flour to a creamy consistency with cold water, then gradually add boiling water, stirring constantly until the mixture thickens. Add a solution of 125 grams of washing soda, mix thoroughly and allow to cool. This will make about 4 litres of paste, which does not run down over other surfaces and remains wet and active for a longer period than the liquid cleaner, giving a better soaking of the dirt and grease and saving time and energy in its removal.

Grease and crayon marks For small grease marks, sprinkle some bicarbonate of soda onto a dry cloth and rub over the marks, or rub with a piece of stale bread, or with a ball of plain

Painted woodwork was fashionable long before paint appeared on the walls, and it wasn't long before special cleaning products were developed to aid the housewife in this regular chore.

flour mixed with cleaning fluid. Remove crayon marks by covering the area with several folded pieces of white tissue paper and pressing with a warm iron. Change the paper as it absorbs the stain so that the grease does not come into contact with the heating plate of the iron.

CLEANING WOODWORK Oil-painted and enamelled surfaces can become soiled over time without the protective qualities of the paint being affected. With a little care you can remove surface dirt without damage. Washable water-based paints are water-resistant but not waterproof, so they cannot be scrubbed or washed down to the same extent as oil paints and enamels.

New paint Do not clean fresh paintwork unless it is absolutely necessary because the binding film will be affected by even mild cleaning agents. Treat fingermarks on fresh paint with lukewarm water wiped on with a pad of cotton wool. If this is not sufficient, use a little mild face soap on the pad. Remove all traces of soap to avoid dull, smeary spots. Rinse with fresh water and wipe over with a chamois leather to leave the surface dry.

Painted and varnished woodwork Wash varnished wood as little as possible – a daily wipe with an oiled duster is generally all that is necessary. If grime has accumulated, try this simple old method. Steep some tea leaves in water for half an hour, strain, and use the liquid as a wash. Wipe off immediately and polish with a clean cloth.
To clean painted woodwork, dust well and wash with warm, soapy water; wring the cloth almost dry, as drops of water may mark the paint. Rinse with clear warm water, dry well and polish with a soft duster. For painted cupboard doors in frequent use, dissolve 1 tablespoon of borax in boiling water and add to a bucketful of warm soapsuds. Wash down, rinse with clean water and rub dry. A little paraffin added to the soapy water will help to remove fingerprints and greasy smudges.
   Dust polished wood carefully and use a soft brush for any crevices. If marks have to be removed with a damp cloth, wring the cloth out in warm water to which you have added 1 tablespoon of vinegar. Polish when the wood is dry.

PAINTING As with many jobs, preparation is vital for successful painting. It can feel like drudgery, but an hour or two spent getting the existing paintwork spotlessly clean is time well spent.

Preparation Surfaces to be painted must be perfectly clean, dry and dust-free. An economical and efficient method of dusting walls is to attach a thick pad of cotton batting to the end of a broom. Go over the entire wall surface with this, discarding and replacing the cotton pad as it becomes soiled. To remove dirt from mouldings, use a small, perfectly clean sweeping brush.
   Wash down and rinse the area to be painted. Swab any mildewed patches several times with strong peroxide, then apply an all-purpose sealer. Wash down with clean water and dry thoroughly.

The Way We Were

By the early 1930s, a grand style of wall treatment had made its way from the stately homes of England to the homesteads of Australia:

'Fresh cream paint covered the walls and the ceiling, every molding and carving painstakingly picked out in gilt, but the huge oval-shaped flat spaces in the paneling had been papered with faded black silk bearing the same bunches of roses as the three carpets, like stilted Japanese paintings in cream and gilt surrounds.'

– *THE THORN BIRDS*, COLLEEN MCCULLOUGH (1977)

Scrape off any blistered paint from window frames and other woodwork. Remove badly cracked or blistered paint with a blow-torch, hot-air gun or chemical paint remover and scraper. If using a blowtorch, take care not to char wood or crack glass. A strong borax mixture in hot water will remove old varnish.

When the surface is quite dry, patch-paint any discoloured parts with undercoat. Also paint any cracked or damaged parts that require filling. Leave for about half an hour, when the paint will have become tacky, then fill with putty, finishing off as smoothly as possible.

Fill gaps between the woodwork and walls with plaster. Allow at least 24 hours for the filling and patching coats to harden, sand lightly, and then apply an undercoat all over.

Painting tips Over the years, people have developed a number of tricks and techniques for successful painting.

• After pouring paint from a large tin, pierce the inner rim of the tin several times; the paint will drip back into the tin, leaving the rim clean and enabling the lid to fit without sticking.

• Before using a paintbrush, run a wide comb through it to remove loose bristles, which have a tendency to come off in the paint or on the surface you are painting.

• Use small brushes for sills, large brushes for walls. On rough surfaces use a worn brush for the first few coats and a new brush for the final coat.

• When painting window sashes, dress the edges of the glass with a band of fairly hard soap; when the paint has dried hard, remove the soap and with it any paint streaks. Use a 2.5 cm brush for painting window sashes. Put the paint on in little dabs close to the glass, and pass the brush along sideways. Pressure control is the secret – press the brush down lightly so that the bristles will straighten and come away from the glass.

• To catch paint drips when painting ceilings, cut a hole in a piece of sponge and push it firmly up the handle of the paintbrush.

• Alternate paintbrushes daily, so that each brush is thoroughly dry before you use it again. If you want your brushes to last, hang them in raw linseed oil.

• Paint every second step of a stairway you still need to use, and when these are dry paint the remainder.

• Use a piece of sponge instead of a brush to paint wrought iron – it gives you better control and is a great time-saver.

Paintbrushes Invest in good paintbrushes – they are not cheap, but if you take care of them they will repay the expense in the long run.

Before using a new paintbrush, suspend it for 12 hours in a container half filled with linseed oil. This will ensure that paint pigment does not cling tightly to the bristles, so will be easier to clean. Never put a new brush into water: the bristles will swell and become flabby and separate into 'fingers'.

Taking Care of the Pence

Pressing a paintbrush against the rim of a paint tin to remove excess paint damages the brush and accumulates paint under the rim of the tin. Fit a wire ring around the top of the tin and fasten another piece of heavy wire about a third of the way across the mouth of the tin. Wipe your paintbrush against this crosswire to get rid of excess paint – you will save money in both paint and brushes.

Paints of all types and colours were available by mail order at the beginning of the century, as this 1908 catalogue illustrates.

Cleaning paintbrushes Mineral turpentine is the best cleaner for oil-based paint on brushes. As soon as you have finished painting, clean brushes thoroughly and shake them out by holding them low down in a bucket or deep jar and twirling the handle between your palms. Dry them with newspaper, dip them in linseed oil and store them wrapped in oil-coated paper.

For water-based paints, wash the brush in plain cold water, dip it into a solution of vinegar and water, comb the bristles straight and then hang it up by the handle so that the bristle flag does not touch anything. A stout piece of wire poked through a small hole in the handle will keep a brush supported and the bristles out of contact with the bottom of the container.

WHITEWASHING Whitewash is inexpensive and lends an old-fashioned charm to buildings. It should be applied warm; stand the tin in a container of hot water, replenishing the water to keep the whitewash warm while you work for much better results.

Despite its name, whitewash can be tinted. The best colours are those used for colouring cement, but dry painters' colours such as yellow ochre, Venetian red, lampblack, raw and burnt umber or burnt sienna can also be used. Stir well so that the colour is thoroughly incorporated. Do not use chrome yellow, chrome green or Prussian blue – these colours are adversely affected by the alkali in the whitewash mixture.

WALLPAPERING Wallpapering is one of the simplest ways to transform a room. The first wallpapers were handpainted and imported, mainly from China, and were mounted and hung, like tapestries.

Choosing wallpaper Scrutinise wallpaper samples under artificial light and in daylight at various times of the day; colours change with light, and a pattern may not be as attractive under a different light.

Texture adds interest to a plain-coloured paper, and textured papers in subdued colours make a dignified and subtle background for formal rooms. However, avoid flock papers, which tend to collect dust. A 'busy' pattern can disguise imperfections in the surface it covers and in your paper-hanging technique; on the other hand, symmetrical patterns must be hung carefully, as they will accentuate any faults.

Different papers for different rooms Take into consideration the purpose and size of the room in which a wallpaper is to be hung. Vertical lines lend height and dignity to a room and are suitable for formal rooms such as a dining room. Horizontal patterns reduce ceiling height and have a calming effect. Patterns with curves can be interesting, but they must have elegance of style.

Large-patterned papers are dramatic but they make a room seem smaller, whereas small patterns can make a small room seem larger. Bedroom wallpapers should be either plain or have simple, light designs; strong colours and large designs do not make for restful sleep.

Bathrooms and other areas that are subject to condensation need specially glazed wallpaper. Designs with tile patterns give a sense of brightness and are easily kept clean.

Words of Wisdom

'Anybody can attempt to distemper a wall or paint a door – but few people can do the job really well. The amateur decorator, like the amateur in so many other fields, fails by being unwilling to give time, thought and care to the preliminary stages of the work. Watch a decorator's man, next time you have the chance, as he prepares walls, floor or ceiling for the treatment chosen by his client. The care he takes, the time he spends, will provide excellent examples for your own efforts.

It seems hardly necessary to add that all the decorating materials you buy should be of the best possible quality. Don't waste time and effort on a job that will not be worthwhile in the end.'

– *The Book of Good Housekeeping* (1944)

Preparation Using wallpaper to disguise a dirty or damaged wall is not a solution in the long term; it may look good for a short time, but the effect will not last. Like new paint, wallpaper requires a smooth, clean and dry undersurface. Prepare the walls as for painting (see pages 77–8).

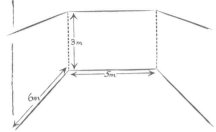

Clear the room of as much furniture as is possible, or move as much as you can to the centre of the room and cover with dropcloths. Do any painting before hanging the wallpaper – it is easier to wipe paste off a painted surface than to remove paint splashes from wallpaper.

To strip off old wallpaper, score the surface of the paper with a fork and then soak it with hot water painted on with an old brush. The perforations will allow the water to penetrate, making removal easier – but be careful not to damage the surface beneath. Difficult parts may require several soakings before they peel off easily.

If the walls have been previously painted with a gloss paint, sand them lightly to provide a 'key' for the paper.

Where to begin This depends on the design of the wallpaper and the layout of the room. If you are using a plain or small-patterned paper, start at a corner on a wall without features or windows and work your way around the room. If you are using paper with a large pattern in a room with a feature such as a mantelpiece, centre the first piece over the mantelpiece to balance the scheme.

Measure the height of the wall from the ceiling, or wherever you wish to position the top of the paper, to the skirting board. Unroll the paper along a working table, measure, and mark the length with a pencil, allowing a good 10 cm extra. Place a ruler across the paper, draw a line across it, then use sharp scissors to cut along the line.

Pasting Methods vary; you can apply paste to the wall or to the paper, or you can soak pre-pasted paper in water. Whichever method you use, pick up the paper by its two top corners, with your thumbs positioned on the unpasted side of the paper, and, checking that you are holding the paper the right way up, place the first length at the top of the wall. Allow the paper to overlap about 5 cm onto the ceiling for trimming. Use a paper-hanging brush or a large sponge to push the top edge of the paper gently but firmly into position, making sure that the paper does not move from its vertical alignment. Working down the length of the paper from the centre to the edges, smooth out any creases or bubbles.

Return to the top and mark the junction of the wall and the ceiling with a pencil; then pull the paper away from the wall and cut along the pencil line. Smooth the top edge of the paper back into place. You may require some extra paste to make sure the top of the paper adheres perfectly to the wall. Use a clean, slightly moistened sponge to wipe off any excess paste. Trim the bottom of the paper so that it is flush with the top of the skirting board, using the same method as for the top. Continue to hang each section of wallpaper using this technique.

BUYING WALLPAPER

When you buy wallpaper, bear in mind that papers with a large repeated pattern will produce more waste than those with small patterns. All the rolls of paper should come from the same batch, otherwise you may find slight differences in pattern or colour.

1. To calculate the quantity of paper you need, measure the height of the walls to be covered from floor to ceiling, or as far up the wall as you wish to paper. Then measure the perimeter of the room and multiply the perimeter by the height to calculate the quantity of wallpaper you need in square metres.

Height :- 3m
Perimeter : (6 + 5 + 6 + 5) = 22m
Area : 66 square m.

2. Divide this number by the area size of your chosen wallpaper, and the result will be the number of rolls you need to purchase. A standard roll of wallpaper measures 52 cm wide by 10 metres long (= 5 square metres).

Rolls requ: 66 ÷ 5 = 13

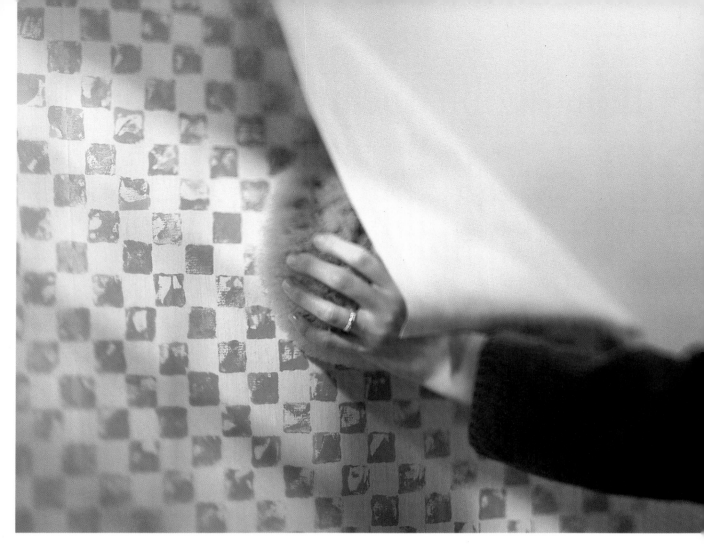

At the corners, cut the paper to overlap the crease of the corner. Paste the overlap firmly down, and then hang the next length of paper on the adjoining wall overlapping the pasted length and matching the pattern carefully. Use a spirit level to ensure that you start the second wall with a perfectly vertical drop of paper.

Wallpapering tips Take advantage of the wisdom of the past for achieving the best possible results when wallpapering.
• Tie a piece of string across the top of the paste bucket and rest your brush on this between pastings.
• If you are using ready-pasted paper, keep a small jar of wallpaper paste to hand in case the edges of the paper dry out.
• To mark the position of a screw hole for a fixture when wallpapering a room, place a matchstick in the hole so that it protrudes slightly. The matchstick will poke through the new paper, showing the exact position for refixing the screw.
• Keep leftover pieces of wallpaper for future repairs.

Cleaning wallpaper To remove marks from wallpaper, a paste of fuller's earth spread over the blemishes and left overnight is often effective. Brush off the next morning and repeat if necessary. Another method is to make a stiff dough with flour and water, take a handful and knead it into a ball. Carefully rub the paper with it, discarding the soiled portions of the dough from time to time and taking fresh pieces as required.

One of the secrets of successful wallpapering is gentle but thorough smoothing of the paper with a dampened sponge to get rid of creases and air bubbles.

Hanging on the wall

OVER YEARS OF TRIAL AND EXPERIENCE, SOME
SOUND PRINCIPLES HAVE EVOLVED CONCERNING THE
CHOICE AND DISPLAY OF WALL HANGINGS.

People sometimes take enormous pains with colour schemes and
furnishing but do not think about wall hangings, contenting
themselves with large, heavily framed prints or a collection of
mismatched pictures. But even a sparsely and inexpensively furnished
room can acquire distinction if the walls are hung with a few well
chosen prints and carefully positioned mirrors or plaques.

PICTURES It is well worth taking time and trouble over your choice of
pictures; some that seem attractive at first sight may give no lasting
pleasure. Some art dealers will let you take a picture home and 'live
with it' for a time before making a final decision – a commendable
practice that has survived from the more relaxed and less
commercialised good old days.

The next thing to consider is the room in which you intend hanging
the picture. A large room might accommodate several oil paintings,
while a small room may require just a few etchings or watercolours.

To show your pictures to advantage, hang them against a plain
background, never against elaborate wallpaper. Hang all pictures at
eye level and do not overcrowd them – one picture on a wall shows to
much better advantage than four or five.

Small pictures can sometimes be grouped together, but only on a
wall that looks sufficiently detached so that they do not interrupt the
continuity of the other pictures in the room.

Picture rails Moulded picture rails are a common feature of old
houses, and they are a much better way of displaying pictures than
hammering nails into walls. Pictures hung on railings are easily
repositioned, and are completely secure once they are hung.

Picture cords should be long enough for a seated person to see the
picture comfortably. Hang a group of pictures so that the lower edge
of each picture frame is at the same level. When hanging a particularly

*A feature of many period
drawing rooms was the artfully
arranged collection of favourite
pictures and family portraits.*

Words of Wisdom

'Above all things, help your tapestries by your scheme of lighting. In a hall, for
instance, the rays that filter through a leaded diamond pane or a mellow stained
glass by day will most likely give the true tone values woven in a period tapestry. At
night-time an unshaded modern electric bulb would be too crude and harsh to be
even dreamed of. A well-chosen Moorish or old buckhorn lanthorn should serve to
shade the jet. A period lamp shade is a wonderful help when some particular style of
furnishing is aimed at. It is possible now to have practically any chosen design or
style reproduced by local firms; the results are astonishingly good as a rule.'

– HOME AND GARDEN BEAUTIFUL (1913)

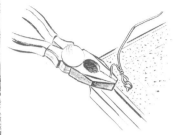

heavy picture, use chain instead of cord and attach a separate piece of chain to each side of the picture.

Care of picture frames

Simple, old-fashioned methods of caring for picture frames are very effective and will help to protect your treasured works of art.

Clean unpainted wooden frames with a soft cloth dipped in linseed oil. Painted frames can be cleaned with a cloth dampened with a mild soap solution. To remove discoloration from gilt frames, rub them with a piece of lemon, sponge with a solution of 1 teaspoon of baking soda in 500 ml of warm water, then polish with a chamois leather. Alternatively, mix an egg white with 1 teaspoon of bicarbonate of soda and rub the mixture on, or wipe the frame over with a solution of equal parts of methylated spirits and water.

It is best to keep picture frames and mirrors slightly away from the wall to allow the air to circulate and to prevent moisture in the atmosphere from accumulating and damaging the backs of the pictures. To keep a picture backing from direct contact with the wall, press a large drawing pin into each corner of the frame or glue small pieces of rubber or thick felt to the back. Use methylated spirits on a soft cloth to clean picture glass; never use water – it could seep beneath the glass and ruin the art work.

MIRRORS Mirrors can brighten and even enlarge a room, collecting light in dark corners and reflecting interior or exterior scenes. Hung over a small table or desk, a mirror provides balance and gives an impression of spaciousness by borrowing the perspective of the scene opposite. Grouped with a flower arrangement, a mirror is of great decorative value. Elegant frames fitted with mirrors instead of pictures will lighten a small, dark room, and a rectangular mirror can be used to offset a symmetrical group of furniture.

Mirrors must be carefully positioned, however, as they will reflect dull as well as interesting surroundings; for example, a mirror placed opposite a door may merely reveal a bleak passageway.

PLATES AND PLAQUES Group china plates or plaques in self-contained nooks – their effect is often lost if they are mingled with pictures. Or arrange them symmetrically around a mirror to make a wall feature, particularly if their designs, colours, shapes and sizes differ.

TAPESTRIES Tapestries, including carpets, were one of the earliest forms of wall decoration. They had practical as well as decorative value, as they were used to block the cold emanations from medieval castle walls. We no longer need tapestries for insulation, but they can lend distinction to a formal room. Keep the wall area surrounding a tapestry clear so that it has plenty of space to assert itself.

REPLACING A PICTURE BACKING

Mounted pictures have a backing to keep out dust and moisture. From time to time, the backing needs to be replaced.

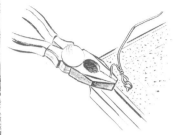

1. Remove the cord and the eyelets with fine pliers.

2. Cut away the existing backing with a scalpel along the inside edge of the frame.

3. Use the pliers to ease out the panel pins that hold the backing board in place.

4. Dismantle the picture into its component parts and clean them all. Reassemble the parts, using the same holes for the panel pins. Cut a piece of strong brown paper to fit the frame and glue it into place, pressing gently from the inner edge of the frame outwards. When it is completely dry, replace the eyelets and the cord.

A TOUCH OF CLASS

There were a number of distinctive styles of architecture and interior decorating in our grandparents' days. The Arts and Crafts movement popularised country furniture, and its descendants – the country kitchen, rustic furniture and folk art decoration – are with us still. This developed in the 1890s into Art Nouveau: a new style for a new century. Art Nouveau's sinuous lines, languid ladies and trailing peacock tails are quite unmistakable.

Art Nouveau went as far as it could in a tangle of tendrils, and then lines became cleaner with Art Deco, which took root between 1908 and 1912 and flourished in the 1920s. The style is more hard-edged, accepting the role of machines and machine-made products in society and everyday life. Then the German style known as Bauhaus, set up after World War I, went further, asking technicians and artists to work together to produce original designs that could be made by machine. They were severe, simple, but breathtaking in their clarity.

BREAKFAST AT TIFFANY'S
Tiffany glassware, with its generous use of leaded glass and sturdy, rich-looking metals such as bronze, is probably the most famous product of the Art Nouveau movement. The Tiffany style is enjoying a renaissance in the late 1900s.

A LEGEND IN ITS LIFETIME – AND BEYOND
Walter Gropius, shown in the photo on the left imbibing with the French architect Le Corbusier at the *Café des Deux Magots* in Paris, established the *Bauhaus* (the building house) in Weimar in 1919. As an institution it survived for only 14 years, having to move cities twice before the Nazis shut it down in 1933, but the impact of the design principles that drove it has been profound.

A FUNCTIONAL STYLE
The underlying principle of Art Deco was that form must follow function. Charles Rennie Mackintosh's oak chair (left) was designed with the sitter's comfort in mind, but with the aim of creating a thing of beauty as well.

A MAN FOR ALL SEASONS

The 19th century craftsman, poet and socialist William Morris was possibly the first interior decorator: his designs, such as the anemone design (right), provided much of the impetus for the Art Nouveau movement.

ANYONE FOR COFFEE?

The invitation would be irresistible if the coffee were served in this exquisite coffee service by Clarice Cliff. Its strong, elegant lines, design and colour are characteristic of Art Nouveau at its peak.

THE MARRIAGE OF ART AND CRAFT

The principles of Bauhaus style were to go back to the roots of design and create fundamental forms that would 'meet all technical, aesthetic and commercial demands.' The idea was to create forms that could be manufactured by machines but would be beautiful too, such as this Marcel Breuer chair of laminated wood.

CREATING AN ART NOUVEAU STENCIL

Stencilled patterns on walls or floors were popular in the early part of the 20th century. Copy this original three-coloured triangular design from the 1930s, or devise your own.

You will need stencil paper, a craft knife and a stencilling brush (all from craft shops), and oil or acrylic paints in three colours.

1. Trace the design elements for the first colour onto the stencil paper and carefully cut out the shapes. Tape the stencil template to the surface you wish to decorate, apply the first colour and allow to dry.

2. Repeat the process with the second design element and the second colour.

3. Repeat the process with the third design element and the third colour.

Light and shade

IN FASHIONABLE HOMES OF THE 1920S AND 1930S, ELECTRIC CANDLES HUNG IN THE DINING ROOM ON MATCHING WALL BRACKETS.

In the bedroom, a centre ceiling fixture, perhaps shaded with silk or covered with an opal glass bowl, would cast a soft light, tinting the room. The dressing table would be glarelessly lit by means of a rise and fall pendant or a table standard lamp and a reading lamp would illuminate the area near the head of the bed.

The kitchen would be flooded with light to make the cook's work easier, and to minimise shadow the light source would be totally enclosed in a close-to-the-ceiling globe-shaped shade, with an extra light bracket over the sink. The bathroom would be lit with another enclosed lamp to prevent steam from dimming it, and there would be an extra light over the shaving mirror.

LIGHTING EFFECTS AND SHADES In the 1920s, most electric lights were adorned with frilled silk shades, and there was an extraordinary array of exotic shades to choose from for standard and table lamps and wall light brackets. A parchment or silk shade or a single alabaster bowl was generally used for the main suspended light in dining or living rooms. Opal glass bowls were popular because they softened the light and were shadowless. Leadlight shades were still popular, and glass bowls in amber, pink or blue were gaining favour.

Cove lighting was sometimes used to add artistic effect to draperies or special features of a room, and translucent glass wall urns or wall brackets in crystal or metal were installed to improve and soften the lighting of large rooms. A single lamp or a pair of table lamps on a sideboard or small table, as well as standard lamps, were invaluable in supplementing lighting, because often the reflected light from the ceiling bowl was not strong enough to sew or read by.

By 1934, built-in panel lighting had begun to gain ground as the latest style in direct and indirect lighting. In a 'model bedroom', for example, this consisted of a combination of a large, central, rectangular panel with wall brackets holding small, luminous panels positioned above mirrors or in the soffit above the bed. These indirect lights were sometimes supplemented by standard or table lamps in the simple shapes that marked the decorating style of the 1930s.

CLEANING LAMPSHADES Lampshades quickly become stained and dirty. Dry-cleaning is the safest course for hand-painted shades and for those made of linen or cotton or containing unwashable

Words of Wisdom

'Light to the home is like charm to the personality. A house without expressive lighting, though its furnishings be faultless, will yet be wanting.'

– AUSTRALIAN HOME BEAUTIFUL (1926)

Leadlight shades – in which pieces of coloured or patterned glass were framed in lead – made a strong fashion statement in the early 1900s.

Make a 1920s lampshade

The parchment lampshades that were so fashionable in the 1920s were often decorated with a pattern cut out of the parchment, so that it was shown in relief against a silk lining when the lamp was lit. You will need a wire lampshade frame, 60 cm of artificial silk, 60 cm of parchment (from art supply shops), a skein of strong embroidery silk, a mixture of 1 part turpentine to 3 parts boiled linseed oil, a craft knife and some carbon paper.

The late 1920s saw the rise in popularity of pottery lamp bases, often topped by elaborately frilled silk shades.

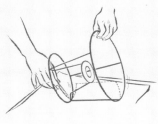

1. Roll the frame over a piece of newspaper firmly enough to leave an impression and cut out the shape. Test the fit on the frame and make any necessary adjustments. Trace the final shape onto the parchment and cut it out.

2. Place the parchment shape on a sheet of thick plastic to protect the table and smooth the turpentine and linseed oil mixture evenly over it with a soft cloth. Leave it to dry for at least a day.

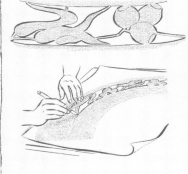

3. Find or design a simple pattern for the cut-out silhouette – the example shown here is a traditional Australian gumnut design. Trace your design lightly onto the parchment using the carbon paper. Place the parchment on the protective plastic, and then carefully cut out the pattern with the craft knife.

4. Cut a strip of silk 5 cm wider than the depth of the shade. Turn down the long edges about 2.5 cm, gather them, and sew the silk to the wire frame with the raw edges on the outside. Hold the ends of the parchment together with paper clips, slip the parchment over the frame, and use the embroidery silk to sew it to the frame over the silk lining with large buttonhole stitches about 2 cm apart.

Early lighting sources ranged from decorative cut glass ceiling fittings to short-lived fads such as the Glow-Worm – an enclosed candle designed to burn in a saucer of water.

glue, but you can wash silk shades in the bath. Use tepid water and mild soap, making sure that any trimmings are colourfast before you start. Rinse the shades by dipping them several times in clean water, and then dry them quickly in front of a fan, turning them frequently so that the fabric dries evenly.

Rub parchment shades with a slice of white bread to remove dirt and grease marks.

Mopping up

INDISPENSABLE THOUGH IT IS TO MODERN LIVING,
THE VACUUM CLEANER CANNOT ERADICATE STAINS
OR SHINE FLOORS.

Patterns are more practical for floor coverings than plain expanses of colour, which are inclined to reveal every blemish.

These chores still have to be done in the old way, with water, polish and elbow grease. Being able to boast floors so clean they could be dined upon was once the aspiration of every housewife, and the development of materials that were easy to wash – linoleum, and then vinyl – made this ambition possible. Later, the invention of the vacuum cleaner boosted the popularity of carpets as floor coverings.

CLEANING AND POLISHING WOODEN FLOORS Be sparing with water when cleaning wooden floorboards. Use a damp mop and put a mild detergent in the water. Wipe along the grain to prevent smearing, polish off with a clean mop then buff with a dry cloth. Once a month, lightly polish clear-finished floors with a liquid wax.

To restore the shine to sealed floorboards, clean thoroughly and allow to dry completely. Sand the area lightly by hand and then coat with clear varnish. Apply a second coat after 24 hours.

Parquetry Never use soap and water to clean a parquetry floor. Remove the dirt with one of the patent restorers sold by the manufacturers of hardwood floors. Apply the restorer with a woollen cloth and plenty of elbow grease, then rub a thin coating of wax over the entire surface of the floor. Polish with a brush, moving in straight lines, first one way and then the other. For the finishing touch, wrap a clean flannel cloth over the brush and rub the floor with this.

Removing stains Oil and grease stains can often be removed from wooden floors by applying a paste of fuller's earth mixed with soap and water. Sponge this mixture onto the stain and leave for a day or two before removing, repeating the treatment if necessary.

CLEANING OTHER SMOOTH FLOOR SURFACES Most smooth floor surfaces improve with a little polish, but do not overdo it; too much polish causes a messy build-up of wax.

Rubber When choosing rubber flooring, avoid a plain colour, as it will show every footmark. Rubber floors are very easily cleaned and should be washed only with warm water and detergent. Unlike other surfaces, they should not be waxed, and cleaning with turpentine or kerosene is also not recommended.

Vinyl Wash vinyl floors with warm soapy water, rinse and mop dry. Stubborn marks can be removed by rubbing with kerosene and superfine steel wool, then washing over with a mild detergent or soapy water and rinsing with clean water. Polish vinyl regularly to keep the surface flexible and smooth. You can make an excellent surface polish by grating 30 grams of beeswax, placing it in a jar and pouring on a

Taking Care of the Pence

In 1925 the *Australian Home Budget* published this recipe for a cheap, effective floor polish: 'Collect a jar full of candle ends, melt them, remove the wicks, and add sufficient turpentine to make a soft paste. Allow to set, then apply to stained floors and lino with a soft rag.'

cupful of turpentine. Stand the jar in hot water until the wax dissolves and shake well. To brighten up old lino, polish and then rub over afterwards with a flannel cloth that has been warmed in the oven.

Cork Wash cork floors with a cotton mop and warm water. Every month add 2–3 capfuls of methylated spirits to the water. After cleaning, rub some linseed oil well into the surface and leave for a week before polishing off. Alternatively, use wax polish alone.

Tiles Clean floor or quarry tiles with warm water and, to remove any grease stains, rub with a cloth moistened with a few drops of cloudy ammonia. Rinse well and repeat if necessary. If the tiles begin to lose their shine, give them an occasional waxing. Slate should never be washed with a soapy cleaner. A little lemon oil applied after mopping over with warm water will make the floor shine. Remove any excess with a clean mop. Do not use alkaline cleaners or steel wool on terrazzo floors; clean them with warm water and a dash of detergent.

CARPETS AND RUGS It pays to take good care of your carpet. It will wear better and last longer if kept thoroughly clean. This means frequent vacuuming, and treating any spills or stains immediately. To revive colours in carpets and rugs, vacuum first, then wash over with a cloth wrung out in vinegar and water.

Remember when choosing carpets that plain colours tend to show dirt and marks more readily than patterned ones. Prevention is better than a cure, so make sure everyone in the house uses the doormat, and keep paths and entrances to the home well swept and clean.

To remove indentations caused by heavy furniture, raise the pile by pressing lightly with a hot iron over a damp cloth. Brush the carpet upwards with your hand or an old hairbrush. Avoid excessive heat on synthetic carpets. To pick up thread and animal hair from carpets or upholstery, use rubber gloves or brush with a damp sponge.

Stain removal After cleaning a carpet, mop up as much excess moisture as possible then use a fan to dry it quickly.

Grease and oil Apply a paste of fuller's earth and French chalk, allow to dry, and brush off gently.

Ink Apply blotting paper, then sponge with soda water. For stubborn ink stains, use equal parts of white vinegar and water. Rinse and blot up well.

Mud Mud is much easier to remove if you let it dry completely and vacuum or brush off. Use warm water and vinegar to remove any remaining stain.

Urine and vomit Sponge well with cold water, then with warm water, detergent and a teaspoon of white vinegar. Apply ammonia straight from the bottle to bad stains.

Wine Sponge red wine with white wine, white vinegar or soda water. If the stain is dry, sponge with a cloth moistened with methylated spirits. Sponge white wine with warm water or soda water.

STAINING A WOODEN FLOOR
This old-fashioned dark finish has become popular in recent years. It is easy to do it yourself – just follow the steps below.

1. Prepare a mixture of 1 part turpentine to 2 parts boiled linseed oil and a little japan dryer. Blend a can of burnt sienna thoroughly with the mixture. This will turn it a rich, reddish-brown. Mix the paint quite thin, so that it will run readily.

2. Apply the stain with a good-sized brush, stroking the brush with the grain of the wood. Apply several coats, allowing each one to become perfectly dry before applying the next one.

3. Lastly, give the floor a coat of clear varnish.

Colour your world

COLOUR FASHIONS IN THE VICTORIAN ERA TENDED TOWARDS A RICH DARKNESS, BUT WITH THE NEW CENTURY THEY BECAME LIGHTER AND FRESHER.

No other aspect of decorative work requires more thought than the selection and use of colour. Like many artists, the most successful colourists of the past broke all the accepted rules and standards in their use of colour. However, before you follow their lead, prepare yourself by becoming familiar with colour theory.

COLOUR THEORY The primary colours are red, blue and yellow. Most people know that mixing two primary colours creates a secondary colour: for example, red and blue produce violet, red and yellow produce orange, and blue and yellow produce green. Each secondary colour is a complement of the primary colour that has been left out of its composition, so red has green as its complement, blue has orange, and yellow has violet or purple.

Secondary colours are complemented in the same way as the primary colours; green is complementary to brown, orange to slate, and purple to olive. A colour's pure complement is formed of equal parts of each; different tones are made by mixing unequal proportions.

Black and white are not really colours: black is the absence of all colour and white is the presence of all. Mixed together they form a neutral grey. Colours can be darkened or lightened by using either: black tones down a colour, producing a shade of that colour, and white lightens a colour, forming a tint.

HOW COLOURS WORK 'Perfumes, colours and sounds echo one another,' wrote the French poet Charles Baudelaire (1821–1867). Colour interacts with our other sensory perceptions to affect moods and stimulate emotions – to cheer or to soothe.
Red is stimulating and generates a feeling of vitality and warmth. It adds richness, but it can be irritating or aggressive if it is over-used.
Blue evokes coolness and space. It is discreet and reserved and suggests calmness and serenity.
Yellow is a sunny, genial colour, although it can be overwhelming if it is used unwisely.
Violet can be either warm or cool, depending on the whether red or blue predominates in its composition.
Green is more cheerful than blue and more restful than yellow; it is agreeable and refreshing.
Orange inherits the warmth and cheer of its component colours – red and yellow.
White is useful as a contrast to lift a colour scheme.
Black produces a cool contrast and increases the brilliance of the colours that are used with it.

The Way We Were

'Most of us have a favourite colour. Something in us reacts to that colour and we enjoy having it about us. For instance, you may love blue and yet perhaps the room you want blue has a cold exposure and therefore it is not a suitable colour. What to do? You could have warm-tinted walls of cream or buff, a dark stained floor with a blue carpet with the wall tint introduced and perhaps a touch of rose. Blue can appear in the curtains warmed by some rose notes. Upholster the chairs in old blue, and lampshades of rose could complete the picture. Such a scheme will satisfy your taste for blue and at the same time the cold aspect will be counteracted by the warm colours.'

– *HOME AND GARDEN LOVERS* (1940)

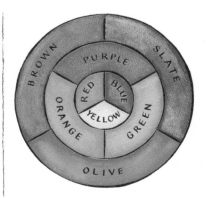

Related colours are next to each other on the colour wheel and are harmonious; complementary colours are directly opposite each other, and are contrasting.

INTERIOR DECORATION Interior decoration as a concept first emerged in the early 20th century, and rapidly developed into a highly skilled profession in its own right, covering the selection of furnishings, fabrics, pictures and household equipment as well as colour schemes.

Choosing colours Selecting a colour scheme is comparatively simple once the influence of colours has been recognised. Sunless rooms need some yellow, red or orange to introduce warmth, while light, sunny rooms call for the cool colours – grey, blue, green or mauve. Rooms with a medium light require yellow or rosy hues.

Choose the main colour first. Pale colours are more easily handled than strong ones, and on large areas such as ceilings and walls, tints and pastels are more suitable, although contrasting colours, used with care, may produce an interesting and attractive combination. As a guide, interior decorators recommend 75 per cent main colour, 15 per cent contrasting colour and 10 per cent 'splash'.

Colours can also give the sensation of weight: dark colours appear heavy and pale ones light. This should be taken into consideration when selecting colours for ceilings and walls.

A wrong colour decision can be a costly mistake. Examine samples under all lighting conditions before making your final choice.

Light colours give an impression of space, especially when all the elements are harmonious.

Colours can also change the apparent size of a room. Light colours tend to increase the size, while dark ones tend to reduce it. Orange, yellow, and particularly red, for instance, seem to bring walls closer, while blue and mauve seem to make them recede.

Light and colour When decorating, bear in mind that colour is affected by light. Not only will a colour change under artificial light, it will also change according to the gradations that occur throughout the day and according to brightness of the day itself. It is unwise, therefore, to select a colour for a room without leaving a sample of the colour in the room to be observed under different light conditions.

COMBINING COLOURS Every colour has a contrast: a colour that is in appearance and sentiment the direct opposite. When juxtaposed, these heighten one another, producing a harmonious scheme. Sometimes one colour changes the appearance of another: for example, green looks yellowish when it is teamed with blue. Colours on a white ground look darker than they are, and on a black ground lighter. You may be seduced by a novel blending of colours and a bizarre effect, but although these may please for a time, you will soon find the scheme irritating and unsettling. A blend of two colours in the right proportions is the best combination.

Changing fashions in colour combinations In the 1890s decorators recommended teaming China blue or turquoise with brown, and sealing wax red contrasted with dun or cream-coloured paint was very popular. Mothers were cautioned against putting dull green in the nursery, as it was believed to make children sluggish and fretful. Instead, yellow or pink walls dotted with bright, coloured pictures were recommended.

Some years later, colour schemes changed and violent contrasts and bright colours were abandoned for gentler and more delicate shades. Fashionable colour schemes for the drawing room were dove grey, old rose, sage green, old gold, buttercup or slate blue.

COLOURS FOR CARPET A carpet forms the background for the furnishings in a room and, as it covers a large area, should harmonise with but not dominate the rest of the room. A gloomy room can be brightened with a light-coloured carpet and a small room will appear larger than it actually is with a pale floor covering. Brightly coloured rugs or cushions appear to greater advantage against flat or neutral backgrounds such as dark polished wooden floors or plain carpet.

The colour of the carpet should also be considered in relation to the purpose of the room. A lighter carpet is probably more suitable for a living room than for a dining room or library, which may look better with a more subdued colour. On the other hand, a light carpet in a lounge room may not withstand the large amount of traffic.

AN ARTIST'S EYE
'Blue and green should never be seen without a colour in between ...' was a common colour dictum at the beginning of the 20th century for both artists and house painters, but in the late 1990s blue and green is one of the most popular and effective colour combinations in the home.

In a large room, sudden bursts of bright, contrasting colours add interest and excitement.

Heaven scent

PEOPLE ONCE STREWED AROMATIC HERBS
OVER FLOORS, WHERE THEY WOULD RELEASE
THEIR SCENT WHEN CRUSHED UNDERFOOT.

The juice extracted from lemon balm and sweet cicely was
rubbed into wooden panelling or floorboards to create a
deliciously perfumed atmosphere and a deep gloss on the wood.
Bowls of potpourri were placed where they would be most
effective, and pomanders hung in clothes cupboards. Little has
changed over the years. Even though the custom of strewing
herbs was abandoned some time ago, they are still used to make
up fragrant potpourris, sachets and pomanders.

*The fragrance of highly perfumed
flowers can linger on in a home-
made potpourri mixture.*

THE PERFUMED HOUSE Potpourri generally consists of dried flowers
and leaves preserved with a fixative of orris root or salt which helps to
retain the natural perfumes. The mixture can be further enhanced by
adding a few drops of an appropriate essential oil. Placed in a bowl
near an open window, the mixture will waft its fragrance throughout
the home.

Lavender and rosemary potpourri Mix together 50 grams of dried
lavender flowers, 50 grams of powdered orris root and 25 grams of
ground rosemary, and add 5 drops of oil of rose geranium. Store for six
weeks in a closed, dark glass jar.

CUPBOARD AND ROOM FRESHENERS To freshen stale-smelling
cupboards, place a mixture of 2 tablespoons of ammonia in water in an
old cup or small bowl and leave it in the cupboard overnight. To remove
the musty smell from a room or a house which has been closed up, burn
a small quantity of eau de cologne or juniper berries in a saucer.

Adding a few drops of oil of cloves, attar of roses or oil of lavender or
pine to your furniture polish is a subtle way to scent your home. Use
in bedrooms and in the hall.

To make sweet-smelling sachets for drawers, add a few drops of
perfume or essential oil to a few teaspoons of oatmeal. Mix well, then
spoon into tiny muslin bags.

Pomanders In the time of Elizabeth I of England, pomanders were
considered essential air purifiers and were carried at all times.

To make a classic pomander, wash and dry a firm, thin-skinned
orange and stud it evenly all over with fresh cloves. Place a teaspoon
each of orris root powder and ground cinnamon in a brown paper bag
with the orange and shake the bag so that the orange is thoroughly
coated with powder. Store the pomander in a dark place for a month,
then remove it and brush off any powder. Tie a ribbon around the
pomander, forming a loop at the top, and hang it in your wardrobe.
It will last for several months.

MAKING A LAVENDER WAND
A lavender wand encloses the
fragrant flower heads in a plaited
cage of stems. You will need about
30 freshly picked lavender flowers
with stems as long as possible.

1. Tie the stems just below the
flower heads with about 3 metres
of narrow mauve ribbon.

2. Bend the stems around the
flower heads to form a cage and
weave the ribbon through the
stems until the flower heads are
covered with a long cylinder of
woven stems and ribbon. Stitch
the ends of ribbon securely and
tie them in a bow.

Window dressing

WINDOWS WERE SMALLER IN EARLIER TIMES,
BUT SMALL OR LARGE THEY HAVE ALWAYS BEEN
AN IMPORTANT PART OF BUILDING DESIGN.

Windows offer a broad palette for artistic decoration, but whether you choose shutters, blinds, curtains, or a combination of all three, the successful decoration of any room must be based upon a balanced relationship between its parts, including the soft furnishings such as the curtains. All must be in relation to the proportions and surfaces used in the building itself. A well decorated room is a combination that has been built up into a harmonious whole and not by sectional treatment. As was astutely observed in the 1920s: 'Curtains are made for the room, not the room for the curtains.'

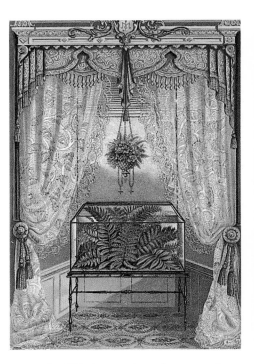

Windows such as these were the main feature of many a room.

CURTAIN CALL By the beginning of the 1920s, the fashion for swathing windows in layer upon layer of lace and heavy drapery had passed. But home decorating experts offered plenty of advice about how to choose, make and care for curtains. Tips ranged from adopting a homogeneous scheme throughout the house to exploring patchwork.

Choosing curtains It is important to consider how curtains will look from outside as well as from indoors. The outside appearance of a house benefits from a uniform treatment, and windows were often dressed with sheer 'glass curtains' of scrim or muslin for this reason. Another way of producing a cohesive external appearance is to use the same lining fabric for all your curtains.

The look of a window from the inside is affected by its outlook; it would be a pity to obscure a pleasant view with curtains, no matter how pleasing the fabric. In such a case, the function of curtains is to soften the glare of the sun, keep the room warm on a cold evening or lend a sense of privacy, and curtaining should be inconspicuous. On the other hand, a window that affords no attractive outlook can be enhanced by imaginative window dressing.

Effects and illusions Study the shape of the window: you will achieve the best effect by following the lines of the room as much as possible. Casement windows can have short curtains on separate rods on the upper and lower halves of the windows; or fine net can be gathered and strung on wires top and bottom with overdraperies arranged on each side.

Bay windows generally call for curtains that follow the curve, but you can have the best of both worlds if you team overdraperies that can be drawn right across the bay with lighter undercurtains following the shape of the bay.

If you have a row of sash windows, you can create a unified effect by connecting them with a valance and a pair of side draperies.

A SIMPLE CURTAIN TO MAKE
You will need fabric one and a half times the width of the window – you may need to join two pieces – and the height of the window plus 30 cm; a dowel 8 cm longer than the window width; and brackets fitted at the top of the frame.

1. Fold the top and bottom edges over 15 cm each, turn the raw edges under and stitch them down. At the top edge, make another row of stitching 5 cm above the first.

2. Push the dowel through the rod pocket, gathering the fabric up on the rod to the width of the window.

Curtains should be equally attractive open and closed. For a large window, do not use a colour that contrasts with the wall tone: the effect when the curtains are drawn will be overwhelming. A lighter or deeper tone of the wall colour will produce a better result.

You can use curtaining to hide design faults. A pleated or gathered valance some distance above the top edge of a low window will make it appear higher. A valance should not be used, however, in a room with a low ceiling, as it will reduce the height of the room. You can increase the apparent width of narrow windows with pelmets, or by fitting curtains that extend well beyond the side frames.

Curtain size Curtains hung close to the glass, such as casement curtains placed inside the window frame, should come to just above the sill. Hung outside the frame, they should just cover its lower edge. When teamed with side drapes, lace curtains should stop just above the floor below long windows.

For bedrooms and other rooms where it is important for drawn curtains to exclude the light, curtains must be ample both in width and in length, or 'drop'.

Materials and finishes Thick materials such as serge, tapestry and velvet do not need to be lined, but cretonne, printed linens and chintz look much better with lining. Casement cloth or sateen is suitable for this purpose. Unlined curtains made of thick material and lined curtains should be pleated rather than gathered.

The modern range of curtain rods, hooks, rings and headers is extremely wide – you can choose gathers, single pleats, multiple pleats or rings and hooks, among many other options. Ready-made curtains are available to fit standard-sized windows; it is worth spending the extra money to have curtains made for an odd-shaped window.

If you are on a really tight budget, you can make your own simple rod-and-pocket curtains for narrow windows. The instructions in the side column at the left show you how to do this.

Curtain tips There are some time-tested secrets of success for both making and hanging curtains.
• Allow generous hems on curtains; the extra weight helps them to hang properly.
• Do not machine stitch the hems of new curtains – just tack them down. If they shrink after the first wash, you can adjust the length before hemming by machine.
• Allow extra width so that if the curtains fade you can trim and rehem the inner vertical edges, which fade the most.
• If there is more than one pair of curtains at a window, change the order at intervals to spread the fading effect.
• Rub furniture polish or wax onto a metal curtain rod to prevent rust and promote smooth running.

WINDOW BLINDS AND AWNINGS Blinds and awnings keep the sun from fading curtains and carpets and keep interiors cool in summer. Over the years a variety of fabrics have been used to make blinds. In the 1920s and 1930s, the most common fabrics were dyed or

A cheap, easy window cleaner if the glass is not very dirty, is to rub over with wet newspapers and then polish with dry ones. The printers' ink is very effective in leaving windows with a just-polished look.

Leading decorators agree that too much design in one room can be tiring on the eyes. With this patterned rug, plain curtains would be a better choice.

unbleached linen and cotton or a mixture of both. These were available in a range of light and dark colours and were attached to spring rollers.

Canvas awnings that could be attached to the outside of the house came into vogue at the turn of the century. These gave protection from the sun and could be rolled up when not needed.

Cleaning blinds After dusting, wipe linen blinds with a cloth wrung out in methylated spirits and vinegar to refresh the colour, then wipe with a dry cloth. You can give old blinds a new lease of life by painting both sides with plastic paint.

To remove small stains from a blind, rub it with a piece of white bread or a ball of cornflour dough. However, a really dirty blind needs a bath. Choose a good drying day, and take down the blind, but do not remove the roller; this part is usually not exposed to dirt anyway. Thoroughly wet the blind and leave it for a few minutes. Run about 20 cm of tepid water into the bath and add a quarter of a cup of washing-up liquid and half that amount of ammonia and mix in well.

Place the rolled blind on the floor parallel to the bath and bring the bottom up and over the side and into the water, sponging as you go, until the whole blind has been dunked except the spring end. Holding the spring end out of the water, run the blind backwards and forwards in the bath a few times.

Use the same technique to rinse the blind with several changes of water, then let it drain over the clothes line for a few minutes. Do not allow it to dry.

Cover a table with a large towel and place the blind on it. With a second towel, wipe it dry from the roller end, rolling up as you go, making sure that the blind keeps its proper shape. Press with a warm iron if needed.

In the good old days, fine scrim curtains filtered the light and provided privacy, and heavier drapes could be looped back to the wall during the day and released at night to retain heat and provide a sense of security.

Cleaning awnings Use a strong salt and water solution to scrub awnings clean. Never use detergents, and do not use household bleach on old canvas, as it will damage the fabric.

To remove mildew from awnings, spread a mixture of soft soap, starch, salt and lemon juice on the canvas and leave it in the sun. As the mixture dries, apply further layers. Rinse thoroughly afterwards with warm water.

CLEANING WINDOWS Every generation seems to have had a favourite window cleaning product, but whatever you use, follow these tips for perfect results every time.
• Wash the window frames before cleaning the windows to prevent dirtying the glass again.
• Do not clean dirty windows with a dry cloth – the dirt will scratch the glass.
• Never use soap to clean windows; the resulting smears can be very difficult to remove.
• For perfectly smear-free windows, clean the outsides with horizontal strokes and the insides with vertical strokes, or vice versa. You will quickly be able to see any smears and wipe them away. Washing window panes in bright sunlight also makes any imperfections easier to see.

Full many a flower

IN THE WESTERN WORLD, FLOWER ARRANGING AS A DECORATIVE ART BEGAN IN VICTORIAN TIMES.

The Victorians favoured elaborate formal arrangements. Massed round bouquets were the most popular form of arrangement, and so strong was the passion for symmetry that flowers were often arranged in tight concentric circles. By the 1930s a simpler style had taken over. The Art Nouveau movement made much use of extenuated line and trailing, plant-like motifs. Stylistic influences from the East also had a powerful effect, in particular ikebana – the highly developed Japanese philosophy of flower arrangement, which simulated the natural growth of plants and created balance through the use of asymmetry.

The delicate Japanese art of ikebana had a profound stylistic influence on European flower arrangement in the early part of the 20th century.

VICTORIAN STYLES The bounty brought back by plant collectors from America, the Middle East and Asia aroused an interest in exotic flowers such as rhododendrons, fuchsias and camellias, but commoner plants such as ivy, lilies of the valley, and bluebells were favourites as well. Dried and artificial arrangements of feathers, wax or shells were also popular, often encased in glass domes.

The Victorians liked to have matching pairs of vases, again in the interests of symmetry. Vases and bowls were of glass or porcelain, especially lustreware. Around the middle of the century a vogue developed for dressing the dining table with flowers arranged in an epergne – a trumpet-shaped container with a shallow bowl at its base and branching offshoots, sometimes supporting hanging baskets.

ART NOUVEAU AND IKEBANA Stems and foliage played as prominent a role as flowers in these arrangements. Sometimes a single flowering branch was placed alone in a vase. Water lilies or irises grouped at one side of a shallow, water-filled bowl became popular.

Subtle colours were fashionable, and there was a marked preference for arrangements using only one or two varieties of flowers or a selection of flowers of the same colour, such as pink roses, carnations and sweet peas.

BETWEEN THE WARS The poppies that flourished in the fields torn apart by the trenches of World War I became a symbol of the illusory new age of peace. This optimism was reflected in the popularity of bright flowers, often arranged in black containers to heighten their colour.

Pyramid arrangements, with vegetation fanning out along the width of a vase, gained popularity. Monochromatic schemes gained favour: for example, white rooms decorated solely with white flowers. A fashion developed for mixing cultivated with wild plants, for example lichen-covered branches with kale.

Taking Care of the Pence

A simple and inexpensive way of arranging a home table decoration is to use a flowerpot saucer filled with wet sand. Disguise the outer edge with fern fronds and insert short-stemmed flowers with a few sprays of maidenhair fern into the sand so that it is hidden.

LIFE OUT OF DEATH
In Flanders fields the poppies blow
Between the crosses, row on row.
– 'IN FLANDERS FIELDS', JOHN McCRAE (1872–1918)

FUN WITH FLOWERS

Flowers bring beauty, colour and perfume into our homes. It is believed that the first home flower arrangements were collections of herbs and flowers gathered for their particular properties – medicinal or mystical – rather than for their purely decorative value.

But by the high point of the Victorian era, when flower arrangement had become a household art, even quite modest homes featured 'flower rooms' equipped with vases, knives, florist's wire and running water. And people quickly worked out how to extend the lifespan of cut flowers. They knew that stems should be broken or cut with a sharp knife (never scissors), and leaves stripped from the lower stalks. They added a piece of charcoal to the water to keep flowers sweet and prevent the water from discolouring. They topped up vases with fresh water at night and moved flowers to a cool place. They even discovered that an aspirin or a little sugar in the water prolongs the lives of cut flowers.

MAKING A FLOWER PYRAMID

A flower pyramid is an easy and inexpensive way of arranging flowers in the symmetrical style favoured by earlier generations of home-makers.

Stack three bowls of decreasing sizes inside one another, supporting them on small, shallow bowls. Fill each bowl with damp sand and arrange the flowers to form a pyramid shape. For the best effect, use no more than three kinds of blooms.

CRAZY VICTORIAN ROCOCO

The 'Hope Vase', held in the Victoria and Albert Museum in London, is a prime example of the Victorian passion for elaborate ornamentation in the early 18th century French rococo style. Made in 1855, the vase depicts the Greek myth of Perseus and Andromeda. The Ethiopian princess Andromeda was to be sacrificed to a sea monster to save her country, but Perseus, son of Zeus and Danäe, fell in love with her and claimed her in marriage after killing the monster.

AUSTRALIAN WILDFLOWERS

Sturt's desert pea is the focus of this 1892 illustration by Italian painter Signor Guglielmo Autoviello. The painting documents the growing acceptance by white settlers in Australia of flowers that must at first have seemed utterly strange.

A NEW STYLE IS BORN
In this spectacular flower arrangement by Anna Airy from 1940, stems and foliage are just as important as flowers.

A LADYLIKE OCCUPATION
In the late 1800s flower arranging, along with other 'genteel' pursuits such as embroidery and painting, came to be considered a suitable occupation for young ladies, and books of instruction soon appeared.

THE PATRIOTIC SPIRIT
In 1915, a Frenchwoman arranges red, white and blue flowers in a *bouquet tricolore*. Throughout the great upheavals of World War II, the women of the Allied Nations kept their spirits up and supported national morale with the traditional occupation of 'doing the flowers'.

MAKING A DAISY CHAIN
Daisy chains can provide hours of childlike pleasure. Any soft-stemmed flower can be used.

1. Cut the stems to about 10 cm long and make a slit about 1 cm long. Thread a second daisy through the slit. Continue until your chain is long enough to slip loosely over your head.

2. To close the chain, cut a slit in stem of the last daisy and very carefully ease the flower head of the first daisy through.

All that glitters

TWINKLING SILVER, BRASS AND COPPER AND
SPARKLING GLASS WERE THE PRIDE OF MANY A
HOUSEHOLD IN THE GOOD OLD DAYS.

Brass and copper ornaments that have been in the family for
generations deserve to be looked after and displayed with pride, and
it is a joy and a pleasure to seat your dinner guests at a table dressed
with gleaming silver and glass.

BRASS AND COPPER Clean slightly tarnished brass and copper by
applying a mixture of salt and lemon juice and then rinsing. A small
brush is useful for pieces with inlaid patterns or filigree.

Brass An old method of cleaning brassware is to rub it briskly with a
cotton wool pad wrung out in vinegar. Then wash it thoroughly in hot
soapy water, rinse it and rub it dry with a soft towel.

For stubborn marks, try a mixture of Worcestershire sauce and salt;
apply it with a toothbrush, scrubbing well into any grooves. Wash in
warm water, dry well, and rub with a clean cloth. Alternatively, use
ordinary toothpaste – the cheaper brands are best because they are
coarse. Leave the paste on for a while, especially if the stains are old,
then rinse off with warm water and polish dry.

Copper To restore the warm shine to copper ornaments, mix
2 tablespoons of vinegar with 1 tablespoon of cooking salt. Rub this
mixture on with a soft cloth, then plunge into hot water and rinse.
Dry thoroughly with a soft, absorbent cloth.

PEWTER It is usually enough to wash pewter in warm, soapy water.
However, if it has been neglected and needs a stronger remedy, you
could mix some finely powdered whiting with a little oil and apply
with a soft cloth. Rub in well, then polish with a clean cloth, giving a
final rub with a chamois.

Always rinse the article in fresh, warm water after cleaning, as
pewter tends to absorb dirty soap marks. Use a soft, clean towel to
wipe it dry. Remove grease from pewter by rubbing it with a cloth
moistened with methylated spirits.
Caution: Never store pewter in oak cupboards – it will corrode.

SILVER Cleaning silver is a rewarding job, as the results can be
quite dazzling. Always rinse silver very carefully after washing it –
the slightest soap residue will cause it to tarnish. To prevent silver
from discolouring after polishing, wipe it with petroleum jelly.

Cover the silver to be cleaned with sour milk, allow it to stand
for half an hour, then wash and rinse. Egg yolk is notorious for
blackening silver; gently rub egg stains with wet salt. Treat
other stains with fine whiting moistened with ammonia or

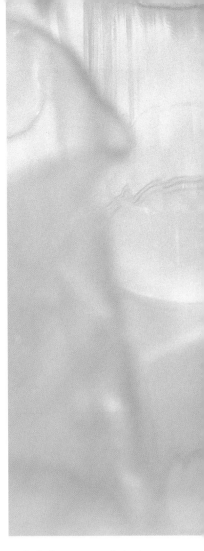

*Polished to a crystal clarity, even
plain tumblers impart a touch of
elegance to the simplest cool drink.*

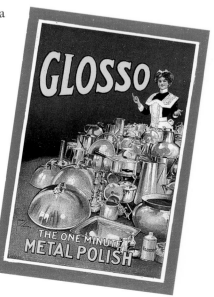

alcohol, then wash and polish the silver. Coarse whiting can damage silver, so if you cannot obtain fine whiting, sift coarse whiting through a piece of muslin before using it.

Clean tarnished silver plate with starch mixed with methylated spirits to form a paste. Allow to dry on the article and then rub off with a soft cloth.

MIRRORS, CRYSTAL AND GLASS Polish mirrors and glass with old stockings moistened with methylated spirits for a lint-free high gloss. Wipe glass tabletops with lemon juice and then dry with newspaper to make them sparkle. Scratch marks on glass can be removed with a mixture of equal parts of silver or brass polish and toothpaste. Apply with a soft, clean pad, working to and fro.

Crystal Place a clean towel in the bowl to prevent chipping. Wash the crystal in warm, soapy water and rinse in cold water. Dry and polish with a lint-free, fine-textured towel. If the crystal is very dirty, add a little ammonia to the washing water.

MARBLE To clean marble, paint the surface with a mixture of one part each of powdered pumice and powdered chalk and two parts of bicarbonate of soda. Leave for a day, then moisten with water and scrub lightly with a soft nail brush. Rinse and wipe dry. Polish with a piece of felt, rubbing from the centre outwards in a circular motion.

BREAKING A MIRROR
The belief that seven years of bad luck follows a broken mirror is widespread, but some European cultures also hold that it is bad luck to see yourself in a mirror by candlelight, or for a bride to see herself ready for the wedding – but a newly married couple can be assured of a long and happy life together if they stand together to admire themselves in a mirror in their wedding regalia.

Feeding the furniture

SOLID, WELL MADE FURNITURE IS AN
INVESTMENT; IT IS EASY TO MAINTAIN
AND CAN LAST A LIFETIME OR MORE.

Adopt a practical approach when buying
furniture. As well as usefulness, consider a piece
in relation to the room it is to occupy, and find
one that matches your budget. Do not skimp on
quality, however; reject anything that is built of
cheap materials and is badly made.

*The bigger the room, the bigger
the furniture can be ... and
treasured items deserve to be
shown to their best advantage.*

CHOOSING AND ARRANGING FURNITURE In the best of all possible
worlds, we would be able to decide on an interior decoration scheme
and choose furniture at the same time. In the real world, however, we
are more likely to be faced with the task of bringing inherited pieces
and pieces bought piecemeal into harmony with each other.

Tastes in interior design have changed radically since the days of our
grandparents, but many of their principles about the placement of
furniture are still sound. They knew that the size and purpose of a
room should dictate the kind and amount of furniture; that large
pieces are not right in small rooms; and that an unusual or especially
beautiful piece needs space to be appreciated.

Furniture should be arranged with the comfort and convenience of
users in mind. Avoid the appearance of regularity and symmetry – the
best arrangements are usually those that look natural and uncontrived.

Beds Medical references often stressed the importance of breathing
fresh air, especially when asleep, and as windows provided the only
ventilation in a bedroom, it was thought wise to place the bed near
one of them, positioning it so as to allow free circulation of air on at
least three sides. This advice still makes good sense.

*Dusting, cleaning and polishing
led to the development of a
profitable industry for home-care
product manufacturers.*

WOODEN FURNITURE In the old days, furniture was made of solid oak,
mahogany, walnut or rosewood, often elaborately carved. Dusting and
polishing was a major part of the daily routine, and over the years
efficient techniques developed for making short work of these chores.

Polished furniture You can greatly improve the appearance of
polished furniture that is in constant use by washing it down with a
mixture of equal parts of water and vinegar and then rubbing in cold-
pressed linseed oil. Repeat the rubbing after two days. Wipe freshly
painted, varnished or polished wood with a cloth dipped in mineral oil
and then polish with a soft duster. This treatment will also work
wonders for even the shabbiest paint.

Mahogany For a high polish, rub with lemon oil then polish with a
soft cloth moistened with alcohol. Old oak does not require a high
polish, and warm beer or vinegar and water are effective revivers.

This treatment may have a darkening effect on the wood, and the slight acidity tends to brighten without polishing. Linseed oil, which also darkens, may be substituted for wax polish.

Raw pine Hot water will turn untreated pine furniture yellow; use cold water and soap. If the wood is greasy, rub the dry surface gently with fine sandpaper and wipe it down with a damp cloth.

Cane and bamboo The best way to clean cane and bamboo furniture is to wash it with lukewarm, salted water in which a little washing soda has been dissolved. Use a quarter of a cup of salt and a tablespoon of soda to a litre of water. Add a little household ammonia to the water for very dirty varnished cane. Rinse well, dry thoroughly away from direct sunlight, and then rub lightly with linseed oil.

To extend the life of bamboo furniture, polish it once a week with a mixture of equal parts of turpentine and linseed oil. To protect it, apply a coat of white shellac.

Carved wood A small paintbrush is ideal for dusting carved wooden furniture. Pour a little liquid polish into a saucer and dip the brush in this from time to time as you dust. Use the polish sparingly. Finally, wipe over with a soft cloth.

SOFT COVERS Soft covers and upholstery used to be made of damask, velvet, tapestry or even silk, and there were many gentle but effective methods of cleaning them. Test any first on a piece of fabric on the underside to make sure that the colour is not damaged.

All fabrics Add a handful of soap flakes to a bucket of warm water and churn to make frothy suds. Using only the froth, gently rub any stains and dirt then dry the material with a fresh cloth. Do not use any water. Repeat if necessary.

Cotton Use shaving cream to remove a fresh stain from cotton upholstery. Carefully rub a little onto the area and wipe off with a damp cloth, then dry the patch with a fan.

Loose covers Before washing loose covers for the first time, test the material for colour-fastness by placing a piece on an old towel and covering it with a piece of wet, white cloth. Press with a hot iron.

Make your own polishing cloth by mixing two tablespoons each of paraffin or linseed oil and vinegar or turpentine in a screw-top jar. Insert a soft cloth to absorb the fluid then hang the cloth to dry. Store the cloth in the jar. It will absorb dust and help to preserve your furniture.

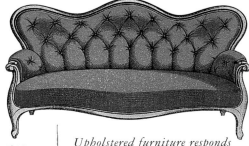

Upholstered furniture responds well to gentle cleaning — as long as it doesn't get wet!

The Way We Were

English novelist Howard Spring describes a typical household in the West Riding of Yorkshire in the closing years of the Victorian era:

'The floorboards and the hall table gleamed, and mingling with kitchen smells was the smell of furniture polish. I was to hear Mrs Ramsden later speak of feeding the furniture – which was not surprising seeing how well-fed everything in that house was – and certainly, as I stood there hesitant, twisting my cap in my hand on that May morning, the table and the chair alongside it had an opulent look as though every pore oozed an oily nourishment.'

– *THESE LOVERS FLED AWAY*, HOWARD SPRING (1955)

If the white cloth shows any colour stain, don't attempt to wash the fabric. After washing, replace the covers while they are still slightly damp – this makes them easier to fit and prevents shrinkage.

Velvet If you would rather not risk soapsuds, try this method. Dip a cloth in powdered magnesia and rub in gently with a fine brush. Leave for an hour then vacuum off. Another method is to sponge the fabric with equal parts of methylated spirits and water.

Tapestry Clean tapestry stools or chair seats by rubbing vigorously with warm bran or powdered magnesia. Leave for a few hours and then vacuum or brush off. Powdered magnesia will also brighten dull thread colours.

Leather If leather chairs become dull, brighten them by rubbing with half a lemon or stale beer, then polish with a dry cloth. To remove grease spots from leather lounges or chairs, rub well with eucalyptus oil, then polish.

If the leather is very dirty and stained or mildewed, add a tablespoon of vinegar to half a bucket of warm water and wash, drying thoroughly with soft towels. Another effective treatment is saddle soap, worked into a heavy lather. Saddle soap also polishes and feeds leather furniture; apply with a dampened cloth and buff with a velvet cloth.

Vinyl Wipe with warm soapy water and rub dry with a soft cloth. To remove greasy marks such as shoe polish or lipstick, wipe off as much as possible with a dry cloth then gently rub with a cotton rag moistened with turpentine or methylated spirits. Wash with warm, soapy water and rub dry.

To remove ballpoint or felt-tipped pen stains, mix equal parts of fuller's earth and calcium chloride with a few drops of methylated spirits. Mix into a thick paste, adding more methylated spirits if necessary, and apply with a knife on the stain. Allow to dry, then wipe with a damp cloth. Wash the area with a wet cloth and polish dry.

BRASS BEDSTEADS Polish a bedstead with sweet oil and whiting. Wet the whiting or tripoli with the oil, spread a little on a piece of soft flannel and rub the soiled brass with this. Next, dip a soft flannel in dry whiting and rub the brass briskly. Polish with a chamois. A bedstead should stay clean for months after this treatment.

An occasional rubbing with a piece of chamois will keep brass bedsteads bright and clean.

PIANOS Dust a piano frequently with a feather duster, as dust can affect its sound, and hang a bag of mothballs inside. Clean the keys with a piece of silk moistened with a little alcohol. At night close the lid and the top, if it has been opened.

Never place pianos close to windows or radiators; if the air becomes too dry, the wooden components will shrink and the joints and soundboard may separate. You should also guard against the accumulation of moisture. Condensation can form on the metal components when a room is suddenly warmed. Do not stand a vase of flowers on a piano: if the vase is knocked over, the water could destroy the internal workings.

Words of Wisdom

'The gravest sin in furnishing is ugliness, and the next is inconsistency. Even people who have a flair for picking out a nice piece are liable to fall into the latter. It is ridiculous, for example, to place a time-worn, weathered, primitive chair, no matter how attractive, next to a highly polished, finely carved writing table. Irrespective of whether they are the same period or not, they are an age apart, and will never harmonise together.'

THE AUSTRALIAN HOME BEAUTIFUL (1928)

Brass bedsteads can be kept delightfully bright with just a little spit and polish.

Splish, splash!

CLEANING THE BATHROOM CAN BE A LABORIOUS
AND TIME-CONSUMING TASK BUT IT IS A ROOM WE
COULD NOT DO WITHOUT.

Before the end of the 19th century, the bath, washbasin and toilet
were generally located in different parts of the house. It took a shift in
public attitudes to hygiene and subsequent improvements in
plumbing before they were collected together in one room.

KEEPING IT CLEAN Nothing could be more inviting than a clean
bathroom, with fresh towels, sparkling floors, shining taps and
fittings, clear mirrors and polished tiles. It is quite easy to keep the
bathroom clean and tidy if each member of the household takes a few
moments before leaving it to make sure that it is left as it was found.
Here are some tips from our grandmothers for keeping the various
areas spotlessly clean.

The shower area Before hanging a new shower curtain, soak it in a
solution of salt and water to make it less susceptible to soap residue.
To prevent mildew forming on the shower curtain, leave it spread out
to dry after showering. Sprinkle powdered borax over a plastic shower
curtain while is still wet to remove soapy film. Wash a woven shower
curtain in Epsom salts to remove mildew and soap scum.

Kerosene, methylated spirits or mineral turpentine are all excellent
for removing the soap film on a glass shower screen, and are much
cheaper than modern proprietary preparations. Afterwards, rub the
screen with a cloth moistened in vinegar to make it shine.

Plain household vinegar and bleach will remove bathroom mould.
Pour into a spray bottle and spray over the mould, leave for
ten minutes and rinse off. Kerosene also works well.

Tiles Clean tiles with a mixture of equal parts of vinegar and kerosene.
Shake well and apply with a soft cloth. You could also use lemon juice,
and polish off with a chamois for extra sparkle. Toothpaste
is excellent for cleaning the grouting between tiles. Apply
it with an old toothbrush then wipe away with a damp
cloth. White vinegar is a natural acid and works well on
greasy ceramic tiles and inside toilet bowls.

BATH AND BASIN Keep chrome or nickel fittings shining
by rubbing them over daily with a damp cloth sprinkled
with bicarbonate of soda. Rinse and dry thoroughly
afterwards. Soap shavings mixed with kerosene will shine
bath enamel. To remove green copper stains in the bath,
cut a lemon and smear the juice on the marked areas. Leave for a few
minutes then rinse off. Use a mixture of salt and turpentine to polish
a yellowed bath.

*Then, as now, the joys of a heated
tub were one of life's pleasures.*

*With the advent of indoor
plumbing, bathroom fixtures and
fittings – either plain or
elaborate – became essential.*

Keeping an orderly house

Queen of the May

MAINTAINING A TIDY AND CLEAN HOME IS IMPORTANT AS MUCH FOR APPEARANCE AND COMFORT AS IT IS FOR GOOD HEALTH.

We no longer have an army of servants or as much time to devote to housework as we did in the old days, but we can, instead, recruit everyone in the family to help us care for the home. It is a good idea to establish a timetable for all tasks, from the simple ones like washing up and keeping the bath clean, to others that are done on a regular basis, such as cleaning the windows and polishing the silver. Draw up a detailed cleaning list, noting how often the tasks need doing; use headings to group chores done yearly, monthly, weekly and daily. Adopt general housekeeping rules which will serve as a basis for the weekly cleaning and the annual spring cleaning.

TIDY TIPS A tidy house is much easier to keep clean than an untidy one. Our grandmothers, who usually had large families, would often have a list of house rules, such as the following – and they made sure that everyone obeyed them.
• Don't put it down, put it away in the right place.
• Keep floors, tables and benches clear.
• Make your bed before you leave your room for the day.
• Wipe the bath after use and leave the bathroom tidy.
• Put magazines and books away when you have finished with them.
• Hang up clean clothes and put dirty clothes in the laundry basket as soon as you take them off.
• If you use up something, write it down on the shopping list.

Taking Care of the Pence

Make a slit in a sponge, fill it with scraps of left-over soap and use it to clean kitchen and bathroom surfaces.

WIPE YOUR FEET In grandmother's time, a foot brush was placed in the hall to avoid trekking dirt indoors. Today, you can make it easier to keep floors clean by placing door mats at all external doors and asking people to wipe their feet well before stepping inside.

EQUIPMENT Essential cleaning tools include a vacuum cleaner or carpet sweeper, a long-handled soft floor broom, a short-handled soft brush with a dust pan for taking up dry dirt and cleaning corners, a separate soft brush for the fireplace, a stiff, short-handled brush for the stair carpet, and a mop for washing floors. A good scrubbing brush is useful for particularly dirty floors and doorsteps and a stiff broom is essential for porches and outside steps and paths. For the kitchen and bathroom, an old toothbrush is an excellent tool for cleaning awkward spots around the sink and for tile grouting. A feather duster is useful for picture frames, bookshelves and high shelves and for cleaning away cobwebs.

Dusting and cleaning cloths should be washable, and it is advisable to keep special soft cloths for polishing windows and mirrors separately from those used for polishing furniture. Cloths for cleaning the bathroom and toilet should always be rinsed thoroughly in very hot water after use.

Good results cannot be obtained with dirty implements, so it is advisable to check the condition of your cleaning equipment regularly to ensure that it is free from dirt.

Brooms and brushes Brooms and brushes will last longer if washed in warm, soapy water. It is easier to do this job outdoors. If the brooms are very dirty or greasy, add some washing soda to the water. First, remove any fluff from the bristles, then clean the wooden parts according to the nature of the finish. Beat the brushes up and down in the soapy water until they are clean, then rinse to remove the soap. Give a final rinse in cold water containing a tablespoon of salt to every litre of water. Shake the brushes well to remove as much water as possible, then hang them to dry in an airy place so that the water does not soak into the wood and soften the fixing. It is preferable to hang brooms with their heads down on a line, or if drying indoors, across two chairs or boxes. Brushes used for wet work should always be rinsed well after use, as soap residues will cause them to deteriorate.

Soft brooms will collect dust and fluff much more easily if you sprinkle a few drops of kerosene on them about once a week. Make sure that all broom handles are smooth. If they begin to splinter, they could injure your hands. To avoid this, rub the handles down with sandpaper and repaint, or renew altogether.

Early vacuum cleaners tended to be narrow-bodied upright models. Pictured here (left to right) are the Proctor, the Goodhousekeeper and the Star.

Mops Mops used for dusting as well as for polishing need to be washed occasionally. Some mops have heads which unhook for washing. To clean, steep for about half an hour in 2 tablespoons of soda dissolved in half a bucket of hot water. This will loosen and remove the dirt. Next, place in fresh hot water containing the same amount of soda and enough soap to make a good lather, and beat up and down. Rinse well and hang up to dry. When the mop is thoroughly dry, stand it in a tin in which you have sprinkled a little polishing oil.

Vacuum cleaner and carpet sweeper Clean these thoroughly at regular intervals – if residual fluff or dust has accumulated they will not function with complete efficiency.

CLEANING AGENTS Always keep a range of good cleaning products. Handle them with care and store away from children. As well as the usual detergents and scouring agents, you will find the following substances useful:
Baking soda (bicarbonate of soda) For grease spots
Cloudy ammonia For cleaning bathroom surfaces, painted walls and stainless steel

No matter what the cleaning product, there was no substitute for old-fashioned elbow grease.

Kerosene For cleaning and polishing tiles, paint work and marble.
Methylated spirits For polishing bathroom fixtures, mirrors, porcelain and crystal ornaments, and for brightening woodwork
Turpentine For dusting cloths
White vinegar For removing grease and for cleaning glass

DAILY AND WEEKLY CLEANING To keep your home in good, basic order, every room should be given a certain amount of tidying and cleaning every day. It is a good idea to do this work early so that you can enjoy the clean and tidy rooms for the major part of the day.

Keep your cleaning goods in a bucket as you move from room to room. This will save you the trouble of going back to where you last used an item. When cleaning very dirty areas, apply the cleaner to the worst spots first – it will do its job while you are busy on another area.

DAILY CLEANING In the days when most women did not go out to work and had household help, they followed a strict daily cleaning routine, which often began well before breakfast.

In the early morning, they opened the doors to the house and the windows of the living areas if the weather was fine to allow the stagnant night area to be replaced.

They then cleaned each room, shaking any rugs outdoors and replacing them, and doing any necessary tidying. Dusting as far as they could reach while standing on the floor was considered sufficient for daily work, and then wooden floors and surrounds were swept.

Beds were left open for at least two hours before making them to allow air and sunshine to freshen the bed linen.

Sweeping any fireplaces that had been in use came next, and then cleaning the toilet and rinsing washing areas in the bathroom. Wet towels were hung up to dry and windows opened.

After breakfast, they cleaned and swept the kitchen and tidied the front entrance.

WEEKLY CLEANING Set aside a few hours once a week to thoroughly clean the house. Bear in mind that the more careful the weekly clean, especially in difficult-to-get-at spots, the less exhausting will be the annual spring clean of the entire house.

For each room, ventilate and tidy the area, remove flowers, collect any articles in need of special attention such as ornaments, and shake any cushions, rugs and table covers outside. Collect all cleaning equipment needed for the room.

Dusting and vacuuming Dust the furniture and shake any curtains and pin them up out of the way. Clean the fireplace and grate if it has been in use, and lay a fresh fire. Polish the grate and wash and polish the surrounds after dusting. Dust the skirting boards then the high places not attempted daily, such as the tops of doors and cupboards and ceiling corners, using a cornice brush or duster over a soft broom if the vacuum cleaner will not reach. Let down any blinds, dust, and

All non-carpeted floors respond well to a weekly mop and polish.

roll up. It is not necessary to dust the walls at every weekly clean, but the wall behind any pictures and the pictures themselves should be done. Walls brushed down or vacuumed occasionally will remain clean longer and wallpaper will require less frequent renewal than if left untouched for a considerable period.

Thoroughly vacuum every upholstered piece of furniture and the carpet, making sure you clean under all the furniture.

Special jobs Now turn your attention to any articles which require special cleaning such as paintwork and windows, and do any necessary polishing of furniture. The dining table and other heavily used pieces generally require polishing every week or so, but other articles need polishing only every few months if they are well cared for in between.

Floors Wash, mop or polish the floor if it is not carpeted. In an ordinary room that does not have very hard use, once a month is often enough to polish a floor – a well-polished floor keeps clean easily. In bedrooms, or where the floor is almost entirely covered with rugs or is carpeted, once in every three months is sufficient. Finally, unpin the curtains and replace any rugs and furniture that have been moved. Change the water in the vases and rearrange the flowers.

Bedrooms In the bedroom, use a clean, stiff-bristled brush to brush the mattress thoroughly after airing, then remove it so that every part of the bedstead may be dusted. Remove the underlay and shake well. Shake all blankets and comforters outdoors if possible, as they get very dusty. Make the bed with fresh linen, then proceed with other dusting, vacuuming and polishing as detailed above.

Bathrooms In the bathroom and toilet, thoroughly clean the bath and hand basin, polish fittings, clean the windows and mirrors and clean and polish the floors. Pour strong hot soda water into the toilet pan using 50 grams of soda to 1 litre of water and brush vigorously. Flush while holding the brush in the pan. Pour in a little strong disinfectant and leave to stand.

Finishing off After all the rooms are complete, polish the stair edges, banisters and wainscotting or skirting boards and the hall furniture. Vacuum the stairs and hall.

SPRING CLEANING With the onset of warmer spring weather comes a feeling of expansiveness and a natural desire to make the home fresher and more attractive for the longer days ahead. It is sometimes better to tackle this task when most of the occupants are away if the family is large, and it is a good idea to begin with areas which are used infrequently, leaving until last those occupied constantly.

Preliminaries Turn out and clean all drawers, wardrobes and cupboards, dust thoroughly, scrub and dry the woodwork if necessary, and reline the drawers with fresh paper before sorting and replacing the contents. Take this opportunity to throw away objects that are never used. Put aside clothing that can be cut up for cleaning rags, or others that will need attention at a later time. Unpack all stored summer things for the house and personal use and put away tidily. Clean and relabel all boxes, bottles and jars used to store household

The cover of this 1937 magazine makes amusing work of an otherwise heavy-going chore.

Words of Wisdom

'A bicycle pump or a pair of bellows is excellent for removing dust and fluff from carved furniture, under wire mattresses and so on. It will reach crevices which defy dusters and feather brushes.'

– *HEALTH* (1932)

items. Wash or clean winter garments and heavy blankets as required and pack away with moth repellents. Also wash mattress covers and underlays.

Wash or clean curtains, drapes, blinds and upholstery. Mend any broken items of china or wood which can be repaired at home, and deal with any small household repairs. Check window frames and similar paintwork, noting any areas that need attention. Any painting or redecorating should be done now. If the chimneys need sweeping, make sure you engage the chimney sweeper before you clean the rooms affected.

Remove all books from shelves and dust each one separately. Clean and polish display cabinets and their contents. Repair or patch any torn wallpaper. Make any home-made cleaning agents and polishes that you will require and ensure you have a good supply of other cleaning products, brushes and cloths.

Cleaning procedure Start at the top of the house and work downwards. Also, try to finish one room before moving on to another. Once the rooms have been completed, the stairs, landings and hall follow, then finally, the kitchen and laundry. The procedure for each room is the same as for the weekly cleaning, only more thorough.

Open all the windows, remove small items of furniture, pictures, blinds, curtains, rugs, cushions and ornaments for subsequent dusting or cleaning, and group large pieces of furniture, covered with protective cloths, in the centre of the room. Check the floors and floor coverings for marks or damage and remedy as appropriate.

Ceilings and walls With the aid of a step ladder, clean the ceiling and walls. For the latter, use long, downward strokes. Clean ceilings with a soft cloth tied over the brush of the vacuum cleaner. If the ceiling is of plaster, do this very lightly to avoid damage. Also remove dust from picture rails and cornices with the vacuum cleaner. Examine ceilings and walls for any signs of damp and arrange to have any necessary repairs made.

Wallpaper can be partly cleaned by sweeping, and any marks removed by rubbing with stale bread, but take care not to roughen the paper by rubbing too hard and make sure that no dough remains on the walls. Cover the floor where you

will be working with newspapers to catch the bread as it crumbles away.

Dismantle and clean all light fittings and wash the windows inside and out. Remove all dust from the furniture and clear, clean and polish the fireplace. Vacuum or polish the floor, depending on whether it is carpeted or not, and wash all paintwork and other parts of the room where appropriate after dusting. Use warm water in which a little soap has been dissolved. Rinse with fresh, warm water and give a final polish with a dry cloth.

The Way We Were

Many of the details of this weekly house-cleaning schedule are not relevant in the 1990s, but the system it advocates is still valid:

'*Monday* – wash day, leave time to clean the bathroom, stairs and laundry.

Tuesday – after ironing is finished the linen closet can be cleaned and the clothes folded and replaced.

Wednesday – for cleaning silverware and putting the china closet in order, repapering pantry shelves and with the midweek change of table linen, the dining room might receive special attention.

Thursday – sweeping bedrooms, and while this is being done it is a good plan to air all the bedding thoroughly; this adds greatly to the freshness of the nicely swept and well-dusted sleeping apartments.

Friday – sweep the parlors, reception and sitting rooms, have the rugs well cleaned and windows and mirrors polished.

Saturday – bed linen and table linen changed, towels and soiled clothing gathered, baking done and special preparation made for the day of rest. This will afford the satisfaction of having conducted a well-ordered system and will leave some time each day for reading, sewing, visiting and resting.'

– *THE HOUSEHOLD GUIDE OR DOMESTIC CYCLOPEDIA* (ABOUT 1900)

Restoring order When all is clean and polished, replace the blinds, curtains, cushions, ornaments and rugs and rearrange the furniture.

Take the pillows, bolsters and mattresses from the bedrooms to the outside of the house and thoroughly beat and air them. Also shake out eiderdowns and blankets. Dust or vacuum the springs of the beds. While the bedding is airing, take apart each bed and dust and polish it thoroughly. Place the head, foot and side pieces on the floor, grooved sides up, and, with the windows of the room open, pour naphtha into all the grooves and crevices. Then reassemble the bed and make it up with fresh linen.

THE FINISHING TOUCHES For a lift of the heart and a sense of real achievement, give your home that finishing touch that means so much. After cleaning, adorn the main rooms and the entrance hall of your sparkling, clean home with fresh flowers.

Dusting and polishing can seem like boring chores, but your reward will be a fresh, bright home that is a pleasure to live in.

The versatile veranda

IN THE FIRST DECADE OF THE 20TH CENTURY,
THE VERANDA BECAME A COST-EFFECTIVE WAY OF
EXPANDING THE CAPACITY OF A HOUSE.

In the extreme Australian climate, the veranda provided protection from the elements.

Australia, with its temperate to tropical climate, was ideally suited to the use of the veranda as an extension of the standard enclosed living space. Because of the need to protect dwelling places from climatic extremes ranging from searing heat to raging winds and torrential rain, verandas were a feature of Australian domestic architecture from the earliest days of European settlement.

The veranda provided opportunities for the ingenious modification of existing buildings: gradually, especially in the cities, veranda spaces started to be used as living spaces – as sleep-outs, as family rooms or rumpus rooms, as studies, as dining areas for warm spring and autumn evenings, and even as supplementary living rooms, closed in with glass and furnished with rugs, curtains, tables, bookcases and easy chairs, often of cane, wicker or bamboo.

It was the introduction of electricity for domestic lighting and heating that made the whole development possible.

EARLY VERANDAS In Australia, it had become the trend by the 19th century to widen the verandas of large homes and to extend them from the front of the house to the sides, and sometimes right around the house, to give more protection from the weather.

In homes where an encircling veranda was precluded by lack of space, the veranda originally tended to be situated on the most sheltered side of the house, so that the occupants could enjoy the open air without being roasted by the sun or buffeted by winds. Later, as the potential of the veranda as an enclosed extension of the living space became obvious, home owners were advised, if at all possible, to position the veranda on the side of the house that afforded the pleasantest outlook.

By the 1920s, the veranda had evolved into an entertainment and recreation area.

The Way We Were

'It is possible to combine simplicity with artistic appearance and good taste. The porch may be made very pleasing to the eye and, therefore, grateful to the senses. Good taste ensures restfulness, an air of homeliness and peace, and thus the porch is to be made a sanctuary, where we may be surrounded by comfort and whence we may contemplate at leisure all the beauties of our garden and inhale the fresh air laden with the sweet and invigorating perfumes of the flowers and shrubs and trees, and watch the birds and butterflies and bees sporting in our domain.'

– *HOME AND GARDEN BEAUTIFUL* (1913)

Verandas offered many advantages, even before their usefulness as auxiliary living space became obvious. The protection from the weather that they afforded increased the durability of the building; maximum ventilation of the inner part of the house was possible because the windows could be left open at any time without fear of damage by sun, wind or rain; and the veranda was a convenient place to leave muddy boots and to dry and air clothes in wet weather. Above all, the veranda imparted a sense of added spaciousness – an important consideration, especially in a relatively small house.

SLEEP-OUTS Sleep-outs to supplement night-time accommodation were a natural development from the widening of the veranda, especially in the cities and rapidly developing suburban areas where space was at a premium. In single-storey buildings, wide verandas simply evolved into supplementary bedrooms. In multi-storey buildings, such as the Victorian terrace houses that proliferated in the inner cities, second-floor and even third-floor balconies were often enclosed and converted into bedrooms or annexes.

THE INTEGRATED VERANDA Little by little, the veranda and its decor and furnishing became an important consideration in home design. It was thought to require only simple and inexpensive furniture, being seen as an area for informal relaxation where and family and friends could recline on a cushioned bench or laze in a hammock, with potted palms swaying in the dappled shade nearby. It soon became the fashion to eat luncheon and afternoon tea on the veranda, and even to serve dinners there, and the use of such a pleasant area as a bedroom became less common.

In the 1940s, many smart renovations included the addition of picture windows or French doors opening out onto the veranda to integrate it more closely with the rest of the home and to provide greater access to the fresh air. Discreet fly wire came into use to protect the occupants from insects while preserving the view. Sliding glass doors were also installed, making it possible to use the area all year round. For those with extensive gardens, the verandah became the perfect transitional area, linking the house with the garden and bringing the contemporary idea of indoor–outdoor entertaining one step closer.

VERANDA FURNITURE Large sheltered verandas were sometimes divided into sections with screens of solid materials, canvas or wicker. A divan or day bed served as a sofa during the day, disguised with a frilly cover-up and matching cushions. Rugs added comfort underfoot, and the other furniture was usually of light lacquered bamboo or wickerwork, which was easy to move and impervious to damp.

Bamboo blinds were often used to provide shade, as they were more airy than canvas, and if painted green looked pleasant and were just as durable. However, if the aspect was rather exposed, roll-up canvas blinds were thought more suitable. They gave better protection from the heat of the sun as well as rainy and windy weather, yet could be rolled up out of the way on fine days.

Words of wisdom

Home decorating magazines had definite views about the type of furniture suitable for the porch:

'It is impossible to furnish the porch extravagantly, for it has too much the character of the summer-house or arbour, and even if rusticity of appearance is not desirable, at least simplicity and lack of costly decoration are absolutely necessary. Comfort is an important consideration. Lightness and durability are the essential characteristics, so that furniture may be easily moved and the decaying influences of the weather resisted.'

– *HOME AND GARDEN BEAUTIFUL* (1913)

Lazing in a hammock in the shade of the veranda became a popular pastime on a hot day.

On the

home front

**HINTS FOR TRADITIONAL DO-IT-
YOURSELF HOME MAINTENANCE**

Surveying your castle

NOT SO LONG AGO, PEOPLE RELIED ON THEIR OWN RESOURCES IN A HOUSEHOLD CRISIS, RATHER THAN CALLING IN A SPECIALIST.

Many problems around the house can be rectified using basic tools and common sense. The best preparation for maintaining your home is to learn a little about it, so that you can deal with minor emergencies, spot problems and tackle small repairs before they become major difficulties.

GET TO KNOW YOUR HOUSE Make sure you know where the main supply points are for electricity, gas and water.

Electricity Find the power cable, the meter, the fuse box and the main switch to turn off the power in emergencies. Mark which fuses govern which electrical circuit. If a circuit is overloaded or a fault occurs, the fuse will 'blow' as a circuit breaker trips or a fuse wire melts and breaks the current. Always replace fuse wire with wire of the same gauge; keep spare wire in the box, together with a torch. A fuse can be replaced with a plug-in circuit breaker of the same rating.

Gas Gas reaches your house through a meter, and the main gas tap is usually nearby. Locate the meter, so that if there is an alarming smell of gas or an emergency, you can close the tap to cut off the gas supply.

Water The cold water pipe runs underground from the street, surfacing as needed in the kitchen, bathrooms, toilets and laundry. Before attempting any running repairs, make sure that you know where the stopcocks are for the hot water tank, cisterns and toilets. To turn off all the water supply to your house, close the main stopcock; you will find it with the meter, near your front gate or door.

Drainage Sewage pipes are separate from those used for waste water, as are rainwater pipes. All pipes drain into the public sewer system, which may carry household waste and rainwater separately. Find the drain covers, near the house, and the soil pipe leading from the toilets.

PLANNING Our grandparents used almanacs to remind them of tasks throughout the year. Like them, you should make a seasonal check on the house, list jobs to be done and budget for upcoming major work.

Tradespeople Use local tradespeople – they value their reputation and will give good service. Keep a list of tradespeople recommended by friends. Establish contact with someone in a local hardware outlet; your custom will pay dividends in advice drawn from experience.

With the advent of electricity, the future of gas seemed dim for a while, but today it is as popular as ever for cooking and heating.

When you need a tradesperson, get several quotes listing the work to be done and the materials involved. It pays to choose someone who will do a good job, not just a cheap one.

ANNUAL INSPECTION Checking your house every year will alert you to potential problems.

Roof Without a torch, check the roof space for light, which may mean that repairs are needed. Inspect the woodwork, wiring and plumbing. Check the timber for borers and termites; look for small holes or small piles of dust below the timber, and check under the house in dark or damp areas where termites build their mud galleries from the nest to the woodwork. If you find them, call in a pest-control specialist immediately.

As recently as the 1950s, the local ironmonger could be relied upon to supply everything the handyperson or home decorator would ever need.

Interior Small cracks are not a worry, but wide ones above windows and doors may indicate weak framing, and large cracks in the wall, if visible on the outside wall as well, may mean subsidence. Large cracks and bulges in plaster may mean that a replastering job is needed. Peeling or blistering wallpaper or patches ringed by stains indicate that damp is penetrating and needs attention.

Rap the skirting in each room. It should sound solid. If it feels soft and sounds dull, look under the floorboards for dry rot, indicated by masses of fungal 'cottonwool' or dark, damp stains around the affected area. Dry rot spreads quickly, so get it treated right away.

Check that all windows, doors, locks, taps, cisterns, and electrical and plumbing fittings are working properly.

Exterior Inspect the house from the outside, using binoculars to check lead flashings, the roofing and the gutters. (Rusty stains on woodwork may mean gutters need replacing.) Test that the mortar between bricks is firm. Crumbling mortar can let in water.

Check outside woodwork by inserting the point of a penknife. If the blade slides in easily, the wood is probably rotten. Inspect window flashings, doorsteps, drains, gratings and dampcourses, paths, fences and boundary walls to ensure they are in good condition.

The Way We Were

In a pioneering community, people had to make do with whatever came to hand for building, such as the stringybark and greenhide recommended in these verses:

'If you want to build a hut, to keep out wind and weather,
Stringybark will make it snug, and keep it well together;
Greenhide if it's used by you, will make it all the stronger,
For if you tie it with greenhide, it's sure to last the longer.

New chums to this golden land never dream of failure,
Whilst you've got such useful things as these in fair Australia;
For stringybark and greenhide will never, never fail yer,
For stringybark and greenhide is the mainstay of Australia.'

– *COLONIAL BALLADS*, HUGH ANDERSON (1962)

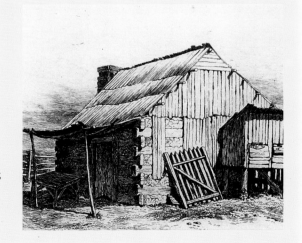

Jewels of Tools

Woodworking techniques haven't changed much over the years, and tools are basically the same as they always were. However, technology has made tools stronger, faster, and in many cases more precise.

Tools are acquired gradually. Some are bought, some given or inherited, some made. A first principle of craft workers throughout the generations has always been: Use the best tools you can acquire – they will save you money and time in the long run. When buying tools seek the advice of professionals or experienced friends, and if possible try out the tool before you buy.

The second principle of good workmanship is to look after your tools. That way they will last your lifetime, and probably longer. Use the right tools for the job: there is no quicker way to ruin a screwdriver than to use it to open a tin of paint. Store tools correctly and they will stay in top condition.

HAMMERING IT HOME

Although nails have been around for 4000 years, it wasn't until 1833 that they were used to build houses. Critics predicted that the houses would blow down in the first good storm, but were quickly proved quite wrong.

SCREWING IT DOWN

Standard sizes for screws were not finally agreed upon until well into the 20th century. In World War II, American bomber planes could not be repaired with British screws, and American manufacturers had to retool.

SHARP AS A CHISEL

Some new chisels are already sharpened when you buy them. Others, just as in the past, must be honed on the back edge before use. Rehone chisels from time to time to keep the blade sharp. Better quality chisels stay sharper longer. When not in use keep chisels wrapped to prevent damage.

DON'T PLAY WITH PLIERS

If the jaws of pliers are likely to damage a delicate surface, place a piece of cloth between the pliers and the work. Don't use pliers as a spanner, as the pliers' serrated edge will slowly cut a nut into a rounded shape.

SAW SENSE

After using a saw, wipe the blade clean and coat it lightly with oil to prevent rusting. Remember to wipe the blade clean before use, as the oil may stain the wood. To prevent damage to the teeth, always hang up hand saws when not in use. To clean a rusty blade, rub with steel wool dipped in mineral turpentine. If a blade sticks as you saw, lubricate it by rubbing the blade with a candle.

DRILLS THROUGH TIME

The first drills were prehistoric bow drills. In about 1400 the brace and bit drill was invented. The first electric hand drill was developed in 1895 by Wilhelm Fein in Stuttgart, Germany. Electric drills were first mass-produced in 1905.

PLANE BUSINESS

One of the Romans' most important inventions was the plane. A fine example of a plane with an iron blade was found in the ruins of Pompeii, destroyed by a volcano in AD 79.

POWERING ALONG

By the 1950s most of the power tools we take for granted in the home workshops of today had already been developed. Modern technology has made these tools more powerful, easier to handle and more accurate, but they are basically the same tools and are used for the same purposes.

SHARPENING A CHISEL

Keep the blades of chisels and planes razor-sharp by rubbing them along an oilstone.

First oil the stone, then rub the honed angle to and fro along the stone, holding the blade at an angle of about 30°.

When the tip of the blade has worn into a thin burr, hold the flat edge of the blade across the stone and, keeping the blade flat, rub it from side to side. Repeat until the blade is sharp.

To help those without the manual dexterity and experience to keep the blade at a perfect 30°, a wooden guide was devised that sat on top of the stone and slid back and forth.

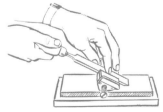

Today the Stanley honing guide, built following the same principles as the older wooden device, keeps angles uniform.

A place for everything

IT PAYS TO KEEP YOUR TOOLS AND MATERIALS
IN GOOD CONDITION, AND THE BEST WAY TO
ACHIEVE THIS IS TO STORE THEM WISELY.

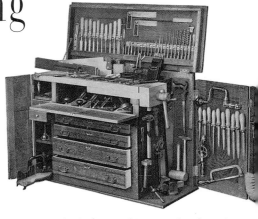

Whether you are lucky enough to have a workshop dedicated
to home handywork or must work wherever you can find space
and clear eveything away after you have finished the job, it is
important not to keep your tools jumbled together any old how
in a drawer or a toolbox – they will spoil each other's edges, and
finding the right implement for the job will try your temper.

WORKSHOP STORAGE In a workshop, hang tools on their own hooks
on a wall-mounted panel. It is sometimes better not to have drawers or
lockers in a workshop – that way, there will be nowhere to throw
something that should be put back in its proper place.

It is essential, however, to have containers for storing small items
such as screws, nails, washers, bolts and hinges. Your grandfather
probably used tobacco tins for this purpose; these days, small glass jars
or the lids of aerosol spray cans make an excellent substitute.

Save space and avoid mess by suspending coils of wire, electrical flex
and rope from large cuphooks screwed into the ceiling.

*A timber combination bench and
tool cabinet from earlier this
century would be treasured by
many a handyperson today.*

*Well made woodworking tools
are things of beauty, and the
craftsmen of old treasured them
and looked after them so that they
would last a lifetime.*

Another tried and tested storage method for tools is to tack a piece of webbing in loops of various sizes along a batten attached to the wall, or to the wall itself. Support the tools in the loops.

PORTABLE STORAGE Lidded boxes with a number of compartments that open outwards on hinges provide compact and well organised storage for tools. Old-fashioned wooden versions are durable and attractive, and provide a nostalgic link with the pre-plastic era, but the best modern versions are designed on the same principles. They are available in metal, and also in tough transparent plastic, so that you can readily see the contents.

A compact storage option for the proficient home woodworker is to make a portable rack, like a small bookcase with a handle, which you can then stand on the floor or a table. Make the shelves only a few centimetres wide, for ease of access, and perforate them with holes of different sizes to hold your various tools.

MAGNETS Use a magnet in your work area to pick up spilt nails or screws, and use magnets on a rack to hold small metal tools in place, or to hold small paintbrushes so that their bristles hang down and keep in good shape.

A canny old idea is to use a magnet attached to your wrist to carry a supply of nails, screws and nuts. Screw a large cylindrical magnet onto a wide, strong leather watchband. The magnet should be quite powerful, so that you will not dislodge the nails when you use your hammer. So that you can pick the nails off easily, wear the magnet on your left wrist if you are right-handed and on your right wrist if you are left-handed.

TIPS WITH LIGHT Make a movable light so that you can illuminate any area of your work bench easily. Simply suspend your light, with its shade and switch, from a curtain runner on a tight supporting wire strung over the bench. Suspend the flexible lead to the light from the supporting wire in a series of loops also anchored by curtain runners. You can change the height of the lamp by shortening or lengthening the lead.

When you have to use your electric drill in a dark area and need to have both your hands free to work, tape a small torch to the top of the drill with masking tape.

A FILE WALLET Store your metal files in a file wallet made from a piece of cardboard folded concertina-fashion and kept together with a pair of sturdy rubber bands, one at either end.

PAINTS Keeping paints and brushes in a paint locker will mean that you waste less paint and have fewer spoilt brushes. Hang your brushes up or place them flat so that the bristles will not be bent, and make sure that you store brushes used for paint in a separate place from those used for varnish and those for shellac.

Close paint tins firmly and turn them upside down to prevent a skin from forming on the surface of the paint.

Words of Wisdom

'According to rumor, a clever woman can fix anything with a single "tool" – a hairpin. We cannot verify this as a fact, since we have no hairpins handy. But we do have saws, hammers, screwdrivers, and so on, and they work just fine. The question of which tools we think you ought to buy is something we cannot answer without quite a few "ifs." If you plan to do such-and-such a job, then you will need such-and-such tools. About all we can do is to tell you the names of tools, what each one will do, and how you should use it.'

– *Complete Home Encyclopedia,* Dorothy Pace (1947)

Piping sweetly

THESE DAYS, WHEN THE DRAINS SMELL OR THE PIPES
ARE NOISY, WE CAN CALL THE PLUMBER, BUT IN
EARLIER TIMES PEOPLE HAD TO BE SELF-SUFFICIENT.

In many countries these days, plumbing work must be carried out
by a licensed plumber if it is to be legal, but in earlier times people
generally had to be able to carry out simple maintenance tasks and
cope with emergencies on their own. Using their know-how, there are
a number of things you can do with a few simple tools while you wait
for the plumber to come. And when the plumber arrives, it helps to
have an idea of what the problem might be.

BLOCKED DRAINS One job that has not changed much over the past
hundred years is unblocking drains. To some extent you can guard
against the problem by keeping your drains clean – in particular,
never pour hot fat or fatty water down a drain. Blockages in main
drains are best left to the professionals.

Sink drains Many blockages build up gradually, when debris collects
around hair or fragments of food. If a sink or basin is draining slowly,
pour boiling water and washing soda down it. Or put a handful of
bicarbonate of soda then half a cup of vinegar down the drain, put the
plug in right away and leave it for half an hour. After this, flush the
drain thoroughly with clean water. Turpentine is also useful for
cleaning the sink, removing grease and getting rid of smells.

To unblock a pipe, place a plunger over the drain hole and push
the plunger up and down several times. If this fails, unscrew the water
trap beneath the sink. With a bucket below to catch the waste water,
unscrew the nut at the base of the U-trap, or unscrew a more modern
P- or S-trap, and clear the trap with a bent wire coat-hanger. Then
pour boiling water followed by cold water through to clean the pipe.

REPAIRING TOILETS The flushing mechanism is straightforward, and
many problems with toilets just need a little know-how.

Cistern overflow This is usually caused by a faulty ball valve. Take
the top off the cistern. If the float or ball has deflated, replace it. If this
is not the problem, turn off the water and replace the valve washer,
which is at the end of the piston.

Reluctant flush If you need to operate the flushing mechanism
repeatedly, the valve that controls the water leaving the cistern
probably needs replacing. Turn off the tap that controls the water
supply to the toilet, tie up the ball valve to stop the cistern filling and
replace the float valve at the bottom of the cistern.

Blocked toilet The trouble is usually in the trap leading out of the
bowl; use a special large plunger. Tying a plastic bag over a mop head
makes an emergency plunger to help unblock a toilet.

EARLY SHOWERS were usually hand-
pumped, and one described in *The
Scientific American* in 1878 recycled
the water by pumping it up again.

As running hot water became
common, baths and showers became
more important. Elaborate mahogany-
encased showers towered over ornate
bathtubs in Edwardian homes, and
early baths ranged from wooden tubs
lined with sheet lead, zinc or copper,
through porcelain baths, to cast-iron
baths, either enamelled, galvanised or
painted. An ingenious folding bathtub
was featured in *The Scientific
American* in 1881.

TAPS If water leaks up past the spindle and comes out at the top when the tap is turned on, there is a simple solution.

Repacking Find the small brass tube or sleeve under the handle, surrounding the spindle. Unscrew the sleeve and pick out the old packing with a knife. Poke some soft string or torn-up rag softened with grease into the space and screw the sleeve down again. The new packing will make the spindle watertight.

PIPES Copper or brass pipes are the best, since they have very smooth interior finishes that discourage the build-up of scale.

Lagging All pipes should be insulated, or 'lagged', to prevent heat loss from the hot water system. Lagging is also necessary in cold areas to stop pipes bursting in freezing weather. Straw was a popular lagging material in the old days, and corrugated cardboard or hay can be used as temporary lagging.

If you are caught without lagged pipes in a cold snap and a portion of pipe is in danger of freezing, heat the area with warm air from a safe form of heating such as a radiator.

Frozen pipes If a tap is not working, check for cracked pipes or fittings that have moved as the ice has expanded them. Place buckets under cracks to catch any water, and turn off the main water supply.

Warm the pipes gently by wrapping rags around the pipes and then saturating them with hot water. Since water usually freezes first at the points where pipes bend, start at those points. Then apply heat at the side closest to the tap, keeping the tap turned on.

In an emergency, if a pipe has frozen and is in danger of bursting, bore a hole in it. You can plug the hole later.

Burst pipes Turn off electricity, water heaters, and the water supply. Stop the supply to the cold water tank by turning off the stopcock. Block the tank outlet pipe with a pad of cloth tied to a broom handle. Make temporary repairs by wrapping a paint-soaked rag around the split, rubbing it with soap or sealing it with sticking plaster.

Leaking joints If a leaking pipe is sending out a jet of water, tie a rag around the pipe so that the squirting stops and the water drips or runs straight down. Use putty, roofing cement or even chewing gum for temporary repairs to pipes.

Air locks If you have emptied the water system because of a burst pipe, you may end up with an air lock, indicated by a metallic tapping in the pipes. Take a short length of hose, attach one end over the hot tap and one end over the cold, then turn both taps on to force the air out of the pipes.

Noisy pipes Noise in water pipes usually results from too much pressure. Have the pressure checked and, if necessary, put in a pressure regulator.

If pipes are too small, the strain on the system may cause thumping. If pipes have been installed without fittings to prevent them from contacting other metal, they will also be noisy. Valves, taps and fittings must have rounded edges and washers must be tight.

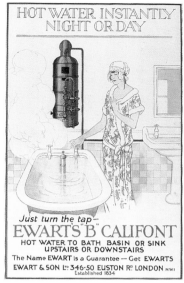

Instant hot water … we take it for granted now, but back in 1925 it was both a luxury and a novelty.

Frozen pipes often called for desperate measures, as this 1955 magazine cover clearly illustrates. In frost-prone areas, lagging pipes will ensure that you are not caught out in a cold snap.

Let there be light

ONE OF THE GREATEST TECHNOLOGICAL ADVANCES
OF THE PAST HUNDRED YEARS HAS BEEN THE
DISCOVERY AND APPLICATION OF ELECTRICITY.

Electricity is useful and powerful, but household current can kill. While our grandparents may have fixed the wiring themselves, today most electrical work must be done by a qualified electrician. Even so, there are some simple electrical problems that we should be able to fix.

FUSES Most new fuses are of the circuit breaker kind, which simply need to be reset. However, if you have old-fashioned wire fuses, you will need a supply of fuse wire of different gauges. Fuse wire is thinner and softer than the main circuit wires, so that if a circuit is overloaded or shorts, the fuse wire heats and melts, cutting off the power to that circuit. In the fuse box, keep fuse wire of the correct gauges, a small insulated screwdriver and a torch.

A damaged fuse can usually be identified by a sooty smudge on the white porcelain holder. Turn off the current at the main switch, remove the old wire, wipe off the soot and fit another length of wire of the same gauge. Make the replacement wire slightly slack or it may snap. If the new fuse blows right away, find out why: you may be running too many appliances, or the insulation on the wires may be damaged. If you cannot find the trouble, call an electrician.
Caution: Never replace fuse wire with thicker wire.

LIGHT FITTINGS If you need to change a light bulb, first make sure the switch is off. If you cannot remember whether the switch is on or off or if you have a two-way switch, turn the electricity off at the mains.

Let a blown incandescent light bulb cool before removing it, protecting your hand with a cloth. Never use a damp cloth to hold a hot bulb – the moisture may cause the bulb to explode.

If you turn on a fluorescent light fitting and the glow at each end is redder than usual, with the lamp flashing to begin with and then shimmering, change the tube or the starter mechanism will be ruined. If a fluorescent light fitting is flickering, replace the starter.

ELECTRICAL LEADS Replace damaged electrical leads immediately. Wrapping electrician's tape round them should never be more than a temporary measure.

POWER FAILURES Power failures are less common than they once were, but they do still happen. If the power fails at night, bring out the candles and have an old-fashioned evening of charades or cards and toast marshmallows on sticks over the candles!

MICHAEL FARADAY discovered how to generate electricity in 1831, but it was a long time before electricity was used around the home. After 1878, the production of incandescent light bulbs – a light source that was clean, steady and efficient – prompted the widespread connection of electricity to homes. Even so, in the early twentieth century many poorer people preferred gas lighting to electricity because of the free heat generated.

Electric labour-saving devices became more popular as domestic servants declined in numbers and electricity plants were built in cities. By about 1920, electric motors were driving food mixers and hair driers, and electricity was being used to power heaters, stoves and kettles.

Open, sesame!

STAINED GLASS PANELS, SHINY BRASS KNOBS AND
INTRICATE MOULDINGS OFTEN CHARACTERISED OUR
GRANDPARENTS' FRONT DOORS.

Modern doors are more likely to have deadlocks and peepholes, but
we still have doors that stick and hinges that squeak, and the solutions
to these problems are the same as they always have been.

STICKING DOORS Doors may stick because the hinges are loose;
because the wood of the door or the frame has swollen; or because the
building has settled and the alignment has shifted.

*Cylinder locks of the Yale type
have been around since 1865, but
most dwellings in the 19th and
early 20th centuries would have
been secured with simple spring
locks operated with keys like those
illustrated above.*

   If the door sags, open it and pull it away from the hinges. If there is
movement, the hinges need adjusting. If the wood around the screws
is chipped or the screw holes are enlarged, remove the hinges, put
hardwood plugs in the screw holes and screw the hinges in place again.

   If the door is latch is not catching in the jamb, the door may have
shrunk. Try inserting thin cardboard or wooden shims (wedges) under
the hinges. Take off the hinge leaf, insert the shim and screw the hinge
leaf back with longer screws.

   For minor sticking, rub chalk on the outer edge of the door. Close
the door and the chalk will mark the frame where the door is sticking.
Sandpaper or lightly plane the edge of the door opposite the mark.

BADLY SHRUNKEN DOORS Remove the door and the hinges and screw
a strip of wood to the frame on the hinge side or to the door itself.

REPAIRING DOORS If the wood is broken around the hinge on a door,
you can insert a new piece of wood. Make the new piece in a dovetail
shape, then cut away the damaged part. Drive the new piece in from
the side and glue and screw it into place. Make new hinge sinkings by
chiselling out the new piece to the required depth, then rehang the
door. Follow a similar procedure to replace wood on the door jamb.

Door knob

Door knocker

Door chains

SQUEAKING DOORS Prise the hinge pin up with a screwdriver and
hammer until it is almost out, then rub it with dry soap or petroleum
jelly. Swing the door to and fro until the pin works down again.

REMOVING A DOOR When taking a door off, open it and support the
outer corner with cardboard to take the weight off the hinges. Ease the
pins from the hinges with using a screwdriver between pinhead and
hinge. Remove the bottom hinge first, and replace the top hinge first.

STIFF LOCKS Oil stiff locks by dipping a feather in oil, squeezing it out
slightly and applying it to the workings.
Caution: Never oil the cylinder section on a cylinder lock – use
powdered graphite, available these days in a graphite puffer.

*Ornamental brass door fittings,
sometimes bronzed or coppered,
were popular in the early 1900s,
as these 1911 examples show.*

Look out below

AFTER THE VOGUE FOR FITTED CARPETS, MANY
OF US ARE REVERTING TO RUGS SCATTERED OVER
VARNISHED BOARDS FOR A MORE RELAXED LOOK.

We no longer get down on our knees to give the floorboards a good
scrub, or face the drudgery of floor polish or carpet beaters, but our
grandparents knew some surprisingly effective and easy ways to deal
with squeaking boards and wrinkled rugs.

WOODEN FLOORS Those treasured wooden floorboards can shrink,
creak and vibrate, but it is usually quite easy to fix such problems.

Shrunken floorboards Floorboard sometimes shrink, leaving gaps
between them. These can be filled with plaster of Paris. Wet the edges
of the boards then ram the plaster in the gaps, having coloured it with
paint to match the boards. If the cracks are wide, insert nails sideways
into the boards to hold the plaster and fill the cracks in several stages.

You can also fill cracks with a mixture of sawdust and shellac; mix it
in small quantities only or it will dry out before you are able to apply
it. When you have finished, sandpaper the top of the filler smooth.

Creaking boards Creaks are usually caused by loose nails in the subfloor. If you can get at the subfloor, ask a helper to walk on the boards
while you are below until you pinpoint the squeak. Then nail a wedge
between the joist and the subfloor at that point.

If the subfloor is not accessible, find the joists under the floorboards
by tapping lightly with a hammer; there will be a hollow sound
between the joists and a solid sound above them. Nail the boards
down with small-headed nails into at least two joists at the offending
spots, ensuring that the nail heads are below the level of the top of the
board. Fill in the holes with a mixture of sawdust and shellac.

Tiny canary-like squeaks are
probably caused by the edges of
boards rubbing together. They
can be quietened by sifting a
little talcum powder between
the cracks in the floor.

A TERMITE TALE
Some primal termite knocked on wood
And tasted it, and found it good,
And that is why your Cousin May
Fell through the parlour floor today.

– OGDEN NASH (ABOUT 1930)

*Rare was the homemaker who
really enjoyed scrubbing the
floors, but the sense of
satisfaction at a job well
done was immense.*

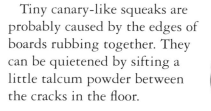

Vibrating floorboards Floors that vibrate when they are walked on point to inadequate support for the whole floor, a much more serious problem than isolated loose boards. The joists may be too light, or there may be too long a span between the bearers that support the joists. To remedy these problems, double the joists by nailing extra pieces of wood to those already in position. It is also possible to jack up the floor from underneath and instal extra bearers or piers.

Painting floorboards Before staining or painting floorboards, wash them with water in which a lump of washing soda has been dissolved, and fill any holes with wood filler. You can stain light floorboards dark with a solution of permanganate of potash, but remember that the boards will darken with each application.

SQUEAKY STAIRS These squeaks usually occur when the wedge under the stair works loose, leaving the tread free to move up and down a little. If you can reach the underside of the stair, simply drive the wedge in again. If this is not possible, drill a hole through the tread and right into the stringer, or upright. Screw the tread firmly into the stringer, and then cover the screw head with a masking plug. Both methods are illustrated in the right-hand column.

FLOOR COVERINGS Whether you have rugs or carpets, they need to be looked after. There are some easy ways to keep them looking good.

Stair carpets Always lay a stair carpet from the top to the bottom of the stairs. Buy carpet a metre or so longer than you need and fold the extra underneath at each end so that portions at the top and bottom of the stairs are of double thickness. Then you can reposition the carpet from time to time to distribute wear more evenly. Tack the carpet at the top stair, fit it tightly under the first stair rod and then work your way down to the bottom.

Curling rugs Sew or glue a small magnet or a flat curtain weight on the underside of a curling rug. If a rug develops a bubble or a fold, glue a strip of felt beneath the offending area.

Laying vinyl flooring Put a vinyl floor covering in the room where it is to be laid at least 24 hours before you intend to lay it, in order to let it become acclimatised. To lay two sheets and achieve the best possible join, overlap the edges and cut through both sheets where they overlap, using a sharp knife braced against a steel rule.

PATCHING CARPETS AND VINYL When you lay new carpet or vinyl, keep the offcuts for later use as patches, as our thrifty grandparents did. To make a patch, place an offcut over the damaged area and match any patterns. Use a Stanley knife to cut right through both the offcut and the carpet or vinyl below, cutting out an area just a little bigger than the damaged part.

To patch carpet, stick a piece of hessian in the space using double-sided carpet tape, then stick down half the patch and wait till it dries. Stick the other half down and tap the patch lightly around the edges to make a good bond. To patch vinyl, simply remove the damaged piece and stick down the patch.

REPAIRING SQUEAKY STAIRS
You can repair squeaky stairs yourself quite easily.

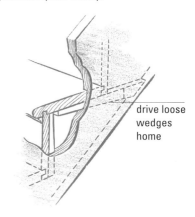

drive loose wedges home

Method 1. Working from below the stairs, drive any loose wedges firmly back into position.

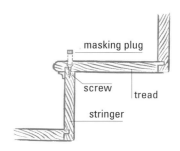

masking plug

screw | tread

stringer

Method 2. If the underside of the staircase is inaccessible, work from the outside. Drill a hole in the tread, screw the tread firmly into the upright (the 'stringer'), and mask the screw head with a plug.

Taking Care of the Pence

Stair carpets carry a lot of traffic. Put three layers of corrugated cardboard instead of expensive underfelt under the carpet on the stairs – it is easily replaced when it has flattened out. Another thrifty tip with carpets is to lay newspaper beneath the underfelt to keep out dust and deter moths.

Around and above us

MAINTAIN THE PLASTERWORK AND THE WALLPAPER IN AN OLDER HOME AND THE ROOMS WILL LOOK AS CHERISHED AS THEY DID IN EARLIER TIMES.

There are two great advantages of plasterwork: it takes paint and wallpaper readily, and it is easy to maintain, as long as the underlying structure is sound. There are time-honoured ways of mending and patching plastered surfaces, and with sufficient patience and care you can even repair a damaged moulded ceiling.

WALLS Do not fill cracks in a plaster wall until you are sure that your house has stopped settling and the framework is no longer moving – otherwise you will need to do the job over and over again. Mark the ends of cracks with a pencil and check them periodically to see if they are still growing, allowing a few extra weeks to make sure.

Fine cracks Fill very fine cracks in plaster walls with a mixture of patching plaster, three parts of boiled linseed oil and one part of turpentine, or with a putty made of oil and whiting putty. Sandpaper the filler afterwards for a smooth finish.

Large cracks To fill larger cracks, use an undercutting tool to cut the plaster round the cracks so that the sides of the cracks taper and are wider at the bottom, providing a dovetail joint for the new plaster. If you do not use an undercutting tool, the job will not last as well.

When you have cut the walls along the cracks, insert patching plaster or plaster of Paris with a little glue mixed with the water to keep it from drying too quickly. Match the texture of the patch to the original surface. Make sure the new plaster has dried thoroughly before priming it.

If the plaster is bulging, the bond between plaster and lath has broken and the plaster could fall. Remove all loose plaster before attempting repairs.

Holes in plaster If a hook has made a hole in a plaster wall, remove the hook. Shred some rag, pour liquid glue over a few pieces and force them into the hole, then finish the hole with plaster of Paris. Before the glue hardens, replace the hook. Leave repair for a day or two before putting any strain on the hook.

REPAIRING WALLPAPER If wallpaper is loose at the edges, stick it down with paper paste, pressing firmly with a clean, soft cloth. If a bulge forms, slit it with a

A MOUSE CAUGHT IN A CAGE
I'm only a poor little mouse, ma'am!
I live in the wall of your house, ma'am!
With a fragment of cheese, and a very
  few peas,
I was having a little carouse, ma'am!
– *COLES CHILDLAND* (1902)

A decorative moulded cornice gives the finishing touch to a period drawing room.

Plaster mouldings were widely used in elegant homes in the 19th century.

razor blade. Use a knife to force paste through the slit then press paper down with a soft cloth.

If wallpaper is badly torn or spoiled, it will need patching. There is no need to take off the old paper. First tear a patch of extra wallpaper large enough to cover the damaged area, matching the pattern or design as closely as possible, then glue the patch into place. Do not cut a patch – sharp edges are hard to conceal. For a really good job, sandpaper the back of the paper at the edges to tissue-paper thinness before gluing. Press the patch down firmly with a clean soft cloth.

Before you hammer a nail into a papered wall, cover the spot with sticky tape. Remove the tape by pressing with a warm iron.

CEILINGS If a plaster ceiling is cracked, mount a stepladder, put your hand flat on the ceiling and press slightly upwards. If there is any movement, the plaster may fall and must be replaced, but if the ceiling is still firmly keyed into the lath you need only fill the cracks.

Replastering a ceiling Move or cover the furniture and take up rugs or cover the carpet. Cut away loose plaster and a little beyond it using a hammer and chisel. Place a board under the working area to catch any drips of mortar. When the laths are bare, wet them well with a broad brush. Mix one part of plaster with two parts of sifted sand and enough water to make a wettish dough. Wet the laths again and apply the plaster with a trowel.

Apply only about a third of the total amount needed, or it may all fall out. Roughen the surface by criss-crossing it with lines using the edge of your trowel to help the next batch of mortar adhere.

Apply this the next day if the first is holding up well, again scoring the surface. For the third application use plaster of Paris, smoothing the surface with the back of the trowel. Mixing a handful of hair (ask your local hairdresser) with the first two applications of mortar will help the mortar to hold.

Filling cracks Remove any loose plaster, scraping at the crack edges, and brush away any dust. Wet cracks well, working the water into them with a fine brush, then fill the cracks with plaster of Paris mixed to a thick cream with water. Force the plaster right into the cracks.

Drilling a ceiling When drilling a ceiling, fragments tend to fall into your eyes. Prevent this by putting a piece of compressible hose (like those used in car heating systems) over the front bearing of the drill. Pull the hose back at first, so you can see what you are doing, then as you start drilling, release the hose and let it spring up to contact the work surface. The hose will surround the bit and catch the chips.

The Way We Were

'The ceiling, of gloomy-looking oak, was excessively lofty, vaulted, and elaborately fretted with the wildest and most grotesque specimens of a semi-Gothic, semi-Druidical device. From out the most central recess of this melancholy vaulting, depended, by a single chain of gold with long links, a huge censer of the same metal, Saracenic in pattern, and with many perforations so contrived that there writhed in and out of them, as if endued with a serpent vitality, a continual succession of parti-coloured fires.'

– 'LIGEIA', EDGAR ALLAN POE (1809–1849)

Clues with glue

IN THE OLD DAYS, BREAKING SOMETHING WAS NO REASON TO THROW IT AWAY — INDEED, THERE WERE WHOLE TRADE ASSOCIATIONS DEVOTED TO GLUES.

If you break something precious, don't despair; simply do what your grandparents would have done: call on your patience and the right glue. Your precious possession may never be quite as good as new, but it will be intact once more. With sufficient determination, you can glue a remarkable number of fragments back together again.

THE ART OF GLUING The secret is to use exactly the right amount of glue. More is not better — in fact, if you use more glue than necessary, its sticking power is lessened. So use as little glue as possible and make sure the edges to be bonded are pressed tightly together.

Technique Ensure the surfaces to be joined are free from dirt, grease and old glue. Apply the glue to both surfaces to be joined. After gluing, hold the pieces together using string or cloth strips tightened by looping them around a stick and twisting it, or with wire bound over padding to protect the object being repaired. String and cloth tend to stretch, so use wire if you need a stronger bond. Simpler mends may just need pressure from a heavy object.
Note: If you break a joint once the glue begins to set, no amount of clamping will rescue it; clean the glue off and start again.

Wood The aim is to knit together the wood fibres, so the parts to be glued must fit together closely and there should be the least possible glue in the joint. If the wood you wish to glue is very porous, such as the end-grain of timber, it is best first to seal it with a thin layer of the glue you are going to use. Some woods, such as teak, are greasy, and must be thoroughly dry or glue will simply peel off rather than set. You may need to screw or nail these woods as well as gluing them.

Veneer Slightly roughen the base to which the wood veneer is to be attached so that the glue will hold.

GOOD OLD GLUES Nowadays there are specialist glues for everything; we do not have to melt cakes of glue into syrup that smells like beef extract, nor do we have to endure the stink of fish glue. But some of the simple glues used by our grandparents will do well if you do not have the right commercial glue to hand.

Glue for glass Mend glass using gelatine and acetic acid. Soak 150 grams of white gelatine in 180 ml of water for 12 hours or so. Then heat the softened gelatine and water until the gelatine has dissolved, add 150 ml of acetic acid and then water until you have made 600 ml of glue. Use this to cement glass sheets together, to glue photographs to glass, and whenever you need a transparent glue.

The Way We Were

As recently as 1936 this was a popular recipe for preparing glue:

'Scotch glue is prepared as follows: Take a cake, wrap it in paper and strike it with a hammer to break it into small pieces. Then put the pieces in the inner chamber of a glue pot and cover with cold water. Leave for a day and then the glue will resemble pieces of jelly. Pour off the water and cover with hot water. Fill the outer chamber of the pot with warm water and boil slowly for about half an hour. Recharge the outer chamber if the water boils dry and stir the glue constantly with a stick until it has become a liquid. Test the liquid by dipping in the stick and noticing how it runs off the end. If it runs off like water it is too thin; it ought to fall much as golden syrup does. When too thin, continue to boil; when too thick add more boiling water.'

– *THE HOUSEHOLDER'S COMPLETE HANDBOOK*, HAWTHORNE DANIEL (1936)

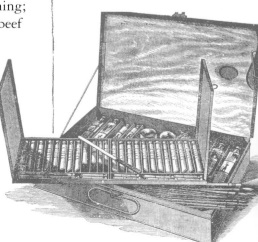

Once you have mended a treasured item, you may need to disguise the remaining cracks with a little paint.

Glues for china or glass Garlic juice will join china or glass leaving little or no mark if it is done carefully, though there is a slight smell of garlic. Another way to mend china is with artist's white oil paint. Clean the broken edges and make sure they are dry. Cover both edges with paint, press them together gently and wipe off the surplus.

Fire and waterproof cement To 300 ml of vinegar add the same quantity of milk, separate the curd and mix the whey with the whites of five eggs. Beat mixture well and sift in enough quicklime to produce a thick paste. This cement will mend broken china very satisfactorily because it resists the action of both fire and water.
Caution: Be careful not to touch the quicklime, since it can burn.

Gum arabic Dissolve gum arabic in water in the proportion of 1 kilogram of gum arabic (from art suppliers) to 1 litre of water to make a very viscous gum that will stick well to paper. Prevent the gum from going mouldy with a drop of oil of cloves.

Another recipe for gum arabic glue is to take one part of sugar, three parts of starch and four parts of gum arabic. Dissolve the gum arabic and the starch separately in a little water, mix them, add the sugar and boil it in a double boiler until it reaches the desired consistency.

An economical glue For an inexpensive glue that keeps well in warm weather and does not discolour, put a level teaspoon of powdered alum (from pharmacies) into 600 ml of water and bring to the boil.

Mix a generous cup of plain flour to a smooth paste with about a cup of cold water. Stir this into the alum water and keep stirring until the mixture is as clear as boiled starch. Stir in a few drops of oil of cloves and pour through a wire strainer. Bottle the glue in a wide-mouthed jar and line the lid with greaseproof paper.

GLUES FOR PAPER Starch was the basis for old-fashioned paper glues. Apart from the familiar flour and water paste, there were several other ways of making starch glues.

Rice starch glue Mix powdered rice with cold water and then gradually add boiling water until the mixture reaches the consistency you want, keeping it well stirred. Boil the mixture for one minute, and you will have a glue that is beautifully white and almost transparent. Use it to make objects from paper, to glue paper to trays for a decorative effect, and for anything else that requires a number of layers of paper to be glued together.

Potato starch glue A gum widely used last century was made from dextrine, a substance obtained by heating potato starch. Potato starch still makes an excellent gum. It will hold paper together, but the papers are also able to be peeled apart again. To make potato starch glue, use the starchy water left over from boiling potatoes, reduced to a thick consistency.

An advertisement from a 1930s magazine leaves the reader in no doubt as to the purported strength of this particular adhesive.

You can make your own glue brush from a piece of bamboo. Scrape off the hard skin to about 4 cm from the end of a 15 cm piece of bamboo, soak the end in boiling water for a minute or two, and then tease the fibres out with a small flat hammer.

As good as new

RESTORING FURNITURE IS ENJOYABLE AND
CONTEMPLATIVE, PUTTING YOU IN TOUCH WITH
THE PERSON WHO MADE THE PIECE AND THOSE
WHO MAY HAVE REPAIRED IT BEFORE YOU.

Nothing beats the satisfaction of restoring a battered piece of furniture
to usefulness and beauty, particularly if it has been passed down to you
or rescued from an old shed or a junk shop. Our grandparents rarely
threw furniture out, and their loving repairs add character to a piece.

REPAIRING FURNITURE A piece of furniture often just needs a little
attention to make it serviceable again, and many repairs are easy to do.
Before you start mending something, consider your approach, bearing
in mind how strong the repair needs to be.

There are two golden rules: never use nails and screws without glue;
and use as few nails and screws as possible, because too many will
weaken the mend. When you do use nails, make sure they are the
right size for the job. Choose round wire nails for strength and thin
panel pins with small heads for finer work.

If you need to dismantle a piece of furniture, mark each piece
carefully so that you know where it belongs.

Table legs and chair legs These repairs need to be strong. The
favoured methods developed by cabinetmakers over the years are
gluing, nailing and screwing; dowelling; and splicing.

Repairing loose joints Tighten loose joints on chairs and tables by
scraping all the old glue from the hole and the dowel and then
replacing the dowel, using a thin coat of wood glue. Bind the joints
with rope or string until the glue sets. Wipe up any spills quickly.

If the top rail of the back of a chair has come loose, take it out
completely by tapping it gently with a mallet. Then cut off and drill
out the dowels that hold the rail on and replace them with longer

dowels. Glue the dowels fully and
make sure the dowel extends past
the short grain of the top rail to
strengthen the join. While the
glue is setting, clamp the join with
wire pulled tight by twisting a
stick through the middle (see page
130 for glueing technique).

Joints between the seat rails and
the legs of a chair also often work
loose. If a corner block or brace has
worked loose, mark it before
removing so that you can put it
back in exactly the right place.

Knock the joints carefully apart using a mallet, and scrape off all the old glue. If the tenons are too loose, they will need to be made larger or 'blind wedged' by using two small wedges. Then reglue the chair in the following order: first the front rail and the front legs; then the two wide rails to the front legs and afterwards to the back; lastly, making sure the frame is square, glue the braces back into position.

Straightening boards Try straightening warped boards by removing them from the furniture and holding the rounded side in front of a heat source to shrink them. If this fails, wet a piece of flannel with hot water, place it between two warped boards and clamp them together. When dry they will almost certainly have straightened up.

FITTINGS Fittings often give furniture its character: do not discard them just because they are stained or broken. They can always be cleaned and they can often be mended.

Brass fittings Remove stains on brass fittings with steel wool dipped in salt and lemon juice or vinegar. Then polish them.

Stubborn fastenings Smear a small amount of petroleum jelly on nuts and bolts that will not move easily.

To remove stubborn screws, scrape away any rust or paint that has accumulated around the head, then insert the screwdriver blade in the slot, and rap the handle of the screwdriver with a light hammer. First turn the screwdriver clockwise to loosen any paint or rust, then anticlockwise to remove the screw.

Nothing can beat beeswax and a healthy dose of old-fashioned elbow grease for imparting a rich, deep lustre to a polished table.

Buy broken old furniture very cheaply at garage sales or opportunity shops to give yourself a supply of old wood for making repairs.

133

If the screw still will not budge, paint the head of the screw with a little thin oil and leave it for 24 hours or so. Then press a red-hot poker on the screw head before trying to turn it again.

DRAWERS Elderly chests of drawers often have damaged drawers or ones that tend to stick. Repairing them is quite simple, once you have identified the cause of the problem.

Damaged drawers If the dovetails that hold the sides of a drawer to the front have been badly damaged, you can strengthen the drawer by gluing corner blocks inside the drawer, using light ones at the front and heavier ones at the back (see right-hand column).

Loose drawers If the rails on which the drawers run are very badly worn, replace them by gluing in a slightly tapered strip of wood at the bottom of the sides of the drawers. Alternatively, fit a false bottom (see right-hand column).

Sticking drawers Drawers sometimes stick because the chest of drawers is balanced unevenly on the floor. If one or two of its legs are on the edges of carpets or rugs, pack thin pieces of cardboard under the other legs to even them up.

If this isn't the cause, try rubbing a little floor polish on the sides of the drawers and polishing them well, or smooth the runners with fine sandpaper and then rub both the runners and bearers with petroleum jelly, beeswax or candle wax. Do not use soap on drawers that are sticking: it will harden and cut into the wood.

RESTORING FINISHES Small blemishes on furniture can often be made less obvious, even if they cannot be eliminated.

Dents To remove shallow dents, scrape varnish from the area, then fold a damp cotton cloth to form a thin pad over it. Press the cloth with a hot iron – it will force steam into the dent and make the wood swell. Repeat until the dent disappears. Sand the surface smooth and refinish it with matching varnish.

Scratches on waxed wood You can treat scratches on waxed surfaces by rubbing them thoroughly either with wax or with half a shelled walnut or Brazil nut.

Scratches on polished wood Treat surface scratches on polished wood by rubbing them lightly with a cork dipped in camphorated oil and then polishing.

Treat scratches on dark furniture by rubbing on either iodine or a mixture of two parts of olive oil and one part of vinegar, and then polishing it.

Heat marks Treat a heat mark on furniture by rubbing in a few drops of raw linseed oil and turpentine, working in a mixture of cigarette ash and olive oil, or rubbing it with a damp bluebag until the mark is dark blue, then drying it well and polishing.

REPAIRING DRAWERS
Drawers that are falling apart are easy to repair and strengthen.

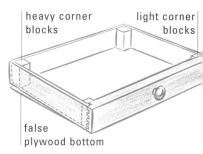

heavy corner blocks

light corner blocks

false plywood bottom

Glue hardwood blocks into each corner of the drawer to add strength. If the runners are worn down so that the drawer is loose, glue a false bottom cut from thin plywood over the old bottom and secure it with brads or panel pins.

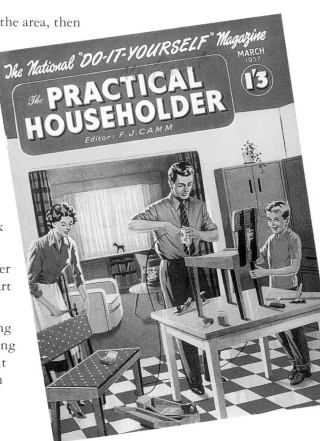

The National "DO-IT-YOURSELF" Magazine MARCH 1957

The PRACTICAL HOUSEHOLDER 1'3

Editor: F. J. CAMM

Water marks White water marks on timber surfaces can be made less noticeable by rubbing on a mixture of salt and olive oil and leaving it for a while before polishing.

Unwelcome patinas Remove the grey or blue bloom that sometimes develops on finely finished wood by wiping it off with a cloth dampened in a mixture of a tablespoon of vinegar to a litre of water. Mildew can be removed with a slightly stronger solution. Wipe it off, dry well and polish as normal.

Stains Many stains can be removed by a little gentle sandpapering. Remember to sandpaper with the grain.

Ink Remove ink spots if they are fresh by blotting up the surplus, and then pressing a damp cloth firmly on the spot until it disappears.

Paint Remove paint spots immediately with warm soapy water and then polish. Cover old spots of oil-based paint with linseed oil and leave it until the paint has softened. Remove remaining paint by rubbing with rottenstone (powdered limestone) and linseed oil, mixed to the consistency of thin cream.

Perfume marks Rub a thin paste of powdered pumice and raw or boiled linseed oil lightly along the grain of the wood and then wipe with a cloth dampened with plain linseed oil.

Another method is to sand off the stain with fine steel wool or sandpaper, and then apply a very sparing coat of equal proportions of oil and vinegar, or oil, vinegar and turpentine, using a dark vinegar for dark furniture, a white vinegar for light furniture. Repeat, if necessary, after it dries.

Candle grease Chill any spots of spilled grease with an ice cube and then prise them off with a spatula or a blunt knife.

Burns Rub a paste of powdered pumice and linseed oil in the direction of the grain and remove it with a cloth dipped in plain linseed oil. Then repolish the furniture.

Repairing veneer Lance blistered veneer with a sharp knife, using an x-cut. Scrape out the old glue with a nail, one end of which has been flattened and sharpened, and roughen the base surface to give the glue the best possible grip. Do not bend the flaps of veneer too much or they may break off. Spread glue under the veneer flaps, then cover the repair with a sheet of greaseproof paper and a flat block of hardwood and clamp it until the glue is thoroughly dry.

Ornamental carving Carved surfaces can become dusty, making furniture look shabby. Dip a 2.5 cm brush into paraffin and hang it up to dry, then work the bristles vigorously into the recesses of the carving. This will remove accumulated dust and give a pleasant shine.

REFINISHING FURNITURE Before you embark on refinishing, check the condition of the piece of furniture – you may find that a complete refinish is unnecessary. Wash the piece thoroughly with warm water and soap, using a soft clean rag, adding three tablespoons of boiled linseed oil and a tablespoon of turpentine to each litre of warm water. After this, apply a good furniture wax, and possibly rub down the

The Way We Were

'One does not brush lacquer out sparingly or with leisure. Lacquer awaits no miser or fussy worker. The brush is dipped deep, the immediate surface is flooded with the lacquer and the workman brushes furiously fast to achieve an even distribution before the escape of the solvents which are powerfully volatile. If the lacquer has been thinned sufficiently before the application, the procedure is not nearly so difficult as it sounds. In fact a certain state of mind might help. Let the worker not become panic-stricken before the application.'

– *How to Repair Furniture*, Frank Yates (1950)

As a temporary measure, mend small tears in upholstery by inserting a wide piece of sticky tape under the tear, sticky side up, to hold it together.

surface using a mixture of oil and pumice with a piece of old felt. Be careful not to cut through the varnish on the edges of the furniture. It may be worth testing a small area to begin with.

If the furniture is affected by tiny cracks, it may still be possible to avoid total refinishing if you remove the top flaky layer with fine steel wool and then treat the surface with a warmed mixture of two tablespoons of boiled linseed oil, one tablespoon of turpentine and one and a half tablespoons of clear varnish.

Do not use solvents and paint strippers in full sunlight, since the strippers will evaporate before they can do their job properly. Apply solvent to horizontal surfaces only, if possible.

Oil finish Linseed oil diluted with turpentine in the proportions of two parts of oil to one part of turpentine will give a good oiled finish but will considerably darken the wood. The simple secret of a good oiled finish is plenty of rubbing to generate friction and heat.

Lacquer When refinishing lacquered surfaces, make sure the surfaces are clean and as free of stains as possible, and that all dust has been removed from the pores of the wood. Work in a dust-free space and in warm, dry conditions, so that the finish sets quickly.

Apply a number of coats of thinned lacquer rather than one or two thicker coats. The waiting period between coats is not long and the finish will be much better. Use a good quality brush that is used only for lacquering. Work fast, as lacquer dries swiftly, and keep the surfaces as horizontal as possible to avoid runs.

CANE FURNITURE Use a spray gun when repainting wicker and rattan – it will give a much better result than a brush.

PIANO KEYS Whiten piano keys with a cloth dipped in lemon juice, vinegar and alcohol. Or spread a lemon juice and French chalk paste on the keys and then wipe it off with a cloth soaked in hot water and wrung out tightly.

UPHOLSTERY Nothing gives an armchair or sofa a more effective facelift than fresh-looking upholstery.

Renewing upholstery Covering old fabric with new rarely works. Strip off old cloth to see whether the canvas covering the springs and the edges and webbed bottoms of seats also need replacing. To strip a piece of furniture, first turn it upside down, rest its top edge on a pad on the floor to protect it, and support the arms of a chair on a stool. Strip off the bottom cover, and it will then be easy to see how to untack the back and side covers. Use old covers as a template to cut new ones, allowing 2–3 cm all round for trimming. When re-covering an easy chair or a sofa, put the back cover on first, followed by the arms and then the seat and outside covers.

Drive tacks in only part way until you are sure they are in the right positions. For a good finish, make sure that the material is as taut as possible.

Words of Wisdom

Our grandparents knew the value of buying secondhand, and of changing the function of outmoded furniture or objects:

'In browsing not only secondhand stores but rummage sales as well, let us also keep our eyes peeled for such welcome things as old wooden chopping bowls (choice!), scoops, wooden spoons and forks, rolling pins (how about a gay towel rack for the bathroom where this forms the roller?), old ladles, clocks, bookends, and what have you.'

– *New Furniture From Old*, Raymond F. Yates (1951)

Seagrass and cane furniture was very much the vogue in the 1920s, and an effective way to have an item match your decor was to spray it with lacquer or paint.

Reflections

HERE ARE SOME TRIED AND TRUE WAYS TO KEEP YOUR MIRRORS UNFLAWED AND RESTORE THE SHINE TO RUSTY METAL.

Our grandparents set great store on keeping their belongings shining and in good working order. Whether you are caring for new additions to your home or cherishing family heirlooms, try using some of the techniques handed down through the generations.

MIRRORS To keep mirrors in good condition, protect them from damp. Make sure air circulates behind them by sticking a slice of cork about half a centimetre thick, one at each corner, on the back of the frame.

GLASS Polish glass in furniture with a piece of old silk. Eliminate shallow scratches on glass and mirrors by applying a water, glycerine and iron oxide paste. With a felt pad dipped in the paste, rub the area until the marks disappear, then rinse with water. Use the same method with an emery powder and glycerine paste to remove deep scratches.

Frosting glass Fill a muslin or fine cloth bag with a thick paste of emery powder and water. Spread fine sand over the glass and rub it in with the muslin bag, a small area at a time.

Removing broken stoppers Pour a little glycerine round the stopper, stand the decanter in warm water and wrap a cold cloth around the top. Repeat if necessary.

CLOCKS Wind clocks at the same time each day; irregular winding eventually makes them gain or lose. Move standing clocks as little as possible.

Dust is the worst enemy of clocks; cover them with a sheet to protect them when you are dusting.

METAL You can clean rusty iron and steel by soaking them in paraffin or turpentine and then rubbing them with emery paper.

Beware of cleaning brass, copper and other metal ornaments too vigorously if they have been lacquered. If lacquer has become damaged, clean the metal in washing soda and hot water, rinse it with water and dry it thoroughly. Then buff the metal with an emery cloth or very fine glass or sandpaper and relacquer it with a soft fine brush.

Metals can be polished with toothpaste – soldiers did this in the long boring intervals between fighting during World War II when making jewellery out of the metal from fighter planes.

WHAT AM I?
Two hands without fingers,
Two feet without toes,
A round white face,
But never a nose.
It always stands still,
But it always goes.
[*Answer: a clock*]

Before the days of chrome finishes, people would spend hours rubbing and polishing to keep metals glossy and gleaming.

137

DON'T LET THE BUGS BITE

Remedies available in the good old days helped people to keep pests under control but did not entirely eradicate them. Today we have harsher products that can stop many common household pests in their tracks, but as people become more environmentally aware they are returning to the milder remedies of earlier generations. Taking precautions to keep pests away from the house and reducing their numbers if they do enter is less harmful to our fragile environment than strong chemicals.

A little knowledge of the pests we loathe will help us beat them at their own game. If we know what pests eat, for example, we can remove or lock away their favourite food. And if we know how and when they breed, we can take measures to prevent them doing so.

AN END TO FLIES

Make sure flies don't find ideal breeding spots near the home by covering rubbish and picking up animal droppings. To keep flies out of the house rub kerosene or lavender oil over door and window frames. Plant horehound, basil or peppermint around outside eating areas.

A HOME MADE INSECT SPRAY

The flowers of the pyrethrum, a small species of chrysanthemum, contain a natural insecticide that is nontoxic to mammals. A pyrethrum spray will kill many insect pests and can also be used to kill pests on the skin.

3. Strain the liquid and add six parts of water to one part of the pyrethrum liquid. Pour the mixture into a spray gun.

1. Pick the pyrethrum flowers early in the morning, when they have just opened.

2. Place the flowers in a dark, well ventilated place until they are dry, then cover them with enough kerosene, mineral oil or alcohol (brandy works well) to saturate them. Leave overnight.

4. Use the spray immediately, because it begins to deteriorate on exposure to light.

BAN BEDBUGS

If you think you have bedbugs, don't panic! First, be sure you have identified them correctly; they are wingless and have eight legs, all well forward on the body. They are about 50 mm long and smell nasty when squashed. Destroy them by superheating the house in summer, by using pyrethrum powder, or by painting turpentine or kerosene into the cracks in the bed frame. Wash bed clothes in very hot water.

RID YOURSELF OF RODENTS

Unless you know how to contact the Pied Piper of Hamelin, the best way to rid your house of mice and rats is to block up or screen all points of entry. Digging a trench around the house and filling it with concrete will prevent rats burrowing through the soil. Use steel wool to plug up mouse holes because mice can't chew through it.

Both rats and mice hate certain strong smells. Keep rats at a distance with creosote, kerosene, oil of peppermint, wintergreen or strong cayenne pepper. To keep mice at bay, try oil of peppermint, oil of cloves or naphthalene flakes in front of mouse holes and at the back of cupboards, or leave sprigs of mint in the cupboard and behind the refrigerator.

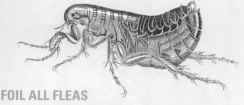

FOIL ALL FLEAS

First, get rid of the source of fleas by making sure the cats and dogs, and their bedding and kennels, are clean. Then spray with pennyroyal. To keep rooms free of fleas, swap carpet or matting with rugs and sweep the floor frequently. Eucalyptus oil on your clothing will act as a flea deterrent. Late last century in parts of China, flea traps made of small pieces of cardboard smeared with scented birdlime were hung under people's clothing.

IDEAL BAITS

Good baits for rat traps include cheese, bread, fat and oatmeal. Mice will risk death for toasted cheese, bacon rind, herring or pastry.

Cosy and warm

T OASTING YOUR TOES IN FRONT OF A
CHEERY OPEN FIRE IS ONE OF THE GREAT
JOYS OF WINTER NIGHTS.

But fireplaces and chimneys need constant cleaning
and upkeep, and the risk of fire must not be
overlooked. Luckily, we have access to the practical
wisdom of the days when open fires were the main
method of domestic heating.

Our grandparents, too, knew the value of keeping
draughts out. Most heat is lost through gaps around
doors and windows and through glass, but you can also
lose heat through the roof. It makes economic sense to
reduce all forms of heat loss from your home.

FIREPLACES Because of the intense heat from an open fire,
fireplace surrounds often need attention. Soot stains,
discoloured metal and cracked tiles can all be fixed.

Cleaning a fireplace front A mixture of 750 grams of caustic soda
and 4 litres of hot water cleans soot stains from a brick fireplace front.
Caution: Caustic solution burns skin and corrodes painted surfaces;
wear thick rubber gloves and avoid splashing the solution around.

Restoring fireplace metal Repaint a metal fireplace surround with
fireproof enamel paint. Rub the surface with wire wool and wipe it
over with methylated spirits, then apply the enamel with a soft brush.

Repairing fireplace tiles Fix cracks and dents in tiles surrounding a
fireplace with a cloth dipped in a thinly mixed filler.

You may be able to replace badly damaged tiles, but if not you can
disguise the gaps with commercial filler. Wet the gap well and fill it
with thickly mixed filler, smoothing it level with other tiles. Leave
overnight to harden, then lightly scour the entire surface with fine wire
wool and wipe it over with a soft cloth impregnated with methylated
spirits. Paint the filler with several coats of fireproof enamel.

FIRE PRECAUTIONS An open fire must be screened by a
fireguard, and the area in front of the fire should be paved
with fireproof bricks or tiles to prevent sparks igniting rugs
or floorboards.

CHIMNEYS The heat above the flames of an open fire creates
a vacuum that draws air through the room and into the
chimney. If the chimney is faulty or blocked the fire will
refuse to burn well.

A chimney that won't draw Poor draught can be caused
by an obstruction in the flue, brickwork leaks, a poorly

*A brass fireside companion to
hold poker, tongs, hearth brush
and shovel is perfect for tending
an open fire.*

*In a well kept home in the 1920s
special cleaning creams were used
to remove sooty marks from
around an open fireplace.*

designed chimney stack, or a build-up of soot. Obstructions, leaks and design problems need the attention of an experienced builder. Accumulated soot is a fire hazard; call in the chimney sweep.

Creosote This corrosive, tarry substance forms when acids from burning wood combine with water. When a fire is burning well the creosote is carried away, but if it is burning poorly and the chimney stack is cool because it is cold outside, the creosote condenses inside the chimney. If creosote catches fire, it may crack a brick chimney.

Chimney fires CALL THE FIRE BRIGADE! In the meantime, as an emergency measure, throw lots of salt into the fireplace and hold a wet blanket over the opening to block the inflow of air.

INSULATING TIPS Don't forget to insulate dormer windows and attic flooring. Choose insulation that is fireproof, safe for your health and does not attract birds or pests.

Attics and roof spaces When fitting insulation in areas under the roof, leave some ventilation or condensation will form. Work on a piece of floor-weight board; falling through a ceiling is dangerous and expensive. Check the wiring and if there appear to be problems call an electrician. When you leave the roof space, fit the trap door closely to stop warm air escaping.

DRAUGHT-PROOFING Seal gaps around doors and windows with weatherstripping – strips of foam rubber or plastic, available in rolls.

Doors You can make an effective draught excluder from a tube made of close-weave fabric; fill it with sand and push it snugly against the bottom of a door. Our grandparents sometimes ornamented these draught excluders with embroidered snake eyes and tongues.

'A gas heater brings the sun into your home,' claims this French advertisement from the mid 20th century. Fifty years ago, if an open fire was not an option, the last word in keeping warm was a gas heater.

Windows To weatherstrip a double-hung window, fit the weatherstripping for the upper part of the window outside, on the frame adjoining the sash, and that for the bottom window on the inside, applying it to the beading at the sides of the window and to the top and bottom of the sash so that the sashes press firmly against the inside sill and the other window. Metal-framed windows often have gaps between the sash and the frame. Scrape the metal clean before gluing on the weatherstripping.

This hot-air fan may not have been very safe.

You may decide to seal a window that is never opened with caulking compound. Clean away any dirt and grit first.

Skirting boards Check for gaps that let cold air in between the skirting board and the flooring and block them with wooden beading.

CONDENSATION Condensation occurs when warm air from kitchens or bathrooms comes into contact with a cold surface. The simplest remedy is better air circulation: open windows to carry the warm air away. More lasting solutions include installing insulation or fitting more windows or bigger ones.

Taking Care of the Pence

If a metal draught excluder has broken, try nailing a strip of felt to the bottom of the door as a stopgap measure.

A room with a view

WINDOWS ARE NECESSARY TO PROVIDE LIGHT
AND AIR, BUT THEY ALSO GIVE PLEASURE BY
FRAMING A VIEW OR BEING A CONSIDERED PART
OF A ROOM'S INTERIOR DESIGN.

Nowadays some new windows are made of aluminium, some of PVC
and some of timber. Many older houses still have old-fashioned
wooden sash or casement windows. These are very attractive, but they
are prone to minor ailments such as leaking, jamming and rattling.
You can save money and give yourself great satisfaction by following
time-honoured methods of correcting such problems.

LEAKING WINDOWS Many leaks originate around window frames, and
often the water runs for a good way along the timbers before the leak
becomes obvious. Fix leaks above windows by attending to the
flashing – the metal protection above the window. If it has become
rusty, or is too narrow to prevent water from entering, it will have to
be replaced. Seal leaks at the sides of windows or below them with
caulking compound, using a caulking gun or putty knife.

JAMMED SASHES Try these methods of freeing a stiff or sticking
window sash. Rub paraffin or candlewax along the channels in the
sides of the frame where the sash rides; move the sash sideways by
wedging a screwdriver between the bottom of the groove and the side
of the frame; using a hammer, gently tap a block of wood all along the
side where the latch holds the windows closed.

RATTLING WINDOWS Wooden windows often rattle because the catch
has worked itself loose or the frame has too much play in it. To fix a
loose catch, unscrew the fitting and replace it, positioning it so that

*Stained glass was used in some
of the windows of grander homes
in the 19th century and with a
little know-how can be quite
easily repaired today.*

To restore dried-out putty, remove any
crusty lumps and knead it in hot water.
When it is thoroughly softened, like
plasticine, roll it in greaseproof paper
smeared with a light coating of linseed
oil. Make sure you squeeze out any
excess water before you store it again.

The Way We Were

New Zealand born writer Ruth Park describes the cleaning
of a window in Sydney's Surry Hills, then a slum area, in
the early 20th century:

'The next day the Chinese, having spent a mysterious
night of bumpings and thumpings, and sharp staccato
hammerings, cleaned out his window. To Dolour and the
other children, standing spellbound before his door, he was
at first only a ghost amidst the yellow dust. Then, before his
polishing cloth, crystal lanes and highways appeared on the
coated glass, and they saw him, calm and ivory and smiling,
chasing the last cobwebs and dirt clots from the window.'

– THE HARP IN THE SOUTH (1948)

the catch just slips into the slot. If there is too much play between the sash and the frame, try taking out the upright strips of beading at the edge of the window and refitting them a little closer to the sash frame to grip the window. If the beading holding a window in position is loose, you can tighten it by hammering the nails that hold it more firmly into position.

EXPERTISE WITH GLASS With some confidence and a little practice you can be your own glazier, at least for the smaller jobs.

Cutting glass Cutting glass is best done with a diamond cutter, or you can use a hardened steel cutting wheel. Cover a perfectly smooth, solid surface with a piece of thick underfelt and place the glass on it. Scratch the surface with the cutter, guiding it along a straight edge. The cutter must be drawn towards your body rather than pushed away, and must be held upright. Make only a very light scratch on the glass, and run the cutter across the glass only once.

To separate the pieces, either put the sheet of glass on the table with the scratch aligned with the table edge and press down sharply on the waste piece, or place a matchstick under the glass at each end of the scratch. Press firmly and sharply on both pieces; the glass should break cleanly along the scratch.

Flowers growing up against a gleaming window pane diffuse and colour the light and add that final touch to an interior.

Repairing leadlighting The panes in leaded glass windows are held in position by thin strips of lead. Protecting your hands with several layers of thick cloth, remove a damaged pane of glass by pressing from the inside, forcing the pieces outwards to spread and bend the edges of the strip of lead. Have a piece of glass of the correct size, weight and colour cut by taking an undamaged identical piece of the old glass with you to the glasscutter's.

You may need to lever the edges of the lead strip forwards to insert the new pane. Press the edges of the lead against the pane with your fingers, and finally firm the edges by rubbing them all round with a piece of soft wood. Repair split corners of the lead with a soldering iron, taking care not to overheat and melt the lead of the main strips.

AWNINGS Canvas awnings have a tendency to develop stains from weathering but they can be cleaned with a strong solution of salt and water. Never use detergents on canvas, and do not use household bleach on old canvas, as it will damage the fabric.

To remove mildew from awnings, spread a mixture of soft soap, starch, salt and lemon juice on the canvas and leave it in the sun. As the mixture dries, apply more. Rinse it carefully afterwards.

Revitalise faded and dirty awnings by dying them (first removing all the metal fittings), or by painting them with house paint that has been thinned with about a litre of turpentine to 4 litres of paint. Awnings painted like this can be rolled for storage but must not be folded, since this will crack the paint.

FLYSCREENS An old-fashioned but effective trick is to paint wire screens black on the inside and white on the outside; this prevents people from looking in and helps you to look out.

Mending flyscreens Nowadays many screens are made of plastic mesh, which is best mended with black button thread, but if you have metal screens, mend them as follows.

Trim the edges of the hole, then cut a patch from matching screen wire; the patch should be about 5 cm larger all round than the trimmed hole. Unravel the edges of the patch for about a centimetre all round and bend the unravelled edges inward at right angles. Place the patch over the hole so that the bent wires of the unravelled edges push through the screen, catch the ravelled edges onto the screen, turn them under and press them down.

Another method, which is a little more fiddly, is to sew the patch onto the screen with a piece of screen wire.

Replacing flyscreens If you need to replace a flyscreen completely, begin by tacking the new screen along one side of the frame; start at the centre point of the frame and work out towards the ends, positioning the tacks close together. Then stretch the screen as tightly as possible and tack along the opposite side, again starting from the centre point of the frame. Tack the third side without stretching the fly wire, but stretch the last side tightly and then tack it in place. Finally, trim off the excess screening.

Repairing a screen frame Wooden screen frames have to take a lot of hard wear and sometimes come apart at the corners. Drill a diagonal hole through the corner of the frame and hammer in a tight-fitting wooden dowel. This method is illustrated in the right-hand column.

WINDOW BOXES For old-fashioned charm, nothing beats pretty window boxes, either placed on the windowsills, if they are wide enough, or resting on brackets fastened to the wall.

Before you fill the window boxes with soil, seal the inside joints with oil putty. When this is dry, coat the insides with clear varnish to prevent moisture from rotting the wood. Then line the base of the boxes with several layers of newspaper to stop the soil from drying out too quickly after watering. To prevent the soil from window boxes from spattering the window when it rains, scatter a layer of gravel on the surface of the soil.

The Way We Were

A famous 19th century novel described the art of placing windows so as to resist the violence of stormy weather:

'Pure, bracing ventilation they must have up there, at all times, indeed: one may guess the power of the north wind, blowing over the edge, by the excessive slant of a few stunted firs at the end of the house, and by a range of gaunt thorns all stretching their limbs one way, as if craving alms of the sun. Happily, the architect had foresight to build it strong: the narrow windows are deeply set in the wall, and the corners defended with large jutting stones.'

– *WUTHERING HEIGHTS*, EMILY BRONTE (1847)

MENDING A SCREEN FRAME
Mend a disintegrating wooden screen frame with dowelling.

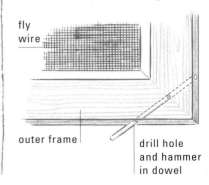

fly wire

outer frame

drill hole and hammer in dowel

Lay them straight

WINSTON CHURCHILL, BRITAIN'S PRIME MINISTER DURING WORLD WAR II, USED TO LAY BRICKS AT HIS COUNTRY RETREAT AS A FORM OF RELAXATION.

You are unlikely to want to build a whole house yourself, but you can learn to do repairs and keep brickwork in good order. And you will have the pleasure of mastering an ancient craft.

CHOOSING BRICKS Bricks should ring when struck, to show they are well fired. They should be free from cracks, and when broken they should be closely textured with no small stones. To test a batch of bricks for porosity, weigh one, stand it in water for 24 hours, and then reweigh it. If its weight increases by more than 10 per cent, the brick will not be weathertight.

EFFLORESCENCE The white crust that sometimes forms on brick walls is crystallised salts, brought to the surface by moisture. On new walls, it may mean that excessive water was used; scrubbing the crust off with water and a stiff brush is all that is needed. On older work, it may be caused by leaky flashing or gutters or poorly applied mortar. If a crust appears under windows, check the sills and the caulking around the frames. Markings near the base of a wall may mean water is being drawn up, so check the dampcoursing.

The practical householder can put his bricklaying skills to good use when building a garden wall.

TRICKS WITH BRICKS There is an art to using a trowel and mortar. Watch a bricklayer at work to learn some of the tricks of the trade.

Handling mortar One way to keep the mortar on the trowel is to 'snap' your wrist as you lift the trowel from the tub. This imparts a slight suction that drives out air between the mortar and the trowel.

Spread mortar evenly. Holding the trowel at a sharp angle, trowel a ridge in the centre of the brick. Remove any twigs, stones or mortar lumps before laying each brick. After laying a brick, cut off excess mortar with the trowel; you need not clean the inside face of the bricks. Wet bricks well before laying, and do not lay bricks in freezing weather.

Replacing bricks Badly bonded or poor quality mortar will fall out. Mortar can be replaced – this is called repointing. Remove loose mortar and brush each join clean. Dampen the join and nearby surfaces, pack the new mortar in tightly with a trowel, and then smooth it, sloping the mortar downward so that it will shed water.

WATERPROOFING Check that all joins in the brickwork are tightly filled, that openings around the doors and windows are caulked and that roofs and flashings are sound. Repoint any porous joins, then waterproof by applying several coats of a mixture of one part powdered waterglass and four parts water; apply only during warm weather.

A BRICKLAYER'S CREED
The line and plummet guide the tool,
And keep the trowel under rule.
The firm foundation lay with care
Nor build thy castles in the air.
– *FLOWERS OF DELIGHT*, LEONARD DE VRIES (1765–1830)

A roof over our heads

ALL SORTS OF MATERIALS, FROM SLATE TO SHINGLE, WERE ONCE USED FOR ROOFING AND IT IS HANDY TO KNOW HOW TO MEND THE ROOF ON AN OLDER HOME.

A thatched roof must be repaired by a thatcher, but you can repair or replace tiles, slate and corrugated iron yourself. Work carefully; it is easy to inflict further damage instead of solving the problem.

FINDING THE PROBLEM Water often seeps along roof timbers for a long way before making its presence known. Play a hose on the roof to locate the hole; once you have found it, if your roofing material permits, drive a long thin nail through it from the inside to the outside so that you can find the leak from the upper side of the roof.

TILED ROOFS Removing a tile means disturbing at least the course above the damaged tile. Carefully lift the two tiles above the one to be removed and pull the damaged one out.

METAL ROOFS Keep metal roofs well painted to protect them against rust. Repair holes in metal roofs by inserting a piece of strong canvas, painted on both sides, into the leaky area. Nail the canvas on with galvanised nails and apply a heavy coat of roofing cement to the patch, its edges and the adjacent area of roof. Tiny holes may be closed with a drop of solder. If a tin roof is riddled with small holes, a thick coat of bitumen affords a temporary solution.

SHINGLE ROOFS Remove old shingles by splitting them and pulling them out. Cut the nails that secured the old shingle with a small saw or a hacksaw blade. Nail the new shingle in place, and do not forget to renail the shingles above the one you have replaced. Use nails that will not rust. You can make a new shingle look weathered to match the others by painting it with linseed oil and turpentine.

To replace rows of shingles, start from the eaves, and use a long piece of wood to tack in place after you have completed a row of shingles, to line up the next row. Make sure the overlap of shingles is large enough to prevent further leaks.

FLASHING Flashing seals joins and angles in roofs. It leaks when leaves or other debris collect and prevent water from draining away, resulting in water backing up under the roof covering. Clear away any obstruction. If you have tin flashing, examine it regularly for rust.

Do not try to repair flashing unless you are quite confident of your skill, and avoid nailing it unless you are sure that the nail holes will not themselves create leaks. Fasten the lower edge of a flashing sheet with nails only if the edge hangs over a vertical surface. The upper edge of a sheet of flashing should never be nailed.

CORRUGATED IRON ROOFS were a characteristic feature of the Australian landscape in the good old days, and many are just as effective today.

In 1836 a French chemist dipped iron into baths of molten zinc, galvanising it and stopping it from rusting, and eight years later an Englishman discovered how to bend sheets of iron between specially designed rollers – an improvement on the older, slower method of making one curve at a time with a heavy press.

Corrugated iron was soon being shipped to Australia, where it was used by the gold-diggers who flocked there after gold was discovered in 1851. Diggers made lean-tos from two sheets; settlers used corrugated iron for walls and roofs; and the new material soon covered many a makeshift leaky roof.

Outside the house

IN AN URBAN ENVIRONMENT YOU'LL FIND THAT WELL MAINTAINED EXTERIOR WALLS, PATHS AND FENCES MAKE FOR HAPPY NEIGHBOURS.

The outside of your house is important to the neighbours; choose finishes and colours that harmonise with the houses next door as well as with the style of your own house and garden. And keeping your house itself and your fences, paths and driveways in good condition adds to the value of your property.

STUCCO If stucco walls are bulging or there are large powdery areas, the metal lath behind the stucco may have disintegrated. The stucco mixture itself may be at fault; magnesium stucco is corrosive and will eventually cause the whole stucco facing to fall. If this is the case, the only solution is to replace the metal lath and stucco the wall again.

If repair is all that is needed, nail new metal lath over the old stucco with extra-long nails. This will also add an extra layer of insulation to the walls.

Random-cut stone is a great way to lead friends and family up the garden path.

CONCRETE Concrete is one of the cheapest and easiest finishes for paths and driveways. Planned and laid intelligently on a well drained foundation, it will last for years.

Repairing concrete Clean holes in the concrete and straighten the sides with a hammer and chisel. Roughen edges with a wire brush where the old and new cement will join, and wet the inside of the hole well. Mix a small amount of rather watery cement and slosh it into the hole and any cracks. Then fill the hole with a stiffer cement mixture and tamp it down. Trowel it smooth, leaving it a little above the level of the surrounding concrete, since it will compact when it dries.

CLEANING AN OIL-STAINED PATH Mosses and tiny plants add a patina of age to a concrete path, but oil stains are much less attractive. Clean up oil spills with paraffin or petrol rinsed off with a solution of caustic soda solution, being careful not to let it touch your skin. Swab the concrete well with water to remove all traces of the caustic soda. Or remove oil stains with turpentine, mixed with a fine powder of fuller's earth; the turpentine dissolves the stain and the powder soaks it up.

FENCES Stone and brick fences are the most permanent and relatively maintenance-free; wooden fences will last for about 40 years; hedges need regular attention to keep them looking good.

LADDERS If you need to stand a ladder on a treasured piece of lawn, stand it on a board with a batten nailed along the centre. Rest the foot of the ladder on the board against the batten to protect your lawn.

WORDS ABOUT WALLS
Something there is that doesn't
   love a wall,
That sends the frozen groundswell
   under it,
And spills the upper boulders
   in the sun;
And makes gaps even two can
   pass abreast...
– 'MENDING WALL', ROBERT FROST
   (1874–1963)

Soapsuds

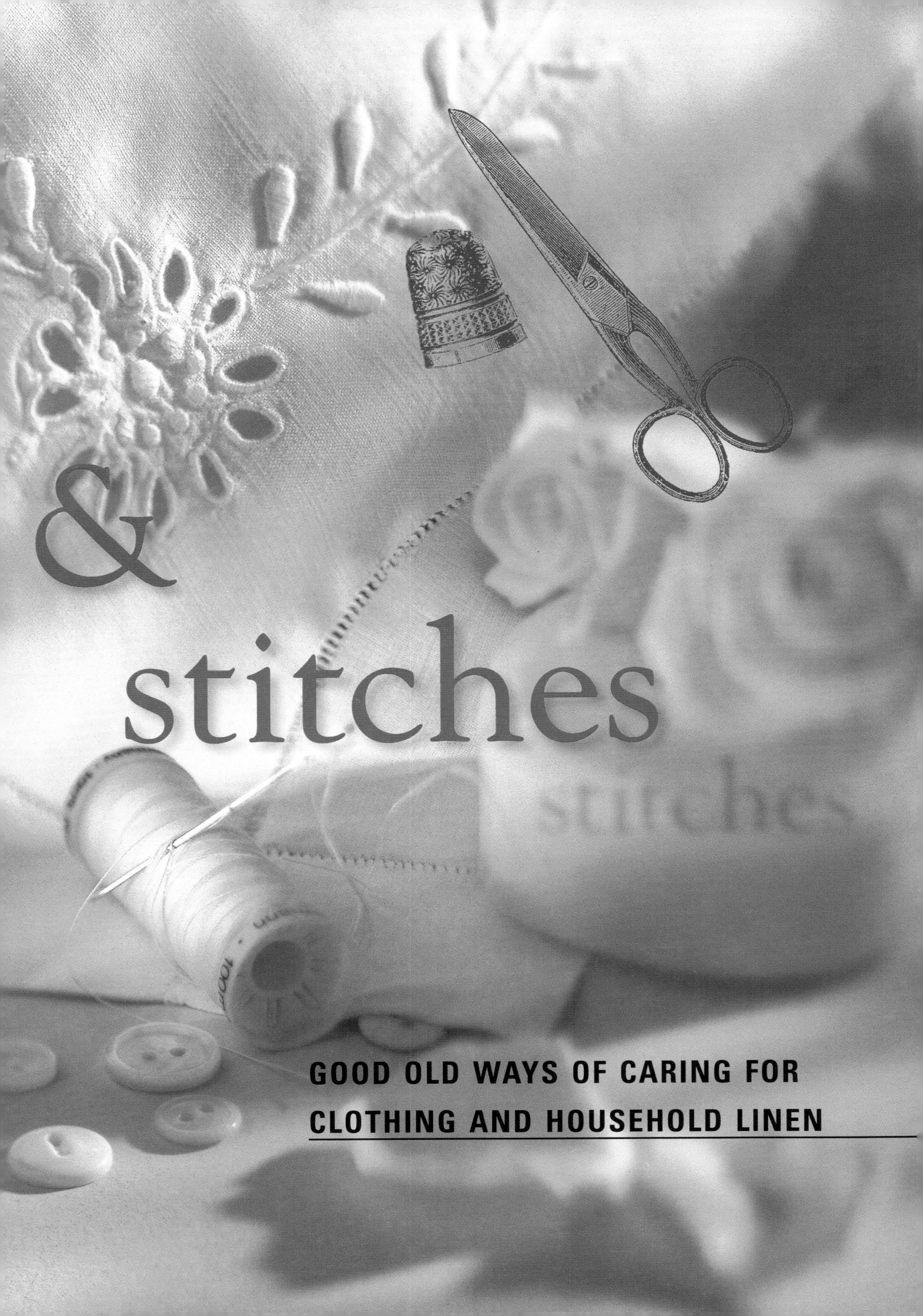

&

stitches

stitches

**GOOD OLD WAYS OF CARING FOR
CLOTHING AND HOUSEHOLD LINEN**

Pre-wash rituals

WASHDAY IS NO LONGER THE CHORE
IT ONCE WAS, BUT MANY OF OUR
GRANDMOTHERS' LAUNDRY
TECHNIQUES ARE APPLICABLE TODAY.

In the old days, the smooth running of the
household was jeopardised if domestic tasks did not follow
a strict routine. Traditionally, Monday was washday, although
many housekeeping experts – including the British home
economist Mrs Beeton – favoured Tuesday, so that tasks such as
sorting, mending and soaking could be done the previous day.

*Then, as now, advertisements
tried to lend a touch of romance to
the most mundane of chores – as
witnessed by this soapflakes
advertisement of 70 years ago.*

KNOW YOUR FABRICS Synthetic fibres first appeared towards the end
of the 19th century. The first artificial fibre, rayon, was made in the
1880s in France from a chemical extracted from plant cellulose, and
the viscose process of producing cellulose fibres soon followed. The
year 1921 saw the launch of acetate fibres under the trade name
Celanese. By 1935, chemists working on plastics had produced nylon;
polyester Terylene made its debut in Britain in 1941; and acrylics hit
the market in the United States in 1950.

Even so, before 1950 virtually all domestic fabrics were made from
natural fibres – cotton, wool, silk or linen.

Cotton Cotton fabric is made from the soft, white, downy fibres
surrounding the seeds of the cotton plant. Absorbent and hard-
wearing, it is today often combined with synthetic fibre to make it
more crease-resistant. Cotton fabrics range from fine muslin to sturdy
furnishing fabrics and mattress ticking.

Wool Woollen thread is spun from the fleeces of sheep. Woollen
items range from bulky knitted jumpers and cardigans to finely woven
luxury fabrics that are scarcely distinguishable from silk. Wool is
warm because the fibres have insulating qualities. Knitted wool is
springy and soft to the touch.

Silk Silk is a fine, lustrous fibre spun from the unravelled cocoons of
silkworms. It is woven in different weights and textures. Many silk
fabrics are indeed 'as smooth as silk', but some are coarsely woven and
have a slub – a pronounced knobbly texture.

Linen Linen is woven from the fibres of flax plants,
Heavier than cotton, it is a very durable
fabric that is often used to make
household linen as well as clothing.
Damask is figured linen, very popular
in earlier years for use in formal
tablecloths and table napkins and
now making a comeback.

The Way We Were

This recipe for making marking
ink is from an unknown source,
but it obviously dates from the
days before steel-knibbed pens:

'5 scruples nitrate of silver,
2 drachms gum arabic,
1 scruple sap green,
1 ounce distilled water.

Mix together. Before using on
the article to be marked, apply
a little of the following:

1/2 ounce carbonate of soda,
4 ounces distilled water.

Let this last, which is the
mordant, get dry; then with
a quill pen write what
you require.'

SORTING THE WASHING The purpose of sorting is to group the soiled washing into articles that can safely be washed together. It is still an essential preliminary for the best washing results.

Sorting by fabric Separate delicate fabrics, such as woollens, from stronger fabrics, such as cottons. Fabric texture determines the water temperature: for example, wool tolerates warm water only but tough cotton and linen items such as tea towels can be boiled. Modern manufacturers often provide care labels – some articles must be hand washed in mild soap; others are marked 'dry-clean only'.

Sorting by colour It is advisable to place light-coloured articles in one wash and dark blue and black articles in another. White cottons can withstand higher water temperatures than coloured cottons and should be washed separately. Be careful with deeply dyed garments, especially when they are new – the colour is liable to run.

Sorting for soiling Some articles need soaking or treating for soiled areas and stains. Rub the insides of shirt collars and cuffs gently with soap to dislodge the grease during washing. Trouser knees are other suspect areas. Treat stains before clothes are washed: pages 154–5 provide some tried and true advice about removing common stains.

Other sorting tips Finally, before loading the washer, you should:
• Check all pockets. (Anyone who has inadvertently let a paper handkerchief go through the washing machine will know how valid this tip from the good old days remains!)
• Brush loose dirt and fluff from pockets, cuffs and turn-ups.
• Close zips, buttons and all other fasteners.
• Tie sashes, ribbons, tapes and strings to avoid tangling.

COLOUR FIXING The colourfastness of fabric dyes has improved greatly, but some articles still require pre-wash treatment to fix the colours. A washing manual published in the 1940s proposed various ways of setting different colours. Steep the articles in the fixing solution for about an hour before washing them; if the colour still runs after fixing, add some of the solution to the last rinse.
Salt and water Use 2 cups of salt in 4 litres of water for cottons of all colours except blue, mauve and green. (Never soak wool in this mix.)
Strong vinegar Use half a cup of strong vinegar to 4 litres of water for blue and mauve fabrics.
Alum Use a tablespoonful of alum to 4 litres of water for green fabrics.
White wine vinegar Use half a cup of white wine vinegar to 4 litres of water for all white materials with stripes, light-coloured woollens and delicate silks.
Caution: Never soak fabrics made from cellulose, such as rayon.

TEA-TOWELS To remove fabric dressing from new tea towels to make them soft enough to use, soak them overnight in a solution of 2 tablespoons of borax dissolved in a bucket of hot water.

FABRIC SOFTENER Clothes will become soft to the touch if they are soaked overnight in a solution of one part vinegar to three parts water and rinsed well before they are washed.

Hilaire Chardonnet, a French chemist, invented the first artificial fibre in 1884. Known as rayon or artificial silk, it was strong but extremely flammable.

Tough fabrics such as denim can tolerate any amount of washday wear-and-tear; delicate fabrics such as silk will benefit from the addition of a little vinegar to the final rinsing water.

A stitch in time

MENDING CAN SAVE A FAVOURITE ARTICLE OF
CLOTHING FROM THE RAGBAG, AND IS A SOOTHING
AND SATISFYING WAY TO PASS THE TIME.

In the old days, girls learnt to sew and mend at their mothers' knees
and at school. People had fewer clothes than they do now and replaced
them less often. From around 1930 to well past 1945, shortages and
wartime rationing made thrift a necessity, and mending was essential.

BUTTONS Use strong thread to sew on buttons and check them now
and then for firmness, particularly metal ones, as over time they can
cut through even the strongest thread. Collect a treasury of spare
buttons, storing them in a screw-top jar for easy visibility.

Button keepers Buttons at stress points such as shirt necks tend
to pull away, and those on knitted garments may pull threads in the
fabric. To prevent this, attach the button to a 'keeper' – a square of
fabric or tape, or a small flat button – on the wrong side of the garment.

Button shanks If the fabric of the garment is thick, make a shank, or
stem, to allow for the thickness of the upper layer of material when
the button is pushed through the buttonhole. (See below right.)

DARNING Darning is a weaving technique to repair a thinning area
or a hole caused by wear. Thinning areas are much easier to darn than
actual holes, so take preventive measures early.

How to darn Use a fine needle for fine fabrics and a darning needle
for wool. Choose thread that matches the fabric in colour, texture and
thickness. Place the area to be darned over a firm surface, such as an
ironing board, and run parallel threads across the hole or thin area, well
beyond the edges. Then weave a second set of parallel threads over and
under the first ones, at right angles. Do not pull the thread too tightly.

FRAYED BLANKET EDGES Blanket edges tend to fray long before the
blanket itself is worn. Trim off loose threads, then use thick woollen
thread to blanket stitch around all four edges.

L-SHAPED TEARS These tears are caused when clothes catch on a sharp
projection. Draw the edges of the tear together and tack them to a
piece of finely woven cloth on the wrong side of the fabric. Then,
using threads unravelled from a hidden part of the garment, stitch
diagonally across one side of the tear from the outside to the centre.
Repeat the procedure on the other side. Then stitch at the opposite
angle along both sides of the tear to make a trellis of stitches.

PULLED THREADS Correct loops of pulled thread in knitted fabric by
gently stretching one side of the pull along its width, then the other,

The Way We Were

'Scarlett could not imagine her
mother's hands without her
gold thimble or her rustling
figure unaccompanied by the
small negro girl whose sole
function in life was to remove
basting threads and carry the
rosewood sewing-box from
room to room, as Ellen moved
about the house superintend-
ing the cooking, the cleaning
and the wholesale clothes-
making for the plantation.'

– *GONE WITH THE WIND*,
MARGARET MITCHELL (1936)

MAKING A BUTTON SHANK
This is an easy way to create the
necessary space between thick fabric
and a button.

Place a matchstick on top of the button
and take the thread over the match as
you sew the button to the fabric.
Remove the match and lift the button
away from the fabric, pulling so that
the stitches are taut. Wind the thread
firmly around the stitches several
times before finishing off at the back
of the fabric.

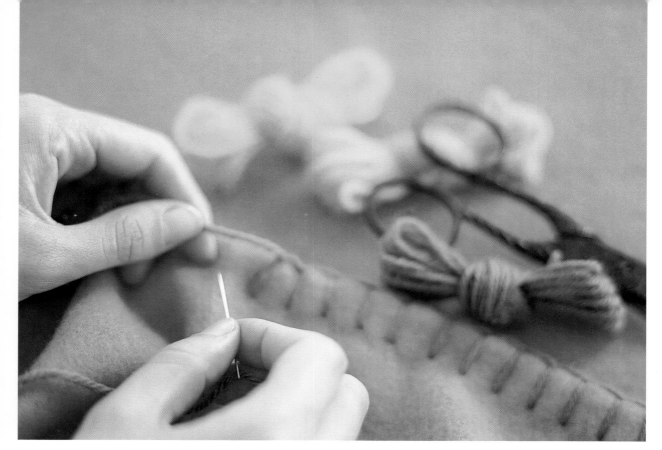

until the loop is taken up. Draw large loops that will not take up completely to the back of the fabric with the blunt end of a needle or thread them through a needle and weave them into the back of the fabric. Never cut pulled threads.

SEWING TIPS The golden rules of yesteryear still apply today:
• Store dressmaking pins in a felt pincushion stuffed with raw sheep's wool. The lanoline in the wool will prevent the pins from rusting.
• Never allow anybody to use your sewing scissors to cut paper, as it will quickly blunt the cutting edges.
• Prevent double threads from becoming tangled by knotting the ends separately instead of together.

SEWING NEEDS Once, every home had a sewing box, which could be an elegant marquetry creation or just an old biscuit tin. Stock your sewing box with these pieces of equipment.
Scissors Small pair with sharp points for snipping threads and unpicking seams; dressmaking shears for cutting fabric.
Needles Sharps for general use; crewels for embroidery; darners; curved and straight upholstery needles; bodkins for threading elastic.
Thimble Essential if you do much hand sewing, to protect your middle finger as you push the needle through the fabric. Choose carefully from the various sizes. A silver thimble used to be a popular gift for a little girl.
Threads Neutral-coloured sewing threads; strong button threads; tacking cotton. Your collection will grow as you match fabrics.
Pins Long and short pins; dressmaking pins; safety pins.
Fastenings Press studs; hooks and eyes; buttons.
Tape measure Flexible, with both imperial and metric markings.

Do as your thrifty grandmother did and give blankets a new lease of life by repairing frayed edges. Add a designer touch by choosing a colour to tone or contrast with the colour of the blanket.

In earlier times a sewing machine would probably have been used as much for mending worn or torn clothes as for creating new ones. This model was made in 1882.

Out, damned spot!

PROMPT ACTION IS VITAL FOR REMOVING STAINS. IN AN EMERGENCY, GO TO THE KITCHEN CUPBOARD FOR HELP.

Before proprietary stain removers, people immediately plunged nongreasy stains on washable fabrics into cold water and applied something like lemon juice or milk. Some traditional treatments, such as rubbing salt into fruit stains, have become folklore; others, such as applying gin to obstinate spots, have disappeared from the repertoire.

PRINCIPLES OF STAIN REMOVAL Identify the fabric and the stain, then quickly get rid of the offending substance. Mop up liquid spills from washable fabrics with a cloth; remove solids with the back of a knife. Before you attack residual marks with a stain remover, test it on an inconspicuous part of the article. Work from the back of the fabric, so as to push the stain out the way it came in. Clean in a circle from just outside the stain to the centre to avoid forming rings. Fuller's earth or talc will absorb liquid spills on unwashable fabrics; for treating any residual stain, see pages 168–9, 'Cleaning without water'.

Do's and don'ts of stain removal Always work in a well-ventilated room and keep children and pets away. Handle stain removers with care. Do not use solvents near a naked flame as they are highly flammable. Never use hot water on a stain – it 'cooks' the stain and sets it for ever. And never soak dyed silks, moiré fabrics or wool.

STAIN REMOVAL EQUIPMENT Basic household items are all you need to remove stains. Your kit should include:
Solvents The most useful are acetone, bicarbonate of soda, borax, cream of tartar, dry-cleaning fluid, eucalyptus oil, glycerine, kerosene, ammonia, hydrogen peroxide, petrol, methylated spirits and turpentine.
Clothes brush Buy the best you can afford.
Cosmetic sponges Ideal for applying solvents.
Cotton wool Use to apply solvents and testing.
Absorbent materials White, lint-free cotton rags are the best. Replace them regularly. Absorbent kitchen paper is also useful.
Scraper A spatula or the back of an old blunt knife work well.
Droppers Keep one for each liquid chemical; wash well after use.
Spray bottle A must for applying water.

DIFFICULT STAINS The following treatment is worth trying on old stains. Mix the juice of a lemon with a quarter of a cup each of cloudy ammonia, glycerine, methylated spirits and hydrogen peroxide. Strain and apply to the stain. Leave for several hours, then wash.

MILDEW Mildew is a mould that keeps growing if left untreated. These time-honoured remedies for removing mildew are still effective.

Check for stains before putting items in the wash. Some marks come out readily in the suds; others need to be treated first. This machine from the 1920s used the principle of the mill wheel to force soapy water through the dirty clothes.

Fresh mildew comes out in the wash. If the entire garment is mildewed, put it in a mild solution of bleach and rinse well.

To treat mildewed bed linen, rub soap on the mouldy spots; follow this with finely powdered chalk. Lay the article on the grass to dry. Moisten the stains and repeat the process until the stains disappear.

Mix a teaspoon of starch with 2 teaspoons of salt and a few drops of lemon juice. Rub into stain, leave for at least three hours, then wash.

Cover stain with lemon juice and salt. Dry article in sun, then wash.

Apply a paste of ammonia and whiting to the spot, then wash.

STAIN SHIFTERS Many of the stain shifters described below work just as well today as they did before 1950, and the ingredients can be found in supermarkets, pharmacies or hardware stores. Modern fabrics may react to some of these substances, so test before you treat. For home methods of cleaning without water, see pages 168–9.

Words of Wisdom

'Silk handkerchiefs require to be washed alone. When they contain snuff, they should be soaked by themselves in lukewarm water two or three hours; they should be rinsed out and put to soak with the others in cold water for an hour or two; then washed in lukewarm water, being soaped as they are washed. If this does not remove all stains, they should be washed a second time in similar water, and, when finished, rinsed in soft water in which a handful of common salt has been dissolved.'

– *Mrs Beeton's Book of Cookery and Household Management* (1861)

STAIN	TYPE OF FABRIC	TREATMENT
Blood	Washable	Soak in cold water for several hours, then wash in tepid soapy water.
Chocolate/cocoa	Washable	Soak in cold water then wash.
	Nonwashable	Rub gently with petrol.
Coffee	Washable	Pour hot soda water through the stain, then wash as usual.
Fruit juice	Washable	Fresh stains: sprinkle generously with salt, then soak stain in cold water. Older stains: as soon as possible, sponge with cold water and ammonia.
Grass stains	Wool	Rub with butter and rinse in petrol.
	Washable	Fresh stains: wash with cold water. Older stains: cover the mark with kerosene, then wash in soap and water.
	Nonwashable	Rub gently with household alcohol.
Ink	Coloured	Apply a paste of mustard and water and leave for 15 minutes, then wash.
Lipstick	Washable	Sponge with kerosene.
	Nonwashable	Apply methylated spirits or eucalyptus oil.
Perspiration	Wool	Sponge with lemon juice and water.
	Washable	Soak in mix of water and soda water.
Tea	Linen	Rub a little glycerine into the stain, then wash in warm water.
	Washable	Soak in mix of borax and warm water.
Urine	Washable	Sprinkle with salt, then soak article in cold water and wash in warm soapy water.
Wax	All	When wax has hardened, scrape off all you can with a spatula; place blotting paper over and under spot and press with a warm iron – the paper will absorb the wax. Use ammonia to take out any residual colour stain.
Wine	Washable	Sprinkle generously with salt, then soak stain in cold water and wash.

Soap advertisements at the turn of the century depicted washing as a graceful pursuit.

Rub-a-dub-dub

WHETHER THE WEEKLY WASHDAY WAS MONDAY
OR TUESDAY, THE WASHING ROUTINE IN THE DAYS
BEFORE DOMESTIC WASHING MACHINES WAS
COMPLEX, TIME-CONSUMING AND LABORIOUS.

*A woodcut advertisement for
shirts published in 1912 took full
advantage of Australia's
reputation for riding on the
sheep's back.*

After sorting and soaking, some articles were washed,
rinsed once, boiled, rinsed again, blued, squeezed
through the wringer and starched before they reached
the clothesline. Handbooks on laundering included tips
for removing rust and verdigris from tubs and coppers,
and advice on caring for other long-obsolete equipment,
such as scrubbing boards, boiler sticks and mangles.
Labour-saving machines have done away with most of this
drudgery, but sometimes the old ways are still the best.

TYPES OF WATER Soft water is best for washing clothes and
linen because it allows soap to lather easily. Rainwater and meltwater are
soft, and so is water that flows through granite or slate country. Hard
water, which occurs in limestone or chalk country, curdles soap, but the
hardness can be counteracted with a water softener.

Water softeners To soften hard water, use three-quarters your normal
amount of soap powder in the washing machine and make up the
difference with bicarbonate of soda. Or add a handful of washing soda
(from supermarkets) to the washing and rinsing cycles.

SOAP Soap consists of fat, which is classified chemically as an acid,
and a neutralising agent such as caustic soda or lye.

Soft soap This preparation lathers more quickly than soap flakes
and is suitable for both machine and hand washing. Finely grate
250 grams of good washing soap into an old saucepan and add 1 litre
of water. Heat slowly without boiling, stirring thoroughly until the
soap dissolves. Pour into a jar, cap, and allow the mixture to cool.

BORAX Borax is available from pharmacies and hardware shops. It
took pride of place in the laundries of the past, and is still used in
many commercial laundry products. It softens water, removes grease
and some other stains, and gives linen and laces a fine gloss. Dissolve
borax in boiling water; it is not soluble in cold water.
Caution: Borax is poisonous; keep it away from children and pets.

WASHING TIPS
• Strong soap hardens and shrinks woollens, turns white silks yellow,
and fades the dyes in coloured materials.
• Hard rubbing wears all fabrics, hardens woollens, gives silks a rough
and wavy look and damages colour.

*Soapmaking is an ancient
technique; as early as the first
century AD, Pliny the Elder
reported that the ancient Romans
made soap with goat fat.*

*Before the advent of modern
laundry equipment, ingenious
engineers fashioned mechanical
aids from whatever was to hand.*

• Water hotter than lukewarm damages silks and may alter or fade the colour in dyed fabrics.

COTTONS AND LINENS White cotton and linen can stand soaking, hot washing, starching, drying in full sunlight and a high ironing temperature. Be more gentle with heat when laundering coloured cotton and linen fabrics, and dry them away from direct sunlight.

Boiling Boiling is recommended only for heavily soiled cottons and linens. Use 30 grams of soap shavings to 4.5 litres of water. Put the clothes in when the water is warm. Boil the cleaner articles first, and heavily soiled articles last, adding a little washing soda.

WOOLLENS Woollens shrink and become matted in hot water. Wash delicate knitted woollens carefully by hand, using lukewarm water.

Lavender wool wash This fragrant mixture keeps woollens smelling sweet. Pour a litre of boiling water over 4 teaspoons of dried lavender in a ceramic bowl. Cover and let soak overnight, then strain out the flowers. Bring the lavender water to the boil in an old saucepan with 500 grams of grated pure soap and a tablespoon of borax, stirring with a wooden spoon until the ingredients are thoroughly blended. The mixture will cool into a white jelly; store this in a screw-top jar and label it clearly. Use half a cup to hand wash woollens or two to three cups in the washing machine. Rinse well.

SPECIAL WASHES Whether you wash by hand or with a state-of-the-art washing machine, some items need special treatment.

Baby clothes Modern babies rarely wear fine muslin or cambric, except perhaps for the family christening robes, but the traditional rules for the care of baby clothes are just as valid today as they ever were. Wash baby clothes every day; use only mild soaps and rinse well; dry in the open air. Iron or air baby clothes thoroughly to make sure they are completely dry.

Neck ties Washing a tie and keeping its shape is a delicate operation. Baste the tie a short distance from the edge with tacking cotton to prevent the lining from wrinkling. Then wash the tie carefully by hand; when almost dry, iron under a cloth. Silk ties should not be washed.

Heirloom lace Gum water is perfect for stiffening net and lace. Crush 30 grams of gum arabic (from art supply shops), soak until soft then cover with 600 ml of boiling water. Strain the solution through muslin, bottle and keep airtight. Immerse old lace in warm soapy water and squeeze it gently, then rinse until the water is clear, adding 1–3 tablespoons of gum water to every half litre of the final rinsing water, depending on how stiff you want the lace to be. Roll the lace in a towel until it is almost dry, and then iron it on the wrong side over a towel to raise the pattern.

Silk Some silks must be dry-cleaned, but most can be washed and ironed with care. The water should be comfortably warm; add a little salt to fix the colour and keep the fabric soft.

The Way We Were

'To a fairly healthy woman washing day is the least trying of all her working days; the hanging out and bringing in of the clothes is as good as a half day out, while the steam arising from the copper clears the skin of the face. Many girls are absolutely at their best on a Monday evening, the work of a beauty parlour having been vicariously performed. "Hanging out clothes" the maid had a better chance of health and beauty than the king in his counting-house, or the queen in the parlour eating bread and honey.'

– *THE COUNTRYWOMAN IN NEW SOUTH WALES* (1937)

Save scraps of soap from the bathroom and laundry. Grate and melt them in a little water, and then use the mixture for washing delicate articles by hand.

EIDERDOWN Eiderdown quilts are not as common as they once were — today's equivalent is the doona, or duvet. If you want to wash down-stuffed items yourself, pick good drying conditions, as the feathers should not remain wet for long. Use plenty of warm, soapy water and thoroughly knead and squeeze the article by hand. Rinse well in at least two lots of water – this is important. Do not wring or spin-dry, but gently squeeze out as much water as possible and then place the article flat on the grass on an old sheet. Turn and shake it occasionally. When quite dry, shake it well again, and then hang it on the line and beat it gently with a light cane to separate the feathers.

BLANKETS Choose a warm windy day, use plenty of soapy water and a cup of ammonia, and rinse thoroughly. Spin-drying has replaced the labour of wringing out wet blankets; our hard-working predecessors had to do this by hand or force the great weight of wet material through a mangle. After spin-drying, shake the blanket vigorously and stretch it into shape before hanging it on the line.

RINSING TIPS Take as much care with rinsing as with washing.
• To stop woollens from felting, add 1 teaspoon of olive oil to every 4 litres of warm rinsing water. Two tablespoonfuls of vinegar in the final rinsing water prevents the itchiness of wool against the skin.
• Sprinkle eucalyptus or lavender oil on a small piece of cloth and add it to the final rinse for articles that are to be stored; the odour will repel moths and silverfish and give your laundry a delicate perfume.
• Washing by hand can leave your hands in a sorry state: rub them with vinegar or salt to take away the wrinkles.

Sweet-smelling lavender and pure, mild soap will permeate all your laundry with a delicious old-world fragrance.

The mangle was a labour-saving device invented in 1779. This model was marketed in about 1900.

158

WHITENING Our grandmothers brightened tired-looking white articles with methods that were much less hard on fabrics than modern commercial preparations.

Blueing Washing blue, made from indigo, was once widely used to counteract the yellow tint that perspiration and the use of soap and soda gave to white linen and cotton. A liquid form is still available. Do not soak clothes in blueing water, as they will become streaky.

Other whiteners Add a cup of methylated spirits and a cup of cloudy ammonia to the washing water occasionally to keep whites sparkling and restore brightness. Half a cup of borax added to the normal washing machine cycle serves the same purpose, particularly when the clothes are dried in the sunshine afterwards.

Whitening wool White woollens tend to go yellow after several washes. To restore their brightness, soak them for an hour before washing in a solution of one part hydrogen peroxide (from pharmacies and supermarkets) to ten parts water, plus a few drops of ammonia. Rinse well, putting a little blue in the water.

STARCHING Starching makes linens and cottons look fresh and crisp and helps to stop dirt and stains from soaking into the fibres. After rinsing, dip articles into starch and water: experiment with the proportions until you achieve the required stiffness. Squeeze out excess moisture and hang the articles until nearly dry or roll them in a clean cloth to be ironed when damp. Iron on alternate sides till quite dry. Do not store starched items for long, as the fibres will deteriorate.

Potato starch Cover three or four large grated potatoes with water. Shake well and let stand for two hours. Shake again, and mix the pulp and water thoroughly with your hands. Remove the pulp and let the starch settle at the bottom of the container, then siphon off the water.

Rice starch Boil 1 cup of white rice in 1 litre of water until soft. Mash it with your hands, then strain out the grains while the mixture is still cloudy. Refrigerate this liquid in a sealed container, shaking it from time to time to stop the rice particles from settling.

Taking Care of the Pence

In the good old days, nothing was wasted in a well run household. Eggshells, known for their bleaching properties, were no exception. To bleach with eggshells, place a good number of eggshells in a cotton bag, tie the bag tightly, and boil it with clothing that needs whitening.

A WASHING RHYME

They that wash on Monday
Have all the week to dry;
They that wash on Tuesday
Are not so much awry;
They that wash on Wednesday
Are not so much to blame;
They that wash on Thursday
Wash for shame;
They that wash on Friday
Wash in need;
And they that wash on Saturday,
Oh! They're sluts indeed.

– TRADITIONAL

The Way We Were

The English writer Laurie Lee was born in a small valley in the Cotswolds in 1914. When he was three, the family moved house. Here he recalls the scullery in his new home:

'The scullery was water, where the old pump stood. And it had everything else that was related to water: thick steam of Mondays edgy with starch; soapsuds boiling, bellying and popping, creaking and whispering, rainbowed with light and winking with a million windows. Bubble bubble, toil and grumble, rinsing and slapping of sheets and shirts, and panting Mother rowing her red arms like oars in the steaming waves. Then the linen came up on a stick out of the pot, like pastry, or woven suds, or sheets of moulded snow.'

– *CIDER WITH ROSIE* (1959)

Sunshine and breezes

FOR MOST WASHABLE FABRICS, SUNSHINE AND FRESH
AIR ARE BY FAR THE BEST DRYING AGENTS, LEAVING
CLOTHES AND LINEN FRESH AND SWEET.

In earlier times, if washday was fine the clothes were hung
out as early as possible; in some neighbourhoods the back
yard or garden became a measure of housekeeping prowess,
with the state of the washing and the time it appeared
keenly judged. A wet washday brought the ordeal of drying
indoors, with clothes draped damply over racks and lines.

THE DRYING DAY Unhampered by the rigid routines of the past, we
can choose to wash on days other than Mondays or Tuesdays, and a fine
day with a good breeze is ideal.

NATURAL BLEACH Sunlight in summer and frost in winter are nature's
cost-free whitening agents for tough fibres such as cotton and linen.
Remember, however, that wool, silk and synthetics are easily damaged
and should not be frozen or exposed to direct sunlight.

Bleaching with sunshine Hang or spread out the washed articles
in bright sunlight. When they have dried, wet them once again, and
then leave them in the sun all day. This method of bleaching will not
weaken the fibres of the material.

Bleaching with frost Peg the wet articles on the line firmly or
spread them on the grass. Once the fabric fibres are hardened by the
frost, handle the articles with extreme care, removing them only after
they have thawed and the fabric is limp again. Frozen fabrics may tear
where they are attached to the line with pegs. To prevent this, wipe
the clothesline with a solution of equal parts of boiling water and salt.

CLOTHESLINE CLUES Your clothesline should be fixed securely,
stretched taut and kept clean. Wipe the line before use each time to
remove dust, bird droppings and other pollutants. A neat trick from
the past is to cut a slit in a large
cork and use this to clean the
clothesline. The cork can be kept
handy in the peg bag.

Clothes props Raise and tauten
a low, slack clothesline by means
of a clothes prop – a long, sturdy
piece of timber with a V-shaped
notch at one end to support the
line. In some parts of Australia,
during World War I, elderly
men made their way from door

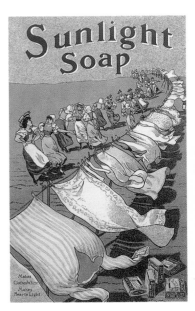

*In our grandmothers' day, women
took great pride in their washing.
Here, a seemingly endless line of
washing advertises the virtues
of Sunlight Soap to a string of
admiring women.*

The Way We Were

Writer Ruth Park, born in
1923, remembers washday
during the time of her New
Zealand childhood:

'Everything white . . . had to
be soaked, boiled, rinsed,
blued, and some starched,
before they were lugged out to
the clothes line, weighing a
tonne. Then the coloureds were
done, treated gently in case
they "ran" . . .

When the washing was dry it
was all lugged in again, the
tablecloths and sheets shaken
and cornered between my
mother and myself, other items
damped down for ironing, and
almost all ironed in the end.'

– *A FENCE AROUND THE CUCKOO*
(1992)

to door selling clothes props and relaying the latest on the Gallipoli campaign and other news from the battle front.

PEGGING OUT The humble clothes peg is a small, unobtrusive home appliance, not often found in the catalogue of really useful things but definitely worthy of a place there. Until the invention of plastics, clothes pegs were made of wire or wood. Split wooden pegs have been around for centuries; spring-action ones are a more recent invention. Although most clothes pegs these days are made of plastic, wooden ones are still available.

To prolong the life of new wooden pegs and prevent them splitting, soak them in cold water for 12 hours before use, and afterwards keep them clean and dry. It is not wise to leave pegs on the line between washes, as exposure to the elements quickly rots them. Store them in a hanging bag made of loosely woven fabric with a coat hanger sewn into the top and a slit opening, or in a small wicker basket, so that air reaches them when they are not in use. Scrub or boil wooden pegs occasionally, and discard faulty ones at once – it is surprising how often the broken ones come to hand if you do not do this.

DRYING Sunlight has its virtues but it hardens and shrinks woollens, yellows white silks, and fades colours, especially when fabrics are wet. While it is advantageous to dry white household linen and cotton clothing in sunlight, you should hang coloured items, flannels and woollens in breezy places away from the sun.

Hang out articles as soon after washing as possible – do not leave wet washing piled in the laundry basket while you wait for a break in the weather. If rain prevents you from drying things outdoors, hang them inside, allowing air to circulate through the drying space.

DRYING TIPS Grandma's drying rules can save you time and money.
• To minimise fading, turn garments inside out before hanging them.
• A good general rule is to peg out garments by their strongest parts: for example, skirts and trousers by the waistband; shirts, dresses and blouses by the shoulders or yoke; stockings and socks by the toes.
• Use enough pegs to ensure that garments are properly supported and do not pull at the pegged points as they flap in the breeze.
• Group garments as you peg them on the line, and hang socks in pairs. This pre-sorting saves time when it comes to putting things away, and is a good preventative measure for the lost-sock syndrome.
• If possible, dry knitted garments flat, spread out on an old piece of sheet or a towel. If you must dry them on the line, slip an old stocking through the sleeves and peg the stocking to the line to help support the weight of the jumper and to prevent peg marks.
• Dry lace curtains and thin fabrics in calm weather only.
• Peg one hem of a sheet or a large tablecloth straight along the clothesline, then bring up the two lower corners and peg them two thirds of the way along the top hem. The article will billow out like a sail and dry speedily in even the slightest breeze.
• If you have a garden with rosemary or lavender, spread articles such as pillowslips on the bushes to dry – they will smell wonderful.

THE HILL'S HOIST rotary clothesline was a refinement by Adelaide motor mechanic Lance Hill of an existing design. In 1945, Hill invented an 'easy-lift winder' to raise the hoist so that the washing would catch the breeze. Mass-production started in 1948, but there was a postwar shortage of metal tubing, so many of Hill's early hoists were made from parts of the submarine boom that was placed across the Sydney Heads during the war. The one millionth Hill's hoist rolled off the production line in 1991, and hoists are now marketed in Europe, Asia and North America.

Before the 1950s, clothes pegs were made of wood or wire. The split wooden pegs were called dolly pegs because of their rudimentary resemblance to the human form.

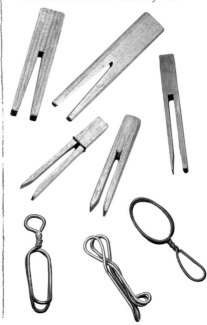

The smoothing iron

TEMPERATURE-CONTROLLED ELECTRIC IRONS HAVE MADE IRONING MUCH EASIER, BUT THE PRINCIPLES OF SUCCESSFUL IRONING HAVE NOT CHANGED.

Before the introduction of synthetics, ironing clothes was essential, not just to give that freshly pressed look but to drive out the last traces of moisture, especially in damp climates. Ironing used to be arduous, and sometimes painful, too, as burns frequently occurred. Flat irons, in pairs or threes, were heated on the stove or beside the fire and used in rotation; box irons contained hot coals or charcoal. Irons had to be free of smuts and the temperature tested by touch: a 1940s handbook sensibly cautioned against holding an iron against the face, advising instead a quick dab with a wet finger.

PREPARING TO IRON Always do your ironing on a smooth surface – several thicknesses of blanket covered with a piece of soft sheeting will be adequate, if you do not have an ironing board, although skirts, trousers and shirts are a good deal more difficult to iron without one. A ready-made ironing board should be firm, rigid and well padded with felt. Adjust the board to a comfortable height and keep the cover clean. A reasonably heavy iron is less tiring to use than a lighter one because you need to exert less pressure. Heat the iron to the required temperature before beginning, and test its effectiveness first on an inconspicuous part of the garment.

DAMPING DOWN In the past, many fabrics had to be damped with water before they were ironed. Steam irons have largely done away with this need, but damping just before ironing can still pay dividends, as it spreads the moisture deeply and evenly through the fibres. Sprinkle items with warm water, which penetrates the fabric more quickly than cold, and then roll them up tightly and put them to one side. Do not

FOLDING AND STORING A SHIRT
Here is a time-tested way of folding a shirt that you want to pack or store in a drawer or on a shelf.

1. After ironing (if necessary) and airing, button the shirt.

2. Turn the shirt face down and fold the first side halfway across the shoulder, placing the sleeve at a right angle to the side of the shirt. Then fold the sleeve down parallel to the side of the shirt. Repeat for the other side.

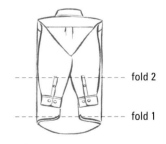

fold 2

fold 1

3. Fold the tail of the shirt up so that it covers the cuffs. Then fold it up from the bottom again to make a neat rectangular shape.

4. Pack or store the shirt face up, making sure that the collar is lying flat.

damp too long before ironing or put away articles that are still damp, as mildew may develop. Articles stored before they have been properly aired will also have a limp appearance, and coloured things may run.

IRONING TECHNIQUES Iron across the thread of the fabric, otherwise the article will not hang properly. Pull square and rectangular items, such as tea towels, scarves, napkins and handkerchiefs, into shape before ironing. Iron tucks from the top of the garment towards the bottom, and tack pleats into place before ironing them through a damp cloth. Immediately after ironing, hang dresses, blouses and shirts on coat hangers to air before putting them away.

Coloured fabrics 'Care should be taken that the iron is not too hot for coloured garments – which, by-the-bye, should always be ironed on the wrong side of the material', advised Mrs F. B. Aronson in *Twentieth Century Cooking and Home Decoration*, published in 1900. Her advice was right: the heat from an iron fades colours, just as sunlight does, but you can keep the damage to a minimum if you iron on the wrong side.

Linens and cottons Iron all household linens and cotton items damp and with a hot iron. If you iron sheets, fold them first in half, lengthwise, to make them less cumbersome to handle, and then iron them dry, making further folds as you go.

Silk Silk must be evenly damp when ironed; sprinkling silk with water to dampen it before ironing is not a good idea because it has a tendency to leave watermarks. Instead of fully drying the garment after you have washed it, roll it in a towel if the colours are fast. Just before ironing, shake the garment out and hang it up. Iron on the wrong side of the fabric with a moderately hot iron (never with a hot one) and then lightly finish it on the right side.

Woollens Knitted woollen garments and woollen fabrics need gentle treatment and should be pressed rather than ironed. Press them on the wrong side through a damp cloth, using a cool iron.

REMOVING SCORCH MARKS If the scorching is only slight, dampen the area that has been affected and place the article in strong sunlight for a few hours. For restoring whiteness to linen that has been severely scorched, provided the threads of the fabric have not been burned through, soak a piece of linen or muslin in a solution of three per cent hydrogen peroxide (from pharmacies), place it over the damaged area and then press with a hot iron. Before applying the peroxide, use a small pad to test it on an inconspicuous part of the fabric to make sure that it does not lift the colour.

CLEANING THE IRON Keep the bottom of your iron clean by rubbing it from time to time with a cloth that has been soaked in strong cold tea, and then wiping it with a clean, soft cloth. Rub a cold iron with a cut lemon to remove accumulated brown stains, then wipe it with a damp cloth and polish with a dry one. If the iron has become sticky, run it back and forth while hot over a sheet of clean paper that has been sprinkled generously with salt.

A box iron had a hollow base that was filled with red-hot coals or charcoal. When the iron began to cool, the user would swing it around to create a breeze that would reignite the coals.

Save the legs of old pyjama trousers to make covers for the ironing board. One leg, secured with large safety pins, will fit smoothly over the board. It is easily removed for washing and cheap to replace when it is scorched or worn.

A Glorious Washing Day

The availability of alternating current at the beginning of the 20th century led to low-priced electricity supplies. By 1911, many homes in Europe and America were all-electric, but wiring Australian houses for power-driven appliances took a little longer. And what a difference the miraculous current made! With electricity came the electric iron, the electric-powered washing machine, and constant running hot water, which cut short the hours of dreary household drudgery and made backache on laundry day and injuries from 'sad irons' (heavy irons) things of the past.

The first electric washing machines appeared on the market in 1910. They replaced a partially mechanised system of washing, in which clothes were placed in a tub of boiling water known as a copper, and stirred with a 'wash dolly' – a short wooden pole with handles at the top and prongs or paddles at the bottom – to loosen and remove the dirt. Before their electrical equivalents, irons had to be heated on top of the stove and their temperature gauged by holding them against the cheek or the back of the hand.

WASHING BY HAND

In rural areas, such as in Tennessee, where this photograph was taken, doing the washing was an even more primitive affair than it was in the cities. Until well into the 20th century, it was not unusual to see women scrubbing garments in water and then pounding them on the side of a trough to loosen the dirt.

SOAP BARS AND SOAP POWDERS

Research into the constituents of oils and fats and improvements in soap manufacture resulted in wide-scale production of bar soap towards the end of the 19th century. Soap powder was developed in 1903 by two German chemists, Hermann Geissler and Hermann Bauer.

"PRESERVES MY HANDS"

KENDALL MFG. Cos
ESTABLISHED 1827
Soapine
THE Dirt Killer
WILL NOT INJURE HANDS & FABRIC
PROVIDENCE.R.I.
SOLD BY ALL GROCERS

ELECTRIFYING THE IRON

Double-pointed irons in sets of three with a detachable handle were devised by a Mrs Potts of Iowa between 1867 and 1871. By 1938, domestic steam irons came with an adjustable thermostat.

IRONING PLEATS

Ironing complicated garments such as pleated skirts was a routine matter for our grandmothers. These days most pleats are ready pressed, but the older garments in your wardrobe may require special attention.

1. Tack each pleat down with large cross-stitches, working from the top of the skirt to the bottom.

2. Place a damp cloth over the skirt and, working again from the top, press with a hot iron.

3. Hang the garment to dry the moisture out, and then carefully remove the tacking from the pleats.

THE AUTOMATIC WASHER

The American inventor Alva Fisher mechanised the wash dolly in 1907 and produced the first automatic washer. Machines using Fisher's system, such as this Míele model, were produced until the 1950s.

LOOK WHAT I'VE GOT!

Proudly she shows off her new acquisition – a Kelvinator washing machine with a removable agitator. Fully automatic washing machines did not come onto the market until the early 1950s.

Ring up the curtain!

RENOVATING CURTAINS IS AN ECONOMICAL
ALTERNATIVE TO FITTING NEW ONES. HOUSEWIVES
IN THE FIRST HALF OF THE 20TH CENTURY KNEW
HOW TO GET THE VERY MOST FROM CURTAINS.

It is not just the outlay on fabric that makes curtains costly: replacing
curtains draws attention to other decorating needs, and paintwork,
carpets and upholstery may then need changing too. You can often
give curtains a lift with some simple strategies and a little sewing.
Many curtains are washable and laundering will keep them fresh, but
if they are not washable there are other ways of sprucing them up.

WASHING TIPS Curtains require some specialised washing know-how.
• Take curtains outside and shake them vigorously before washing to
get rid of the worst of the dust.
• Before washing curtains for the first time, soak them overnight in
water to which plenty of salt has been added. This will remove the
dressing from the fabric and help to set the colours.
• After washing fringed curtains, comb the wet fringe with a wide-
toothed comb; it will look like new when dry.

WASHING CRETONNE AND CHINTZ Cretonne is a heavy printed cotton
with a matte finish used to make curtains and loose covers; chintz is
similar, but has a glazed finish. These instructions are for hand washing.

Light-coloured cretonne Wash in the same way as coloured prints,
making sure the water is not too hot. Starch with equal quantities of
starch and cold water. Dry until still quite damp to the touch all over.
Iron on the wrong side to preserve the matte finish.

Dark-coloured cretonne and chintz Prepare bran water as given
in the recipe below. Add a little melted soap to it, and salt in the
proportion of 1 tablespoon to 4 litres of water. Wash by squeezing; do
not rub. Rinse in bran water with salt added. Cover with a cloth, fold
once, then wring. Iron immediately on the wrong side with a hot iron.

Preparing bran water Place a cup of bran in a litre of water and
bring slowly to the boil. Simmer 20 minutes, then strain. Combine
with an equal quantity of tepid water. Bran water has both stiffening
and cleansing properties, ideal for washing cretonne and chintz.

HAND WASHING WHITE MUSLIN AND NET CURTAINS Prepare a tub of
warm water and melted soap, and borax or a little vinegar. Shake the
curtains well, then leave them to soak overnight in the prepared
liquid. Squeeze the surplus water from the curtains and place them in
a tub filled with warm water. Knead to remove the dirt; do not rub.
Place the curtains in a pillowcase and boil for 20 minutes. Rinse well.
Starch in thin, boiled starch. Squeeze out excess water; do not twist.

*Simple or dressy, curtains repay
careful handling by remaining
fresh and attractive for years.*

The Way We Were

In Britain, World War II and
the black-out forced people to
adopt a new, unfashionable and
unwelcome style of curtaining,
which did not always keep its
place as window dressing:

'Black-out material was soon
covering almost as many
British women as windows; a
black dirndl skirt, decorated
with rows of brightly-coloured
tape, could, one woman found,
look very attractive. A Woking
woman bleached black-out
material to make a "glamorous"
evening top to wear with a long
black skirt – "black-out
material of course" – and a
Hereford woman wore "black-
out slacks and a blouse made
from a net curtain." Black-out
material was also used for
petticoats.'

– *HOW WE LIVED THEN,*
NORMAN LONGMATE (1971)

Fold the curtains, wrong side out, over the line and peg each end. The centre must be on the line, and the edges gently pulled straight, with corners meeting. Pull gently into shape occasionally while drying; this should save you the trouble of ironing.

IRONING CURTAINS Ironing curtains can be tricky, especially if they are long. Our grandmothers reduced the labour in a number of ways.

Long curtains Fold a long curtain lengthwise and iron it to within about 2.5 cm of the fold, keeping the selvage straight. Unfold it and iron the strip in the middle that you omitted. The curtain will then have no trace of a centre fold.

Madras curtains Dampen the curtains with warm water, then roll up and leave for 30 minutes. Beginning with the hem and frill, iron the wrong side only with a moderately hot iron.

FRESHENING VELVET CURTAINS Take velvet curtains outside to freshen them. Place a curtain face down on a table and whip it with a cane to remove dust. Brush the back of the fabric, then turn it over and brush the pile with a stiff brush. Make a dryish mix of oatmeal and petrol and sprinkle it on the right side. Brush it all over the curtain, then brush it out and shake the fabric. Do not touch the damp pile, as you will leave fingermarks. If possible, hang the curtains in the bathroom over a hot bath to lift the pile.

DYEING FADED CURTAINS Sunlight tends to fade curtains unevenly. Dyeing may not entirely hide the streaks but it certainly minimises them. Choose a colour that is deeper than the original but similar, and follow the instructions carefully. Let down hems before dyeing to allow for shrinkage, re-hemming when the curtains are dry. Curtains should be clean and still thoroughly damp when you immerse them in the dye. Press newly dyed curtains before they dry; if you dampen them as you iron, the material may develop a spotty look.

RESTORING SHRUNKEN CURTAINS If curtains have shrunk, lengthen them with a band of harmonising fabric – choose plain for patterned curtains, patterned for plain. Or a valance can be used to conceal a band of fabric added to the top of a curtain.

Nothing evokes the carefree summer days of childhood like fresh, fragrant curtains caressing a leadlight window.

Cleaning without water

IN THE PAST, THE HIGH PRICE OF GOOD COMMERCIAL
DRY-CLEANING ENCOURAGED PEOPLE TO DEVISE
HOME METHODS OF CLEANING WITHOUT WATER.

In fact dry-cleaning is a misnomer, as many processes require articles
to be treated with fluids other than water or sponged with substances
dissolved in water. Some old-fashioned dry-cleaning processes dowsed
garments in highly flammable liquids. These methods, risky both for
people and the environment, are not recommended now, but cleaning
with dry ingredients from the pantry – such as bran, salt, rice and
cornmeal – can be successful. Virtually all home dry-cleaning
techniques tend to be messy, and are best practised out-of-doors.

PREPARING FOR DRY-CLEANING Do not put soiled garments away for
long periods; stains that have been allowed to soak into the fibres and
set may be impossible to dislodge. So treat winter clothes at the end of
the season, not only to make cleaning easier but also to deter moths
and silverfish. Whatever the material, go over it thoroughly with a
soft-bristled clothes brush to remove all the dust. When brushing
satin or broadcloth, be careful to brush with the nap of the fabric.

GENERAL-PURPOSE DRY-CLEANER A mixture of water and fuller's earth
(from hardware and craft shops) will remove grease and oil from felt
hats and other smooth fabric surfaces. Fuller's earth is an absorbent
clay with a gentle cleaning action. Mix the fuller's earth with water to
the consistency of paste and spread it over the soiled area. Allow the
paste to dry, and then remove it with a stiff brush.

BRAN DRY-CLEANER A bran and flour mixture is effective for cleaning
light-coloured fabrics. Heat equal quantities of bran and flour in the
oven, turning frequently to avoid browning. When the mixture is as
hot as you can get it, spread it over the soiled fabric and rub it well in
as quickly as possible. Immediately fold the hot garment in a towel
and put away for two or three days. Then unwrap the garment and
give it a good shake. Brush off any remaining bran.

DRY-CLEANING LEATHER Leather is best cleaned by a professional, but
you can give a facelift to a well-worn leather garment. Cover it with a
paste of pipeclay – a fine, white, pure clay – and water, rubbing one
way only, working from the base to the top. Allow the paste to dry
completely and then shake the garment until all traces of
the clay have disappeared.

Restoring suede To restore a suede coat,
rub all over with a piece of towel dipped
in bran. Shake well, then rub lightly
with fine sandpaper to restore the pile.

*Fur collars or muffs were once
treasured possessions which also
benefitted from dry-cleaning at
home. Heated bran was gently
rubbed into the fur, then a soft
brush was used to remove the
bran before the items were hung
outside on a clear day to air.*

Words of Wisdom

'Really, I cannot see any more
sense in a grand cleaning day
for clothes than I can see it in a
huge turning out period for the
home. Repairing and cleaning
as the individual article needs it
saves time; keeps one's self
respect in working order; makes
one's goods and chattels last
longer and saves one's friends
from developing spots before
their eyes.'

– *HELEN'S WEEKLY* (1927)

DRY-CLEANING VELVET AND PLUSH Fabrics of this kind have a fine, delicate pile that can collect dust, making them look tired and dull. Treat them with a brush of medium stiffness, brushing against the pile for velvet and with the pile for plush, then hang them in a bathroom over a hot bath for a while to allow the steam to revive the pile. Do not attempt to clean dirty marks from velvet or plush – this is best left to the professionals.

Rejuvenating a velvet collar Mix 3 teaspoons of ammonia with 300 ml of water, moisten the corner of a towel with the mixture, and rub the velvet collar thoroughly. Use a wooden paper knife to remove the froth that forms as you do this. Repeat the process three or four times, using a clean portion of the towel each time. Finally, place a clean, damp piece of linen over the collar and press firmly but carefully with a moderately hot iron.

DRY-CLEANING WOOLLENS Many modern woollen fabrics are washable, by hand or even in the washing machine, but nonwashable woollens can still eat up a good proportion of your dry-cleaning budget. Try some of these old methods instead.

Salt Dry salt is excellent for cleaning woollen coats, dresses and skirts. You will also need a pad of linen, folded a number of times. Lay the garment on a table and scatter a thin layer of salt all over it, spreading it evenly with your fingertips. Next, use the linen pad to rub the salt into the cloth, using long sweeping strokes towards the hem of the garment. Do not rub in a circular motion, as this roughens the surface of the fabric. Ensure that every part of the garment is thoroughly rubbed in this way. Slip the garment onto a coat hanger and then brush it vigorously with a stiff clothes brush to remove all the salt. Vulnerable areas such as cuffs, collars and hems may require a second application of salt before they are really clean.

Ground rice Finely ground rice is an effective cleaner for white or light-coloured wool garments. Ground rice is available from large supermarkets, or you can grind rice grains to a fine powder in a coffee-mill. Apply as described above for salt, but leave the powder on the garment for several hours before brushing it out. Tie a scarf round your head so that your hair will not become coated and sticky with powdered rice.

REMOVING RAINDROPS Being caught in the rain in a nonwashable garment may leave you with the problem of rain spotting. The droplets are easy to remove while they are still damp. Keep a scrap of clean, soft silk cloth in a pocket or your handbag and use it to gently rub the rainspots off. Always rub with the weave of the material, not against it, and the marks will disappear.

Try removing lint or hair from woollen clothing by dabbing the surface of the fabric with a moistened rubber sponge. This is more effective and kinder to clothing than a brush, which means that good garments will last longer.

Before World War II, few men owned more than one suit. This 1930s pressing business came up with a novel way of bringing in the customers.

In store and in transit

WHEN STORING CLOTHES, GIVE THEM ENOUGH SPACE — THERE IS LITTLE POINT IN IRONING THINGS ONLY TO SQUEEZE THEM INTO FRESH CREASES.

In 1914, one fashion writer lamented that 'the crowded state' of the wardrobe was responsible for coats emerging looking 'fit only for the rummage sale', and that carelessly stuffing 'unfortunate neck and waist wear' into drawers 'all anyhow' made it look 'deplorable'. When packing, remember that too little space crushes the clothes and too much allows them to move about, with equally disastrous results.

THE IMPORTANCE OF AIRING Clothes should be well aired before you put them away: ideally in the sunshine, or else in front of a heater. It is important to air things that have been damped for ironing or ironed with a steam iron.

Air winter coats, dresses and suits after wearing and give them an outdoor airing from time to time. Do not wear the same winter clothes day after day: fabrics appreciate a rest.

Air household linen before storing it. Slip articles that will not be used for a while inside old pillowcases or cover them with old sheets.

COAT HANGER COMFORT Use padded coat hangers for jackets and topcoats — simply wrap old stockings securely round a wooden coat hanger and cover with pretty fabric. Or buy wooden tailor's hangers, especially made to support weighty garments. Make sure you centre garments properly, one to a hanger, otherwise your clothes will look lopsided next time you wear them. Do not hang skirts and trousers by the belt loops; support the whole waistband in a spring-clip hanger. Fasten all buttons and zips.

SPREADING THE WEAR Put freshly ironed linen, towels, underwear and handkerchiefs underneath existing piles. This ensures that they are used in rotation, and avoids that crushed, slightly dingy look that items acquire from having been at the bottom of the pile for too long.

CLOTHES MOTHS The larvae of clothes moths feast on woollens and furs. Fabrics made from synthetic and plant fibres, or that are stained with perspiration or other animal products, attract them, too. Adult clothes moths do not feed: they concentrate on producing the next generation, the females often depositing their eggs in the folds of clothing. Put things away clean.

Caution: If moths have already laid their eggs in your blankets and clothing before you put them away, none of the following repellents will prevent the larvae beginning to munch as soon as they hatch.

Moth repellents were available in the 1940s, but anything sharply aromatic, such as cloves, will keep moths away.

The Way We Were

In parts of Australia, not only do moths and silverfish devour fabrics, but plagues of hungry mice also appear:

'There was a very wet year about 1916 and the same year we had a terrible lot of mice. Oh I tell you we did. We had to take all the curtains from the windows and pack 'em in a case; they'd eat everything … All the blankets and sheets had to be packed away. Ooh they did so much damage … At that time we only had straw in our mattresses and you'd hear them nibbling at that in the night. They'd run all over your head to get to it and there was nothing you could do except wait until they were ready to leave the place.'

– WHEN GRANDMA WAS JUST A GIRL, MARTIN MCADOO (1983)

Moth repellents The secret of keeping moths at bay is to make your wardrobes and drawers unattractive to them by keeping them free from dust and fluff, vacuuming them regularly and, from time to time, wiping them over with a repellent, such as eucalyptus oil. Alternatively, you could scatter cotton wool balls dipped in oil of cinnamon among your woollens.

Newsprint was once popular for lining drawers, as it was thought an effective moth deterrent, but today's newsprint is too dirty for the purpose. Instead, line your drawers with brown paper, butcher's paper or wallpaper off-cuts. Cut a piece larger than the drawer by about 5 cm all round, place the paper right side down in the drawer and fold in the edges. Then remove the paper, scatter cloves or powdered camphor in the drawer, and put the paper back in right way up.

Fragrant sachets Sachets in drawers and hung in the wardrobe give freshness to your clothes and discourage silverfish and moths. Make the sachets of light fabric such as muslin, and fill them with a mixture of 30 grams each of ground cloves, nutmeg, mace, caraway seeds and cinnamon, and 90 grams of orris root powder. Trim sachets with ribbons or beads – they make pretty and useful gifts. Replace them when the scent begins to fade.

SILVERFISH Silverfish – wingless insects, so called because they are covered with silver scales and move rapidly – normally live indoors and are found virtually worldwide. They like materials containing starch and, while their preferred diet is wallpaper and bookbindings, they also eat fabrics. Like clothes moths, silverfish are repelled by sharp scents – eucalyptus oil is particularly repugnant to them.

THE ART OF PACKING Travelling was altogether more leisurely before 1950. While fabrics have become ever more resilient and uncrushable, magazine articles from the 1920s on the art of packing clothes still have value, especially if you are packing for long-term storage.

Basic rules Collect everything for packing in one spot before you start, so you are not tempted to cram articles in at the last minute. Hats should be placed in their own boxes with the crowns filled with tissue paper. Mount shoes on shoe trees or stuff them with paper. Heavy articles should go at the bottom of the case or be packed separately. Then pack in layers, putting in the heaviest clothing first, then underclothes and socks, then shirts, dresses and blouses.

Folding Tissue paper is seldom used for packing these days but it deserves to come back. Turn jackets and coats inside out. Stuff sleeves with tissue paper and spread the garment on the bed, pulling the collar up. Put the sleeves in their proper position, fold the fronts over at each side, and the coat down the middle. Double to fit in the case.

Fold trousers along their original creases down the legs. Insert a roll of tissue paper when they fold back to fit into the case. Lay skirts flat and fold in the fullness on either side. Cover with tissue paper and fold the skirt in three, from the waist downwards, with tissue paper between the folds. Pack pleated skirts in cardboard cylinders.

It is the larvae of clothes moths that eat your woollies, so the aim is to deter females from laying their eggs in your wardrobe.

We generally travel lighter than our grandparents did, but the packing techniques they used are ideal for folding garments for long-term storage.

Colour changes

DYEING FABRICS, USING EITHER NATURAL
DYES EXTRACTED FROM PLANTS OR COMMERCIALLY
AVAILABLE DYES, IS AN AGE-OLD ACTIVITY.

*Commercial dyes have been used
for years to transform clothing
and household items. This 1921
advertisement is for a washing
powder and dye combined.*

In the good old days, all sorts of fabrics, from cheesecloth
to silk georgette, were dyed successfully. People also dyed
woollen yarn and fabrics. The key to home dyeing is
experimentation – try plants from your garden, or create
shades by mixing commercial dyes. Some fabrics dye better
than others; synthetics are not easy to dye at home.

WHAT DYEING CAN DO Cold-water dyes are best suited to
tinting fine-textured materials, such as silk or muslin;
boiling dyes are more satisfactory for obtaining fast colours.
Remember that fast-coloured cloth can be dyed darker but
not lighter. White, cream or neutral shades take colour
changes best, and loosely woven fabrics generally dye better than
closely woven ones. Wool dyes more readily than cotton, and cotton
more readily than silk. Test scraps of fabric beforehand.

Caution: Dyeing will not restore an even colour to articles that are
already badly streaked or blotchy, nor will it cover up stains.

Over-dyeing The original colour of the fabric affects the result. Blue
dye on red is apt to produce purple. Green fabrics can be dyed dark
blue, dark red, purple and brown. Blue fabrics generally do best if
limited to dark green or dark brown. Pale pink fabrics will take
almost any colour. The following chart is a useful starting point.

USING COMMERCIAL DYES Commercial dyes are now available in a
wide range of both liquid and powder forms, and processes use either
cold, warm or boiling water. Follow the instructions on the packet.

Preparing to dye Using hot-water dyes is simple, if messy, so wear
rubber gloves and protective clothes.

The quantity of dye depends on the weight of the fabric, and results
depend on the proportion of fabric to dye. If in doubt, make the dye a
little light, as you can always add more. Before adding extra dye,
remove the articles from the vessel, then pour in the mixed dye and
replace the articles. The dye darkens as the boiling proceeds.

The metal vessel for dyeing must be rustproof and large enough to
hold enough water to cover the article and leave room for you to move
it around. Mix the dye and add salt as directed.

Remove buttons and metal fittings from the articles to be dyed and
let hems down in case of shrinkage. Articles must be clean and moist,
so wash them first and put them in the dye while they are still damp.

Stirring the dye Hot-water dyes should boil before you place the
article in the solution. Bring to the boil again for about five minutes

ORIGINAL COLOUR	DYE	FINAL COLOUR
Red	Yellow	Scarlet
Red	Blue	Purple
Blue	Yellow	Green
Pale blue	Pink	Lavender
Yellow	Pink	Coral
Green	Brown	Olive
Purple	Yellow	Light brown
Orange	Pink	Coral

and then simmer for up to to 45 minutes for a fast colour. Keep the cloth submerged. The colour must reach every part of the fabric: use a long-handled wooden spoon to stir the brew and lift the material to spread the solution through seams. When the boiling is finished, allow the contents to cool, continuing to stir. Rinse well in running water and hang the articles to drip. Iron while still damp all over. *Caution:* Wash home-dyed articles separately and always iron them damp. Dampening dyed articles before ironing may cause spotting.

NATURAL DYES In 1920 an Australian women's magazine claimed that the German discovery of aniline dyes, derived from coal tar, had 'dealt a death-blow to many a pleasing and romantic home industry'. But, of course, it is still possible to gather plants that yield subtle colours that are well suited to dyeing cotton and homespun wool.

Preparing natural dyes This takes time, and most require a mordant – a compound to fix the colour. The mordant is usually alum, in the form of crystals (from pharmacies, craft shops and hardware stores). Other mordants are chrome, tin and copper.

To yield good dyes, flowers should be fresh and leaves and stalks tender. Berries work best when fresh and overripe. Be sparing with alum and tin, and handle chrome with care because it is poisonous.

Many plant materials – flowers, leaves, berries, roots and bark – make superb dyes in softly vibrant natural shades.

Words of Wisdom

'When tinting white clothes any colour, mix a pinch of bicarb of soda in the hot water used for making the dye mixture. This makes the dye spread evenly and avoids patchiness and streaks.'

– *MY MOTHER'S WAYS,*
MARY MURRAY (1996)

Soak flowers, leaves or roots for at least 12 hours in just enough cold water to cover them – rainwater is best. Soak bark for a month. Then boil the mixture for one to two hours for leaves and at least 45 minutes for flowers. Leave for 24 hours, boil again, and strain. You will need about a litre of solution to every 25 grams of cloth. Place the fabric or yarn in the dye and heat to a simmer. Remove the article, add the mordant – a level teaspoon for every 100 grams of yarn or cloth – and mix. Return the articles to the vessel and simmer for one to 24 hours; the colour will intensify with time. Do not boil, as it may destroy the colour. Let the article cool in the dye, or take it out and rinse well, first in hot water and then in progressively cooler rinses.

Dyes from some common plants Comfrey leaves yield a yellow dye with a tin mordant, or an orange-yellow dye with a chrome mordant. You can also make a pale yellow dye with dandelions, using either flowers with a tin mordant or roots, scrubbed and chopped, with an alum mordant. Lily-of-the-valley leaves and stalks give a blue-green dye with an alum mordant, or a green dye with a chrome mordant.

Dyes from lichen Lichens produce a wide range of lovely yellows, browns and reds. Simmer lichens for several hours to produce a good colour, which will deepen when you add a mordant.

Dyes from native Australian plants The leaves of many eucalyptus species yield soft-coloured, fast dyes when boiled without a mordant, although alum enhances the results. Kangaroo paw leaves or the flowers and leaves of Sturt's desert pea produce pretty pinks.

TIE-DYEING AND BATIK These are specialised dyeing techniques that produce intricate and original patterns. In tie-dyeing, fabric is tied or stitched together to prevent the dye from penetrating. Batik uses melted wax to prevent the fabric from absorbing the dye.

Combining techniques A 1920 issue of an Australian women's magazine describes a way to combine tie-dyeing and batik on the same fabric. You will need a material that will accept dye, plus marbles, thread, fabric dyes, beeswax melted in a saucepan, and a brush.

Twist portions of the fabric around several marbles (see diagram, top right). Tie with multiple strands of thread dipped in the melted beeswax. Dip the fabric into the first dye and leave it for a few minutes; the thread round the marbles prevents the dye being taken up and forms intricate abstract patterns.

When the first colour is dry, remove the threads; the fabric is now ready for the second dye. If you want to keep the first shade for any part, use the brush to coat both sides of that area of the fabric with beeswax. For easy spreading, keep the wax quite liquid over a low heat.

Dip the fabric in cold water and rinse carefully, then put the fabric into the second dye while it is still damp, ensuring that the dye is not hot enough to melt the wax. After about five minutes, lift it out and put it into cold water, stirring with a stick. With a hot iron, press the fabric between sheets of paper until all the wax is removed.

MARBLES, KNOTS AND BEESWAX
You can make intriguing tie-dyed patterns by using a mix of readily available materials.

Before tie-dyeing, use waxed thread to tie portions of the fabric around various small objects. Instead of marbles, you could use cherry stones, pebbles, corks, buttons, or anything else that your imagination suggests.

Colourful dyes are readily available from nature; you can use dandelion flowers to achieve a pale yellow dye.

Making over and making do

REFURBISHING OR ALTERING GARMENTS IS
A REWARDING CHALLENGE, PARTICULARLY IF
YOU HAVE A GROWING FAMILY.

When Lewis Carroll's Alice fell down the rabbit hole and
swallowed the *Drink Me* potion and *Eat Me* cake that made her
small and large, her clothes shrank and expanded with her.
Real children's clothes are not so accommodating – kids grow,
leaving their hemlines behind them. Our foremothers knew ways of
making skirts and dresses last two or three seasons for little girls, who
grow upwards more quickly than they grow outwards.

*With basic sewing skills and a
little time, you can give an outfit
a new lease on life in an hour or
two at the sewing machine.*

HEMLINES Sewing for children is frequently a race to keep up with
their rate of growth. Tucks and inset bands are simple but effective
strategies for lengthening garments (see side column). False hems are
another way to solve the problem.

Tucks Include one or two tucks in skirts and dresses for growing
girls. Placed a short distance above the hemline, they will be a design
feature – and they can be unpicked when the extra length is needed.

Bands Bands of contrasting fabric can be added to lengthen skirts:
at the bottom to make a wide hem; as an inset above the original hem;
or as hip bands. Choose the fabric carefully, and the bands will look
like an attractive feature rather than an attempt to economise.

False hems A false hem is an invisible way of letting down a coat
or skirt to its extreme length. Unpick the existing hem and brush the
inside fold to get rid of any fluff. Press under a damp cloth, treating
the original hemline mark as outlined below in 'Vanishing tricks'.
Stitch a strip of matching material or toning lining fabric to the hem
edge with the two right sides facing. Turn the strip over to the inside
so that the joining seam is at least 5 mm up from the new hem crease.
Pin and tack, then stitch down the false hem securely.

Vanishing tricks To remove old hemlines, dissolve ¼ teaspoon of
borax in 1 cup of hot water and add ½ teaspoon of vinegar. Wring a
cloth out in this solution, place it on the wrong side of the garment
and press firmly with a hot iron. Brush the garment when dry; the
hem marks should have disappeared.

  Sometimes nothing will shift a fold mark, so try a cover-up. With a
small amount of machining, you can hide the fold mark beneath a
length of contrasting or matching braid. Placing matching braid on
other parts of the garment, such as the cuffs and the neckline, creates
an overall trimming effect.

TUCKS AND BANDS
Try these fashionable tricks to keep
pace with your child's growth needs.

Make horizontal tucks in the skirt of a
new dress and unpick them when the
time comes for that extra length.

Lengthen a skirt by insetting a band and
adding a hem piece in a fabric to
contrast with the main garment.

Alternatively, add extra length by
insetting contrasting bands of fabric
around the hip area.

SLEEVES To slow down the rate at which children outgrow long sleeves, you should cut out the sleeves 2.5 cm longer than the pattern when making the garment. Take up the extra material in a tuck just above the cuff band on the inside, where it will not show. When necessary, the tuck thread can be easily unpicked and the sleeve instantly lengthened.

WORN POCKETS It is hard to imagine that in Britain during and immediately after World War II, fabrics were in such short supply that pockets were regarded as superfluous and government regulations did not permit the 'utility' styles to have them.

In these less difficult times we take pockets so much for granted that they suffer a fair bit of strain from carrying sharp or heavy objects, such as pens, coins and keys. Repairing or replacing a pocket is not a difficult operation.

There's a hole in my pocket With a little skill, you can replace holed pockets in jackets and trousers with strong new bottoms of hard-wearing drill or calico. Cut off the worn part well above the damage and open the side seams a little. Stitch a generous piece of new fabric to each cut edge with a run-and-fell seam, which avoids raw edges and bulky seams. Then seam around the edges to make a pocket shape, and trim and bind the seam to ensure that the new pocket piece is firm and secure.

Patch pockets Patch pockets have a tendency to tear away at the corners. To remedy this, unpick the pocket corner and place a strip of cotton over the torn area on the wrong side of the material. Fasten the strip in position with firm running stitches in matching thread. Turn to the right side of the material and reinforce the repair with light darning, then firmly reattach the pocket corner. The repair will be unobtrusive and strong.

LEATHER PATCHES Tweed sports jackets are invariably 'old friends', much loved by their owners, and the natural processes of wear and tear and possible separation cause pain. Leather elbow patches and leather strips along sleeve ends, fronts and pocket edges reinforce the worn fabric, have a certain sartorial distinction, and will delay the final moment of parting for several years. Elbow patches are a good remedy for worn elbows in a favourite woollen jumper, too.

Out at the elbows Choose soft, supple leather in a colour that tones with the material of the jacket. Cut out two ovals, making sure that they are large enough to completely cover the hole or worn patch with a generous allowance all around. Use button thread, or any other strong thread, to sew the patch over the hole with buttonhole stitch or blanket stitch. Do not make the stitching too tight or the leather may split when the elbow is flexed.

Pockets, sleeves and fronts Bind the frayed edges of pockets, sleeves, and jacket fronts with strips of toning leather.

ISAAC MERRIT SINGER'S 1851 invention, the sewing machine, was one of the first significant domestic labour-saving devices. Singer's was not the first sewing machine to be invented, but it was the best. By the early 20th century, many women throughout the western world owned a Singer, with its distinctive solid wood and cast iron stand and gold detailing on a black enamel background.

Words of Wisdom

'Sometimes "making over" can have a value that has nothing to do with thrift. When my father died suddenly and we had the sad task of sorting his clothes, I found a shirt that I had loved to see him in. The collar and cuffs were badly frayed, so I cut them off to make a close-fitting round neck and three-quarter sleeves, which I bound with fabric trimmed from the shirt tails. I wore that shirt for years, until it literally fell to pieces on my back. And every time I wore it, I thought of my father.'

– ANONYMOUS (UNPUBLISHED)

TOO GOOD TO THROW AWAY Cotton dresses and skirts that have lost their original appeal can often be made over into serviceable aprons – coat, pinafore, smock or waist in style. Remove the sleeves and enlarge the armholes for ease of movement. Cut away other restricting or worn parts of the garment and hem or bind the raw edges. Garments that already have external pockets are useful, but it is easy to add large patch pockets in plain or contrasting fabrics to hold household items or pegs.

THE LEGACY OF LACE Romantic and alluring lace blends well with almost any other material: it is the fabric of the Church, of brides, of grand old ladies and elegant femininity. Use old and new lace to rejuvenate garments in as many ways as your imagination and sewing skills allow. It is especially effective when used to recycle evening wear, which does not wear out but does go in and out of fashion. The old saying, 'A lady might as well be off the earth as out of style', does not apply to garments that have been rescued with lace collars, bows, bodices, peplums, belts or jackets. And lace is equally at home in the daytime, where it looks especially charming as insets in full skirts.

MAKING OVER CLOTHING Women's periodicals, especially during World War I, encouraged the practice of making over adult garments for children. Articles advised that those coats, dresses, trousers and skirts that had already done 'yeoman service' and might have a 'hopeless look about them' could still be turned into smart and serviceable juvenile clothing. If you embark on this thrifty activity, the following hints may be helpful.

Tips for clothing remakes
- Unpick the garment and remove all the fluff from around the seams.
- Wash and press the pieces.
- Check if the material might be better re-used wrong side out.
- Avoid using places where pockets have been.
- Use a paper pattern for the 'new' garment and move the pieces about until you have the best fit. If you have to join the material to accommodate the pattern, make the joins as inconspicuous as possible.
- Double stitch seams where you can.
- Use new stiffening, where required, and new trimmings, such as buttons and braid.

RECYCLING KNITTING WOOL Used knitting wool can be revived by steaming it. Unravel the knitted garment, winding the wool around a fairly large square of cardboard. Next, hold the card over boiling water. Keep turning the card and moving it to and fro until the wool is evenly damp. Leave the wool on the card until it is dry, then wind it into balls, and it is ready to be knitted up again with much of its natural resilience restored.

The Way We Were

'After the Depression, Mum was good at making do and going without. She made my sister's first long "deb" dress out of white curtain net, trimmed with green ribbons, and she unpicked clothes to remake them as well as jumpers to reknit the wool.'

– *THE HOME FRONT FAMILY ALBUM* (1991)

Knitted garments for children were amongst the most versatile of all clothing. When they started to look tired, or were outgrown, the wool could be unravelled and used to knit something else.

New lease of life

UNTIL ABOUT 1950, 'WASTE NOT, WANT NOT'
WAS A WAY OF LIFE, NOT FOR ENVIRONMENTAL
REASONS BUT BECAUSE OF SHORTAGES.

One 1930s magazine contained instructions for placing newspaper
layers between two old blankets and then covering them with flannel
to make a 'warm' rug. In the Australian bush, where the tyranny of
distance led to many innovations, 'waggas' made from sacks, old clothes
and blankets were popular bed covers. Other recycling ideas abounded.

BEDSPREADS INTO BATH MATS Thick cotton and candlewick
bedspreads that have seen better days become useful again when they
are transformed into bathmats. Cut out two or three pieces of the
desired shape and stitch together firmly, lengthwise and crosswise, to
achieve an adequate thickness. Bind the edges with a wide binding of
cotton fabric, cut on the cross – gingham is especially effective.

TOWELS INTO FACE CLOTHS Cut pieces 25 cm square from the good
parts of worn towels and neaten the edges by crocheting round or
binding with bias binding. Choose a different coloured edging for
each family member and match it with their toothbrushes.

LIFE AFTER TEARS When linen tablecloths have seen their best days,
make unworn pieces into table napkins with machined or hand-
stitched hems. These will protect clothing better than paper napkins,
and are kinder to the environment. The less presentable remnants can
be used as tea towels – great for drying glasses.

   Worn cotton or linen sheets are equally adaptable. Make the decent-
sized bits into under-pillowcases or cot sheets, or use them as ironing
cloths. Stitch two thin pieces together to make good tea towels of
regular thickness – linen sheets are especially good for this. Use
smaller bits as dusters, pudding cloths, strainers or nappy liners.

SANTA'S HELPERS Recycling became an art form during World War
II, when Christmas toys were in short supply. Determined to maintain
children's faith in Father Christmas, resourceful British women turned
old stockings into rag dolls with buttons for eyes, embroidered faces
and wool for hair. They reshaped pieces of coats and trousers into
stuffed animals, and unravelled seaboot socks to knit them up again
into teddy bears. And when ragbag contents were too worn for use on
the outside, they were shredded to make filling.

USING FABRIC SCRAPS Today's ragbags yield much richer pickings
than the wartime ones, and home dressmakers always have leftover
fabric scraps, which occupy precious storage space. Make these into
smaller items such as sun-tops, aprons, soft toys or doll's clothing.

The Way We Were

During World War II, the
British Board of Trade sent
shopkeepers the following
practical instructions:

'In wartime, production must
be for war and not for peace.
Here are examples of the
changeover from peacetime
products to wartime necessities:

• corsets become Parachutes
and Chinstraps;
• lace curtains become Sand-fly
netting;
• carpets become Webbing
Equipment;
• toilet preparations become
Anti-Gas ointments;
• golf balls become Gas Masks;
• mattresses become Life
Jackets;
• saucepans become Steel
Helmets;
• combs become Eyeshields.'

– BOMBERS AND MASH: THE DOMESTIC
FRONT 1939–45 (1980)

Pure woollen socks that are too far
gone to be darned make perfect
polishing cloths; stuff them with rags to
make polishing pads. They also make
useful liners for the bases of vases to
stop them marking or scratching
polished wood; cut a round from the
sock, the size of your vessel, and
simply glue it to the base.

VERSATILE CURTAINS The linings and header tapes of curtains often wear out long before the fabric in the curtains themselves. After dry cleaning or washing, superannuated curtains can be turned to a variety of uses.

Curtains into cloaks Convert an old velvet curtain into an evening cloak. Line it with silk, and use leftover pieces to make a matching evening bag.

Curtains into costumes Elderly velvet and brocade curtains can be transformed into colourful fancy dress costumes – Robin Hood's doublet or Tudor Elizabethan court costume. Make ruffs and collars from old lace curtains, dress up old felt hats with imitation ostrich feathers, and move your family back through time. It makes a refreshing change from robots and astronauts.

Curtains into clothes care 'The swansong of an old cretonne curtain is "Useful to the End",' according to an article in a 1920s issue of an Australian women's magazine. Fold each curtain in half and machine a seam along the sides and across the bottom to make long bags for storing evening dresses and winter coats. Sew moth-repellent bags inside these protectors. Hang the garments on coat hangers and tie the open end of the curtain bag tightly round the hook of the hanger to exclude moths and dust.

If the cretonne is beginning to split, seam up the rents and use the curtains to protect the contents of the linen cupboard. Lay a curtain on each shelf with a long flap protruding that can be wrapped around the pile of sheets and pillowcases. Or use curtains split beyond redemption as dustsheets during redecorating or spring cleaning.

Curtains into cushions An effective way of recycling the good parts of curtains is to make them into scatter cushions. Stuff cushions with recycled materials, too: down from an old quilt, or pieces of soft fabric from the ragbag, cut very small to avoid lumpiness. Trimmings give a professional finish: try fringing at the ends of an oblong shape, silken cord on a round cushion, or piping around a square one. Loose covers can also be recycled in this way; almost any weight of fabric will do.

When the family budget could not extend to the services of a professional dressmaker, party gear and fancy dress costumes – especially for children – were recycled hand-me-downs, and often started life as part of the household furnishings.

MAKING A CYLINDRICAL CUSHION Scattered on sofas and chaise longues, vividly coloured bolster-shaped cushions can give your decor a touch of the exotic.

Make an inner cushion from calico or sheeting 60 cm wide by 75 cm long. Join the long sides and hem and gather in one of the shorter sides to form a cylindrical bag. Stuff the bag firmly with filling, and hem, gather and sew up the other end.

To make the cover, cut three broad strips of velvet or satin 62 cm long by 22 cm wide, and two strips of a contrasting luxury fabric 62 cm long by 10 cm wide. Join alternating wide and narrow strips along the 62 cm edges to make a whole piece measuring about 62 cm by 78 cm. Join the long sides, gather one end and disguise the gathering with a button covered with the velvet or satin. Attach a few strands of black or coloured braid, ornamented with bead ends.

Slip the inner cushion inside the cover, then gather the other end and finish it off with braid and beads to match.

PATCHWORK PIECES

Aboriginal women were the first Australians to make patchwork quilts. They fashioned possum and kangaroo skins into blankets and cloaks, sometimes using whole pelts, and at other times cutting them into roughly rectangular shapes and stitching them together using bone awls and the sinews from kangaroo legs. Sometimes they decorated finished articles on the inside by slashing or scouring the inner surface of the skin to make patterns.

Even before they arrived in Australia, many early immigrant women whiled away the long sea voyage sewing together any scraps of fabric they could lay their hands on. Many also brought quilts with them from England, and the practice of quilt making continued in the new country, both from custom and out of necessity. Early Australian quilts were mainly of log cabin or hexagonal design, but a greater variety of patterns evolved as fabrics and time became more plentiful.

PIECING OVER PAPERS

Newspapers and old letters were often used to make paper templates for quilts, and remnants of these, found in old unfinished quilts, reveal fascinating details of the life and times of earlier quilters.

QUILTS FROM HOME

Many early settlers brought their precious quilts with them, and they became a great source of comfort as well as warmth in an alien land.

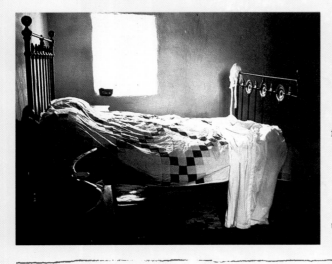

RAGS AND RICHES

Crazy patchwork quilts of plush and other rich fabrics (above right) were popular at the end of the last century. At the other end of the scale, during the 1930s Depression even men's used suiting was recycled into 'waggas' (right).

THE MARRIAGE QUILT

In the 19th century, the fashionable pastime of quilt making kept many middle class women occupied making quilts for their trousseaus.

ENGLISH PIECING

Using paper templates to cut and neaten patchwork pieces ensures regular shapes.

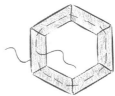

1. Cut out the fabric, allowing a 0.75 cm seam all round, then make a paper template for each hexagon. Place the paper template on the wrong side of the fabric, turn back the seam allowance and tack in place.

2. With right sides together, oversew along one side of the covered hexagon. Do not sew through the paper template.

3. Continue joining patches in this way. When the work is finished, pull out the tacking and remove the paper templates.

LOG CABIN QUILTS

The design concept is simple, but log cabin quilts give great scope to the quilter's ingenuity in arranging thin strips of fabric in various colours and shades to make a unique pattern.

THE DRUNKARD'S PATH

Made up of quarter circles set into squares, each wavy line in the drunkard's path quilt design is supposed to be reminiscent of the lurching gait of a drunken wanderer.

Hand and foot

IN BYGONE DAYS, ETIQUETTE STATED WITH
CONFIDENCE THAT YOU COULD ALWAYS TELL A
WOMAN'S CHARACTER FROM HER FOOTWEAR.

Fashion pundits were adamant that no one could be dressed in the best
of taste if their shoes were out of harmony with the rest of their
outfit, or – even worse – if they were scuffed or dirty. Australian
women were reprimanded for wearing 'open, strapped shoes' with
a plain coat and skirt, instead of 'a nice pair of boots'; and boots
teamed with a light cotton frock constituted an equally dismal
lapse in fashion etiquette. Spotlessly clean gloves and an
immaculate leather handbag were other prerequisites for the
well dressed woman.

SHOE CARE In the good old days, every respectable household
maintained a shoe-cleaning outfit. Now, as then, this should
contain a moderately stiff brush for removing dried mud and
dust, soft woollen rags or old woollen socks for applying polish;
and a soft polishing brush and a velvet pad or soft cloth for
bringing up that mirror shine. Separate brushes should be kept
for black and coloured shoes.

Keeping in shape Immediately after taking shoes and boots off,
place them on shoe trees or stuff them firmly with soft tissue paper
to maintain their shape.

Damp footwear Stuff wet shoes and boots with newspaper to
preserve their shape and then dry them slowly, away from direct heat.
When dry, fine leather shoes often will regain softness and suppleness
after being coated in oil or vaseline. Boots and tougher footwear
benefit from being rubbed down with saddle soap.

   When boots and shoes are even a little damp, they can be difficult to
polish. To counteract this problem, first place a few drops of kerosene
on a cloth and rub it carefully all over the leather. Then apply polish
in the usual way.

*No lady would ever be seen
in public without her gloves,
and manufacturers in the 1890s
publicised a large range.*

Waterproofing Melt together equal quantities of beeswax and
mutton suet. While the mixture is still liquid, rub it over leather
boots and shoes, including the soles. Wipe off any excess. This is a
messy business, but it will keep water from penetrating the footwear
and is particularly effective for walking boots.

Leather softeners The juice of a lemon will soften patent leather
shoes that have become hard and dry. Rub them all over, and when
dry, polish in the usual way. Or, to prevent them cracking in the first
place, rub patent leather shoes with a soft rag dipped in olive oil. Let
the oil soak in for about half an hour, then polish with a clean, soft
cloth. This treatment is also good for patent leather handbags. A good
rubbing with castor oil will soften other kinds of leather.

In 1927, an issue of *Helen's Weekly*
advised readers to varnish the soles
of their shoes lightly to make them
harden and last much longer, and to
help to keep out the damp. (If you want
to try this thrifty tip today, it would be
wise to sand the varnish lightly in case
of slipperiness.)

Removing spots and stains Petrol followed by an application of beaten egg white removes grease stains from leather. Petrol will also take tar off shoes. Grease spots on suede shoes can be removed by rubbing them with a rag dipped in glycerine (from pharmacies and supermarkets). Remove other stains from leather by sponging with a solution of warm water and vinegar. When dry, polish the article with a soft cloth soaked in linseed oil, and then vigorously with a clean soft cloth to remove all traces of oil.

Deodorising and storing shoes A generous sprinkle of bicarbonate of soda inside shoes freshens them. Leave them for a day or two, then shake out and air the shoes. Sprinkle starch inside shoes to keep mildew at bay in the bottom of the wardrobe.

NEW SHOES Many shoes now are not as well made as they were in the past, but some traditional care tips still apply. New shoes frequently cause painful blisters. Pour methylated spirits or rubbing alcohol into the heels of the shoes and let it soak in. Wear the shoes while they are still wet. If a shoe pinches over a toe or a joint, press a cloth wrung out in very hot water over the trouble spot. Leave it there for a few minutes and the leather will expand a little and soften.

Polishing new boots and shoes To protect the leather, give new footwear a dressing with a good shoe cream before wearing. If new boots are difficult to polish, rub them all over with a cut lemon. Allow the juice to dry then apply shoe polish as usual and shine with a hard brush.

WORN SHOES Have heels repaired as soon as they begin to wear. Use a good household glue to stick down the little pieces that sometimes get skinned from heels, or to fix loose inner soles.

LAUNDERING LEATHER GLOVES Some leather gloves can be washed; other need dry-cleaning. Consult the manufacturer's label before taking the plunge. Mend any rips or tears before washing.
Washing: Make rich suds by adding mild soap to lukewarm water, never hot. Wash the gloves on your hands, remembering to removing your rings first so that you do not pull or puncture the leather. Rub your hands together gently. Remove the gloves by rolling them carefully back from the wrist.
Caution: Do not wash chamois or doeskin gloves on your hands because they tear easily when wet; just work them gently around in the water. Add a few drops of olive oil to the washing water.
Rinsing and drying Rinse in lukewarm water then work the gloves around again in mild soapy water to keep them supple. Squeeze out excess moisture in a towel, rolling from the fingers towards the wrists. Gently pull the gloves into shape. Blow into them to make them dry more evenly. Dry indoors away from excessive heat or cold.

SUEDE REVIVER Give a facelift to a handbag or a pair of suede shoes that have developed that flattened look by holding the article in the steam from a boiling kettle. At the same time, brush it firmly with a wire brush to freshen up the pile.

The Way We Were

In the mid-19th century, gloves were to be found in every woman's social wardrobe:

'You *must* have gloves, or I won't go,' cried Meg decidedly. 'Gloves are more important than anything else; you can't dance without them, and if you don't I should be *so* mortified.'

– *LITTLE WOMEN*, LOUISA M. ALCOTT (1868)

These elegant boots and shoes were among the fashion items illustrated in the 1912 edition of PENROSE ANNUAL.

Hat tricks

UNTIL WELL AFTER WORLD WAR II, EVERYONE WORE A HAT OUTDOORS, AND WOMEN WERE OFTEN EXPECTED TO WEAR THEM INDOORS AS WELL.

Hats are no longer compulsory except with uniforms, but they are making a comeback. They protect us from the sun and make fashion statements at formal occasions and race meetings. There are many useful tips from the past about keeping hats looking spruce and new.

CLEANING STRAW AND PANAMA Use a clean vegetable brush to remove loose dirt from the hat. Then place it on a flat surface that will not colour the damp straw. Dilute a measure of hydrogen peroxide (from pharmacies and supermarkets) with an equal quantity of cold water. Apply to white straw or panama hats with a cloth, beginning with the top of the crown, and wetting only a small part at a time. After scrubbing each portion, rub it as near dry as you can with a fresh towel. Dry in a dark room or in the shade. Re-shape the hat, while it is quite damp, by moulding the crown over a pudding basin the shape and size of the crown: this is called re-blocking.

Revitalising panama The pantry can often furnish cheap chemical-free treatments such as this one for restoring a panama hat; the technique cleans with salt, whitens with lemon and stiffens with egg.

Beat together the white of an egg, the juice of half a lemon and a teaspoon of salt. Apply the mixture evenly to the hat with a brush, then wipe off the excess with a damp cloth. Dry well away from the direct sun. The hat should take on a new lease of life.

Stiffening straw To stiffen straw, brush on the wrong side with white of egg, white hard varnish (from hardware stores) or gum arabic (from art supply shops).

CLEANING FELT HATS Brush the hat carefully to remove dust and clean as recommended below. Press felt hats through a damp cloth until the cloth is dry, then pull the cloth off; this will raise the pile.

Dark felt Rub with a cloth dipped in household ammonia and brush firmly in the direction of the nap.

Light fawn felt Rub with hot oatmeal or hot fuller's earth (from hardware and craft shops).

Grey felt Clean by brushing with hot bran.

White felt Brush all over with a thin paste of magnesia and water, leave till thoroughly dry, and then brush off. Or rub gently with emery paper and then lightly with block magnesia, and then leave for a day before brushing.

HAT TRIMMINGS FROM THE ROARING TWENTIES

Shirred flowers: Make these simple flower shapes by lightly stitching narrow shirred ribbon to the hat. Use tiny beads of pearl, enamel or wood to make the stamens.

Leaf motifs: In 1927 these were 'newest among trimming ideas'. Make them from silk or velvet upholstery cord.

Vandyke points: Fold and stitch grosgrain ribbon in two or three contrasting tones, as shown. In 1929, this trim was suggested for winter hats of plush or felt, but it would be just as effective on a fine straw.

RENOVATING VELVET HATS Brush the hat well and give it a good shake to dislodge any dust. Ask a friend to hold the velvet taut while you place a well moistened cloth on the wrong side and iron with a hot iron to force the steam through to the right side and lift the pile. Keep ironing until dry, taking care not to scorch the material.

LAUNDERING A BERET Many berets can be hand washed carefully with perfect safety. Roll the beret gently in a towel to remove excess moisture and then slip it over a plate of a suitable size so that the beret keeps its shape while drying. Press with a slightly damp cloth.

TRIMMING A HAT In the days when no well dressed woman would dream of appearing in public without a hat, a quick, effective and economical way of ringing the changes was to trim hats at home, varying the trimmings to suit different outfits.

Three-minute rose Make the rose with soft satin ribbon. You will need 75 cm of ribbon 4 cm wide; as the width increases, so does the length. Two-tone ribbon is particularly effective, as the winding shows first one colour and then the other.

Position a small hatpin where the flower is to be. With a few light stitches secure one end of the ribbon where the hatpin disappears under the surface. Twist the ribbon loosely round and round under the projecting head and point of the hatpin, folding it over at intervals so that sometimes one side of the ribbon shows and sometimes the other. Twist to the end, tuck in the raw edge, and stitch the rosette down lightly here and there before removing the hatpin.

Trimming a hat with ribbon, beads and other bits and pieces is fun and inexpensive.

The Way We Were

Australian humorous columnist Lennie Lower had a gift for tongue-in-cheek advice on women's and domestic matters. Here he notifies his female readers of a new fashion in hats:

'For garden parties and the like the picture hat is again coming into vogue. They are extremely large, and would not suit a short woman as she might be mistaken for a marquee. The trimmings may be of feathers, flowers, fruit, vegetables, or nuts.'

– *THE AUSTRALIAN WOMEN'S WEEKLY* (1933)

How does

How does

your

garden

grow

**DRAWING ON THE STORED WISDOM
OF THE PAST TO CREATE A GARDEN**

Planning your old-world garden

OUR FOREBEARS' GARDENS RANGED FROM FORMAL DESIGNS TO SWEEPING LANDSCAPES TO INFORMAL BLOCKS OF COLOUR.

The typical 19th century garden was a sanctuary – a secluded, romantic place of soft lawns, statuary and beds of European favourites. By the early 20th century, labour shortages had contributed to the rise of the smaller private garden and the popularity of gardening as a national pastime. Bedding out of hothouse annuals became too expensive and labour-intensive, and keen gardeners embraced hardy, easy-to-grow plants. Gardens dominated by lawns bordered by flowerbeds became popular in the 1920s. The 1930s was a golden age of garden design, with poet and novelist Vita Sackville-West's creation of linked gardens at Sissinghurst Castle, in England, the gardens of Edna Walling and Paul Sorrensen in Australia and those of Alfred Buxton and Edgar Taylor in New Zealand.

Variations on some of these themes probably already exist in your garden. You could highlight those you have, or introduce more, to bring the tranquillity of a bygone age to a modern garden.

Over many years these trees have grown until their boughs have arched over to create a vista of filtered green light.

STARTING FROM SCRATCH Most of us have to adapt an existing garden to our own ideas. But, daunting though the task may be, for those lucky enough to start with a blank canvas, there are many possibilities. The final form of your garden will grow out of the interaction between the climate, the soil, the site and your needs and desires. It is most important that you start with a plan – this will force you to think about the whole garden at one time and consider how one space will interact with another. Decide what you want from your garden and how much time and effort you can put in to maintain it and balance this with your budget and the nature of the site.

Weathered tubs of old-fashioned flowering annuals (such as lobelia, alyssum, pansies and nasturtiums) will provide colour and interest while the garden becomes established. For a seasonal touch, fill stone urns with geraniums in summer and bulbs in winter.

The basics On a piece of graph paper, mark the boundaries of your property, the positions of the house, water and sewerage pipes (so you don't plant large trees on top of them), existing features such as trees or rocks, and indicate the general contours. Then use a sheet of tracing paper over the basic plan to draw in your design ideas.

Work out the most suitable places for the activity areas in the garden – for example, the clothesline, the compost heap, the vegetable plot and the tool shed. Also consider the where would be the most logical places for paths.

Garden rooms You might like to think of the entire space as a series of linked 'garden rooms', each with a specific focus or purpose. This has the advantage of breaking down garden maintenance into small jobs in defined areas.

Dividing up the garden will also create an illusion of space. Use old-fashioned arbours, arches and timber trellising to create focal points, define divisions, hide unsightly areas, provide support for climbing plants and supply privacy.

Sunny areas Choose a spot that gets at least four hours sun a day for the kitchen garden. The clothesline should also be located in a sunny place and it should be on the same level as the laundry.

If you want a lawn, it too will require a sunny, well drained spot; shady areas can have 'lawns' of herbs or shade-tolerant ground covers.

Trees Mark on your plan where trees and shrubs need to be planted for screening, privacy and shade; choose a selection that grow to different heights, to provide layers of interest.

Avoid rows or regular order unless the area is large and the lines are of considerable length, and consider the effect the sizes of the mature trees will have on the house, garden and surroundings.

Framing Look for desirable views which may be improved by framing with foliage, arches or gateways, and undesirable views which you may want to screen off. Place fragrant plants near windows, seats and along pathways.

Features Make a feature of a rustic garden bench, or a period birdbath or statue. Affordable reproductions are widely available. Terracing will give an old-fashioned feel to a sloping site, and natural rock outcrops can be used to create fern gardens and rockeries.

NATIVE PLANTS IN OLD-TIME GARDENS From the early years of European settlement in the southern hemisphere, old-world favourites and exotics from South America, Africa and India were planted side by side with local flora. Consider continuing this tradition.

Native flora that were commonly grown in Australian and New Zealand gardens of yesteryear are:

Trees Bunya bunya pine, eucalypt, Illawarra flame tree, lillypilly, silky oak, wattle.

Flowers and shrubs Boronia, Christmas bush, Christmas bells, eriostemon, Geraldton wax, kangaroo paw, mountain devil, old man's beard, red bottlebrush, rock lily, waratah.

Climbers and ground covers False sarsaparilla, wonga wonga vine.

Ferns and palms Cabbage tree, stag horn, slender tree fern.

WISE ADVICE

If you wish to be happy for a day,
   get drunk;
If you wish to be happy for a week,
   kill a pig;
If you wish to be happy for a month,
   get married;
If you wish to be happy for ever,
   make a garden.

– CHINESE PROVERB

Words of Wisdom

'There is a mistaken idea that if the area is small, it must on no account be broken up for fear it will appear even more limited. The smaller the area, the more imperative it becomes to devise some means of making it appear larger. To do this we must conceal the boundaries as much as possible, and break up the remainder with groups of trees and shrubs which form vistas, creating a sense of distance which does not really exist.'

– *GARDENS IN AUSTRALIA*, EDNA WALLING (1944)

Tools of the trade

A PROPER COLLECTION OF TOOLS IS ESSENTIAL IN
ANY OCCUPATION, AND THIS IS PARTICULARLY THE
CASE WITH GARDENING.

Having the right tool for the job saves time and results in better care
of your plants. It pays to buy the best you can afford – quality tools
that are properly cared for will last a lifetime. Spades, forks and
secateurs made of forged steel are stronger than those of pressed steel.

THE GARDEN SHED You'll find an overwhelming selection of tools
available, but some are more useful than others.
Spade The first requirement for digging, edging and cultivating.
Long-handled shovel For digging or scooping up soil or compost.
Four-pronged digging fork For breaking up the soil in lumpy and stony
ground and digging in heavy soils, handling manure and compost,
and lifting delicate plants without damaging the roots.
Hand fork For weeding and lifting seedlings.
Level-headed or garden rake For levelling off after digging, prior to
planting. Also useful for removing small stones and twigs.
Lawn rake For raking up leaves and lawn clippings.
Dutch hoe For getting rid of small weeds in light soils.
Swan-neck hoe For weeding in between rows of plants.
Cultivator For breaking up the soil and removing weeds.
Shears For trimming grass edges around shrubs and near walls and
borders, and for shaping and trimming hedges.
Secateurs For pruning small branches.
Pruning saw For cutting thick limbs and branches.
Trowel For weeding and shallow digging, planting bulbs,
transplanting seedlings and lifting small plants.
Dibbler For forming holes when transplanting seedlings.
Flat file For sharpening the blades of spades and hoes.
Garden line For marking a straight line when planting.
Wheelbarrow For carrying soil, compost and mulch, and for carting
rubbish away.
Watering can For keeping the soil moist during seed germination and
gently watering young seedlings.

CARING FOR TOOLS Time spent maintaining tools will be saved over
and over again in energy, efficiency and temper. Never leave tools
out at night. If possible, hang them on hooks or nails in a shed.
   After use, wash or wipe garden tools clean, then dry them.
Keep a tin of rough grease or oil with a rag in it, and after each
use, rub metal parts with the rag to prevent rusting. Wipe
wooden handles with linseed oil every few months. Sharpen the backs
of cutting edges by rubbing with a sandstone or oilstone every year or
so. Do not stand tools on their blades, especially on a concrete floor.

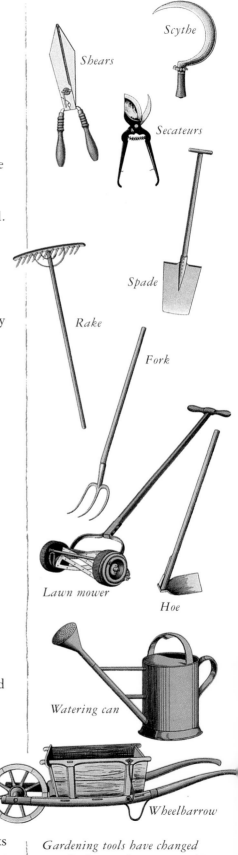

Scythe

Shears

Secateurs

Rake

Spade

Fork

Lawn mower

Hoe

Watering can

Wheelbarrow

*Gardening tools have changed
very little over the years, as this
selection from the 1890s shows.*

The good earth

A PREREQUISITE FOR HEALTHY PLANTS IS GOOD SOIL.
ALWAYS ENSURE THAT THE EARTH HOUSING THEIR
ROOTS IS WELL DUG, COMPOSTED AND DRAINED.

Soils are of three basic types – sandy (light), loam (medium) and clay
(heavy). Loam, containing sand, humus and clay, is the ideal to be
aimed for. Sandy soils drain too easily, leaching away vital nutrients;
clay soils drain poorly, absorbing and retaining water. You can correct
these problems by adding organic matter – if you do this consistently,
over time a poor soil will become fertile and suitable for most plants.

SPADEWORK Digging is the best way to improve your soil, and is the
foundation for successful gardening. When digging, add as much
manure and compost as possible. Take care not to injure the roots of
shrubs and trees with the spade, especially in spring, when the roots
are growing and damage would greatly reduce that season's growth.

Vegetables do best in coarse, crumbly soil. Dig ashes into the soil at
spading time to create this texture, or dress the soil with lime.

Dig deep Dig down to a depth of least 30 cm to break up solidly
compacted earth, expose it to air and sunlight and loosen it so that
roots can penetrate. With your foot, push a spade down to its full
depth, keeping it as upright as possible. Lift out the full spade of soil
and turn the sods over; if they are lumpy, chop them with the spade. A
systematic method of loosening a bed is by 'trenching' it. The steps in
the right-hand column explain how to do this.

When to dig The best time is the day after rain or a good soaking –
when the soil is damp. Do not dig in wet weather, as the soil will
become sticky and less able to admit air. A fork is the best tool to use
when turning over heavy or hard soil. Just before planting, break up
any remaining lumps, loosely repack the soil and smooth the surface.

Sweetening the soil After digging, leave the soil open for few
days to allow the air, sun and moisture to sweeten it. For
maximum sweetening, dig up a bed at the end of the growing
period (early winter) and leave it exposed until spring planting.

MANURING Manured soils absorb moisture well, and soils with
a high humus content hold warmth longer than light sandy
soils. Manure must be well rotted before use. Dig it into beds
you are preparing to plant.

Soils vary in fertility so there are no rules about the amount
of manure to use, but it is impossible to apply too much well-
rotted organic compost.

For heavy clay soils, add either lime or stable manure, but not
together. Instead, add lime six weeks or so after manure – lime
promotes the decomposition of humus and the development of
beneficial soil bacteria and prevents the soil from hardening.

TRENCHING
This old-time method of aerating
the soil in a plot is also an
efficient way to add manure.

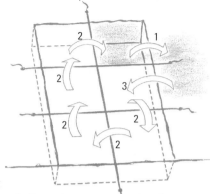

1. Spread manure over the plot.
Using string markers, divide the
plot in half lengthwise, then
crosswise at workable intervals.
Starting from the top right-hand
section, remove the manure and
topsoil to a depth of 50–75 cm and
turn it onto the ground to the right.
Break up the exposed subsoil.

2. Repeat step 1 in the top left-
hand corner, turning the manure
and topsoil into the first section.
Work down the left side and up the
right side, turning the manure and
topsoil from the current section
into the previous section.

3. Fill the last section with the
manure and topsoil that you set
aside from the first section.

*Breaking up the soil before
planting enlivens and aerates it
and results in better crops.*

The everyday miracle

EACH YEAR OUR GRANDPARENTS HARVESTED SEED
OR STRUCK CUTTINGS FROM THEIR BEST PLANTS, AS
PEOPLE HAVE DONE SINCE AGRICULTURE BEGAN.

This selection process developed a precious plant bank to be handed
on to future generations. With their life-sustaining promise of future
harvests, seeds and cuttings of treasured varieties were carefully carried
from the old countries of Europe across the oceans to take root in fresh
fields. The propagation skills of earlier times are easily acquired and –
for virtually no cost – will enable you to fill your garden with your
favourite flowers, shrubs, fruits and vegetables.

SEED As well as the familiar tiny dried-up dark brown specks, seeds
can take the form of root tubers, such as potatoes, and whole fruits,
such as chokos. To propagate from seed, allow one or two of the
healthiest plants in each crop to run to seed after flowering.

Seed-collecting tips Most flowering plants can be grown from
collected seed. However, only plants grown from nonhybrid seed are
suitable; most commercially available seed and seedlings are hybrids.
• Select the best and healthiest blooms while the plant is in full
flower, and tie a piece of bright braid around your choices so you will
recognise them when they are faded and running to seed.
• Do not collect seeds until ripe and almost ready to be dispersed. If
the seed is likely to drop before you can collect it, put a bag over the
flower as it begins to dry out.
• Collect seeds on a warm, dry day when the dew has evaporated.
• Store dry flowerheads in a labelled and dated paper bag until the
seeds have fallen out. Scoop out the seeds of fleshy fruits, wash them,
dry them on paper towels and store them in a dark place. Dry peas and
beans in the pod and remove the pod before storing.
• Store seed in an airtight container, marked with the collection date.

CUTTINGS Propagating plants from cuttings will produce new plants
that are identical to their parent plants, and mature plants will be
formed in much less time than growing them from seed. Apart from
annuals and biennials, almost any plant can be grown from a cutting.

Cutting tips There are several types of cuttings, and some plants root
more readily from one type than from another.
• Softwood cuttings are shoots taken in spring from active current
growth. Some suitable plants are buddleias, delphiniums, marguerite
daisies and wallflowers.
• Semihardwood cuttings are firm wood taken when the first flush of
growth has passed. Some suitable plants are fuchsias and geraniums.
• Hardwood cuttings are mature wood taken when dormant. Some
suitable plants are roses, hydrangeas and rhododendrons.

*Rosa inermis; roses are usually
propagated by grafting.*

PARKER & WOOD,
SEEDS AND TOOLS,

*The popular carrot, as featured in
an advertisement for an early
horticultural supplier. Carrots are
easy to grow from seed.*

- Take root cuttings from plants with thick, fleshy roots or runners. Starting at the end nearest the stem, cut a section of root into lengths – top growth will develop from the part of the root nearest the stem (the top), and roots from the bottom end. Some suitable plants are peonies, perennial phlox and wisteria.
- Leaf cuttings are used mainly for indoor plants such as begonias and African violets.

Striking cuttings One part of coarse river sand to three parts of peat hold the cutting firmly. Wash the sand first in a large container such as a barrow; light foreign matter will float to the surface and spill over the edge.

Do not push the cutting into the striking mixture, as this could tear the bark and the injured part may rot. Instead, use a pencil or stick to make a hole of the right depth.

The never-changing pattern of life repeats itself yet again as tender young leaves emerge from the soil.

GRAFTING The scion (a piece of wood from the previous season's growth) is inserted into a host plant or rootstock belonging to the same plant group. This method is used mainly for deciduous fruit trees and roses.

LAYERING You can obtain a good-sized plant fairly quickly by this method, which also has the advantage of letting the new plant continue to draw nourishment from the parent. Some suitable plants for layering include box, daphne, gardenia, magnolia and carnations.

Cut an angled slit in a pliable, low-lying stem and wedge a small pebble or matchstick into the slit to keep it open. Bend the stem over so that the slit is buried in a shallow hole filled with sand and peat. Pin it down with bent fencing wire anchored in the harder surrounding soil. When roots have developed from the slit, sever the stem to cut the new plant away from the parent plant.

DIVISION Clump-forming and trailing perennials can be lifted and divided for replanting. With some plants you can do this with your hands, but for others you will need a knife or a sharp spade. Division will rejuvenate perennial plants that have become large and overcrowded; you may wish to remove the parent plant and replace it with a less woody divided section. Suitable plants for division include anemones, day lilies, irises, lupins, phlox, shasta daisies and violets.

The Way We Were

'To own a bit of ground, to scratch it with a hoe, to plant seeds, and watch the renewal of life – this is the most common delight of the race, and the most satisfactory thing a man can do.'

– *MY SUMMER IN A GARDEN*, CHARLES DUDLEY WARNER (1870)

In the beginning...

GOOD GARDENS BEGIN WITH GOOD SEEDS, SAYS AN OLD ADAGE, AND THE MAJORITY OF PLANTS CAN BE GROWN FROM SEED.

Many plants, like Topsy, just grow, but others require more time and attention from the gardener. As well as annuals and perennials, consider the beauty of bulbs, climbers, bushes and trees.

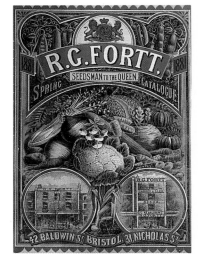

A seed supplier's vegetable catalogue for the spring of 1881.

RAISING PLANTS FROM SEED Our forebears would save seeds each year for planting the following year. Whether you harvest your own seeds or buy them from a garden supplier, draw on the wisdom of the past to raise your seeds successfully.

• To test compost-enriched soil before planting, take a handful and press it as tightly in your hand as possible. It should not clump together but, as the *Journal of Horticulture of Australasia* poetically said in August 1909, 'should open out like a silk handkerchief'. If the soil sticks together, it will set and harden when you water it.

• If the seeds are very small, mix them with sand or dry, fine soil, to make sowing easier.

• Sow a few seeds every fortnight or so throughout the growing season for a continual showing of flowers or a steady harvest of vegetables.

• Do not let water pool on the surface of the soil, as it will cake in warm sun. If this does occur, lightly rake the surface so that germinating seeds can push through.

• Protect tiny seedlings from heavy rain or frost by arching small-leafed twigs (wattle is ideal) over them, or by using a seed bed cover.

SOWING THE SEED To germinate, as our forebears knew, seeds simply need moisture, warmth, air, and a covering of soil. But gardeners of the old days also had their own, often secret, recipes for potting mixture and compost, and their own techniques for raising seedlings.

Many seeds can be sown directly into the garden, without the need for transplanting.

Sowing directly into the soil Most annuals and some perennials can be sown directly into the garden. Label each row as you sow. To get the most benefit from your crops, follow the old-time prescriptions:

• Wait until the weather is settled and warm enough to provide the temperature most suitable for the germination of the type of seeds you wish to grow, and if you live in a cold area make sure the frosts are over. Prepare the soil beforehand and allow it to rest for days – preferably weeks – before sowing. Just before you sow, make sure the soil is finely broken up, dry and level. Don't sow into soil that sticks to the spade – it is too wet.

• Cramped seedlings become weak plants, so sow seed sparsely and evenly in shallow drills, made by pressing a piece of light batten into the soil. Press seeds in firmly with a flat board and cover lightly

with fine sandy soil, or carefully tamp down the soil. A good rule of thumb is to sow seeds at a depth equal to the length of the seed. Water gently each evening using a watering can with a fine rose, and keep the surface moist after the seeds have germinated.

• To prevent overcrowding, thin out seedlings by removing the least robust. Do not disturb the remaining plants – break off unwanted seedlings at ground level rather than pulling them up.

Raising seedlings in sand and gravel Seeds do not need manure, as they have built-in stores of plant food. Sand and gravel lack nutrients but provide warmth and help drainage, preventing seed from being rotted by too much water. They also admit air, which is necessary for the satisfactory growth of seedlings. Once seedlings appear, apply weak manure water occasionally.

Growing seedlings in containers Annuals that are too tender for the open bed can be grown under glass in seed boxes or pots, and transplanted when they can withstand the rigours of the garden.

Seed boxes should be shallow and well drained: cover the bottom of each with a layer of pebbles or broken terracotta. Keep them clean to prevent the introduction of harmful bacteria. Fill the boxes with a good seed-raising mixture and level it off with a board. Press the soil in firmly. Immerse each seed box in a shallow tub of water and leave it there until the water reaches the surface. Sow seeds thinly in drills 5–6 cm apart, and barely cover them with fine soil or sand.

A pane of glass resting on the rim of the container will protect the seeds from damage by heavy rain or watering, and from birds, slugs and snails; at the same time it will help to retain moisture in the soil and, in the winter, it will concentrate the warmth. Tilt one edge of the glass slightly above the edge of the container to admit air, raising it a little more each day until the plants are well enough established to do without it. Provide shade, if necessary, by laying hessian or newspaper over the glass.

Transplanting seedlings The success of your seedlings depends largely on the way they are transplanted. Annuals raised in seed boxes, such as pansies, phlox and asters can be planted directly into the garden, but seedlings of trees and shrubs should be acclimatised by transplanting them first into small pots and, once established, into the garden.

Here is some wisdom from gardeners of the past on transplanting and raising seedlings:

• Put a seedling into a hole made with a dibbler; the hole should be a little deeper than needed and the soil slightly moist. Gently lower the roots into the hole, and while still holding the seedling, fill the hole with water while lifting the plant to the correct height.

• If a seedling's root system is pot-bound, loosen the roots gently with your finger and thumb before transplanting it. Plant the seedling in moist soil, and gently water it in after planting.

• Shade seedlings during the hottest part of the day by pushing a few pieces of twiggy foliage into the ground beside them. The foliage will gradually fall as the twigs die, and by the time the last leaf drops the young plants should be able to look after themselves.

MAKING A SEED BED

Some perennials are best started in a seed bed, then potted, before being planted out in the garden.

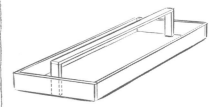

1. Enclose a seed bed about 1 metre wide by any length with hardwood planks. Position the bed so that it runs north–south. Replace some of the surface soil with a good seed-raising medium, water it, allow it to settle, and then level it off with a board. Drive in 20-cm-high hardwood stakes at the centre of each end, and join with a length of timber.

2. Tack some calico to the length of timber and tack the edges of the calico onto strong laths so that the cloth can be rolled up or tied down to provide shelter. Keep the cloth lowered until the seedlings start to come through. Roll up the western side until midday each day, lowering it in the afternoon. Roll up the eastern side after midday. Gradually reduce the amount of shade. Remove the screen when the seedlings are well above ground height.

• An inverted terracotta pot or glass jar placed over seedlings on cold days and at night will shield them from low temperatures and frosts. Do not allow stems and leaves to touch the sides of the pot.

• When lifting seedlings, be careful not to seriously damage their roots.

BULBS Bulbs will survive and bloom with little space or attention. Provide rich, well dug and well drained soil so they will reach their full potential – most are deep-rooting, so break up the lower layers of soil. Never use fresh animal manure. If you are planting bulbs in manured soil, place some poor sandy soil at the bottom of each hole before positioning the bulbs and then fill around the holes with more sand until the bulbs are covered.

Small bulbs such as ranunculus and freesias need a covering of about 5 cm, larger bulbs such as narcissus and hyacinth about 10 cm. Choose an aspect that gets as much winter sunlight as possible – bulbs grown in too much shade tend to make foliage instead of flowers.

After flowering, let the foliage die down slowly. To lift the bulbs, wait until the tops are thoroughly dry, indicating that the bulb below is mature. Store on racks in a cool, dry position, labelling each variety. Tulips and hyacinths should be lifted each year; daffodils, liliums and agapanthus can be left in the ground; crocuses, scillas, chionodoxas and snowdrops should not be lifted. Do not water bulbs that are to be left in the ground, as most require a dormant period before they start growing again.

CLIMBERS Climbers are a versatile addition to a garden, softening raw edges and adding height to walls and gateways. In many parts of Australia and New Zealand, it was quite common to see jasmine, honeysuckle and wisteria forming riotous mantles around buildings, so that, as Edwin Booth noted in his early commentary, *Australia*, 'it was difficult to tell where the wall of foliage ended and the wall of wood commenced.' There are evergreen as well as deciduous climbers, so you can choose permanent shade, or summer shade and winter sunshine. If this is not a consideration, plant an evergreen and avoid the untidiness of leaves shed in autumn.

Most evergreen climbers are best planted in autumn, so that they can start to establish their root system before winter sets in. Many resent being moved in cold weather and take some time to reorientate themselves. Climbers eventually make very deep and often very wide-spreading roots, so remember to allow for this when planting out. They also need ample room above ground.

Raising your plants from seed has several advantages, not the least of which is the satisfaction of growing the plants yourself. You also have a greater range to choose from, you can determine when the seedlings are ready to plant out and, best of all, you will save money!

Garden frames protect plants and concentrate heat and moisture. Portable frames come in a variety of shapes and sizes.

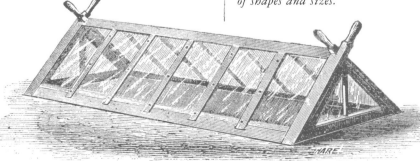

After planting a climber, water it well and stake or tie it to its permanent place on the trellis or fence. Make sure the supports and wires are strong enough to bear the weight when the climber is fully grown. A few leafy twigs pushed into the ground will shade the young plant in the hottest hours. Regularly train the climber upwards. Remove the shoots at the base of the plant and secure the top growths to the climbing structure.

Climbers need good loam with regular nutrient enrichment and watering. They do not like soil disturbance.

ROSES Roses are often sold 'bare-root' (without soil), and so have specialised planting requirements. Plant the bush as soon as you get it home, so the roots do not dry out. Cut away any broken or damaged roots with sharp secateurs, then dip the root ball into a bucket of muddy water thick enough to coat it. Build up a mound in the centre of the bottom of the hole, and drape the roots over it so that they will point downwards when you spread them out. Do not put manure in the bottom of the hole; instead, let the rose become established, then manure it from the surface. Carefully fill in the soil, using a blunt stick to poke soil around the roots and eliminate air pockets.

Choose the site for a tree or bush carefully, as once planted it will be difficult to uproot and replant.

TREES AND BUSHES Plant evergreen trees in autumn or spring, and deciduous trees as soon as all their leaves have fallen and no later than when the buds begin to swell. Dig a hole as deep as the pot the tree grew in, and wide enough to be able to spread the roots out without coiling or bending them. If the ground is hard, break up the bottom of the hole with a pick. To improve poor soil, mix in a little leaf litter, well-rotted compost, peat moss or other plant food – but do not make it too rich, or the roots will be reluctant to leave it for the surrounding soil. Break up any lumps in the soil from the hole so that when you replace it the tree roots will be able to penetrate it easily.

Lower the tree into the hole and carefully spread out the roots on the broken-up soil at the bottom. Replace the soil until the hole is half filled, then water thoroughly and firmly tamp down the soil. Fill in the rest of the hole to just below the old soil line on the trunk, tamp the earth down again, and water.

Choosing a tree for planting Choose a tree with a straight stem and clean bark. Reject any specimens that look old, dry or scaled by insects. Small, young trees are the best choice, as the roots are less likely to be injured when you dig them out.

Examine the root system of a tree grown in a pot. The fine fibrous points should be undamaged and the bark of the root entire. Roots coiled around the inside of a pot may continue growing that way, eventually strangling the plant. Roots that are poking through the bottom of a pot could be damaged when the plant is transplanted.

The water of life

Water your garden in the early evening – water applied during the day quickly evaporates.

LIKE ALL LIVING THINGS, PLANTS CANNOT SURVIVE WITHOUT WATER – BUT A DELUGE CAN BE JUST AS DESTRUCTIVE AS A DROUGHT.

Establishing and maintaining the right drainage and watering patterns is an important key to creating an attractive and productive garden. Fortunately, poor drainage can be corrected quite inexpensively using the ways of yesteryear.

DRAINAGE All ground, unless very sandy or gravelly, is improved by drainage, to carry away excess water and keep the soil well aerated. The stiffer and firmer the soil, the greater the need for help with drainage. Trenching (see page 191), which breaks up the subsoil, is one of the simplest ways of improving drainage. Another is to dig open trenches around each plot as temporary drains.

Raised beds are another way of overcoming the problem of poor drainage. The sides of these beds also provide a wonderful display case for trailing flowers and plants.

Simple underground drains The best permanent method of correcting poorly drained soil is to construct a network of drains. A simple system can be created by digging 1-metre-deep trenches, with 30 cm of rubble placed under the topsoil. Mark out a main, central drain and run side drains into it at 45-degree angles, allowing sufficient fall. If there is no suitable outlet, dig a deep soak hole at the end of the main drain and fill it with rubble.

WATERING Water only when plants actually need it. Allow the ground to dry out, and when watering is required give a thorough soaking so that moisture penetrates deep into the soil. This encourages plants to send their roots down in search of moisture, and so equips them to survive times of water shortage. A surface sprinkle is worse than useless – plants will push their roots upwards, making them vulnerable to the effects of hot sun and drying winds.

The water-efficient garden Water-efficient garden planting can cut domestic water usage by as much as half. Group plants according to their water needs, so that when watering thirsty plants you do not waste water on those that do not need as much. Keep your garden weed-free, as these unwanted freeloaders compete with your plants for water.

In the ranks of the light drinkers are many old favourites suitable for a border, rockery or dry bank; these include annual cornflower; red valerian, a popular perennial; and all wormwoods, valued for their striking silver foliage.

Friends and foes

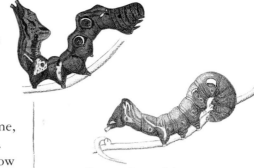

THERE ARE MANY OLD-TIME WAYS OF
OUTWITTING THE PESTS THAT BLIGHT YOUR
BLOOMS OR MAKE OFF WITH YOUR FRUIT.

The insects, diseases and weeds that can attack your precious plants
can seem numberless. Garden hygiene and regular maintenance are
your first line of defence, but you should also enlist the help of the
many animal friends that live in or visit your garden.

*Butterflies are beautiful creatures
but in their caterpillar stage they
are destructive in the garden.*

INSECT PESTS Birds are often chased away from crops at harvest time,
but gardeners have long recognised their role in controlling insects.
Provide water and leave a little fruit on the tree after harvest, or allow
a few plants to run to seed, and the birds you attract will repay you
many times over by hunting down garden pests. And you could try
some of the pest control methods of yesteryear instead of using
modern inorganic pesticides.

Botanical insecticides Plant-based pesticides were much
recommended by gardening
manuals of the 1920s. Now
fashionably 'green', they are just as
effective today as they were in our
grandparents' time.

Quassia spray Bring 30 grams of quassia
chips (from pharmacies and health food
shops) to the boil in 1 litre of water
and simmer for half an hour. Strain
the liquid and mix in 20 grams of
pure soap flakes. Dilute one part of
the mixture with three parts of water
and use as a spray for cabbage moth and other leaf-eating insects. The
bitter taste will also deter birds and possums.

Starch spray Dissolve 250 grams of ordinary household starch in a
little cold water, add it to 7 litres of boiling water and stir it in with
6 teaspoons of kerosene. Use the mixture for scale insects, especially
fern, greedy and oleander scale. Spray the mixture onto plants, leave it
for several days, then hose off the dead scale and the starch; or leave
the spray to flake off, bringing the scale with it.

White oil This is an old remedy against scale. Mix a cup of vegetable
cooking oil with two cups of water in a blender until it turns white.
Apply the mixture immediately, before it begins to separate.

Manual methods Simple measures developed over many years can
help to protect your garden from both pests and poisonous chemicals.
Garden hygiene Snails and slaters live in undisturbed piles of timber
and stones; clear away this material and deprive them of lurking and
breeding places.

The Way We Were

Sparrows, introduced into eastern
Australia in the 19th century,
quickly became a pest of orchard
crops. To this day, sparrows are
ruthless destroyed in Western
Australia.

'The homely sparrow, although
appreciated in town for his
chattering sociable ways, bringing
a message of country outdoor life
to city dwellers, is abused for
wanting to share the food of
poultry and for pulling up young
peas, but he does good service all
the winter in picking up the seeds
of weeds or the larvae of insects, or
helping rid the rose plants of
green fly.'

– *HOME AND GARDEN BEAUTIFUL* (1913)

Crop rotation Long before chemical pest control, gardeners knew that not planting the same vegetable in the same patch of soil two years in succession prevented the build-up of pests and disease; instead, they rotated their crops over periods of three or four years.

Picking off pests Snails come out at night, especially after rain, and are easy to collect. Snail and slug eggs – small and semitransparent – are often found among rubbish, stones and loose soil, and only a little pressure is needed to destroy them. Caterpillars can be squashed, and a strong jet of water from the hose may remove pests such as aphids.

Traps and barriers Wrap hessian around tree trunks to trap the grubs of codling moth; remove the wrappings occasionally and destroy the catch. Smear grease in a band around the trunks of trees to stop the progress of all crawling insects; apply it early in spring, before the caterpillars begin to crawl. Sprinkle wood ash or sand to deter snails and slugs – they find it difficult to cross coarse materials.

FUNGUSES Here too, the wisdom of earlier times highlights the need for garden cleanliness and regular maintenance. Tools can transmit fungal diseases from plant to plant, so keep them meticulously clean. Regularly remove weeds and rubbish.

Armillaria, or root rot, is a common fungus disease of undrained soils. To eradicate it, remove and burn the affected roots. Then improve drainage and apply 125 grams of lime per square metre.

Marigolds planted with spinach keep nematodes away and provide a brilliant colour contrast.

AWAY WITH SNAILS! In 1937 a young Australian, Les Vaughan, noticed large numbers of dead snails clustered around empty packets that had once contained metaldehyde, then used by doctors to sterilise surgical equipment. Vaughan realised the chemical had commercial potential, and soon developed it into a successful snail and slug bait. Scattered in the haunts of these pests, the distinctive green pellets provided gardeners with an easy way to defend flowers and vegetables from attack.

WEEDS Weeds compete with your plants for space, water and nutrients, and should be banished from your garden. Before resorting to modern herbicides, try some of the old ways.

Old manuals constantly stress the most obvious method: remove weeds whenever you see them, by hand or by digging or hoeing, to break the life cycle of annual weeds by preventing them from flowering and running to seed. Lift deep-rooted weeds such as dock and dandelion complete with their tap roots. Weeds with creeping roots are harder to eradicate, as the entire root system has to be lifted. Take heart: continuous cropping, digging and hoeing will eventually get rid of all weeds.

Dense planting and ground cover reduce the need to weed, as weeds find it harder to became established.

INSECT FRIENDS Some insects are your allies in the garden, devouring harmful insects — another reason for not using broad-spectrum pesticides that do not discriminate between friends and foes. Benevolent garden insects include bees, ladybirds, antlions (lacewing larvae), preying mantises, hoverflies, assassin bugs, dragonflies, ground beetles, wasps, hornets and garden spiders.

SIDE BY SIDE Companion planting developed when gardeners of old realised that some plants flourish growing side by side and others perform better apart. In the cottage gardens of yesteryear, blooms brightened the kitchen garden and insect-repellent herbs bordered the flower beds.

• Chives benefit most plants, especially carrots and apple trees.

• Onions, garlic and shallots inhibit beans and peas. Beans thrive best interplanted with carrots and cauliflowers. Peas do well with radishes, cucumber, carrots, corn, beans and turnips.

• Borage and strawberries do well together, and borage flowers are highly attractive to bees. Strawberries are also good companions for lettuce, spinach, and bush beans, but dislike cabbage.

• Lettuce benefits from proximity to carrots.

• Tomatoes grow well near asparagus, basil, carrots, celery and parsley.

• Roses benefit from parsley and garlic, which protect them from aphids and is also said to intensify their fragrance.

• Borders of pyrethrum daisies will discourage insect pests.

• A crop of marigolds (*Tagetes* species) will rid the ground of nematodes (eelworms), and is especially useful planted among tomatoes, which are prone to nematode attack.

• Sage protects carrots against whitefly and cabbages from the cabbage white butterfly.

• Tansy repels ants, flies, chewing beetles, cabbage moth and aphids and bitter herbs such as rue, mugwort, wormwood and southernwood repel slugs and insects.

Words of Wisdom

'A very good way to protect Peas from birds, mice, and slugs is to strew a layer of sawdust half an inch thick entirely over the drill after the Peas have been sown and covered. Mice never touch it; birds do not like it, and never meddle with the Peas when they appear through it; and it bothers the slugs by sticking to them. Any sawdust will do.'

– *BRETT'S GARDENING GUIDE* (1919)

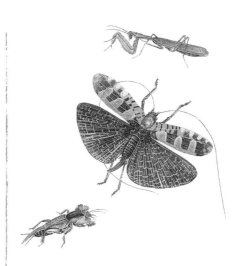

The preying mantis (top) eats insect pests but crickets (above) sometimes devastate grasses.

DESIGNING WOMEN

Among the influential garden designers of the past hundred years, three women are prominent. English garden designer Gertrude Jekyll, along with her mentor William Robinson, developed the concept of 'natural' gardens as a reaction to the formal practice of 'bedding out' of the mid 19th century. Before these two revolutionised garden design, the fashion was to raise flowers in greenhouses and then transplant them into formal flowerbeds to provide spectacular displays two or three times a year.

In contrast, Jekyll championed the herbaceous border, planting hardy perennials in subtle colour gradations and allowing them to bloom and die down naturally. Another keen English gardener, Vita Sackville-West, followed in Jekyll's footsteps when she created her renowned garden at Sissinghurst in Kent. And Edna Walling, who was born in England but spent her working life in Australia, adapted Jekyll's design principles to suit the Australasian climate and lifestyle.

EDNA WALLING

Many gardeners, including Walling herself, have judged Mawarra, a garden in Mount Dandenong, to be her finest creation. It is a peaceful garden that has matured and increased in beauty with time. The original herbaceous borders have recently been recreated.

GERTRUDE JEKYLL

Hestercombe, in Somerset, is a fitting memorial to the long collaboration between Gertrude Jekyll and architect Edwin Lutyens. The sumptuous plantings owe much to Jekyll, while the layout, using natural materials and geometric forms, is Lutyens' contribution.

VITA SACKVILLE-WEST

Beautiful, eccentric writer and passionate gardener Vita Sackville-West designed her famous garden at Sissinghurst in Kent on many of Gertrude Jekyll's ideas. She enthusiastically adopted Jekyll's concept of garden 'rooms', each with a different theme and blooming in a different season. Every year thousands of people visit Sissinghurst, which is now the property of the British National Trust.

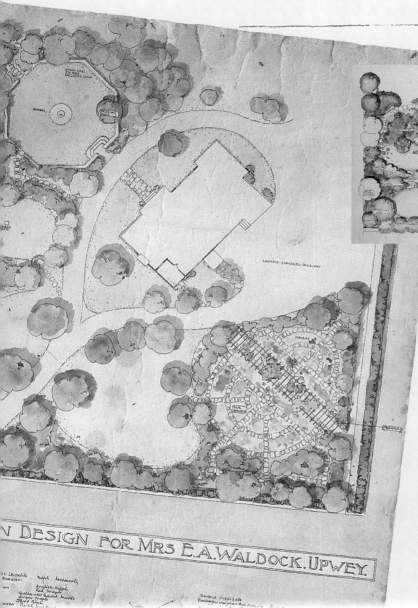

N DESIGN FOR MRS E.A.WALDOCK. UPWEY.

Born in Yorkshire, Edna Walling and her family settled in Australia in 1912, when she was sixteen. At first she was strongly influenced by memories of the countryside and flower gardens of England, but later her involvement in environmental issues and her love of the Australian bush led to a radical change in her style in the 1950s, when she began to press for the inclusion of Australian native flora.

A delightful feature of Walling's work was her beautifully drawn and water-coloured plans, such as those illustrated above and left. Like those of Jekyll and Sackville-West, her designs began with strong architectural elements such as walls, steps, pathways and water features, softened with prolific and exuberant plantings.

GROWING NATIVE PLANTS WITH EXOTICS

Edna Walling began to use native Australian plants in the 1950s, and sometimes combined natives and exotics. She would certainly have approved of these three planting ideas.

For a romantic, fragrant potted arrangement, surround a gardenia with native violets and allow them to spill over the edge of the pot.

You can achieve a dramatic effect by planting arum lilies around a native grass tree.

Plant Dutch or Louisiana irises around the edges of a pool where native water lilies are growing.

Animals in the garden

THE GARDENS OF OLD HOUSED A RANGE OF ANIMALS, FROM DOGS AND RABBITS TO PEACOCKS. MOST SUBURBAN YARDS ALSO HAD A CHICKEN SHED.

As gardeners of the past were aware, striking a balance between your garden's needs and those of your animals is not always easy, but it is simpler if you adopt a practical approach. If you do not keep a pet, another way of bringing the animal world into your garden is to attract wildlife instead.

POULTRY For our great-grandparents, keeping a few hens was more than a source of food; it was also a way of recycling kitchen scraps and controlling weeds and insect pests. But vigilance and good fences are essential if the enterprise is to run smoothly.

Food and shelter Fowls need shade, sunshine, dust, green feed, and plenty of clean water. At night they need a clean, dry, sheltered place to roost. They like variety – cooked potatoes, stale bread or a cabbage head to pick at are welcomed. Poultry can be let loose in the orchard, but ducks are best confined to the vegetable and flower gardens.

PETS You may need to fence off a section for a pet, or else restrict serious gardening to the glasshouse and shade house.

Dogs Dogs are likely to be destructive to the garden: if you cannot live with this, a dog is not for you. However, there are ways of modifying your garden to cope better with the habits of a dog. Select robust shrubs and trees with flexible rather than brittle branches. Strategically placed plants with prickles and spikes can be useful – pets will learn to avoid them.

Cats Cats prefer the ease of digging in newly turned soil. If you abandon a section of your garden to your cats, they may confine themselves to that patch and leave the rest of the garden alone. Or provide a sandpit (for feline use only), which they may prefer to your newly sown beds. Mulch will also deter a cat.

BIRDS, BEES AND BUTTERFLIES You can encourage visits from these beautiful and beneficial creatures by growing plants that will increase your garden's attractions.

A birdbath lends a relaxed, old-world feeling to a garden, while providing water for birds. Birds will find food and shelter among the leafy branches of fruit-bearing bushes and trees. Many birds nest in hollow trees and branches, so do not remove these trees unless they are unsafe.

Butterflies and bees will visit your garden and cluster around flowering plants that are rich in pollen; butterflies are attracted to flat-faced summer flowers, such as buddleia.

Letting poultry wander through the garden occasionally can be beneficial – they will seek out insects and weeds to feed upon.

Taking your dog for a daily walk may discourage it from digging up your garden.

Warmth and shelter

GREENHOUSES WERE ALL THE RAGE IN EUROPE LAST
CENTURY AS GARDENERS SCRAMBLED TO GROW
TROPICAL PLANTS FROM ASIA AND AMERICA.

The greenhouse, shadehouse and cold frame
moderate the environment, allowing gardeners
to raise plants that otherwise could not survive,
and to extend the growing seasons of others.

GREENHOUSES Greenhouses are popular in
cooler climates and during the winter. In
Australia and New Zealand the greenhouse is
usually an extra for special plants. It can range
from a small lean-to against a house wall to an
imposing free-standing affair. In the cooler parts
of New Zealand glasshouses are used to raise
salad vegetables as well as flowering plants.

A position with full sun all day is best, but the
greenhouse should at least be sited to receive unobstructed morning
light. If an even temperature and protection from wind are all you need,
an unheated greenhouse will do. Some plants, however, need extra heat;
this can be provided by whatever means is the most economical and
convenient, such as an electric fan heater. Study your greenhouse inside
and out to establish its water, ventilation and shade requirements.

Regulating light and shade When necessary, usually from spring to
autumn, sunlight can be reduced by using blinds or other shading.
Protect a greenhouse exposed to the north and west from the summer
sun by applying a coat of whitewash in spring. Rain, wind and sun
will gradually remove the whitewash, and by the dull days of winter
abundant light will again be flooding in.

Ventilation Provide adequate ventilation, preferably at the sides.
Open ventilation windows on warm, humid days and close them in
cold, windy weather. The door should not face in the direction of the
prevailing wind. Leave enough space between the shelves for air to
circulate freely. Some plants thrive better on shelves with sides
turned up like trays than on flat, open shelves.

Watering Maintaining humidity is as important as maintaining an
even temperature. Brick flooring is best, as bricks retain moisture
well. In general, water in the morning, when the temperature is
rising; in winter, especially, this gives the plant a chance to adjust to
the water temperature. Water sparingly in winter and, if possible, on
a sunny day to minimise temperature fluctuations.

THE SHADEHOUSE The popularity in the 19th century of ferns, orchids
and tender exotics made the shadehouse – also called a bush house – a

*'Who loves a garden loves a
greenhouse too,' wrote 18th
century English poet William
Cowper in* The Task, *his long
poem on rural themes.*

*Shadehouse plants favoured in
earlier years include begonias; elk
horns and stag horns; tree-ferns;
maidenhair; and such palms as
the kentia, bangalow and fan.*

gardener's essential in Australia. In cooler climates such as New Zealand tropical plants need the full protection of glass to flourish, but in most parts of Australia the shadehouse is sufficient. It diffuses the strong rays of the sun; provides shelter from draughts while allowing free circulation of air; and protects from crushing rain. And a bench near the entrance provides a pleasant refuge in full view of both the garden and the shadehouse plants.

Building a shadehouse A shadehouse is relatively simple and inexpensive to build. In its most basic form, the end walls are about 2.5 metres wide and 3 metres high; the side walls can be whatever length is desired. If possible, site the shadehouse running east–west.

The walls should resemble a paling fence: attach either palings, bamboo or thin, straight saplings to the frame. The palings need be only 2 metres high; fill in the metre gap between the top of the palings and the roof with wide-spaced battens or wire netting. Put a door of closely spaced palings on the western or southern side.

A flat roof is best: place saplings or sawn timber at 1-metre intervals, then stretch lengths of fencing wire lengthways over them and interlace thin branches of pliable plant stems through the wire. Do not put too much shade material on the roof – it must let in more light than the walls – and do not make the roof too low.

Inside the shadehouse Grow plants in beds dug in the floor on each side, or in pots on benches and shelves. Leave enough space to be able to walk easily up and down the centre. Seedlings and tender plants can be raised in boxes and pots in the shadehouse before being planted out in the garden. Exotics can be coaxed along to their flowering or display stage, and then put on show indoors.

Shadehouse conditions are ideal for ferns, palms and orchids. Turn ferns in pots half-way around every two or three weeks so they will grow evenly.

COLD FRAMES A cold frame traps warmth from the sun, helping cuttings to strike and seedlings to grow rapidly at the start of the season. Introduce plants gradually to the garden when the weather becomes warmer, so they are acclimatised when the time comes to plant them out. The frame should face north, to take full advantage of the sun.

Taking Care of the Fence

A simple cold frame can be made from surplus materials. A discarded glazed window frame is ideal for the top; old planking or a cut down wooden packing case will do for the sides. The back of the enclosure should be higher than the front. Attach the window frame to the back with hinges. In hot weather, shade the plants with a blind.

The Way We Were

'The bush house is suited to the woman that is fond of flowers, yet lacks the strength to dig. It is a concentrated form of gardening, somewhat more advanced than the verandah gardening, yet not requiring so much technical knowledge, and such unremitting care as glasshouse work.'

– *THE AUSTRALIAN GARDEN FAIR* (1923)

The kindly fruits of the earth

GARDEN-FRESH FRUITS WERE COMMON IN DAYS OF OLD, WHEN FRUIT OF SOME DESCRIPTION GREW IN MOST BACKYARDS.

Late summer brought succulent grapes, juicy sun-warmed peaches and the astringent taste of passionfruit; crisp apples and wild blackberries were the bounty of autumn; while spring brought the purple-stained delights of mulberry picking and the joy of watching strawberries grow plump and crimson. What was not eaten fresh was preserved in jams, jellies, pickles and chutneys.

THIN AND TRIM After planting, a young deciduous fruit tree – apple, pear, fig, mulberry or stone fruit – should be cut back hard, removing most or all of its head and leaving no more than three upwardly angled, evenly spaced limbs. This sounds drastic, but if you spare the pruning knife, the tree will grow long and spindly, with practically all the new wood at the tips.

Continue to prune hard for three to four years to build up a stocky tree with good bearing wood throughout. Prune to an open-centred vase shape, with evenly spaced limbs rising at an oblique angle from close to the ground – these will sustain a heavy crop better than branches that stretch out horizontally.

Figs Remove the autumnal green fruit from fig trees. They will not develop into usable fruit, and if left on will hinder the growth of the new branches that will bear the next season's crop.

Stone fruits Some trees often bear more than the branch can carry or that the tree can nourish; if all the fruit is left to mature, it will be mostly small and of poor quality. Thin it out by removing the smaller fruits so that those remaining have enough room to grow to maturity.

Branching out Apples, pears, peaches, plums, apricots and cherries are suitable for training as espaliers and cordons, and these trees make an attractive and productive alternative to ornamental climbers.

In a small garden, a tree trained by either system can take up no more room than a row of peas, yet crop as heavily as a full-sized tree. Prune with great care for the first two or three years to obtain well-spaced branches; from then on a yearly trimming is vital if the form is to be maintained. Two or three trees of the same variety are necessary for good cross-pollination and fruit formation.

An espalier is a tree trained on wires, with its branches positioned so that they radiate outwards horizontally from its stem. Espaliered fruit trees make attractive features on warm walls, and are useful screens and garden dividers.

Deciduous fruit trees such as apples and pears require an annual pruning to ensure they yield good crops of fruit.

A *cordon* is a tree kept to a single stem, with evenly spaced, upwardly angled limbs covered in fruiting spurs trained against a wall. A two-stemmed form has branches lined with fruiting spurs trained in opposite directions along wires 50 cm or so from the ground. This method can be used alongside paths in a small garden.

VINES To bear a good crop of fruit, grape vines require plenty of manure every year, placed on the surface of the soil in autumn. Water well during the cropping period. The leaves dropped in autumn make excellent compost. When pruning grapes, leave the largest and strongest shoots, as they produce the plumpest and sweetest fruit.

Passionfruit appreciate compost-enriched soil, regular watering and a sunny position. Cut back after fruiting to allow better air movement and to encourage new lateral shoots, which will produce the next fruit.

BERRY FRUITS Fresh berries picked from the garden were a common treat in days of old. Most berries are easy to cultivate, so why not enjoy the luxury of home-grown berries yourself?

Strawberries Remove flowers from strawberry plants in their first year to ensure that all their strength goes into making strong plants rather than indifferent fruit. In the following season you will be rewarded with a fine crop. Replace each plant after its third year. Cultivate several beds, each planted in a different year, to ensure a regular supply of fruit. Nip off runners in early autumn to separate new plants from their parents. Protect the beds in winter with a covering of straw, grass cuttings or other mulch; remove this in spring. If space is a problem, grow strawberries in recesses cut into the sides of a large upright container filled with rich soil.

Grapes are one of the most cultivated fruits worldwide. A vine or two was an asset in the home garden, and did not need as many people to gather them, as in this 19th-century vineyard at Marlboro-on-the-Hudson, in the United States.

Currants and gooseberries Plant at the back of borders, in soil that should be well trenched to a depth of at least 60 cm. In autumn, prune out excess summer growth (where one or more branches cross, cut one out) to ensure that the bush is not crowded with young wood the following summer, which will make it difficult for the sun to reach the fruit and ripen it. Propagate currants from cuttings of wood taken the previous year, choosing straight, vigorous shoots.

Loganberries These grow quickly and easily, and produce exceptionally good crops. Before planting, dig the ground deeply and manure well. Train plants on wires over a fence. The canes will bear only once; they should be cut back to the ground after fruiting.

Harvest home

HARVEST IS TRADITIONALLY A TIME OF
CONTENTMENT, WHEN THE WORK OF SOWING AND
TENDING CROPS IS FINALLY REWARDED.

Our forebears knew that the harvest represented the provisions that
would see them through the coming winter, so they gathered and
stored vegetables, fruits and grains with great care. On a less
utilitarian level, they also knew how to harvest flowers for both
colour and fragrance.

VEGETABLES Gather vegetables in the early morning, before the sun
robs them of their crispness. If you do not need them at once, store
them in a cool, dry place.

   Pumpkins will last throughout the winter stored in a cool, well
ventilated spot. In the old days they were packed in dry straw in the
stable or barn. Peas, beans, radishes, beetroot, turnips, cucumber and
squash are best picked just before they reach maturity, but tomatoes
have a better flavour if allowed to ripen on the vine.

FRUITS Pick fruit for storage in the middle of the day, after the dew
has evaporated and the fruit is quite dry. It is best gathered before it is
fully ripe. Be careful not to bruise the fruit, as this leads to decay.
Place it gently in a shallow box or basket, preferably in a single layer,
as placing one layer of fruit on another can cause bruising. Store in a
cool, dry, well-ventilated place.

Apples and pears When the fruit is almost ripe, place a mulch of
grass or straw under the tree to prevent falling pieces bruising when
they land. Pick the fruit by raising a piece slightly and twisting it to
one side. If it does not part easily from the branch, leave it on the tree.
To store apples and pears for a long period, place them in boxes of
perfectly dry sand, which preserves them by keeping them cool and
excluding air. Avoid placing pieces of fruit together so that they touch
one another. A cool cellar makes an ideal storage place.

Lemons These can be stored for several months in dry sand, the same
way as apples. Pick when they are fully grown but still pale green.

FLOWERS Gather flowers in the early morning, when they are full of
sap; the stored energy keeps them fresh for a longer time. Place a
bucket of clean, fresh, cool water in a shady spot and put the cut
flowers into it immediately. Pick before the flowers are fully
developed, at the stage between bud and bloom.

   Delphiniums will last longer if the stems are plunged into very hot
water for a few seconds as soon as they are cut, then transferred to cold.
Gum leaves will have a longer vase life if immersed in water for an
hour or two after cutting. All cut flowers will keep longer in water
that is clean and fresh.

A HARVEST HYMN
Come, ye thankful people, come,
Raise the song of Harvest-home:
All is safely gathered in,
Ere the winter storms begin.
– HENRY ALFORD (1810–1871)

Making the most of your garden

THE TYPE OF GARDEN YOU DECIDE TO CREATE WILL DEPEND ON YOUR SPACE, YOUR SOIL AND YOUR TERRAIN, AS WELL AS ON YOUR PERSONAL TASTE.

Study your climate, aspect, soil and natural features before you start to create a garden. A natural rocky outcrop begs for a rock garden, while a sunny corner is ideal for a formal herb garden. These days the back garden is largely the preserve of the swimming pool and barbecue, but there are healthy rewards if you can find space for a kitchen garden. There is also a special joy in creating a garden for children.

ROCK GARDENS The fashion for rock gardens began in Edwardian England, when they were contrived for growing alpine plants. Later, designing rock gardens became an art in itself. The mini-environment of nooks, crannies and crevices allows you to grow plants that would not flourish in a normal garden bed, but you need not restrict your planting to alpine dwellers.

The site Choose a sloping site – a rock garden on flat ground will not look natural. It is best to make a rockery in autumn so the stones and soil will be well settled by spring. Site the garden in full sunshine, away from water run-off from trees.

Drainage is very important. Examine your soil, and if it is heavy and damp, remove enough to build up a more porous foundation – old building rubble, empty tins filled with soil with holes in the sides, bricks, tiles and other building rubble are suitable foundation materials. Bind this together with wire or wire netting, ram soil and gravel into the crevices, and you will have a mound in which you can embed rocks and stones in a natural-looking formation.

Choosing and placing the rocks The keynote is informality. Study rocky hillsides in nature, noting how the rocks are positioned to hold the soil, and try to reproduce such formations in your garden.

The type of rock will be governed by availability as well as personal choice. Light-coloured rocks such as sandstone contrast pleasantly with the greys and greens of rockery plants. Choose large rocks and set them firmly and deeply, with the most attractive face of each showing. Vary the size, shape and angle as much as possible. Make sure all are securely embedded, and make any necessary cementing invisible.

Planting A good nurseryman can advise on the most suitable plants for any given situation. Group plants according to colour and form, providing shelter for those that need shade and placing sun-lovers in the hottest positions. When all the plants are in place, give the rockery a light covering of very coarse sand or broken gravel.

The best site for a rockery is on land with a natural rise.

210

HERB GARDENS

HERB GARDENS Culinary and medicinal herbs have long formed an integral part of the traditional garden. As their number includes annuals, biennials and perennials, this is a very versatile group of plants; whatever the situation, there will be suitable herbs. Most require little more than sunlight and well drained soil. In cottage gardens, herbs were planted among flowers and allowed to self-seed.

Knot gardens A favourite planting arrangement for herbs was to enclose and protect them in a low, clipped hedge tracing the shape of a knot. There were several forms of knot – open, closed or in the shape of a family emblem. Influenced by Continental Renaissance gardens, knot gardens first became popular in England in the 16th century.

To make a knot garden, choose your design, plant a border of box, lavender or rosemary – all these will take hard pruning – and fill the spaces with herbs.

Wheels and ladders Confining each type of herb to its own enclosure can involve some imaginative recycling. Position an old cart wheel or a small wooden ladder on the ground and fill each section with a different herb.

What to plant Always include chives and basil – as well as their delicious and versatile flavour, they have attractive flowers and pest-repellent properties. Sage and thyme, both handsome evergreens, are good companions, but caraway is not happy with fennel, nor will parsley prosper beside mint. Pennyroyal, marjoram and winter savory belong with parsley in a *bouquet garni*, and so should have a place in

Rediscover the tranquil pleasures of growing your own produce.

The common marigold has a place in any herb garden, providing flavour for soups and salads, and colour to pot-pourri.

211

the garden. Yarrow is said to enhance the aromatic qualities of other herbs. Therapeutic herbs include marshmallow, chamomile, dandelion, tansy and wormwood.

THE KITCHEN GARDEN Site this plot in a sunny, well-drained position near the back door. Filled with vegetables and herbs for the table and flowers for indoor decoration, it will be pretty as well as practical. And if you base the design on the formal gardens popular in the mid-19th century, a kitchen garden can be decorative – try a circular bed with even segments divided by pavers, each section filled with a different vegetable and the rim edged with thyme, parsley or strawberry plants. A paved or gravel path around the plot will keep your feet free of mud in wet weather.

Successive plantings Be guided by the tastes of your household and the potential of the soil, so that you do not waste time and space growing vegetables that no one will eat or that will not thrive.

Plant so that you have crops ready to eat throughout the year. A 1923 issue of the magazine *The Garden and the Home* suggested the following row by row guide to keep the garden productive all year:
  a row of peas, followed by cabbages
  a row of spinach, followed by radishes
  a row of carrots, followed by lettuce
  a row of onions, followed in spring by French beans
  a row of beetroot, followed in spring by tomatoes
  a row of lettuce or peas, followed in spring by early carrots
  a row of parsnips, followed in spring by beans
  a row of peas, followed in spring by cucumbers or marrow

COTTAGE GARDENS Historically, cottage gardens were the antithesis of the large formal gardens, orchards and kitchen plots of the landed gentry. Working people had only a small area on which to grow all their needs. The resulting garden, a profuse and harmonious jumble based on productivity, colour and companionship, was practical as well as pretty. Seeds and cuttings were saved from year to year, new plants were acquired by exchange, rather than purchase, self-seeding plants such as alyssum, hollyhocks and forget-me-nots were treasured, and fragrant plants from the wild also found a place. Borders were usually perennials and new acquisitions were placed wherever there was space, resulting in a mixture of plants of different heights.

Although no two gardens were the same, they had in common the need to use the entire area, leaving room for only one or two paths.

Creating a cottage garden Make paths no wider than the width of a wheelbarrow and soften the edges with trailing ground covers or fragrant low-growing herbs. Place shrubs and tall plants towards the

In the old days, many varieties of fruit and vegetables were grown. This selection featuring melons, pumpkins, tomatoes and an unusual variety of capsicum comes from a 1913 edition of the Larousse Encyclopedia.

The Way We Were
The Allied nations responded wholeheartedly to the World War II 'Dig for Victory' campaign, which urged people to grow food in every available patch of soil. Public land in many large cities, including the moat of the Tower of London, was turned over to cabbages, cauliflowers, carrots and potatoes.

'Dig! Dig! Dig! And your
  muscles will grow big,
Keep on pushing in the spade!
Never mind the worms,
Just ignore their squirms,
And when your back aches,
  laugh with glee,
And keep on diggin'
Till we give our foes a wiggin'
Dig! Dig! Dig! to Victory.'

back and low-growing and trailing plants at the front and along pathways. Plant in large drifts, not straight rows, and mix perennials of different heights together. Avoid large masses of one colour, but take advantage of white flowers and the mute greens and greys of many herbs – these will soften bright profusions. If tempted by the colours, forms and longer-flowering periods of hybrids, remember that the sacrifice for these advantages is that hybrids do not have the fragrance of their ancestors, nor will they breed true to type.

Some plants for the cottage garden A typical cottage garden included a range of plants. While your choice will depend upon climate, aspect, availability and personal preference, the following flowering plants and herbs have been popular choices for cottage gardens over many years.

Flowers and shrubs Baby's breath, baby's tears, buddleia, columbine, cornflower, daisy, daphne, forget-me-not, foxglove, gardenia, geranium and pelagonium, gilliflower, heliotrope, hydrangea, larkspur, lilac, love-in-a-mist, lupin, marigold, monkshood, primrose, nasturtium, peony, pinks, poppy, red valerian, rose, shrub rose, snapdragon, sunflower, violet, wallflower

Climbers Honeysuckle, ivy geranium, jasmine, climbing roses, sweet pea, wisteria

Edgings and ground covers Garden viola, lobelia, meadow foam, primrose, sweet alyssum, sweet violet

Herbs Basil, borage, chamomile, chives, feverfew, hyssop, lavender, mallow, parsley, rosemary, sage, speedwell, thyme

A CHILD'S GARDEN In the time before radio and television children were encouraged to spend happy and productive hours in the garden, and absorbed horticultural knowledge as they helped to plant and raise vegetables and blooms. The garden was, and still can be, a place of wonder and discovery for all ages.

Preparation and planting Choose a piece of land with morning sun and dig and enrich the soil – this is a job for the supervising adult: if it is poorly performed, the results will probably be discouraging. Restrict planting to sturdy, fast-growing varieties that can be relied upon to flourish.

Flowers such as honeysuckle, balsam, pansies, snapdragons, golden marigolds and sunflowers are fun. The seed pods of busy lizzie burst open at the slightest touch, the yellow glow of buttercups held under the chin can be analysed and daisies can be threaded into chains. Peas and broad beans are a good introductory vegetable crop, with a border of parsley and red lettuce. Take care not to plant poisonous plants or plants with thorns.

Play areas Make sure the play area is shaded and has a soft surface, such as lawn. For young children, include a sandpit. Tricycle riders will appreciate a wide path with a firm surface and turning circles.

A sturdy tree with low, climbable branches can be a meeting place or a site for a tree house. Suitable trees include the jacaranda (a haze of blue in spring), Japanese maple (silky smooth bark for climbing), mulberry and mango.

Encourage your children's enterprises in the garden by offering to buy the flowers and vegetables they cultivate at current shop prices.

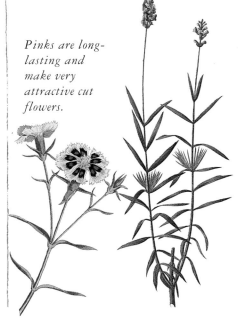

Sweet lavender is a popular choice for the cottage garden.

Pinks are long-lasting and make very attractive cut flowers.

BIRDS IN THE HIGH HALL-GARDEN

Birdsong in the garden makes early mornings and early evenings a delight. A pair of rosellas hanging upside down on a banksia bush or a magpie foraging on the lawn for fine twigs for her nest bring a garden to life. Birds in the garden add colour and movement and a feeling of being at one with nature.

You can easily attract birds to a suburban garden, even a tiny one, by growing a judicious selection of food plants to supply blossoms, berries and seeds, and by planting native shrubs that have a high insect population. If you want birds to regard your garden as home, you also need to provide plenty of cover, a permanent supply of water and high branches or perches that the birds can use as song posts. Dense shrubbery, especially if it has prickly foliage, attracts many of the smaller birds.

SIGHTS AND SOUNDS
A well placed dovecote makes a charming focal point in the garden at any time, and the gentle cooing of doves has a wonderfully calming effect on a warm summer afternoon.

MAGPIES MATES
Magpies are conscientious parents, protecting their eggs with great ferocity and working hard to satisfy the appetite of their demanding young. Magpies need tall trees for roosting and nesting, but come to open garden spaces to forage.

MAKING A BIRDBATH
All birds appreciate a birdbath, and they will provide you with endless entertainment as they stop to bathe and drink. Make sure there is a perch nearby so that they can check that the area is free of predators such as cats.

A flattish earthenware dish set on a piece of clay pipe is one option.

A shallow stone dish embedded in a rockery is another possibility.

CANNY KOOKABURRAS

Kookaburras are frequent visitors to suburban gardens. They tend to stay in the same area and can live for up to 20 years, so they become well known to local human residents. They are patient hunters, perching on low branches to scan the ground for prey, and have also been known to steal a free feed from suburban barbecues.

FEEDING THE BIRDS

A seed ring can provide a healthy supplement when food is scarce.

1. Mix 3/4 of a cup of native bird seed mixture with 1/4 of a cup of unprocessed bran and a beaten egg. Place in a greased, foil-lined container and bake in a moderate oven until solid.

2. Hang the ring from a tree branch with a sturdy ribbon.

SUPERB FAIRY WRENS

These jaunty little birds like low, thick bushes in the garden for protection from larger predators. Wrens live in family groups and they all help to forage in open grassy areas for insects with which to feed the young. Nests are often close to the ground and baby superb fairy wrens are weak flyers, so they need to be protected from cats and dogs.

ROSELLAS AND OTHER PARROTS

At the time of early European settlement, eastern rosellas were common in the Rose Hill area of Sydney and became known as 'Rose Hillers'. This name was later corrupted to rosella, and now describes a group of similarly patterned Australian parrots. Rosellas settle in areas with a scattering of mature trees suitable for nesting and open ground where they can forage for seeds and insects. Like lorikeets, they enjoy the pollen and nectar of native flowering shrubs and trees. They are also partial to a little fruit, which can be a problem if your garden has fruit trees, but native fruit trees such as the Port Jackson pine will provide them with an alternative preferred diet. As well as enhancing your garden, flowering gum trees, paperbarks and banksias will provide nectar for rosellas, lorikeets and other native parrots.

BELLING THE CAT

However cute and furry, cats are natural enemies of birds. Larger birds soon learn to ignore cats, but smaller birds are easy prey. It was once thought that a bell around a cat's neck would warn birds of their danger, but cats are adept at stalking so smoothly that the bell doesn't sound.

Indoor gardens

WITH A LITTLE TENDER LOVING CARE, MANY
PLANTS, INCLUDING MOST BULBS, SUCCULENTS AND
ANNUALS, CAN BE GROWN SUCCESSFULLY INDOORS.

In the 19th century, exotic plants brought back from the tropics
caused great excitement. In Europe, these plants had to be grown
under glass; most grand Victorian and Edwardian houses had a
conservatory filled with ferns, palms, orchids and other delights, while
many a modest house was also graced with a scaled-down version of
this glass garden. In Australia and New Zealand, delicate plants were
grown in shadehouses or glasshouses (see page 205), or else on a
sheltered veranda or indoors.

Indoor plants are within easy reach and can be attended to with
little effort, and fickle weather presents no obstacle.

HOUSE PLANTS As with outdoor gardening, good drainage, feeding
and suitable soil are the keys to success. Space for indoor plants is
limited, so select a choice variety. You will find greater interest in
watching their varied growths and welcoming a range of blooms.

Watering More plants are lost through overwatering than the reverse;
take particular care to not overwater in winter. The evening is the best
time to water in summer, and the morning in winter. When watering
hairy-leafed plants, such as African violets, do not wet the foliage, as
this can cause leaf rot and disease. Most smooth-leaved plants can be
watered on the foliage, and occasionally spraying their leaves with
mist in hot weather is beneficial.

Light Many of the plants suitable for indoor use are natives of jungles
and rainforests, so are accustomed to filtered light and high humidity
like that in a home. No plant can grow without light. A general sign
of insufficient light is weak and spindly growth.
A variegated plant lacking light will turn green
as it tries to take maximum advantage of the
available light – this often happens in winter –
and moving the plant closer to a window
will usually restore its foliage. Plants
that can tolerate less light than most
include the aspidistra, some
philodendrons and English ivies.
Plants will always try to face the light,
and are best positioned against a side
wall opposite a window.

Give your plants an occasional spell
outside – there you will have good
light for carefully checking leaves for
signs of distress, and they will benefit
from a gentle hosing and some fresh air.

*The Victorians were keen indoor
gardeners. There was no shortage
of pots for the purpose, as this
1890 advertisement shows.*

Scraggy plants A few simple remedies can restore scraggy plants to health. Make sure the plant has morning sun and is not in a draught. Arrange your pots so that sun-loving plants get most of the sun's rays, and let others, such as ferns, take the shady spots. Rearrange their positions until you discover where each plant thrives best. Fast-growing, soft-wooded plants need a light, rich compost that allows roots to develop quickly.

Repotting The roots of potted plants, indoors or outdoors, are confined in a very limited space. At the very least, their root systems need fresh soil at regular intervals. Signs of nutrient deprivation are refusal to grow and small pale leaves.

Repot in the same pot, after carefully trimming some of the entangled roots, or in a slightly larger one. Do not put small plants into big pots, as the soil becomes sour before the tiny roots have a chance to use it.

Never repot plants in winter – repotting into cold soil when the plant is inactive can lead to losses, as the roots will not penetrate the fresh soil until growth starts again in the warmer weather.

As with all gardening, good drainage is of prime importance. Place a piece of broken pot, hollow side down, over the drainage hole, and on top of this lay smaller shards, small stones, charcoal or anything similar that will help water to quickly drain away – a third of the pot should be taken up with this material. Top with a layer of potting mixture suited to the plant, then place the plant in position, gently spreading the roots out towards the sides of the pot. Gradually fill in with potting mixture, at the same time turning the pot and compacting the soil evenly all around. Leave ample space for watering.

Soak a new earthenware pot in water for 15 minutes, otherwise the porous clay of the pot will absorb much of the water you give its plant for many weeks afterwards. Scrub old pots clean before re-using them.

Carrot ferns Cut off a carrot top a couple of centimetres below the leaf base, and place it on damp cotton wool or lint, or even just in a saucer of water. It will quickly sprout an attractive green ferny growth

Planters, a little fork, potting mix and some bulbs and seeds – you do not need much paraphernalia for successful indoor gardening

There is no need to spend money on expensive plant pots: old teapots and cracked cups are just two examples of receptacles that can be recycled as planters in the kitchen or living room.

Children will enjoy inspecting a carrot fern each day in case new shoots have appeared.

that lasts for some time. Carrot ferns make an inexpensive decoration in the kitchen and do well on windowsills.

VERANDA FLOWERS For those who do not have a shadehouse or conservatory, a veranda can often provide sufficient shelter, if it is free of draughts. The best aspect is facing north-east (for morning sun), and one or both ends should be enclosed.

The biggest problem is that pots dry out quickly, but this can be overcome by choosing concrete or wooden containers instead of clay pots, which are very porous. Using two containers, one within the other, is another way of slowing moisture loss. Hardy palms, ferns and shrubs are good veranda plants. Fuchsias have always been a favourite, and flower well if cut back yearly; they also root easily from cuttings.

WINDOW BOXES Window boxes, which can be tended from indoors, were popular in the 1920s and 1930s and have enjoyed a revival in recent years. There are two methods of window box gardening. One is to fill a box with plants in pots, then pack leaf-litter or sphagnum moss around and over the pots, perhaps finishing off with a light covering of soil. This suits foliage plants that require little attention, other than correct watering, such as aspidistra, aralia, grevillea, ferns and aucuba. The second is to grow plants directly in the boxes.

Drainage The shape of the window box is a matter of personal taste. Its most important feature is good drainage. If the box is long, it may require more than one drainage hole, or a drain that will funnel all excess water to a hole at one end can be fashioned in the bottom of the box. Attach a short pipe to the hole to prevent water stains on the sill.

Suitable plants The aspect of the box will determine what you can grow. Plants popular in the past include begonias, dwarf nasturtiums, pansies, primulas, mignonette, geraniums and pelargoniums, violas, petunias, alyssum and the fragrant dwarf Virginia stock. Trailing plants are very effective; lobelia, in particular, can provide a mass of colour over a long flowering period. Succulents can be used in frost-free areas and cacti do well in a hot sunny situation. Potted herbs can also be kept in a sunny window box. On the shady side of the house, ferns can be substituted for flowering plants. Bulbs are best grown in pots and placed in a window box when in flower.

Words of Wisdom

Many common household plants are known to remove chemicals from indoor air. These wonder-working plants include many that graced our great-grandparents' homes – peace lilies, rubber plants, palms, philodendrons and spider plants.

'If you are so unfortunately placed as not to have a foot of ground outside of your house, try and grow a few plants and flowers inside your house, even in your bedroom. They will not only be interesting and beautiful to look at, but will purify the room by inhaling what to us would be foul air; for, like us, flowers breathe and even sleep, but they breathe and flourish best by absorbing air which is unhealthy to us.'

– *THE HAPPIFYING GARDENING HOBBY*, E.W. COLE (1918)

The terrarium was another way to bring the outdoors in, in what was really a scaled-down version of the greenhouse.

Enclosures

FENCES AND HEDGES ARE PRACTICAL AS WELL AS DECORATIVE. EARLY SETTLERS IN AUSTRALIA AND NEW ZEALAND OFTEN GREW HIGH WINDBREAKS OF EVERGREENS SUCH AS RADIATA PINE.

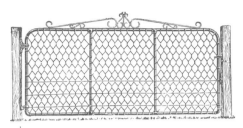

The humblest of huts edged the space in front with a fence of split palings or saplings nailed to rails. Hedges of hawthorn or lonerica (hedge honeysuckle), planted in some areas as cheap, natural fences for stock and as protection against wild animals, also provided privacy, shade and shelter from the elements.

In suburban gardens, fences and hedges, as well as giving privacy, can be used to divide the space into outdoor rooms. Arches can add an element of surprise and pergolas and summerhouses provide welcome shady retreats on hot days.

FENCES A fence with close palings blocking the prevailing winds can make a difference of several degrees in temperature – enough to prevent serious damage to tender plants. A fence is also a barrier against roaming animals, and it provides privacy.

When choosing a fence, consider the type of plants that will surround it. Clothe a bare paling fence in flowering or fruiting climbers. Plant flowering shrubs such as azaleas or hydrangeas close to a post and rail fence to fill it out.

Picket fences Full of old-fashioned charm, a picket fence is ideal for a cottage garden. It shelters plants by cutting down wind flow, and lets in enough light for plants to thrive and to work their way between the pickets. Traditionally, fence pickets were hand-split. With motorised saws came dressed timber with elaborate curved, pointed and spear-shaped tops.

Wire netting fences Woven wire netting was developed as fencing material towards the end of the 19th century as a more durable alternative to wooden pickets. Gates, often with elaborate metal scrollwork, were made to match and were hinged on solid, turned gateposts. Wire netting fences suit simple, cottage gardens.

Wrought iron pickets Used widely in town and city gardens towards the end of the 19th century, iron pickets provide a barrier between the street and the garden that lets sunlight through to the plants behind. Reproductions of classic wrought iron fencing designs are available today in lightweight alloys.

Trellises A simple trellis fence is suitable for separating the front garden from the back, subdividing a garden or cutting off an orchard from a flower or kitchen garden. A trellis fence is relatively easy to build and maintain, being little more than a post and rail fence with battens attached at regular intervals. Trellis fences provide perfect support for colourful climbing plants.

The utilitarian wire netting fence was often enlivened by an ornamental gate featuring intricate metal scrollwork.

To keep an established, formal hedge looking neat, trim it in early and late summer.

GATES AND ARCHES Choose a gate to match your fence – a picket gate for a picket fence, a woven wire gate for a wire netting fence, a wrought iron gate for a wrought iron fence. Wooden and wire netting gates were common in hedges; wrought iron or wooden gates complemented solid brick or stone walls.

A gate framed by an arch is particularly attractive in a hedge or trellis, especially when it leads to another part of the garden. Arches, with or without gates, can be positioned at either end of a path or at intervals along a path, and ideally should frame a view. Arches look especially attractive with flowering climbers trained up the sides.

Gates within gardens A gate surrounded by climbers in a tall trellis screen or a gate in a high hedge can create the feeling of a 'secret garden' – even if the unseen area contains no more than the compost heap or the potting shed.

The moon gate – a circular opening in a wall framing what lies beyond – was very popular in Britain in the 19th century, a reflection of the Victorian passion for *Chinoiserie* – the Oriental influence in all kinds of decorative arts. A simple moon gate can be created with trellis and dense small-leaved ivy.

HEDGES Hedges can enclose a garden for privacy, divide up a large garden, hide a fence or an ugly building, provide a backdrop for flowering plants or a windbreak. A hedge will also swallow dust raised by traffic, but whatever its purpose, it must have ornamental qualities. A low flowering hedge can indicate a break, without blocking a view.

Foundations As hedge plants are usually vigorous growers, and in addition are planted very close together, their food requirements are great, making it important to thoroughly dig and prepare the soil. Think of this as the 'foundations' of your hedge, which must stand it in good stead in the years to come. If the ground does not permit deep digging, it is not suitable for a hedge.

Dig to a depth of at least 50 cm and a width of a metre or more, mixing in well rotted manure. Planting in holes any smaller or shallower is inviting failure – the roots cannot penetrate the undug soil surrounding them, and in wet weather water collects in the hole and is likely to rot the roots. For most screening hedges a single row is enough, but for a windbreak you may need several staggered rows of plants of different heights and densities.

Clipping Do not clip a hedge on a hot, sunny day – the newly exposed leaves will scorch and look unsightly. Clip so that your hedge is wider at the base than at the top, so that light and moisture can penetrate to the bottom of the hedge. Do not let a young hedge become leggy and top-heavy, as this is difficult to remedy in later years and will require cutting back to within 60 cm or so of the ground, followed by regular trimming to correct the shape.

To trim a small hedge evenly, cover the sides and top with wire netting, and clip down to that.

Quick-growing hedges Despite the long years required for a hedge to reach maturity, it is better to plant a steady growing variety than a quick-growing one. Quick growers need far more cutting to keep them

Arches are a well loved device for structuring a garden. Train flowering climbers such as clematis up trellised arches.

The Way We Were

At one time, an ingenious method of hanging a gate on small rural holdings was to sink an empty wine bottle into the ground with the recessed end uppermost. The shaped end of a tree fork was seated in this, and the top was fastened to the gatepost with a horseshoe; horizontal railings were attached to the fork to form the gate. The glass recess formed a socket and the horseshoe a rigid loop in which the tree-fork upright could move freely.

attractive. Macrocarpa, for example, reaches a fair height in a year or so, but from then on needs constant clipping, and this relentless mutilation can cause it to die suddenly, leaving an untidy hole. Slow growers, such as lonicera, need only a little attention once shaped and formed.

Flowering hedges Planting a flowering hedge is an effective way to add more colour to your garden. Escallonia, abelia and lavender make attractive flowering hedges, as do roses, whose thorns also act as deterrents to intruders.

Native hedge plants In Australia, saltbush was commonly used in the late 19th century, but fell out of favour because it had a tendency to die back and leave gaps. Boronia was used in Western Australia and several varieties of dwarf acacia make good native hedges. The red silky oak will make a hedge two metres or so high. In New Zealand, akiraho is a popular choice for hedges.

Patching gaps The death of a hedge plant leaves a sad hole. For an instant repair job, buy or strike three or four spare plants at the same time and keep them in reserve.

PERGOLAS The term 'pergola' is loosely applied to almost any structure that supports climbing and trailing plants. Pergolas originated in Italy and were designed to provide shade in summer while doubling as a support for grapevines. They became popular in English gardens in the early 20th century. Covered with climbing roses, clematis or honeysuckle, a pergola can add old-fashioned charm to the garden. It can also make an attractive covered walkway – but make sure it leads to something. In a small garden, two or three arches can give a similar effect to a pergola.

A pergola will be subjected to the buffetings of weather, so it should be of sturdy construction and made of the strongest and most durable wood available. The wood can either be sawn or barkless 'rustic' but in either case it should be varnished or stained to make it water-resistant. The uprights should be fairly solid, but the beams and cross-pieces can be less sturdy. The bases of the posts that rest in the ground should be treated with creosote.

SUMMERHOUSES The summerhouse, which offers a cool, shady refuge from the heat, was a greatly appreciated addition to many 19th century Australian and New Zealand gardens. *The Garden*, published in 1880, suggests forming a simple temporary arbour by firmly fixing in the ground a few branchy boughs, drawing them together at the top and forming the sides with wooden or wire trellis, ready for the planting of climbers or 'some pretty summer plant of sufficient luxuriance and strength to furnish an agreeable place for retirement and shade during the warmest months.'

The floors of such rustic pavilions were usually laid with pebbles, wood or bricks, and some part of the roof was made showerproof. Summerhouses of a more refined kind were made of iron pillars latticed with wire; these were frequently placed near tennis and croquet courts to provide pleasant resting places for players during breaks in the game. Circular and octagonal shapes were popular.

KUBLA KHAN, the 13th century oriental potentate, was the inspiration for the most famous garden enclosure in English literature:

So twice five miles of fertile ground
With walls and towers were girdled
    round
And there were gardens bright with
    sinuous rills,
Where blossomed many an incense-
    bearing tree;
And here were forests ancient
    as the hills,
Enfolding sunny spots of greenery …

– 'KUBLA KHAN', SAMUEL TAYLOR COLERIDGE (1772–1834)

Lawns and pathways

PATHS AND GRASSY AREAS ARE FUNCTIONAL
ELEMENTS IN A GARDEN, BUT TREATED WITH
IMAGINATION THEY CAN BE DECORATIVE AS WELL.

A narrow, winding path can make a garden look longer.

In the cottage garden, paths are no wider than is needed to reach the beds. Larger gardens demand wider paths (one 1880s gardening book suggests that 'six to eight feet' is sufficient), which often curve mysteriously out of sight. Lawns have been a common feature of the garden since the beginning of the 20th century, their popularity growing with the rise of the suburban garden and the invention of the self-driven lawn mower and the garden hose.

LAWNS Good drainage, thorough spadework and well prepared soil are the keys to success. This done, level the ground, rake and make firm. Sow in late autumn on a calm, cloudy day. Spread seed evenly, rake lightly into the soil, then firm down with the back of a spade. Seeds germinate best in well-packed soil. Water regularly to prevent the soil drying out and the germinating seeds perishing.

In spring, take out all weeds and fill up the holes with clean soil. Cut the grass down hard, then 'dress up' any poor spots with manure lightened with sand. Sow seed in weak places.

You should never put rich top-dressing on healthy lawns but you can improve a failing lawn with a mixture of old turfy soil and well rotted manure. The dressing should not completely cover the grass, or it may destroy it. Repeat in autumn; if dressing is needed again, use a lighter covering.

Mowing Preferably wait until grass is dry before mowing, but if this is not possible, move the hose over the lawn to dislodge the drops of rain or sweep it lightly with a leaf rake. Never mow twice in succession in the same direction: mow first in one direction, then at right angles to the first direction, then diagonally, then at right angles to the previous mowing. Established lawns should be cut regularly from spring to autumn. In the height of summer, it is a good idea to leave the clippings on the lawn to help keep it moist.

Aeration A heavily used lawn tends to become compacted and will need aeration. Use a garden fork to pierce holes at regular intervals. This will allow water and fertiliser to penetrate the soil more easily.

LAWNS have always been an integral part of gardens, and various tools have been developed over the years to make lawn care easier.
Garden rollers were used in the old days to bring lawns to a velvet smoothness. In 1830 Edwin Budding patented a 'machine for cropping or shearing the vegetable surface of lawns, grass-plots and pleasure grounds.' It used the principle of rotating cutters operating against a fixed blade. Cut grass was collected in a box at the front. The first successful petrol-driven mowers appeared in the early years of the 20th century.

Herb lawns Shady areas can be planted with lawns of herbs, which do not require mowing and give off a pleasant aroma when walked upon. Suitable herbs include thyme (slow to establish), pennyroyal (which as a strong peppermint odour) and the single-flowered chamomile, which is the toughest as well as the most successful. However, none is as hard-wearing as a traditional lawn.

UP THE GARDEN PATH With simple, thoughtful treatment, a path can be made one of the most charming features of a garden.

Route A path should take the most logical and direct route to its destination. If you do not want a straight line, put in an obstacle, such as a bench, to explain the curve. Make sure that curves are gentle so that people will not be tempted to take a shortcut across the lawn.

Drainage Drainage is the most important part of making a path. Remove the soil to a depth of 30 cm and form a channel in the centre of this trench. Fill the channel with small stones or gravel, then cover the trench with rough stone or broken brick or earthenware. Ram this in well until it is firm, cover it with a layer of ashes or sand 4–8 cm deep, water well and level it off; it is now ready for its surface.

Surface A path must be made of a firm, all-weather material. To aid drainage, its surface should be slightly convex, the centre being 2 or 3 cm higher than the sides. Paving stone, cinder, gravel, crushed brick and hard-packed earth make suitable materials for paths.

Brick paths are traditionally associated with cottage gardens; worn bricks will lend a feeling of age. In traditional cottage gardens only very simple laying patterns were used.

Edgings Paths can have a living border of low, clipped hedge, or can be edged with tiles, bricks or stones, or with thick wire or green sticks bent in hoops.

STEPS Steps are usually an extension of a path and ideally should be made of the same material. You can also make steps a feature to add interest to an otherwise bland area. As they also serve as a retaining wall, they must be securely anchored to the slope.

The fewer steps you have, the wider they should be. And never have a single step on its own: it is far too easy to trip over. If the difference in levels renders a long flight of steps necessary, incorporate a landing.

Two or three long steps edged with urns filled with flowering plants can double as seating.

Gradient The gradient on a flight of steps is determined by the width of the treads (the flat, horizontal part of the step) and the height of the risers (the vertical parts of the step). Wide treads and shallow risers will give a gentle ascent. Treads must be no narrower that 35 cm; risers should be no higher than 18 cm. Make the gradient as even and gentle as possible.

Drainage On steep slopes, an open drain on one side of the steps will help to channel water away. Even so, water flowing down the steps will make the ground at the bottom wetter than elsewhere, making good drainage particularly important.

TRADITIONAL PAVING PATTERNS
There is an almost infinite variety of patterns that you can make with paving bricks.

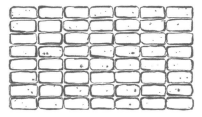

Simple cottage garden pattern

Herringbone pattern

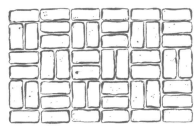

Basketweave pattern

GARDEN BED EDGINGS
An edging of bricks or wire hoops adds definition to a garden bed.

Diagonal brick edge

Wire hoop edge

Completing the picture

CAREFUL CHOICE AND THOUGHTFUL PLACEMENT OF
GARDEN ORNAMENTS CAN TRANSFORM A GARDEN
INTO AN OASIS OF BYGONE TRANQUILLITY.

In even the smallest plot, a classic bird bath or piece of statuary can set
the tone. A larger spread could be furnished with roomy benches,
flower-filled urns, a pond or a tiered fountain – perhaps even a wishing
well or a Japanese bridge. Garden ornaments should look like part of
the overall scheme, and should not be alien to the landscape or its
design. Do not isolate urns and pillars in the centre of a lawn; instead,
let them complement flower beds or fringe pathways. Reserve focal
points for interesting features such as sundials or statues.

MARKING TIME Horizontal sundials mounted on pedestals have long
been favourites in parks and gardens. These ancient timepieces, which
use divisions carved into stone or etched in metal to mark the hours,
lend an ordered, old-fashioned feel to the surroundings. For accurate
operation, a sundial must be correctly installed, with the gnomon –
the arm that casts the shadow – parallel to the earth's axis.

Mottoes, usually sage observations on the fleeting nature of human
life, are a feature of many sundials. Two old favourites are:
• Among ye floures I tell ye houres.
• Let others tell of storms and showers, I tell only sunny hours.

FOR THE BIRDS Providing clean water for birds to drink and bathe in
will encourage them into your garden. Put some water in a large
shallow bowl attached to a pedestal high enough off the ground to
give the birds some protection from cats. Some shrubbery nearby will
help to give them a greater feeling of security. Keep the water clean
and fresh, and top it up daily in hot weather.

A CHANCE TO SIT Seats and benches come in a range of styles and sizes.
Reproductions of the sturdy wooden garden benches popular in the
late 19th and early 20th century are now widely available; they were
traditionally painted dark green. Copies of the elegant garden bench
designed by Edwin Lutyens, with its high, scalloped back and rolled
arms, are also readily obtainable. A hexagonal seat encircling a
spreading, shady tree was another old favourite. It was made of wood
or of cast-iron fashioned to imitate rustic bough work.

As lawns became more widespread, so did lawn seats. These were
often designed to be reminiscent of the marble benches of classical
antiquity, and were placed at the edge of the green sward. Simple
'rustic' arrangements were also popular; these are easily put together

*Courtyards, balconies, terraces,
steps and the approaches to paths
and entrances are good vantage
points for urns.*

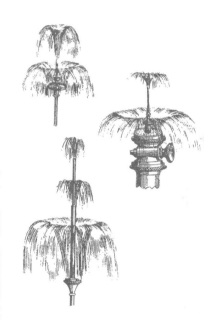

*The height of a fountain's jet
should be in proportion to the
width of its pool.*

in your own garden, being as simple as a bench made of a plank of planed wood supported by bricks or blocks of stone. Half of an old cask makes a handsome and comfortable seat; invert it and sink the edge several centimetres into the ground, and make a backrest from battens nailed onto stout poles and driven about 30 cm into the earth. Drill a few holes in the sides of the cask to prevent water accumulating.

Placement is vital, whatever the type of seat. Choose a warm spot with a good view over the garden; beside a path, inviting you to stop and sit; in the shade of a tree; or near beautiful or fragrant plants.

URNS Urns are important garden accessories because they provide display cases for ornamental shrubs and colourful annuals. An urn on a pedestal can be the focal point of a small garden; a pair of urns can flank an entrance, the start of a path or the top or bottom of a stairway. Urns that rest on pedestals so that their surrounds are warmed by sunlight are especially suitable for trailing, soft-hued geraniums. For a quick garden facelift, buy some decorative seasonal plants fully grown and place them complete with their pots in a few carefully positioned urns. In the past, popular urn styles included the castellated, the rustic and the classical.

The ultimate in garden seating: some benches featured revolving tables and an adjustable awning.

POOLS OF TRANQUILLITY A pond gleaming with goldfish and dotted with water lilies can be one of the garden's delights, inviting relaxation, suggesting coolness, attracting birds, and offering a focal point. The most suitable spot, especially if you want to grow aquatic plants, is in a hollow in a position that catches the full strength of the sun's rays – a pond in the shade will rarely be successful, and will support only a limited range of plants. Most aquatic plants need at least 50 cm of water, and still water and an even temperature are essential to growth. Water snails will consume the algae that grow in still water, and goldfish will eat most water-dwelling pests.

Formal ponds are usually symmetrical and look most appropriate in gardens with balanced geometric designs. A gushing fountain will add drama, but use it only intermittently if you have water lilies, as its spray will lower the temperature of the pool, checking the growth of the plants and damaging their leaves. An informal pond can be of any shape, and can be edged with grass or marsh plants or form part of a rock garden. To replace water lost by evaporation during the day, gently spray the full surface of the pond in the early evening.

Water flowing between several ponds over stone-paved terraces provides the opportunity to grow several types of plants. Water-loving plants will grow happily around the margins, while aquatic plants will thrive in the centre. Plant irises, flowering rushes, small reeds, club mosses and ferns in the chinks between the stones around the edge.

Taking Care of the Pence

Transform old and discarded garden and kitchen equipment into distinctive plant holders. Old buckets and barrows packed with potted annuals can take the place of an expensive stone or terracotta urn, and kettles and saucepans trailing greenery add to the charm of a cottage garden. Wooden barrels were popular planters in the 1920s and 1930s.

remedies

**HOME HELPS FOR STAYING HEALTHY
AND TREATING COMMON AILMENTS**

Health and long life

OUR FOREBEARS KNEW, JUST AS WE DO TODAY,
THAT THE BEST WAY TO ENSURE A PLEASANT LIFE
IS TO STAY HEALTHY.

They also knew that health is more than the absence of disease and
infirmity; it is a positive state of mental, physical and social wellbeing.
Some of us are born with more robust bodies and minds than others,
but we can all work towards achieving and maintaining a healthy
lifestyle. And advice on how to do this has not changed very much
over the past hundred years.

RISE AND SHINE 'Early to bed, early to rise makes a man healthy,
wealthy and wise', runs the old precept, and those who were health-
conscious in the past took it to heart. They began the day with a cool
bath or shower and a vigorous towelling to get the circulation moving.
Next came a brisk 30-minute walk, followed by a hearty breakfast.

Modern advice on healthy living is essentially the same, though
more flexible to suit a diversity of lifestyles. Today we are told that
taking regular, suitable exercise is more important than the time at
which you take it, and that as long as you have enough hours of
undisturbed sleep, it does not matter when you have them.

A proper breakfast Most health experts agree with their earlier
counterparts that a substantial breakfast is a good start to the day. In
fact, many nutritionists say that breakfast is the most important meal
of the day and should never be missed. The good news for weight-
watchers is that eating breakfast helps your body to start metabolising
energy more quickly after the slow-down during sleep, and that
exercise increases your metabolic rate.

THE GOOD TASTE OF HEALTH As early as the 1940s, dietitians were
advising people to include wholemeal flour, unrefined cereals and fresh
vegetables and fruits in their diet; to steam vegetables lightly rather
than boiling them until the vitamins and minerals were destroyed; to
eat more fish, eggs and cheese and less red meat; to drink milk and
fruit juices instead of tea and coffee; and to give children
dried fruits instead of sweets.

Relaxed eating In the past it was not just what
that went into the stomach that was important,
but how it got there. Children were told to chew
their food properly, and sometimes even ordered
to take an exact number of chews: one source
claimed that 32 times for each mouthful was the
correct amount. This number of times may seem
to us to be excessive, but chewing food well
before swallowing is good practice as the saliva
acts on the food to begin the digestion process.

*In the 19th century, many
manufacturing chemists made
fortunes by marketing a great
variety of patent tonics, pills
and ointments that were said to
promote health and beauty.*

*A bowl of cereal for breakfast,
and maybe some fruit, gives us the
energy we need to start the day.*

You'll be less prone to indigestion if you chew your food thoroughly. Eating in a calm, unhurried manner was and is recommended for those who are anxious to avoid the agonies of indigestion.

A little of what you fancy Many modern food 'fads' are based on the view that certain food combinations are beneficial or harmful. This belief is not new: Lawrence Armstrong, writing in *The Housewife* in 1934, argued that 'no person, who values his health, will eat any form of starch at the same meal as protein, which includes meat, eggs, fish, nuts, cheese and dried beans of all kinds.'

A more commonsense view was taken by *Nutrition and Health* in 1943: 'Nature has mixed all her foodstuffs together. Milk, for instance, is an almost perfect food; yet it contains protein, starch and fats, as well as vitamins and mineral salts … Soy bean flour is about two-fifths protein, two-fifths carbohydrate … You can eat meat and vegetables together with an easy conscience. In fact, the more variety you have in each meal the better will it be balanced.'

Words of Wisdom

Much time and care was once devoted to chewing food thoroughly, sometimes with comical results:

'Zara had a patent habit of masticating each mouthful so-and-so many times before swallowing; and the children forgot to eat, in counting their aunt's bites. With their ears cocked for the click at the finish. Mamma said it was her teeth that did it, and it was rude to listen.'

– *THE FORTUNES OF RICHARD MAHONY*, HENRY HANDEL RICHARDSON (1930)

SUNLIGHT For much of this century, sunbathing was promoted as essential for good health and protection against illness. Everyone was advised to spend some time each day in the sun, and sunbathing was encouraged – even for babies.

Nowadays we are aware of the harm of over-exposure, and doctors advise that babies should never be exposed to the sun. Such warnings are not new, however. Writing in 1949, one health writer warned against sunbathing in the heat of the day. He advised his readers to begin with five minutes exposure to sunlight at about 8 am (later in the winter) and to increase exposure each day by two minutes until they reached a maximum of half an hour a day.

Our bodies do need some sunlight because without it we cannot manufacture the vitamin D that is essential for healthy bone structure and strong teeth. Sunlight is also beneficial for the skin and can help to control skin diseases such as eczema and psoriasis.

In any case, most of us are instinctively drawn to the warming rays of the sun and feel both happier and healthier after even short exposure. This may have something to do with the warmth of the sun, which helps speed up the circulation.

The ideal is to protect ourselves from the harmful effects of the sun while still enjoying its benefits. The best way to achieve this is to wear a hat, protective clothing and sunglasses, avoid exposure to the sun between 11 am and 3 pm, and to apply sunscreen regularly.

A BREATH OF FRESH AIR The highly contagious nature of tuberculosis (TB) and the desire to 'strengthen the lungs against disease' accounts in part for our grandparents' insistence on fresh air. Mothers were advised to leave even small babies to sleep in their prams in the fresh air during the day, and many children suffered the rigours of cold winter nights sleeping on open verandas for the sake of their health.

Today we worry less about diseases like TB, at least in developed countries, but fresh air still helps to protect us from airborne viruses such as colds and flu. A crowded, stuffy room is an ideal environment for spreading viruses from sick to uninfected people. It is a good idea to do just what our grandparents used to do – open the windows now and again to admit some fresh air.

HEALTH TONICS People once swore by health tonics, which they believed stimulated their systems to function more effectively. 'Spring tonics' were especially popular, and some modern experts believe that their apparent effectiveness was because fresh fruit and vegetables were less available during winter and people were starved of fibre to keep the digestive system working efficiently. Today, some of these health tonics are still useful for their restorative effect on a slow digestion.

Dandelion leaf tonic stimulates gastric secretions and increases the output from the kidneys, creating a diuretic effect. Steep 1–2 teaspoons of dried dandelion leaves in 1 cup of boiling water for five minutes. Strain, and allow to cool to lukewarm before drinking.

Barley water clears the kidneys and bladder and helps to promote clear skin. For cystitis sufferers, it is also a good substitute for tea and coffee. Place 100 grams of pearl barley in a stainless steel or glass saucepan, cover with water and bring to the boil. Strain and throw away the water. Add 3 cups of water to the barley and simmer for two hours. Add the zest of a lemon and leave to cool. Strain the liquid and refrigerate. Serve with a slice of lemon.

FIT FOR LIFE Healthy lungs and heart play a significant part in reducing the risk of developing heart disease, so maintaining aerobic fitness is important. Correct breathing is also a major factor in physical fitness, without which we could not easily perform our daily activities. Regular exercise benefits every part of your body and contributes to both physical and mental wellbeing.

What could be more apt for the health-conscious of today than the following advice from the 1940s: 'The best exercise is that in which the whole body is involved, that is not too strenuous and is suited to the age and constitution of the individual. Those who walk or swim regularly or play golf are doing themselves more good than someone who plays a hard game of football or tennis and then does no further training until the next game.'

SLEEPING SOUNDLY Rest is as important to good health as exercise, food and sunshine. The amount of sleep needed varies from person to person, but seven to eight hours is normal for most adults. The healthier and happier you are, the more likely you are to sleep well. For a little help achieving restful sleep, try drawing on the wisdom of the past before resorting to patent or prescription medicines.

The Way We Were

'Those means by which we secure strength and retain it are also the best means for recovery from sickness. Important among these are: pure air; pure water; good food; suitable clothing; cleanliness; sunlight; exercise; rest.'

– *HOME AND HEALTH* (1909)

Before the nature of tuberculosis was fully understood, people took all sorts of of patent medicines in the hope of effecting a cure.

Give your stomach a break You are more likely to have trouble sleeping if you are still digesting a heavy meal when you go to bed, so if possible eat your heaviest meal in the middle of the day and have a light dinner in the evening. Try eating nothing at all within three hours of retiring. Alternatively, try a nourishing snack of something starchy just before bedtime – suggestions from one old source included bread and hot milk, bread and honey or a bowl of gruel. Another recommended a few grapes. Tobacco, alcohol and caffeine are stimulants and can cause sleeplessness.

Check your environment A well ventilated bedroom that is not damp, a comfortable bed and warm, light nightclothes all contribute to a good night's sleep. Make sure you are neither too warm nor too cold – both conditions will make you restless – and do not neglect your feet: cold feet are a common cause of wakefulness.

Relax Stress is not just a phenomenon of the late 20th century, and our grandparents were aware that sleeplessness is often caused by anxiety. They advised gentle exercise and relaxation before retiring. 'A relaxed, enjoyable evening is the best preparation for a sound sleep,' one sage advised. 'A hearty romp with the children or a pleasant walk or drive after a stressful day will often dispel excess weariness and prepare the body for refreshing sleep,' said another. A warm bath, not too hot, just before retiring was considered 'a great relaxer when the nerves are on edge after a heavy day.' Many advisers pointed out that daily exercise promoted sound sleep at night.

Students might benefit from this 19th century advice: 'Do not go directly to bed after studying hard, take a short walk, even if it is just around the garden or up and down the veranda. Distract the mind from study by reading a novel or a magazine for a few minutes before going to bed.'

Calming herbs Many old-time sleeping draughts contained opium derivatives, such as laudanum, which were freely available over the pharmacy counter. Herbal teas were also used and are still popular. Steep about 30 grams of any of the following herbs in 600 ml of boiling water for ten minutes and drink just before retiring: rosemary, chamomile, thyme, lemon balm, lavender or skullcap. Valerian, long used as a sedative, gives a refreshing effect rather than causing drowsiness. Boil valerian with water for about 15 minutes to extract the full benefit.

Honey, always known as a mild sedative, is the traditional sweetener for herbal teas. Some modern nutritionists claim that honey stimulates the production of the hormone serotonin, which calms the brain and induces relaxation.

A cure for insomnia from the turn of this century contains valerian and two other ingredients normally used for soothing the digestion. Boil 15 grams of valerian root, 30 grams of dandelion root and 30 grams of slippery elm bark in 1 litre of water for an hour then strain off the liquid. Take a wineglassful just before you go to bed and have no solid food beforehand.

'I must have left it behind!'

Liver salts were often considered an indispensable part of life by our grandparents.

HINTS FOR A HAPPY LIFE
Don't worry.
Don't hurry. 'Too swift arrives as
    tardy as too slow.'
Simplify! Simplify! Simplify!
Don't overeat. Don't starve. 'Let your
    moderation be known to all men.'
Sleep and rest abundantly. Sleep
    is nature's benediction.
Be cheerful. 'A light heart lives long.'
Think only heartful thoughts.
'As a man thinketh in his heart,
    so is he.'
– *HAPPY HOMES* (1891)

Cool, clear water

THE PRESENCE OF WATER ON OUR PLANET MADE
IT POSSIBLE FOR LIFE TO COME INTO EXISTENCE
SEVERAL BILLION YEARS AGO.

The curative powers of water have been known since ancient times:
archaeologists have identified bathing places where early cave dwellers
treated the sick. In its pure state, this most versatile of substances is
extremely beneficial. In its liquid form we can drink it, bathe in it or
soak a compress in it and apply it to the skin. In its solid form, as ice,
we can use it to bring down a temperature or cool a drink. As steam,
we can inhale it. No wonder water is called the essence of life.

HEALTH SPAS Before modern medicine and the belief that most
afflictions can be cured by drugs or surgery, millions of people all over
the world visited spas to take the waters. They stayed at health resorts,
or hydros, built around mineral springs, and relied on water to treat
such ailments as arthritis, high blood pressure, nervous disorders,
depression, allergies, skin problems and diseases of old age. They
bathed, encased their bodies in packs, inhaled steam, took saunas and
drank the water – and many left the spas invigorated and even cured.

In Europe water cures are still popular and doctors often recommend
them. Outside Europe, although many orthodox medical experts do
not acknowledge the benefits of hydrotherapy, a few spas still exist. If
you are anxious or run down, a week or two at a spa may be just what
you need for relaxation and to stimulate your body to heal itself.

SITZ BATHS Sitz baths were popular at spas for the relief of such
ailments as cystitis, constipation and piles. Cold sitz baths increase
blood circulation to the vital organs and were used for their
stimulating effect on the reproductive organs and the spine. Hot sitz
baths were used to relieve pain and inflammation. Alternate hot and
cold baths were used to increase vitality.

To give yourself a sitz bath, run water into your bathtub to a depth
of about 20 cm and sit with your knees drawn up so that only your
'sitz' – your behind, hips and tummy – and your feet are immersed.
Or use two plastic tubs, one to sit in and one to put your
feet in. For an alternate hot and cold sitz, sit in the hot
tub for three minutes with your feet in the cold one,
and then sit in the cold bath for one minute with your
feet in the hot one. Repeat several times.

HOT BATHS A warm bath relaxes the muscles and eases pain. A hot
bath serves the same purpose and also promotes sweating, which
removes impurities from the body. Many ingredients were added to a
bath to hasten healing. Epsom salts, for example, drive off chills and
colds, while 1 kg of oats or bran tied in a muslin bag and placed in the

Words of Wisdom

'Among the simple remedies
which the house-mother will
find most efficacious, hot water
stands first, for many are the
aches and pains which it will
relieve.

A sudden sore throat will be
relieved almost miraculously by
the application of hot-water
cloths, and a spoonful of hot
water held in the mouth for a
few seconds will often relieve a
sick headache. Applications of
hot-water cloths to the soles of
the feet and the back of the
neck will soothe a nervous
headache almost immediately;
the patient should be kept very
quiet and allowed to sleep, if
this is possible.'

– *THE RIGHT WAY WITH BABY* (1914)

*A sitz bath, a hip or half bath,
is a bath taken in the sitting
position. Sitz baths were widely
used to treat everything from
menstrual disorders to fatigue.*

bath relieves the symptoms of eczema and other skin complaints. Seaweed aids relaxation, as do herbs such as chamomile, thyme and lavender.
Caution: Blood pressure may fall after a hot bath, so leave the tub slowly and, after drying, lie down for half an hour.

STEAM BATHS Steam baths, or saunas, have been used for thousands of years to prevent and treat sickness. Even today, many claim that steam baths cleanse and rejuvenate the body both inside and out, because the steam promotes sweating, which helps to rid the body of toxins. It is also claimed that overheating the body speeds up the metabolic process and inhibits the growth of viruses and bacteria. Steam also clears the sinuses.
Caution: If you are pregnant or have a heart condition or high blood pressure, check with your doctor before taking a steam bath treatment.

Steam baths, or saunas, were a popular form of treatment at spas, where people used to go in great numbers for water cures.

COLD SHOWERS A cold shower morning and night increases muscle tone, speeds up metabolism, stimulates circulation, strengthens the nervous system, stimulates the glands, increases hormone production, improves digestion, builds up resistance to colds and infections, helps to prevent premature ageing and keeps you younger.

Cold showers were a popular health measure in the 19th century. Given the benefits claimed for this simple treatment, perhaps we should grit our teeth and try it!

Your skin absorbs beneficial minerals from sea water.

SEA BATHING Sea bathing became popular around the middle of the 19th century, and seaside resorts began to rival the older health spas near mineral springs. Sea water is rich in minerals, which are inhaled from the air and also absorbed though the skin when bathing.

Do-it-yourself sea water You do not have to live near the sea to benefit from the properties of sea water. Make reconstituted sea water by dissolving 1 or 2 kg of sea salt (from health food shops) in half a tub of cool water. Soak in your tub for 15 minutes or so then dry your body briskly with a coarse towel. You can make a sea water substitute by adding to the water 2 kg of common salt, 250 grams of magnesium chloride and 250 grams of Epsom salts.

DRINKING Humans can survive for weeks without food, but no one can live for more than a few days without water. Water is essential for the regulation of body temperature, for digestion, for the elimination of waste products and as a lubricant for joints and eyes. Water flushes out bladder and kidney infections, helps to prevent the formation of kidney stones and improves the complexion.

People who drink too little water may suffer from headaches, poor concentration and bad breath. Vomiting, diarrhoea or excess sweating can cause dehydration unless extra fluids are taken. Water is present in solid food as well as in drinks, but many health experts, both past and present, recommend drinking eight large glasses of plain water a day.

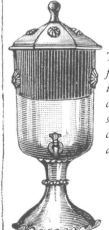

This water filter, made late in the 19th century, was said to ensure clean, bright drinking water.

Good old ways with common ills

COMMON AILMENTS ARE OFTEN SO TRIVIAL THAT WE RARELY BOTHER TO GO TO A DOCTOR – INDEED, MOST EVENTUALLY CLEAR UP ON THEIR OWN.

Still, they can be annoying, embarrassing or temporarily debilitating, so we usually look for ways to speed up the healing process. For alleviating symptoms, traditional folk remedies are often as effective as modern pharmaceutical preparations – if not more so – and in the main they cause fewer side effects. Naturally, for serious conditions you should consult a medical specialist.

ARTHRITIS There is no recognised cure for arthritis, but much can be done to relieve pain, reduce swelling and maintain mobility and strength in the joints. If arthritis has been diagnosed, you may like to try some of the traditional treatments.

Massage In times past, painful joints were often rubbed with a warming embrocation such as camphorated oil or a mixture of one part cayenne to four parts olive oil and eight parts spirit of camphor. A mixture of lemon juice and olive oil was also thought to be an effective massage oil, as was aloe vera juice.

A great treat for anyone who is suffering from arthritic pain is to gently massage the troublesome joints with aromatic oil. Try 10 drops each of rosemary, lavender, marjoram and peppermint essential oils in 30 ml of almond oil.

Poultices A hot mustard poultice was popular for relieving painful joints because mustard draws the blood to the skin's surface and creates a warming effect. Test the preparation first on a small area to make sure it does not burn the skin. Mix mustard powder with the white of an egg rather than water, as this will take the sting out of the mustard. Do not use commercially prepared mustards.

Another widely used poultice was made from crushed fresh peppermint leaves, which contain menthol – an ingredient in many modern pain-relieving liniments.

Detoxification Many older people still swear by a teaspoon each of apple cider vinegar and honey in a glass of warm water taken both in the morning and evening. Other popular detoxifying treatments were dandelion leaf tea and sage tea, which may well help to relieve the symptoms of arthritis, since their diuretic action improves the elimination of uric acid from the body.

Some products available to our grandparents claimed to be an effective treatment for just about anything, and could either be taken or applied externally.

BACKACHE Most back pain will get better with rest, preferably lying on a firm mattress. There are many old recipes for relieving the pain; try these before you reach for modern analgesics.

Caution: If back pain is severe or is associated with weakness in a leg or loss of bladder control, there may be a serious underlying cause; consult a doctor without delay.

Poultices and compresses A hot poultice will provide relief from most back pain. Linseed, or flaxseed, was well known as a pain reliever. Boil 500 grams of ground seed in water until it forms a paste, which you then pack between two layers of gauze and apply to the painful area. Hot moist bran was also recommended as a poultice.

A compress made from a piece of flannel wrung out in hot water brings relief. You could add a few drops of an essential oil such as ginger, rosemary or wintergreen to the water.

Water treatment Raise your spirits and lower your pain by taking a warm bath containing 5 drops of lavender oil mixed with a little olive or almond oil. Then prevail on a loved one to massage you with a mixture of essential oils – 4 drops of ginger, 6 drops of lavender and 5 drops of marjoram in 3 teaspoons of almond oil.

Exercise Modern medical science has proved the efficacy of starting gentle exercise as soon as possible after the onset of back pain, but the idea is not new. More than 60 years ago, family health advisers were recommending sufferers to begin gentle stretching exercises as soon as

You can make inexpensive treatments for common ailments with simple ingredients from the kitchen, the garden and the health food shop.

A SPARKLING REMEDY
How seldom in our life we find
A Remedy and treat combined.
This Effervescent Seltzer fine
A blessing proves to me and mine.

– ADVERTISEMENT (1887)

235

possible and to start walking within two days, even in the severest cases. They also recommended regular, gentle exercise as prevention against further attacks.

BAD BREATH Bad breath is likely to be caused by something you consumed – such as spicy food, garlic or onions – or by smoking cigarettes or drinking alcoholic drinks. In times past poor dental hygiene was often the cause of bad breath, but this is less likely today, at least in cases where people regularly consult a dentist. However, sometimes an abscess in an otherwise healthy mouth can cause bad breath.

At times bad breath can result from a mouth infection, such as thrush, or a respiratory infection such as bronchitis or sinusitis.

While you treat the underlying problem, try one of these recipes for sweetening the breath: chew parsley, wintergreen, mint or peppermint leaves; drink peppermint or fenugreek tea; add a few drops of vinegar to water and gargle each morning; add 30 drops of tincture of myrrh to a glass of warm water and use as a mouthwash; or chew dill, cardamom or caraway seeds, or a couple of coffee beans.

BOILS AND CARBUNCLES A boil is an inflamed, pus-filled area of skin, usually an infected hair follicle. Boils are most common on the neck and in warm moist areas such as the armpits and the groin. A carbuncle is a cluster of interconnected boils. People with diabetes have a tendency to suffer from boils.

Sometimes the body absorbs the boil before it comes to a head and there is no need to do anything. If this does not happen, bringing the boil swiftly to a head so that it will burst and drain is still the best treatment. Do not lance the boil, as some old remedies suggest, as this can easily result in a worse infection. The pus is highly infectious, so make sure that you wash your hands well after touching it and keep your towels and other personal items separate from those of other people. If a boil is more than 1.5 cm across or you develop a carbuncle, it is best to seek medical advice.

Hot poultices are the best way of bringing a boil to a head. A popular poultice in the old days was a stiff paste of Epsom salts and glycerine – exactly the same ingredients found in many modern proprietary treatments for drawing boils. Cold poultices were made with mashed garlic, lemon slices, grated carrot or honey; all these ingredients also have antiseptic properties, so they will help to prevent reinfection. Leave a poultice on a boil for 10 to 15 minutes at a time.

BRUISES The traditional practice of putting a steak over a black eye may have helped – as long as the steak was cold enough! A better and more aesthetic remedy is to apply a cold compress or an icebag – five minutes on, five minutes off. Applied immediately, it will help to stop internal bleeding and reduce swelling. Add a few drops of lavender oil to a cold compress to help soothe the pain.

COMPRESSES AND POULTICES

In our grandparents' day compresses and poultices were used to promote healing and to reduce inflammation or pain.

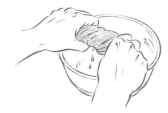

To make a hot compress, soak a clean cloth or face washer in hot water or in a herbal infusion or decoction. Wring out the cloth and apply to the affected area. Repeat the procedure several times while the compress cools.

To make a poultice, bruise fresh herbs or finely chop dried herbs, mix to a paste with water and cook for about 5 minutes. Pack the paste between two layers of gauze and apply to the affected area. Leave on for three or four hours, replacing every hour.

An old remedy for soothing a bruise is to apply hot poultices of comfrey leaves.

Every household medicine cupboard used to contain a jar of arnica ointment, which has an amazing ability to reduce pain and swelling. It is still available in health food shops, but do not apply it too often, and never to broken skin. Arnica can be toxic in large quantities so do not take it internally without strict supervision. Ointment containing St John's wort, or hypericum, is as effective as arnica, if not more so.

Once the bruise has darkened, you can soothe the pain and remove discoloration with one of a number of old remedies. Try frequent hot poultices of hyssop or comfrey leaves, or a mixture of chamomile and yarrow, or apply calendula ointment, aloe vera gel or tea-tree oil. A massage with rosemary oil in a vegetable oil carrier stimulates local circulation and speeds up the healing process.

COLD SORES Cold sores are caused by a virus that tends to be activated if your lips are exposed to strong sunshine or cold winds, or if you are run down or have a cold. Women are more likely to develop cold sores around the time of menstruation.

Act when you feel the first tingling: if you are quick enough, one of the following treatments may stop it in its tracks. Dab the spot with lemon juice, or hold ice wrapped in gauze on it. Dab on an essential oil such as eucalyptus, lavender, lemon or tea tree, or apply calendula or hypericum ointment. Tinctures will help dry out a full blown cold sore. Try tinctures of lavender, calendula, witch hazel or hypericum.

CONSTIPATION Some of our forebears were so obsessed with the need for a daily bowel movement that they used such fierce treatments as castor oil or treacle and brimstone (sulphur).

However, many health professionals, even a hundred years ago, counselled against using laxatives regularly, arguing that they made the bowel 'lazy' so that it would no longer function naturally. They recommended what modern health experts advise – a balanced diet with plenty of vegetables and fruit, plenty of water to drink, and regular exercise.

Preventative measures Establish a set time for going to the toilet and act immediately on any urge to move the bowels. Fruits such as rhubarb, figs and prunes have laxative qualities. Eating liquorice or drinking a decoction of dandelion root also aid regularity.

CRAMP Cramp is a painful muscle spasm caused by a temporary salt deficiency. Pregnant women tend to have leg cramps, and anything that causes profuse sweating, such as a fever or strenuous exercise, can cause cramp. Rub and stretch the muscle for quick relief.

DIARRHOEA Most diarrhoea is caused by contaminated food or drinking water, which produces an inflammation of the large intestine. In healthy adults diarrhoea usually clears up by itself in a day or so. However, see a doctor if it lasts more than 48 hours, as fluid loss can lead to dehydration and shock.
Caution: Small children, the elderly and the frail are particularly at risk from diarrhoea and should be watched carefully. Prolonged diarrhoea can be a sign of serious illness.

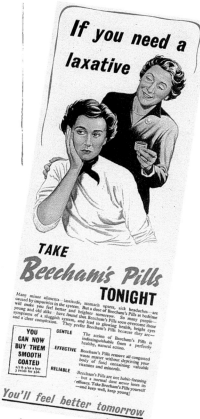

Today, as yesteryear, the best way to avoid constipation is to have a healthy diet and take plenty of exercise.

Home treatment Our forebears rightly saw diarrhoea as the body's method of eliminating poison. Letting the illness take its course is the best thing to do; taking modern antidiarrhoea preparations is likely to prolong the problem. The most effective treatment is a liquid diet for 24 hours, warmth, rest, and plenty of fluids. As the symptoms subside, replace lost nutrients with a light diet of boiled rice, fruit and vegetable juices and soup.

The following old recipes are safe and will soothe the digestive tract. Slippery elm soothes the mucous membrane – add 1 teaspoon to 250 ml of hot water and sweeten to taste. Raspberry leaf tea has long been used to treat diarrhoea, as well as sore throats, colds, fevers and period pain. Arrowroot is nourishing and easily digested, and 1 tablespoon mixed with 2 cups of water was often given for diarrhoea; milk arrowroot biscuits are a palatable modern substitute.

EARACHE Earache is generally caused by an ear infection and is a common childhood complaint. Never put anything inside the ears unless advised to do so by a medical practitioner.

To relieve earache, place a hot compress or a hot-water bottle swathed in a damp towel over and behind the ear. A chamomile infusion can be used in a compress to good effect. Or try massaging around the ears and down the back and sides of the neck with a mixture of 3 teaspoons of almond oil and 6 drops of lavender oil. *Caution:* If earache is severe or prolonged, or there is a discharge, seek medical advice. There may be a middle ear infection, which can cause permanent damage if it is not properly treated.

FOOT PROBLEMS Tight or ill-fitting shoes are responsible for most foot problems, from aching feet to bunions. Change your shoes or – best solution of all – go barefoot for six to eight weeks and most of your troubles will disappear. Some of the following old ways may be of assistance in the short term.

Blisters Blisters usually affect only the top layer of skin and will heal on their own in about a week provided you leave them alone, other than keeping the area clean and protecting the skin from further rubbing. A favourite old-time treatment for blisters was a cabbage poultice, which is worth trying: cabbage contains a substance that promotes healing and relieves pain.

There is usually no need to burst a blister, but if you need to hurry up the process, follow this modern advice. Wash your hands and the blistered area with soap and water, swab the skin with antiseptic and use a sterile needle to puncture the blister in several places, being careful not to tear the skin. Once the blister has drained, cover with an antibiotic ointment and a gauze pad.

If blisters become painful or inflamed, or if there is no apparent cause for them, consult a doctor.

Bunions Pressure on the big toe from tight or ill-fitting shoes can cause the joints to swell and the surrounding skin to become hard and inflamed. Do not neglect bunions – the joints can become so deformed that you will need an operation to cure them. The most obvious

MAKING OINTMENTS

Ointments can be made quite easily by adding a few drops of essential oil to a base such as melted petroleum jelly, paraffin wax, or beeswax and oil.

1. Put 25 grams beeswax and 100 ml cold-pressed almond oil in a glass or enamel bowl over a saucepan of boiling water. Simmer until the wax melts into the oil.

2. Remove the bowl from the heat and stir the mixture continually as it cools and stiffens, gradually adding 10–30 drops of essential oil. A drop or two of tincture of myrrh or benzoin added to the ointment will extend its life.

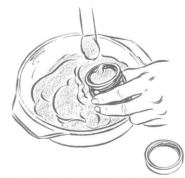

3. Place the ointment in a jar and store in a cool place.

Words of Wisdom

'Constipation is as old as human history. Ordinarily it should be treated by correcting the diet, rather than depending on laxative medicines. The old Greek physician, Hippocrates, whom doctors call the father of medicine, makes this remark: "Persons in good health quickly lose their strength by taking purgative medicines or using bad food." And an American writer has expressed the same idea with a modern touch: "In the race of life, the man with the educated bowels will eclipse the man with an educated brain; and the drugs and chemicals that work while you sleep are a little later going to prevent your working when you wake." Quite so. Don't take purgatives for constipation. Take better food.'

– *Nutrition and Health* (1943)

'treatment' is to discard the offending shoes. Go barefoot as often as possible and do toe flexing exercises every day. Add 1 tablespoon of Epsom salts to a bowl of water and soak your feet for 20 minutes, wriggling your toes while they soak. Massage your feet each night with patchouli and lavender oil, or try chamomile or geranium ointment.

Chilblains Chilblains are caused by circulation problems, especially in cold or wet weather, and prevention is better than cure. Exercise to improve your circulation – try skipping for ten minutes followed by a brisk half-hour walk. Dress appropriately – thick-soled shoes, warm socks or stockings and gloves are essential. To improve circulation, soak your feet every night first in hot water for a few minutes and then in cold, repeating the process several times.

Some old-time experts recommended a ginger footbath; ginger stimulates the circulation. Make a decoction with 30 grams of ginger and 1.5 litres of water and soak your feet for 10 minutes. Drinking ginger or yarrow tea also improves circulation. After bathing, rub your feet briskly with a rough towel until they are rosy and tingling.

At the first sign of chilblains – usually slight inflammation and a tingling sensation – paint your toes with iodine or soak your feet in a warm solution of washing soda. Dry your feet, then paint the affected parts with a mixture of two parts of beeswax to three parts of olive oil.

Full-blown chilblains can be extraordinarily painful. One traditional treatment is an ointment of 25 grams of calamine, 25 grams of yellow beeswax and 3 tablespoons of olive oil. Alternatively, mix 1 tablespoon each of glycerine, honey and flour with the white of an egg and beat the ingredients into a fine paste. Apply to the reddened area and cover with a cloth or bandage, leaving it in place for 24 hours.

Ingrowing toenails This painful condition is caused by the toenail edges pressing into the surrounding skin, which eventually becomes infected. A salt-water foot bath twice a day will bring temporary relief. If the condition becomes chronic, doctors occasionally perform surgery to remove part of the base of the nail so that the nail will be narrower and less likely to dig into the skin.

Prevent the condition from recurring by filing or cutting the nail straight across the top, wearing shoes that fit properly and keeping your feet and footwear clean.

In cold weather, prevent chilblains by wearing footwear that keeps your feet dry and warm.

NATURE'S REMEDIES

Long before the advent of 20th century drugs, people relied on medicines made from plants for the treatment of common illnesses. Some of the 'cures' were based on misconceptions and superstition, but many others worked. Modern studies are now discovering why they were effective and are using this knowledge to produce medicines for ailments that were previously thought to be untreatable.

Although today a large percentage of our medicines contain plant extracts, or are made from synthetic products that mimic the active ingredients in plants, many people are returning to traditional plant remedies. This is partly due to a growing belief that whole plants contain substances that prevent dangerous side effects produced when only the active ingredient is chemically extracted for use in modern drugs. There is also a growing theory that there may be a multiplier effect when the whole plant is used.

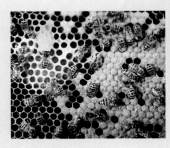

HEALING HONEY
Honey has both antiseptic and healing properties. It is used today in burn and ulcer therapies and to heal sores that are resistant to modern antibiotics. It can also settle the stomach and induce sleep.

THE MODERN PHARMACIST
In the 19th century, scientists began a systematic study of the properties of plants to identify their active ingredients. They learned to extract these ingredients to make medicines with a more consistent strength than had been possible when the whole plant was used, and not long afterwards chemicals based on these natural drugs were being synthesised in laboratories. This was the beginning of our modern pharmaceutical industry, which has taken over the preparation of medicines from the apothecary.

OUT OF THE GROUND
For centuries St John's Wort, or hypericum (left), was used to treat pulmonary and bladder complaints, incontinence and depression. This wonder plant also has healing and antibiotic properties. Today hypericum is becoming a popular alternative to the antidepressant Prozac.

Yarrow (right) is an antiseptic and an anti-inflammatory, as well as promoting tissue repair. In World War I, soldiers carried yarrow as a field dressing.

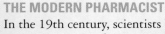

GORGEOUS GARLIC

Modern science has confirmed the age-old claims that garlic is an antiviral and antibacterial agent. Eaten raw, it can clear congestion and combat sore throats, and it is also said to lower cholesterol levels and blood pressure and inhibit blood clotting.

SPRING TONICS

'Spring tonics', taken before meals, were once a popular cure for 'the winter blues'. The root of the sarsaparilla plant was often used in these tonics, and a hundred years ago there was a hardly a household that did not have a bottle of sarsaparilla cordial on hand to offer the weary or hot visitor.

We now know that bitter substances such as sarsaparilla stimulate gastric secretions, thus increasing appetite and facilitating digestion. Modern herbalists use sarsaparilla root to treat skin problems.

LEARNING TO RELAX

Autogenic training, taught by therapists worldwide, helps the body to achieve a state of deep relaxation so it can heal itself.

The trainee takes up any of the positions illustrated here, and, with eyes closed, imagines a peaceful scene – perhaps an ocean view or a mountain range.

Then the trainee induces various physical sensations by silently repeating a set of six phrases.

One sentence might be 'My right arm is heavy'. Other sentences relate to heartbeat, breathing, warmth and coolness.

FLATULENCE Flatulence, or 'wind', happens when gas accumulates in the digestive tract, and it can be both uncomfortable and embarrassing. A common cause is swallowing air during eating – which is generally a direct result of eating too fast. Gastric flatulence occurs soon after eating, and bowel flatulence occurs some time later, when the swallowed air has moved to the lower bowel.

Caution: Persistent flatulence needs to be investigated by your doctor; it can be the sign of a chronic problem, such as irritable bowel syndrome or gall bladder disease.

Eating habits Our forebears believed mealtimes should be calm, leisurely affairs and that food should be well chewed before swallowing, thus ensuring that food is properly digested. Too much fat can cause problems for some people, while eating protein and carbohydrate at the same meal induces wind in others. Modern causes of flatulence include antibiotics and a high fibre diet.

Palatable remedies Herbal teas have been used for centuries to cure flatulence. Experiment with catmint, chamomile, lemon balm, peppermint, dill or fennel, making infusions of single herbs or a mixture of two or three. Try ginger or peppermint, especially, for bowel flatulence.

Other simple remedies from days gone by are also worth trying. In our grandparents' time some sufferers chewed basil or parsley leaves. Another old stand-by was yoghurt, but it must be the kind grandmother ate – unflavoured and containing the 'live' culture.

HEADACHES Most headaches are simply the body's protest against conditions such as hunger, atmospheric changes, too much alcohol, poorly ventilated rooms, anxiety, or even sleeping for too long. Sometimes a headache is brought on by certain foods, or by illnesses like sinusitis or a tooth abscess. The first line of defence is to find the cause and avoid it in future – a tall order if the cause happens to be something like stress at work.

A cup of tea and a good lie-down Herbal teas that can relieve headache pain include willow bark (the 'natural' form of aspirin), rosemary, peppermint, ginger, hops, borage, linden and chamomile.

The best thing to do is to lie down in a dark, quiet room with a cold compress over your forehead. A hot compress on the nape of the neck is good for a tension headache. A cool footbath containing peppermint (either the herb or the oil) is said to draw energy from the head towards the toes. Sit with closed eyes, relax and imagine the pain draining away into the cool water at your feet.

Massage is another old faithful treatment, especially for headaches caused by muscle tension in the neck and shoulders. Add a few drops

The manufacturers of these hot water bottles claimed to have tested them for strength by standing an elephant on them.

Headache powders, combined with a cup of strong tea and a rest, were the way our grandmothers commonly coped with stress.

of lavender or peppermint oil to a good vegetable or sunflower oil and gently but firmly massage the sufferer's temples and forehead, and then the neck and shoulders.

LARYNGITIS Laryngitis, or voice loss, can be caused by an allergy, a polluted atmosphere, or infection due to a cold; it can also be caused by vocal strain from extended bouts of shouting, singing or coughing. The best treatment is to keep the throat moist by a steam inhalation of a few drops of benzoin, friar's balsam, sandalwood or thyme oil. Additionally, a hot compress around the neck may help, or a humidifier in the room.

Drink plenty of water, suck ice or gently gargle an infusion of sage, marigold, thyme or raspberry leaf. Add the juice of half a lemon to hot milkless tea, sweeten with honey and sip slowly – both lemon and honey have antiseptic properties.

And finally, do not strain your voice further – do not try to talk (do not even whisper), and do not gargle strenuously. If hoarseness persists, consult a doctor.

NEURALGIA Neuralgia is intense pain caused by irritation or damage to a nerve. Analgesics can sometimes help, but the best treatments are still those that have been perfected over generations. Again, herbal teas may help: try a combination of skullcap, hop flowers, valerian root, chamomile flowers and St John's wort.

Heat treatment Apply a hot-water bottle wrapped in a towel, a hot compress infused with St John's wort, chamomile flowers or ginger root, or a hot linseed poultice. More comfortable than a hot water bottle is a cloth bag filled with a heat-retaining substance such as salt, which can be heated in the oven. The bag should be only half full, so that it moves and moulds to the body. Health food and 'new age' shops stock these bags, or you can make one yourself from a densely woven pure cotton fabric. Make sure the bag is not hot enough to burn the skin, and wrap it in a towel. It is best to have two bags, so that one can be heated up while the other is being applied.

PERIOD PAIN Women in the old days tended to have fewer periods than modern women because they were more often pregnant. Also, they may have suffered less from period pain because they were usually younger when they had their first child: painful periods are often due to a 'tight' cervix and disappear after the birth of the first child. But they knew many effective treatments for the condition. Applying heat to the lower stomach and back helps to reduce cramping by encouraging blood flow through the muscles. Alternate hot and cold applications are even more effective. Slow abdominal massage using oils such as chamomile, lavender, lemon balm or marjoram also helps to relax muscle spasm and relieve the pain.

Herbal remedies Many herbs have significant hormonal effects, and herbal teas such as lemon balm and chamomile were favourites in days gone by. Parsley and dandelion leaf teas have diuretic properties and were taken to ease the characteristic bloated feeling, and linden flower

MAKING A TINCTURE

A tincture is made by combining herbs with alcohol and water. Tinctures contain a concentrated form of the herbal extract; take medical advice about how much to use and for how long.

1. Put 100 grams of dried herbs or 250 grams of fresh herbs in a glass jar and add 2 cups of alcohol. Brandy and vodka are ideal for home-made tinctures: do not use surgical spirit, industrial alcohol or methylated spirits, as all are poisonous. Seal the jar and store in a cool place for two weeks, shaking occasionally.

2. Strain the liquid through muslin or cheesecloth. Then squeeze out as much of the liquid as possible.

3. Pour the strained liquid into clean, dark bottles. Label and date the mixture.

tea and valerian were recommended to relax the muscles and reduce cramps. Caraway or peppermint tea were also taken to ease pain.

Black haw, or cramp bark, as it is popularly called, was often used in combination with other herbs to relieve period pain. Its effectiveness has been confirmed by modern research, which has found that cramp bark acts as a uterine sedative. Make a decoction of angelica roots, cramp bark and ginger, combine it with an infusion of chamomile flowers and drink one cup three times a day.

SINUSITIS Many people suffer from infection of the sinuses after a cold. The symptoms are a feeling of congestion and an aching head and face. You can clear the airways with an old-fashioned steam inhalation. Add a few drops of a decongestant oil such as eucalyptus, tea-tree, pine, friar's balsam or peppermint to a bowl of steaming water and throw in a handful of fresh lavender or mint or some chamomile flowers. Inhale this up to four times a day. Sprinkling a few drops of decongestant oil into the shower recess just before you shower works well too.

For aching around the eyes a cold cabbage poultice may help, or a warm salt-water compress. Eating natural decongestants may also be effective: try raw or cooked onions or garlic, or spices such as ginger, cinnamon, cloves, mustard and horseradish. Herbal teas that help to reduce nasal congestion include catmint, elderflower and golden seal.

INDIGESTION The best way to prevent indigestion is to follow our grandmothers' advice – eat slowly, chew your food well, and relax during and after meals. Slowly sipping hot water after each meal or, for heartburn sufferers, during the meal, is also recommended.

If indigestion does occur despite these precautions, try this pleasant-tasting old favourite. Boil 1 teaspoon of grated fresh ginger or ground ginger in water for five minutes, sweeten with honey and add lemon juice or cinnamon and cloves if desired. Ginger soothes the stomach and digestive system and will ease most stomach complaints.

Slippery elm is another powerful treatment for digestive problems. Our grandparents made it up as a drink with a flavouring of lemon or cinnamon, but it is more palatable with food – try sprinkling a teaspoonful on mashed banana or muesli.

NAUSEA AND VOMITING There are many reasons for vomiting, from eating tainted food to being extremely nervous. Stomach disorders, pregnancy, travel and migraines can all cause vomiting. Persistent vomiting needs medical investigation, but there are any number of old-time remedies for occasional bouts of nausea. Raspberry leaf, chamomile or lemon balm tea have settled many stomachs in the past. Lemons offer an almost miraculous cure for many: nibble a lemon that has

Words of Wisdom

'Pills – If used too freely injure health, and too much doctor's physic often bring patients down to a shadow, whilst some simple remedy will very often make wonderful cures; but not being generally known what that simple remedy is, by consulting this book it is soon discovered.'

– *SIMPLE HOUSEHOLD RECIPES* (1899)

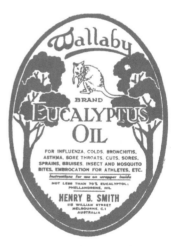

Eucalyptus oil was used to treat a wide variety of troubles, from influenza to bruises.

been peeled and dipped in salt, or suck half a lemon. If you cannot bear the taste of undiluted lemon juice, squeeze the juice into a glass of warm water or weak tea and sip it. Ginger tea is also effective, or suck a small piece of fresh ginger.

Morning sickness A glass of hot water before breakfast can settle the stomach well. Apricot nectar in small amounts also helps. Raisin tea is a nourishing old-fashioned remedy; raisins are high in energy and are a good source of potassium and iron. Soak a handful of washed raisins in water overnight, then bake them in a slow oven till syrupy. Add hot water to taste and strain. Drink hot or cold with a slice of lemon.

Travel sickness Try to stop the onset of sickness by keeping a small amount of food in your stomach all the time. Eat a light meal before leaving and eat a little – even just plain dry biscuits – every two hours while travelling. Ginger is also a proven travel sickness preventative.

Always apply a sunscreen if you are exposing your skin to the sun.

SUNBURN Repeated overexposure to the sun ages your skin and can cause skin cancer; avoid sunburn by using a hat, protective clothing and a sunscreen. If you do get burned, calamine lotion is an effective treatment. Bathing in a tub of tepid water to which you have added 1 cup of apple cider is also soothing, or place a cold compress of milk over the burn. Aloe vera juice was often used on sunburn; interestingly, many sunburn creams contain this ingredient. Calendula or hypericum ointment smoothed over the burn will help to prevent scarring.

TIREDNESS The most common cause of tiredness is too much work, too much play or not enough sleep – or a combination of all three. To perk yourself up, try one of these old remedies. Warm the soles of your feet; take a warm bath to which fresh rosemary or peppermint has been added; massage your feet with eau de Cologne; stand under a cool shower for ten minutes; lie down for 15 minutes with your feet raised.

Sip a herbal tea: dandelion leaf tea was often advised for tiredness and irritability, and rosemary or thyme for exhaustion. Rosehips and rose petals were said to have an uplifting and calming effect, and 1 teaspoon of tincture of myrrh in a little water was considered a great pick-me-up for those who were tired or run down.
Caution: Persistent tiredness can be a symptom of something serious and should be investigated.

WARTS About 50 per cent of warts disappear on their own within a year. This natural end to the problem has given rise to many successful 'cures'. One was to put some pebbles, equal in number to the warts, in a bag and leave the bag somewhere; unfortunately, whoever found the bag was then said to develop the warts!

The sap from petty spurge, or wart weed, has been used for centuries to treat warts, and recent tests have confirmed its value. If you want to try it, protect the surrounding skin with petroleum jelly and apply the sap from a freshly cut stem daily. The sap is toxic, so do not get it anywhere except on the warts.

HEADACHES in the days before aspirins were often treated by wrapping brown paper soaked in vinegar around the head:

Jack and Jill went up the hill
To fetch a pail of water.
Jack fell down and broke his crown
And Jill came tumbling after.
Up Jack got and home did trot
As fast as he could caper.
He went to bed to mend his head
With vinegar and brown paper.

– TRADITIONAL

Colds and flu

WHILE SOME OLD COLD AND FLU REMEDIES WOULD
BE FROWNED ON BY TODAY'S DOCTORS, MANY WORK
AS WELL AS MODERN POTIONS FROM THE PHARMACY.

Colds and flu are virus infections for which scientific ingenuity has not
yet found a cure: remedies, whether traditional or modern, can only
relieve the symptoms and make life a little less miserable while the
virus takes its course. Fortunately, most attacks clear up naturally in
seven to ten days. The best way to shake off a cold or flu quickly is to
do just what your grandmother would have advised – go to bed, rest,
keep warm, drink plenty of fluids and eat light, nourishing food.

ACHES AND PAINS   Before the advent of aspirin, a few drops of lavender
oil in a warm bath or hot or cold compresses to the spine and forehead
were popular ways of relieving the aches and pains of flu. Some of the
herbal tea remedies for headaches may also help (see page 242).

CLEARING THE TUBES   Steam inhalations of herbs such as chamomile
flowers, peppermint and catmint, or essential oils such as eucalyptus
and peppermint, can clear nasal passages. Fill a large bowl with boiling
water and add the herbs or a few drops of the oil. Lean over the bowl
with a towel over your head and inhale deeply for ten minutes.

COUGHING   The old wisdom advised against suppressing a cough, since
a cough gets rid of phlegm in the lungs. Many modern experts agree,
counselling against the use of antihistamines and decongestants, which
may thicken the mucus and make it more difficult to loosen.

Drinking lots of fluids and increasing humidity in the lungs loosens
phlegm. A steam inhalation or a hot shower is effective. Or try a
teaspoon of honey on the back of the tongue.

For a cough that is troublesome at night, sit up in bed and sip hot
water. Sleep propped up on pillows. In the old days a steaming kettle
was kept in many sickrooms to increase humidity; modern humidifiers
do the same job and are easier to keep going all night.
Caution: If a cough lasts much more than a week, see a doctor.

Cough mixture Honey has always been used in
cough remedies because of its soothing, antiseptic
properties. A delicious old-time cough remedy
was a drop of aniseed oil in a teaspoon of honey.

WORKING UP A SWEAT   Hot drinks and a good
sweat ease cold and flu symptoms; a favourite
treatment in the past was to have a mustard
foot bath and a hot lemonade before retiring.
The volatile oils in mustard bring blood to
the skin that is in contact with it.

*A balm for clearing the nasal
passages was a handy standby in
the old days, as an alternative to
a steam inhalation.*

BATH
MUSTARD

Hot drinks Drink a glass of apple juice spiced with 1 teaspoon of lemon juice, a pinch each of cinnamon and ginger and a little cayenne pepper for a pleasant, night-time drink. Not quite so pleasant was a pinch of cayenne pepper, a crushed garlic clove and the juice of a lemon in a glass of boiling water.

Spicy cures Steaming chicken soup has long been a favourite treatment for colds and flu, but spicy foods such as curries will work just as well. If the food makes your eyes water it will cut congestion.

Hot baths Other treatments include taking a hot bath to which ⅓ of a cup of Epsom salts had been added. If chills came with a cold, a few drops of lavender and cinnamon oil were added to the bath.

SORE THROAT Warm drinks or hot or cold compresses on the throat are both effective. A warm salt-water gargle also gives relief – add ¼ of a teaspoon of salt to a glass of water.

We now also know that sweet foods stimulate the brain to produce endorphins – the body's natural painkillers. Sweetened liquids also encourage the production of saliva, which helps to soothe a dry and irritated cough. Add 3 teaspoons of honey and the juice of ½ a lemon to a glass of hot water for almost instantaneous relief.

Bayer-Kreuz
GEGEN KRANKHEIT

Aspirin was introduced in 1888 in Germany, but it was not until 1915 that the Bayer company began retailing this wonder drug in over-the-counter packs.

The vitamin C in citrus fruits may protect you against colds and flu.

Life savers

In 1850 the average lifespan in newly industrialised countries was about 40 years. High infant mortality was partly responsible, but serious illness was also a constant threat. Diseases such as typhoid, cholera, smallpox and tuberculosis killed millions. Measles, or even a simple cold, might turn into pneumonia, from which there was at that time little hope of recovery.

Those who escaped disease might die from infection contracted during an operation to set a broken leg, during childbirth or following a cut or blister. Others were killed by the treatment itself as they were purged, bled and starved in an attempt to rid the body of 'poisons'. The kindest treatments available in the 19th century – and often the most effective – were good nursing, massage, baths, rest and herbal medicines.

Around the turn of the 19th century, discoveries about the nature of diseases and how to treat them became the foundation of modern medicine. By 1900, average life expectancy had risen to about 46 years; today it is 75 years or more.

VIEW OF THE INTERIOR

In Germany in 1895 Wilhelm Röntgen developed what quickly became known as the X-ray. One of the first X-ray photographs (right) was of the bones in a woman's hand – her wedding ring is clearly visible. The following year, X-rays were used to locate an airgun pellet in a boy's wrist.

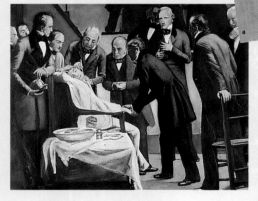

SWEET SLEEP

In 1846, the first surgical operation using ether was performed. Before this, surgery was undertaken only in extreme emergencies, the patients being partly anaesthetised with alcohol or opium.

INTRODUCING BACTERIA

In the 1860s, Frenchman Louis Pasteur expounded his germ theory of disease, which explained how living organisms, so tiny that they could be seen only through a microscope, caused many diseases. This discovery led British surgeon Joseph Lister to experiment with antiseptics in the operating theatre.

DEATH TO BACTERIAL DISEASE

In 1928, Scottish scientist Alexander Fleming discovered a mould, which he named penicillin, that destroyed bacteria. In 1940 this antibiotic was finally developed for medicinal use.

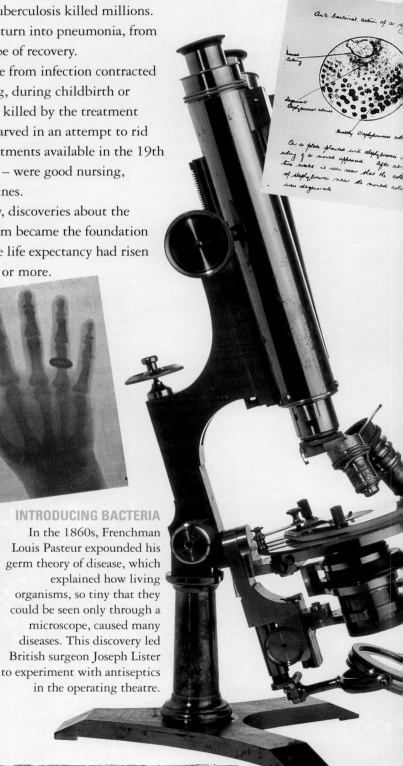

A NEW LINE OF DEFENCE

Edward Jenner's discovery in 1796 of a vaccine derived from the living cowpox virus was to give generations of people immunity from smallpox. But it was another 80 years before scientists understood enough about the human immune system to develop vaccines against other killer diseases.

IT'S NOT OUR FAULT!

In 1848 – years before Pasteur and Lister – a Viennese doctor, Ignaz Semmelweis, markedly lowered the death rate in his obstetrics clinic from puerperal fever ('childbed fever') by demanding strict antisepsis. His colleagues were sceptical – and jealous – and forced Semmelweis to resign. He died in a mental asylum in 1865, and his pioneering work was not recognised until much later.

STUDYING BACTERIA

Building on Louis Pasteur's discoveries, German scientist Robert Koch began work to differentiate between types of bacteria. In 1882 he discovered the tuberculosis bacterium, and the following year the cholera organism. Once these bacteria were identified, scientists were able to begin looking for drugs to fight these scourges.

MEDICAL DISCOVERIES, 1846–1940

1846 William Morton, an American dentist, uses 'laughing gas' (sulphuric ether) as an anaesthetic.

1847 James Young Simpson uses chloroform to relieve the pain of childbirth, paving the way to the widespread use of anaesthetics in surgical practice.

1848 Ignaz Semmelweis fights to introduce antiseptic methods in a Viennese maternity clinic.

1861 Louis Pasteur discovers anaerobic bacteria.
1882 Robert Koch isolates the tuberculosis bacillus.
1883 Koch discovers the cholera bacillus.

1890 Emil Von Behring and Shibasabura Kitasato develop vaccines to protect against tetanus and diphtheria.

1895 Wilhelm Röntgen discovers the diagnostic potential of X-rays.

1896 Scipione Riva-Rocci develops an instrument for measuring blood pressure – the sphygmomanometer.

1899 The Bayer Company develops aspirin.

1903 William Halstead introduces surgical gloves to keep surgeons' hands sterile.

1905 George Washington Crile performs the first human blood transfusion.

1928 Alexander Fleming discovers penicillin.
1940 Howard Florey and Ernst Chain develop penicillin for medical use as an antibiotic.

'I'm not hungry'

IN MINOR ILLNESSES, LIQUID INTAKE IS THE MOST IMPORTANT THING; THE BODY WILL MANAGE PERFECTLY WELL FOR A DAY OR TWO WITHOUT SOLID FOOD.

When the invalid is ready to eat again, serve small, light meals that are easily digested – nourishing drinks, broths and soups are ideal for a convalescent. Include carbohydrates, such as rice or potatoes, and fruit and vegetables for vitamins. Avoid heavy, high fibre breads and cereals for a few days and serve vegetables cooked rather than raw, as they are easier to digest. After a few days, reintroduce protein in easily digestible forms such as poultry and fish.

OATMEAL As well as being easily digestible and highly nutritious, oats have been found to have antidepressant properties.

Oatmeal beverage As an alternative to barley water (see page 231), try oatmeal water. Boil 1 cup of oatmeal in 3 litres of water for half an hour, add a pinch of salt and 2 tablespoons of sugar, strain the liquid and allow to cool. Flavour with fruit juice, such as lemon, or add milk.

Gruel In 1838 readers wept for the orphans in Charles Dickens' *Oliver Twist*, who were given only thin gruel, or porridge, for supper. As part of an invalid diet, however, porridge is comforting and easily eaten. Mix 2 tablespoons of oatmeal to a paste with a little cold water, then gradually add 1 cup of boiling water and cook over a moderate heat for 15 minutes, stirring all the time. Sweeten with honey and flavour with lemon or nutmeg to taste.

LEMONADE Oranges, lemons, grapefruit and limes contain a high level of vitamin C – vital for healthy skin, bones, teeth and gums. Vitamin C also plays an important role in healing wounds and burns, and helps to produce noradrenaline, which regulates blood flow, and serotonin, which promotes sleep. Citrus fruits cannot cure a cold, but plentiful doses of vitamin C may lessen the symptoms and duration.

Homemade lemonade is a pleasant way of taking vitamin C. To make lemonade, wash a lemon and slice it thinly, removing the pips. Place slices in a jug with 4 teaspoons of sugar and the juice of a second lemon. Allow this syrup to stand for 15 minutes then add 1 litre of boiling water. Leave until cool, then strain and serve with ice.

CHICKEN BROTH Chicken is an excellent source of protein and of most B vitamins, and rice provides carbohydrates. Add a few cooked vegetables and you have a light, well balanced and nutritious meal.

Words of Wisdom

'Invalid cookery is a branch in itself, requiring special care and attention. It is important that food for invalids, or very sick persons, should be light, nourishing, and easy of digestion; also, that it be given in as concentrated a form as possible, in order that the small quantity which a patient is able to take at a time may afford sufficient nourishment without taxing the stomach or digestive powers.

Let the food be made as appetising as possible, but carefully avoid highly seasoned dishes. Never over-sweeten any dish, as that is not only unwholesome, but nauseating, to a sick palate.

And, never forget that cleanliness, and daintiness, in the manner of serving food, go far towards improving the appetite of the sick and suffering, for the life of a patient may depend upon the amount of nourishment he can be tempted to swallow.'

– *THE HOUSEHOLD MANUAL* (1899)

Skin and joint a chicken and place it in a pot with 1 litre of water, 1 tablespoon of rice, a pinch of salt and a blade of mace or a bayleaf. Simmer the mixture for 20 minutes then take out some breast pieces and put aside. Let the rest simmer for 1 hour then discard the carcase and herbs. Add reserved chicken pieces to the broth. Heat and serve.

BAKED FISH Fold a boneless fillet of white fish in half. Season with pepper, salt and a few drops of lemon juice and place in a lightly greased ovenproof dish. Cut 1 tomato into quarters and place around the fish. Cover with greased paper and bake for 15–20 minutes or until the fish is opaque. Serve the fish with the tomato wedges.

A substantial meal delights most members of the household, but serve a small, light dish to someone who is unwell.

EGGS FOR INVALIDS Eggs are nature's complete food, containing not only protein and fat but essential vitamins and minerals. Eggs can be hard to digest, and modern health advice is not to eat too many of them. For an invalid, however, lightly cooked eggs, on their own or incorporated in desserts or drinks, are a good source of nourishment.

Steamed eggs Butter a soup plate and place it over a saucepan of boiling water. Break 2 eggs into the dish, being careful not to break the yolks. Scatter tiny knobs of butter over the eggs, cover the dish with another plate and cook until the whites are set, about 4–5 minutes. Serve on a slice of lightly buttered toast.

Orange jelly A homemade orange jelly, when made with eggs, will supply an invalid with needed protein as well as the vitamins provided by the orange. In the top of a double boiler place the juice of an orange, 3 teaspoons of gelatine dissolved in ½ cup of hot water, 2 well beaten egg yolks and 1 teaspoon of sugar. Stir the ingredients continually until the mixture is hot, then turn into a wetted mould and set in the fridge.

Semolina pudding Bring 1 cup of milk to the boil and sprinkle in 30 grams of semolina. Stir mixture till it thickens and then add the yolk of an egg and 1 teaspoon of sugar. Pour into a greased pie dish and bake in a moderate oven for 15–20 minutes. Beat the white of an egg to a stiff froth, heap it roughly on top of the semolina then return the dish to the oven until the meringue topping is golden brown.

Eggnog An alcoholic drink provides energy and gives a temporary lift to the spirits. Beat 3 eggs in 150 ml of water, slowly add 90 ml of sherry or brandy, then add a little sugar and nutmeg. *Caution:* If the patient is on medication, it is advisable to check with the doctor before serving alcohol.

Taking Care of the Pence

In an emergency, toastwater is a cheap, easy and quick way to get some liquid and carbohydrate into a very sick person: simply pour hot water over a slice of toast and add a slice of lemon for flavouring. Toastwater was a great standby in the days when medical help was expensive and sometimes slow to arrive.

Home nursing

IN THE DAYS BEFORE ANTIBIOTICS, RECOVERY FROM MANY COMMON AILMENTS OFTEN DEPENDED LARGELY ON SKILLED NURSING.

Today, at least in industrialised nations, serious illnesses are generally treated by experts in hospitals. However, recent advances in technology and changes in attitudes have meant that more people are opting for home care during terminal illnesses or prolonged recuperation from serious illnesses. Carers are once more learning how to nurse loved ones at home, and the wisdom and expertise of our forebears is a valuable resource in the modern sickroom.

Regular visits from the family doctor were a comfort for the sick in our grandparents' time.

A PLEASANT ROOM A pleasant environment is especially important for someone who is unwell and must spend 24 hours a day in the same room. Choose the sunniest, most airy room in the house for a patient, even if it means disrupting other family members for a while. Sunlight is a tonic for most invalids, except those who are particularly sensitive to light, but take care that the room does not become overheated.

Air conditioning Fresh air is best provided by an open window, but make sure that the patient is not in a draught; if necessary, screen the patient so that the window can be left open. You can improvise a screen by draping a sheet over a tall clothes horse or by rigging a line between the patient and the window and hanging a sheet over it. An old but simple and effective way to keep a room cool during hot weather is to tack a piece of wet muslin over an open window so that the breeze cools as it blows in.

Peaceful surroundings Little things can soon become irritating to someone who is unwell. Avoid banging doors, squeaky hinges or beds, flapping curtains or clinking jewellery. If possible, choose a room that has plain wallpaper and curtains, as strange figures or detailed patterns can become extremely irritating to a feverish patient. Even a ticking clock can be agony for some.

If the patient wishes to have a clock in the room and you are unable to provide a silent one, take a tip from your grandmother: cover a bedside clock with a large drinking glass. In this way the face will be visible but the ticking will be muffled.

Sweet air In the old days, fresh lavender, thyme and oregano were often strewn over hospital floors to sweeten the air. These herbs have antibacterial properties and so provided some protection against airborne bacteria. A favourite room disinfectant was 15 drops each of lavender and lemon oil in a small bowl of water. Another common practice was to chop camphor into small pieces and dissolve it in warm water before adding lavender water. This mixture was often sprinkled around the room when the bed was made.

Taking Care of the Pence

A bed table of some sort is essential for serving an invalid's meals. Provided you are not facing a prolonged stint of nursing, save money by improvising a bed table: rest a flat board, such as a table leaf, over two kitchen stools placed on either side of the bed. Even an ironing board will do at a pinch.

A COMFORTABLE BED A sick person needs a fairly roomy bed, but do not choose a double bed if you have to wash or change your patient, as you will have problems stretching over it; a wide single bed or a three quarter bed is the most suitable choice.

Use lightweight, easily washed sheets that are wide enough and long enough to tuck in well under the mattress – sheets that only just reach under the mattress quickly become rucked and tangled. Position the bed so the light from the window is not shining directly into the sick person's eyes.

Most beds these days are quite low, which makes nursing a backbreaking task. By far the best option for a long stay in bed is a hospital bed on wheels, but if you cannot borrow or hire one, you can raise an ordinary bed by fitting the bed legs into four solid blocks of wood into which hollows have been drilled.

Patient comfort Sitting or lying in bed can become uncomfortable. A rolled up blanket or a pillow or two placed under a bedbound patient's knees will relieve some of the pressure on the spine. A back rest can also be a great help, or sometimes a careful arrangement of pillows behind the patient can be more comfortable than a back rest.

FRESH BREATH AND A CLEAN FACE When someone is ill, nothing is more likely to raise the spirits than a fresh-tasting mouth, clean hair and freshly washed skin – except perhaps the clean, smooth sheets on a freshly made bed. Before breakfast and after each meal, provide the patient with a toothbrush, toothpaste, a glass of mouthwash, a moistened facecloth, a towel and a small flat basin. Brush their teeth for them if they cannot manage themselves, and for a very sick patient use an applicator dipped in mouthwash instead of a toothbrush.

Long hair can easily become tangled in bed, especially if it is not regularly attended to. Go gently when a patient is too weak to comb his or her own hair. Part hair in the middle and draw it to each side. Work on one small section at a time, picking it up in your hand and combing the ends first. If hair is badly tangled, comb a section and then let the patient rest before untangling the next section.

Plaiting the hair in two loose braids or bringing the hair on top of the head in a loose knot can relieve the irritation of hair around a flushed face, but take care not to place the knot on the back of the head or the nape of the neck where it will press into the pillow. Do not scrape the hair back tightly, as this may bring on a headache.

THE ULTIMATE BED BATH For someone who is too weak to leave the bed, a bed bath can be a pleasurable experience, cooling the body, calming the mind and demonstrating the carer's love and concern.

To give a bed bath, follow the steps in the right-hand column. Make sure the room is warm and free of draughts. You will need a hand towel, three bath towels, two thin, single blankets (bath blankets) or large towels, two washing basins and two facecloths.

Half fill one basin with warm water (38–40°C) for washing, and another with cooler water (24–26°C) for rinsing and refreshing. Place a facecloth in each basin. If necessary, change the water several times during the bed bath to keep the temperature constant.

GIVING A BED BATH
Wash a small part of the body at a time, keeping the rest covered. Rinse and dry thoroughly, especially between the fingers and toes and in the genital area, or the patient will feel sticky and uncomfortable. After a bed bath, change the bed linen and the patient's night clothes.

1. Remove top bedding, replace bottom sheet with a bath blanket and cover the patient with the second bath blanket. Wash the patient's face, neck and ears, rinse with cool water and dry.

2. Wash the patient's arms, one at a time, supporting them with your other hand as you do so.

3. Raise the patient's knee with one hand and wash the upper leg, then the lower leg and foot.

4. Roll down the bath blanket and tuck towels down either side of the body. Wash the shoulders, chest, abdomen and genital area. Then roll the patient over and wash the back.

CHANGING SHEETS FOR A BEDRIDDEN PATIENT It is not difficult to change the sheets when a patient is too ill to leave the bed, once you know how. First remove the top bed covers and the pillows and loosen the bottom sheet. Gently roll the patient onto his or her side at the edge of the bed. Go around the bed and roll the undersheet towards the patient. Take the rolled-up clean sheet and tuck the end into the mattress on your side then unroll towards the patient. Roll, or if necessary lift, the patient onto the clean sheet. Remove the old sheet and finish unrolling the fresh one. Smooth it out and tuck it in firmly.

SWEET DREAMS Sleep, wrote Edward Young in the early 18th century, is 'Tir'd Nature's sweet restorer' – but sleep eludes many bedridden patients and they toss and turn the night away, becoming increasingly distressed. Establishing a bedtime routine can encourage the subconscious to accept that it is time to sleep. Wash the patient's hands and face and change the night attire.

Remake the bed, brushing out crumbs and straightening the bottom sheet. Ensure that the evening ends on a calm note. If the doctor approves, give the patient a herbal tea, such as chamomile or hyssop, or a glass of warm milk.

Fresh linen perfumed with herbs can refresh and cheer a sick person's jaded spirit.

SLEEP – THE CURE-ALL
Sleep that knits up the ravell'd
   sleave of care,
The death of each day's life,
   sore labour's bath,
Balm of hurt minds, great nature's
   second course,
Chief nourisher in life's feast.

—*MACBETH*, WILLIAM SHAKESPEARE

TAKING THE PRESSURE OFF When someone is forced to lie or sit in bed for a long time, the blood supply at pressure points such as the hips, the base of the spine, the heels, the shoulders and the elbows becomes constricted. This can cause pressure sores that will ulcerate if left untreated. Modern preventative measures, both in hospital and at home, are exactly the same as they were in earlier times.

Encourage a patient to get out of bed and walk around, even if it is only for short periods. If this is not possible, help the patient to change position in bed frequently. Rub the patient's back with medicinal alcohol twice a day and then dust with talcum powder. A gentle all-over massage with a good massage oil and a few drops of lavender oil will also keep the circulation moving. For centuries people have used honey and sugar poultices to treat ulcerated sores, leaving the skin healed and free of scar tissue. Comfrey ointment can also ease the pain of a pressure sore.

Keep beds wrinkle-free, regularly smoothing wrinkles from the bottom sheet and retucking it tightly. Brush out any crumbs immediately after a meal. In the old days sheepskin fleeces were often placed under the bottom sheet to relieve pressure, and sheepskin underblankets are still sold today for the same purpose.

THE IDEAL VISITOR Unless someone is very ill, a visit from a friend is a great morale booster. But it can be trying for an invalid to be trapped in bed unable to get away from an insensitive visitor. Bear in mind the following rules, summarised from a 1920s issue of the *Ladies' Journal*, and you will always be welcome in the sickroom.

Sit where the invalid can see you without having to move. Keep the conversation light, but discuss events outside the sickroom. Do not talk too loudly or too softly, and do not talk about your own illnesses; a long description of every ailment you have ever had is not pleasant for anyone. If the patient looks dreadful, do not blurt it out, but do not insult a person's intelligence by remarking how well he or she looks if this is not so. Do not ask every few minutes, 'How are you feeling?' – nothing is more irritating. Do not wear strong scent – it can make a person in delicate health feel quite ill. And do not make a person who has recently had an operation laugh.

Talcum is very welcome when caring for small children or bedridden patients as it soothes the skin and prevents chafing.

The Way We Were

'What is necessary to say, speak in a mild but perfectly distinct voice, and never allow whispering in a sick room for any purpose whatever. If there are any secrets to be kept from the patient, no hint of them, or whispering about them, should ever occur in his hearing; yet if it is believed the patient can not live very long, I would most certainly inform them of this belief – 'tis cruel and unjust to withhold it ... Be firm, but kind, in all your relations with the sick. Give them to understand you know best, and what you know best to do you are going to do.'

– *DR CHASE'S THIRD LAST AND COMPLETE RECEIPT BOOK AND HOUSEHOLD PHYSICIAN* (1887)

Looking after the little ones

IN MANY RESPECTS, CHILD CARE TODAY IS AN INDUSTRY: PAST GENERATIONS OF WOMEN PASSED ON THEIR KNOWLEDGE BY EXAMPLE AND WORD OF MOUTH.

As in all aspects of health care, some modern child-care precepts are safer and better than the folklore of the good old days. In other areas, however, baby care has not changed over many decades, and the wise women of bygone days can still offer us useful advice.

A NOTE OF CAUTION Because of their low body weight, small children are very vulnerable to problems such as dehydration that can stem from relatively minor ailments. It is best to be on the safe side: if a baby shows any of the following danger signals, or even if you just feel that something is not quite right, call a doctor.

• temperature higher than 39°C or below 36°C
• breathing at a rate of 60 breaths a minute for more than 5 minutes
• difficulty in breathing
• 'barking' cough
• fits or convulsions
• blood in stools or urine after the age of a week
• tender stomach when it is pressed
• dry, flaky skin, particularly on the stomach or around the mouth
• rash
• discharge from the ears or continual rubbing at the ears
• vomiting or watery diarrhoea together
• repeated projectile vomiting
• listlessness or irritability
• refusal to eat
• fewer than four wet nappies in 24 hours

Words of Wisdom

'Don't try to make the baby laugh every time he is picked up. Some people tickle him until he grins stupidly, and this often done makes his nervous system very sensitive and irritable. The grin produced like this is often the result of nervous irritation. The spontaneous laugh of a baby is beautiful. Play with the baby in moderation. Let him play mostly on his own, except in small doses …

Excessive handling – Do not make a habit of dressing him up for show nor expect everyone to handle or kiss him. Jogging him about makes him uncomfortable, unhappy and overexcited. Jogging, rocking and dancing babies is likely to cause indigestion and nervous upset. A sick baby is often the result of this, whereas judicious handling would have made all the difference.'

– *AUSTRALIAN BABY BOOK* (1931)

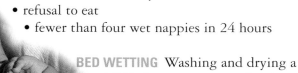

BED WETTING Washing and drying a child's sheets every morning in the days before there were washing machines could not have been much fun – no wonder advice on how to cure incontinence in young children abounded. The more reasonable advised parents not to punish their children for what they could not help, but others saw bed wetting as a sign of laziness or moral weakness and urged mothers to spare no pains to cure the habit and thus save the child! Modern experts are more likely to say that bed wetting up to around five years is quite normal and that there is no cause for alarm – and certainly no reason to turn to drugs or other drastic measures.

There are several old-time measures that may prove effective. Avoid large amounts of fluid near bedtime, but do not refuse the child drinks some hours before bedtime. Wake the child after a few hours and take him or her to the toilet. Make sure the child is warm enough – being cold can cause bed wetting.

If a child has been dry for a year or so and then suddenly starts to wet the bed once more, investigate for possible psychological stress. Children over five who are still wetting the bed may have a physical problem and it is as well to consult a doctor.

In wealthier homes, nanny was the person who cared for the youngest member of the family.

CHILDHOOD VIRUSES Common childhood viral diseases such as chickenpox and mumps were once feared because complications that were sometimes fatal often followed the primary infection.

There is still no cure for these diseases, but antibiotics have virtually done away with the complications. Nursing care while these diseases take their course is the same as it ever was: keep the child comfortable, try to ease the symptoms and watch for complications.

Chickenpox Children may be off colour for several days or have a slight temperature before any spots appear. The rash usually appears in clumps, sometimes on the inside of the mouth as well as on the body. The spots form fluid-filled blisters that later become milky and then dry out, leaving scabs that fall off. Chickenpox is caused by the same virus as shingles. It is highly contagious; children can spread shingles to adults, and adults who are suffering from shingles can infect children with chickenpox.

Chickenpox is not a serious illness and major complications are rare. The rash is extremely itchy, and the main consideration is to prevent the child from scratching, as the blisters can become infected and leave permanent pockmarks. Make sure the child's nails are short and clean to lessen the likelihood of infection from scratching. Calamine lotion is still a good old-fashioned treatment for itchiness, or try a lukewarm bath with two cups of bicarbonate of soda added.

Keep the child at home to avoid spreading the virus to other people and provide light, nourishing meals.

Mumps Pain and stiffness beneath the lower jawbone, often on only one side, are the first symptoms. This is usually followed by swelling that lasts four to six days and changes the shape of the face. There may be fever and headache. Eating and swallowing become difficult and painful. Boys may also have swollen testicles.

Mumps makes children feel very miserable. Keep the child calm and comfortable in bed and give soft foods

A thermometer is a useful item of home medical equipment, but do not take a baby's temperature by mouth. Put the thermometer into the armpit and hold the child still with the arm pressed to the side for three minutes.

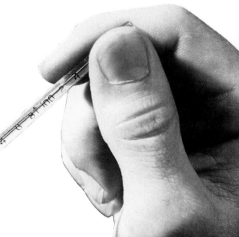

and plenty of cool drinks. A hot water bottle wrapped in a soft towel and applied to the affected area is often a comfort, or you can try a cold compress with a drop or two of lavender oil on it.

COLIC A baby who screams for several hours at night for no apparent reason is often said to have colic. People used to blame 'wind' for this condition, especially as the baby often draws the legs up towards the stomach and seems to be in pain.

Even today, colic is not really understood. There are any number of possible causes: overfeeding or feeding too slowly or too quickly are common reasons. Being cold is one suggested cause, and even wet nappies have been blamed. Some experts believe that over-stimulation may be the culprit.

Some time-honoured treatments may help at least some babies some of the time. Most importantly, keep calm and take heart – this distressing condition usually stops by the time the baby is about three months old. Try giving a little warm water in a bottle and then holding the child over your shoulder. Sometimes applying warmth to the baby's stomach and feet helps, or try a warm bath. Massaging the baby's stomach very gently with warm oil using a circular motion can also ease the discomfort – add 3 or 4 drops of lavender or chamomile oil to 1 teaspoon of warm almond oil for a calming lotion.

If a child continues to cry and seems distressed, there may a more serious underlying cause: consult a doctor.

CROUP Until the age of about four, children have disproportionately narrow airways, and any respiratory infection may bring about a frightening attack of coughing, wheezing and panting. Try propping the child up in bed and giving small sips of warm water. Make sure the room is warm but there is plenty of fresh air. Keeping the air moist will also help; the old-fashioned steaming kettle will do in an emergency, but if croup is a persistent problem it would be easier to invest in a humidifier.

If an attack continues, put the child in a bath of warm water, deep enough for the water to come up to the throat. Dry the child with warm towels, rub the chest and back with warm camphorated oil, roll the child in a warm blanket and keep him or her warm but not hot. A good massage oil for clearing the airways is 6 drops of eucalyptus oil and 4 drops of lavender oil to 3 teaspoons of almond oil. Massage into the chest and back two or three times a day.

If there is no improvement after three days, or if the child coughs up blood or has a high temperature, call a doctor immediately.

EARACHE Indigestion and teething commonly cause earache in infants. More seriously, earache may result from bad teeth, infected adenoids or a middle ear problem. If a baby is irritable and rubs the ears, consult a doctor to eliminate the possibility of any of these underlying causes.

To relieve a transient earache from indigestion or teething problems, apply warmth externally to the baby's ear with a warm compress or a wrapped up hot water bottle, or gently rub warmed almond oil with a few drops of lavender around the sides and back of the ear.

SWADDLING

Confining a newborn baby's limbs and torso with blankets or cloth was used to 'keep the baby's back straight' until early this century, when people realised that it was better for the baby to be free to move. A modified version of swaddling, however, can help settle a restless baby, as it gives a sense of warmth and security.

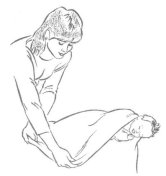

1. Wrap the baby in the natural position without straightening the arms and legs out.

2. Use a light, slightly stretchy shawl or baby's blanket, a flannelette cot sheet or soft cotton netting, depending on the weather.

3. Always position the baby on the back.

NAPPY RASH Fresh air is one of the best preventatives; let the baby spend as much time as possible without a nappy. Change nappies as soon as they are wet and keep both baby and nappies scrupulously clean. After a bath, dry the skin folds carefully. If you are breast feeding, avoid strongly spiced foods, citrus fruits, coffee and alcohol to minimise the irritant content of the baby's urine.

Try dabbing reddened buttocks with oatmeal gruel made by boiling 1 teaspoon of oatmeal in 1 cup of water. If the baby's buttocks are very red and raw, clean them with warm olive oil instead of water at each nappy change. Dry the baby gently and rub in dry cornflour. For more severe nappy rash, apply a little zinc ointment.

PRICKLY HEAT Prickly heat is an irritating skin rash, frequently accompanied by profuse sweating. Prevention, as always, is better than cure: make sure that the baby never becomes too hot and that clothes are clean, loose, and preferably made of cotton.

If a rash does appear, a time-honoured treatment is to sponge the baby frequently with a solution of equal parts of vinegar and cool water, then dust with baby powder or apply calamine lotion. Another effective treatment is to bathe the baby frequently with 2–4 drops of lavender or peppermint oil in a cup of water.

TEETHING TROUBLES Teething should not be seriously uncomfortable for a healthy baby: if the child appears ill, seek medical advice. Do not assume that teething is the cause of persistent crying and discomfort.

The first few teeth usually come through quite easily, but the first molars, which come through at about 12 months, can be painful. Chamomile has been used for centuries to ease teething pain. Add a drop of chamomile oil to 1 teaspoon of good vegetable oil and rub it gently into the baby's cheek – Roman chamomile is more effective than German chamomile. You can also make a warm compress with chamomile oil and press it against the baby's cheek.

Babies chew vigorously when a tooth is about to come through, and a teething ring can provide some comfort. A rusk – a finger of bread that has been dried in a slow oven – can serve the same purpose for babies over eight months old. Do not leave children alone while they are chewing rusks in case they choke.

THUMB SUCKING Some babies will suck their thumbs, their fingers or their clothing no matter what you do to try to prevent it. Some of the old methods, such as tying the child's hands to the side of the cot, keeping mittens on the child or painting the thumb with bitter aloes were cruel as well as ineffective, and probably served to aggravate the problem, since children suck their thumbs for comfort. Neither punishing the child for thumb sucking nor giving some reward for desisting has much effect.

Ironically, one of the reasons parents gave for their objection to thumb sucking was that it looked babyish! Another reason for concern was the belief that constant thumb sucking caused teeth to grow crooked, but modern experts say that this is unlikely to happen unless the child continues the habit after the age of about seven.

A BEDTIME RHYME
Half-past bunny-time,
Possums by the moon;
Tea and bread-and-honey time,
Sleep-time soon.

– *Kiddie Songs*, Furnley Maurice (1917)

If colic is a problem, make the hour before bedtime as calm as possible. Bathe the baby gently and unhurriedly and speak softly.

When new ways are better

MEDICAL EMERGENCIES CAN BE ALARMING, BUT
BYSTANDERS OFTEN HAVE TO PROVIDE FIRST AID
UNTIL PROFESSIONAL HELP ARRIVES.

Alcohol was once a popular treatment for shock, but it is not recommended these days, as it could prevent or delay the giving of an anaesthetic, which may be necessary later. The same applies to hot sweet tea and food.

In the old days a doctor might be hours or even days away, so people had to have some expertise in first aid. But many old-fashioned remedies were unsound, and people often died of injuries that we would view today as minor. First aid is one area where the new ways are often better than the old.

SHOCK When someone is in clinical shock, the oxygen supply to the tissues cannot meet the body's needs. The victim is pale and cold, with a rapid pulse and shallow breathing. The aim of treatment is to ensure that the heart, lungs and brain get enough oxygen. Old-fashioned treatments such as wrapping the victim in blankets can cause overheating, which increases the blood supply to the skin and takes it away from the vital organs.

What to do Get the victim to lie down, stem any obvious bleeding by applying pressure directly to the wound, and then raise and support the legs so that the feet are higher than the head – unless there is an injury to the head, chest or abdomen or the victim has suffered a heart attack or a stroke. Loosen tight clothing, cover the patient lightly and summon medical assistance.

BURNS AND SCALDS Burns were treated with all sorts of substances in the old days, from mutton fat and olive oil to butter or herbs, and many thought it essential to break blisters in order to 'let out the poison'. Such remedies did more harm than good.

What to do Cool the area by immersing it in cold water for at least 10 minutes, or as long as the pain persists. If water is not available, use liquid such as beer instead, but never fat or ointment. Remove clothing and jewellery from around the injury before the skin starts to swell, but do not attempt to remove any loose skin or material that is stuck to the wound, such as bitumen or melted fabric. Leave blisters untouched – they are the body's natural defence against infection – and apply a clean, non-fluffy dressing.

Minor burns A time-honoured, safe and effective treatment for small burns is to dab on some honey with a fingertip. Honey has soothing and antiseptic properties, and will heal minor burns quickly without blistering or scarring.

NOSEBLEEDS Remedies practised in the old days, such as applying cold compresses to the nape of the neck, chewing paper, or immersing the feet in warm water, were really no more than diversions: most nosebleeds stop spontaneously within 15 minutes. Some old remedies, such as plugging the nose with wads of gauze, were dangerous, as they caused the sufferer to swallow blood, which could lead to vomiting or breathing difficulties.

What to do The safest and most effective remedy for a nosebleed is to sit with your mouth open, leaning slightly forward so that blood clots cannot obstruct the airway. Pinch the soft part of your nose together and breathe through your mouth, spitting out any blood that collects. After 10 minutes, slowly release your nostrils. If the bleeding continues, repeat the treatment for a further 10 minutes. Do not raise your head until the bleeding has stopped, and avoid exertion and blowing your nose for several hours. If bleeding persists for longer than 30 minutes or recurs, seek medical advice.

POISONING Many household substances can cause illness or death if they are swallowed. Old-time remedies included inducing vomiting, swallowing milk or bread or taking herbal antidotes.

Remedies have not changed a great deal over the years, but we now know which remedies to use for the various types of poisons. If someone has swallowed a corrosive substance or a volatile fluid such as petrol, for instance, inducing vomiting exacerbates the damage, since a substance that burned going down will also burn coming up. Drinking milk or water, on the other hand, will cool the affected area and dilute the poison.

What to do Today there are information centres that will advise you how to treat for a particular poison; include the number for your region's poisons information centre in your list of other emergency numbers and display the list in a prominent place. If you suspect that someone has swallowed a poisonous substance, try to find out what they took and telephone the centre for advice.

SNAKE BITE Tying a tourniquet around the bitten limb, slashing the wound and sucking the poison out was the traditional remedy for snake bite in Wild West films and boy's own adventure stories. Other old-fashioned remedies included holding the wound under running water or rubbing Condy's crystals into it.

The modern first aid treatment for snake bites is less dramatic but much more effective. The aim is to slow down the rate at which the blood stream absorbs the poison until an antivenom can be administered in hospital.

What to do Get the victim to lie down and stay as calm as possible, and call an ambulance immediately. If the bite is on a limb, apply a pressure bandage over it and wind a second bandage firmly, but not too tightly, around the limb, working towards the trunk. Immobilise the limb with a sling or splint, and try not to move the patient.

Prevention is better than cure: make sure that all poisonous substances – cleaning products, medicines, garden sprays, and so on – are safely locked away.

The Way We Were

'A daughter of Wm. Reed, of the town of Pittsfield, in this country, who was bitten on the arm some three years ago, was cured by drinking whisky until drunkenness and stupor were produced, and she never felt any inconvenience from the bite since, which goes to show that the bite of the *Devil's tea* is worse than the bite of a rattlesnake.'

– DR CHASE'S RECIPES; OR INFORMATION FOR EVERYBODY (1866)

in
Beauty

SIMPLE BEAUTY TIPS FROM THE PAST TO SAVE YOU TIME AND MONEY

The basics of beauty

MUCH OF THE BEAUTY ADVICE OF THE PAST PROMOTED THE IDEAL OF TOTAL BEAUTY, AND IS AS RELEVANT TODAY AS IT EVER WAS.

Many experts preached a holistic approach to beauty that included good nutrition, fresh air, exercise and relaxation, a positive outlook, an attractive personality and attention to deportment and grooming. The lotions, potions and ointments they recommended were the icing on the cake, or the cure when all else had failed.

Caution: All recipes have been checked for safety and every effort has been made to ensure that ingredients are harmless. However, some skins are particularly sensitive to certain ingredients, even though they are 'natural', so test all preparations on a small patch of skin – the inside of the elbow is an ideal spot. Wait for 24 hours; if the skin reddens, blisters, burns or becomes itchy, do not use the preparation without professional advice.

RELAXATION AND EXERCISE The art of relaxation is essential to true beauty from within. If you start to feel flustered, use the following technique, recommended in the days before meditation was the popular way to achie;ve serenity. Lie down with your feet raised so that they are higher than your head. This position is a tonic for your bodily organs and relieves strain on your legs and ankles. Close your eyes and relax your body completely from head to toe, so that you feel like a rag doll. Now imagine that someone has taken a cool sponge and erased every worry and anxiety from your mind, leaving it as clear as a summer sky. Exercise tones up the system, puts a sparkle in the eyes and helps you to relax.

COSMETICS FROM THE OLD DAYS Our grandmothers were rather casual in their instructions for making beauty preparations. Most of their recipes were versions of preparations that people had been making up at home for generations, so readers already knew the methods and the general proportions of the ingredients.

Interpreting the recipes Measurements in spoons and cups have not changed much over the years, and in any case were intended only as close indications of weight or volume. Measurements in drops were just that – a drop is the quantity of a liquid that will form

Words of Wisdom

Yawning in public was, and still is, bad manners, but yawning is a healthy, natural response to the body's need for a deep breath to boost its supply of oxygen:

'People should yawn regularly. If we yawn and stretch ourselves both before going to bed at night and upon getting up in the morning, we should benefit ourselves greatly. Yawning is a healthy function, having a salutary effect on certain tubes in the neck and lungs by exercising all the respiratory muscles.'

– *WORTHS AUSTRALIAN FASHION JOURNAL* (1899)

Apothecaries used scales such as these to accurately measure ingredients, but quantities were not crucial in home preparations.

a small pear-shaped globule. Use an eye dropper, available from pharmacies, to measure drops.

Systems of measurement Confusingly for the modern reader, there were a number of systems of weights and measures in common use in the good old days. There were, for example, three kinds of ounces: the avoirdupois ounce; the Troy ounce, or apothecaries' ounce; and the fluid ounce. A dram (or drachm) was one-sixteenth of an avoirdupois ounce, and the smallest unit of all was the grain – the average weight of a grain of wheat. In 1947, the International Standards Organization was established to standardise units of measurement, basically according to the decimal system.

This was a timely move, but while some countries eagerly embraced the new, simpler system, others clung tenaciously to their traditional systems; even at the close of the 20th century, systems of measurement are far from consistent across the world, or even within countries.

For the convenience of readers, all the quantities except drop measurements have been converted into metric equivalents.

Making up the recipes For the best results, take advantage of some tips developed over the decades.
• Save small screw-top jars to store preparations, or buy pretty containers from gift shops.
• Wash jars in hot soapy water, boil them for 10 minutes and allow them to dry thoroughly before use.
• Keep all equipment scrupulously clean.
• Use stainless steel, glass, enamel or pyrex containers for warming and boiling, and stainless steel spoons for mixing. Never use aluminium implements to make beauty preparations, as aluminium can react with other substances.
• Use only distilled water or water that has been boiled when making up the recipes.
• Make up only small quantities – home-made creams and lotions will deteriorate within a few weeks, some within four days, unless you keep them in the refrigerator.
• Clearly label all preparations, including the date of bottling.
• Some recipes include essential oil of roses as a perfuming agent. Today, this ingredient is very expensive; oil of geranium is an economical but equally fragrant substitute.

Making herbal teas In a non-aluminium container, place 1 teaspoon of the chopped herb or flower for each cup. Pour on boiling water, cover and infuse for about three minutes and then strain. If using fresh ingredients, use twice or three times as much as the dried and infuse for a few minutes more. Strain off the liquid, allow to cool and store in a glass container in the refrigerator for up to five days.

Making decoctions This method is used to extract the soluble components from the roots, stems and seeds of herbs. Place finely chopped, crushed or powdered dry seeds, roots or stems in a small saucepan, add a cup of water, cover and bring to the boil. Simmer for 10–15 minutes and strain while hot.

Relaxing for a few moments each day is an important component of any beauty routine.

The Way We Were
'Beauty, in the old days, used to float into the world like Botticelli's Venus on a shell, natural, breath-taking, divine. Beauty, today, is made from baser metals by an astonishing alchemy totally of our time.'

– VOGUE'S BOOK OF BEAUTY (1933)

Facing the world

THE DEFINITION OF A BEAUTIFUL FACE CHANGES WITH CHANGING FASHIONS, BUT CLEAN, FLAWLESS SKIN HAS ALWAYS BEEN AN ESSENTIAL COMPONENT.

Advice about skin care often involves complicated routines of creams and tonics, scrubbing, steaming and masks, but most practices can be broken down into three simple steps: cleansing, toning and moisturising. Modern commercial skin-care products can be extremely expensive; some of the simple recipes of the past are still practicable.

CLEANSERS Beauty experts have always been divided about whether the best facial cleanser is soap and water or a soapless cleanser. Many believe that soap should never be used on delicate or dry skin but that it is beneficial for an oily skin. Either way, gentleness is the key to success: massage the lather or cleanser liberally but lightly into the skin to loosen all make-up and dirt, and then rinse off with warm water. Cotton wool pads – the modern equivalent of a soft cotton cloth – are useful for removing any residue.

Milky cleansers In the 1920s, buttermilk was recommended as a refreshing skin cleanser in hot weather, and a mixture of equal parts of milk of magnesia, paraffin oil and witch hazel was also believed to be effective. The strained juice of crushed strawberries soaked in milk for two hours was suggested as an excellent cleanser for sallow skin.

Fragrant cleanser Melt 30 grams of hydrous lanolin (from pharmacies) and 15 grams of beeswax in a basin or the top of a double boiler over a low heat. When runny, slowly add 90 ml of olive oil and 2 tablespoons of rose or lavender water. Remove from heat and stir until cool. Store in screw-top jars.

Almond cleansers Melt 2 teaspoons of grated soft soap with 5 tablespoons of almond oil in the top of a double boiler. Gradually add 2 teaspoons each of butter and rose-water, beating continuously. Remove from heat and beat until cool. Store in screw-top jars.
  For an almond preparation that softens and slightly bleaches the skin, whip 2 tablespoons of almond meal and 150 ml of water until blended. Sieve through cheesecloth and bottle.

Cream and cucumber cleanser Put 1 cup of thick cream into a saucepan and heat to boiling point. Let cool. Do this three times and then, while still hot, stir in the strained juice of a lemon, 2 tablespoons of strained cucumber juice, 2 teaspoons of glycerine and 2 teaspoons of honey. Stir until cold. Add a few drops of your favourite scent and store in pots.

Olive oil and honey cleanser Mix 2 teaspoons of olive oil with 1 teaspoon of honey. Rub in with fingertips then wipe off gently and splash the face with warm water.

Since the late 19th century, the market place has been flooded with skin products but effective treatments can be made at home.

Oatmeal cleansers Pour some hot water over a few tablespoons of good quality oatmeal in a firmly tied cheesecloth or muslin bag and let it stand until soft. Use the bag on the face like a sponge. You can also use finely ground oatmeal on your face instead of soap.

TONERS AND ASTRINGENTS Applied with cotton wool after cleansing, toners and astringents refresh the skin and remove any last traces of make-up or excess oil. If you have dry skin, avoid alcohol-based toners: instead, try an infusion of fresh or dried herbs. For example, cooled thyme leaf or lemon grass tea helps to freshen and clear your complexion, and lemon grass tea refines the texture of your skin.

Dry or delicate skin Simply apply rose-water, or make a mixture of 1 teaspoon of cider vinegar and 2 tablespoons of distilled water. Another toner for dry skin is a mixture of two parts of warm milk to one part of warm water.

Oily skin For a simple toning treatment for oily skin, dip a slice of cucumber into a little fresh lemon or lime juice diluted with six parts of water and rub it gently over the skin.

Our grandmothers were proud of their delicate skins and used fruits and other plant products to keep them glowing and flawless.

Skin lotion or toner will go much further if you wet some cotton wool in cold water, squeeze out the water then apply the preparation with the damp pad, rather than with your fingertips.

Juice toners Watermelon juice and cucumber juice are gentle toners and aids to the complexion. They are best used fresh, but you can keep the juice in glass bottles in the refrigerator for a few days.

Rose-water and witch hazel toner Use two parts of rose-water to one part of witch hazel for normal skin – use a little more rose-water for dry skin.

Toner for all skin types Make this refreshing mixture by mashing half a cucumber with 4 mint leaves and blending in ½ cup of water. Strain the liquid into a glass bottle and store in the refrigerator.

MOISTURISERS Moisturising creams replenish the skin after cleansing and toning. In the old days moisturisers were used as night creams, so some of these recipes are very rich.

Honey moisturiser Warm a cup of honey in a saucepan, add 2 teaspoons of rose-water and ½ cup of milk, and turn off the heat. Mix well and allow to cool. Pour the mixture into a bottle and store in a cool place. Shake the bottle well before use and apply the lotion with cotton wool, patting it gently into your neck and face. Use before going to bed and rinse off in the morning.

Rich moisturiser Heat ½ cup of peanut oil with 1 tablespoon of lanolin in a double boiler over low heat. Very slowly, in a thin stream, beat in ½ cup of water. Take off the heat and add a beaten egg. Continue beating until the mixture is thick and creamy. Pour into screw-top jars and store in the refrigerator.

Creamy lavender moisturiser Put 6 tablespoons of lanolin in a bowl and stand in a pan of hot water. Add 2 tablespoons each of avocado oil and almond oil and beat well. When combined, remove from heat and continue to beat while the mixture cools and thickens. Add 2 teaspoons of lavender oil and beat until the mixture is thick and creamy. Pour into small screw-top jars and store in the refrigerator.

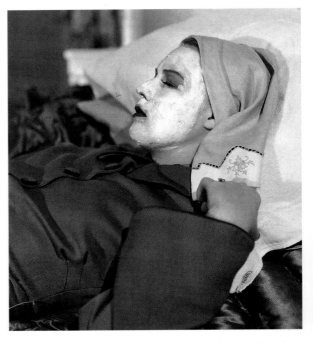

Few women look this good with a face pack, but the results are well worth the inconvenience..

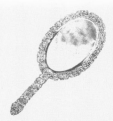

Words of Wisdom

'Rubbing the face over with slices of freshly cut cucumber after washing every morning, or bathing it night and morning with strained barley water or parsley lotion, are methods which were employed by our grandmothers and great grandmothers for preserving the beauty of their complexions during the summer months ... Parsley lotion is made by taking a large handful of freshly picked parsley and pouring over it a pint of boiling water. Allow this to infuse in a covered vessel and when it has become quite cold it may be strained and applied to the skin.'

– *MY LADY'S JOURNAL* (1906)

WRINKLES Cosmetics manufacturers have been striving for decades to produce an effective treatment for wrinkles, but despite many promises, no one has really delivered the goods. A pot of genuine anti-wrinkle cream would be a bottomless pot of gold for the successful inventor! You could try these wrinkle-preventing recipes from the 1890s, but if you are faced with failure, remember Mark Twain's consoling words: 'Wrinkles should merely indicate where smiles have been'.

Masks Mix an egg white with 1 tablespoon of honey and enough ground barley to make a firm paste. Use as a face mask. Or try this: mix equal parts of glycerine and cucumber juice together, then dab onto your face and neck with cotton wool and leave to dry. Rinse off with warm water.

Our grandmothers also used vegetable masks to ward off wrinkles. Mix a grated raw potato with 1 teaspoon of cream, smooth over your face, leave for 10 minutes, then rinse off with warm water. Or mash 3 small boiled carrots and mix to a paste with 3 teaspoons of lemon juice. Leave on your face for about 20 minutes before rinsing off.

Lotions Mix 3 teaspoons each of glycerine, rose-water and witch hazel with 3 tablespoons of honey. Massage the lotion gently into your face and rinse off with warm water. Or mix 1½ tablespoons of coconut oil with 2 teaspoons of sweet almond oil, apply and massage in thoroughly. For oily skin, add 10 drops of simple tincture of benzoin. Always massage your face with an upward movement.

FACE PACKS Some say that a face pack acts on the complexion like a glass of champagne on the spirits! Apply a face pack each week to boost your regular skin-care routine of cleansing, toning and moisturising.

A face pack helps to tone the facial muscles and makes the skin less liable to develop enlarged pores or blackheads. Face packs must be applied to thoroughly clean skin; for a luxury touch, give yourself a steam treatment first but, if you have dry skin, limit these to once every fortnight.

Apply the pack to your face and throat, staying well away from the sensitive areas around your eyes and lips. Cover your eyes with slices of cucumber or tea bags that have been steeped in hot water and allowed to cool to lukewarm, and rest comfortably with your feet elevated. Remove the pack with tepid water, pat your skin dry and apply cold water or rose-water.

Fruity face masks Mashed fresh strawberries or apples make a pleasant and revitalising face mask; mashed ripe pears or bananas enrich and refresh.

For dry or delicate skin If your skin is very dry, add a well beaten egg to 3 teaspoons of warm olive oil. Massage well into your face and neck and leave for 15 minutes. Rinse off with warm water. Or try mashed avocado, or almond oil mixed with almond meal.

For oily complexions Mix the strained juice of 2 or 3 tomatoes with a little lemon juice, rub it in gently and allow to dry. Leave on for 30 minutes then rinse off. Or mash half a small cucumber with a little milk and the white of an egg and beat until a paste is formed. Smooth the mixture over your face and leave for 20 minutes, then rinse off with tepid water.

To enliven the skin Wipe your skin over with cotton wool dipped in fresh cream, then spread a good quality honey over your face and pat it into your skin for 15 minutes.

To refresh the skin Boil 30 grams of dried marshmallow root powder (from health food stores) in 600 ml of cold water and let the

While a face mask is cleansing your skin, revitalise your hair by giving it a hot oil or a conditioning treatment.

Fruit face packs are usually made from mashed ingredients; while the sliced pieces worn here are certainly startling to look at, they probably do little to improve the skin of the wearer.

mixture stand overnight to thicken. You may need to beat it before straining it into a glass jar. Stir in 1 teaspoon of honey for each cup of lotion and mix well.

To nourish the skin Mix together equal quantities of wheatgerm meal and natural yoghurt. Smooth the mixture over your face and neck, leave on for ten minutes, then rinse off with warm water.

To soothe and beautify Smooth the unbeaten white of an egg over your face, leave to dry, then rinse off with warm water. Or mix together 3 drops of olive or almond oil and 1 teaspoon of honey. Apply to your face and leave for about 20 minutes before removing with warm water.

PROBLEM SKIN Some people are plagued by blackheads, pimples or acne. Until quite recently, the only real cure was inner cleansing and a sensible diet low in rich and greasy foods. In modern times, powerful antibiotic and hormone-based treatments have been developed but these are prescribed only when other, gentler, remedies have proved ineffective. Some old-fashioned mixtures are still helpful.

Blackheads Blackheads are nearly always caused by a lack of attention to facial cleanliness. Regular steam treatments followed by a gentle astringent or toner will help in maintaining a scrupulously clean skin. For a refreshing astringent lotion that is especially helpful in preventing blackheads, boil 3 tablespoons of oatmeal in 300 ml of water for three minutes. Strain and cool the liquid, add the juice of half a lemon and dab onto your face and neck night and morning.

The following lotion was believed to correct large pores, and was especially recommended for oily skin and blackheads. Mix 150 ml of orange flower water with 3 tablespoons of witch hazel, shake lightly and add 1 teaspoon of tincture of benzoin. Apply night and morning with cotton wool.

Pimples and acne Mix 45 grams of fuller's earth (from pharmacies and health food stores), ¼ teaspoon of powdered calamine and sufficient water to form a creamy consistency. Smooth the paste evenly over your face, leave until dry, then wash off gently with cold water. Rubbing a steamed sliced onion over pimples can also be effective, because of the sulphur content in the onions.

For acne, some old-time external treatments included lemon or cabbage juice or cold sage tea, which are astringent and mildly antiseptic. For internal use, the following recipe was recommended. Dissolve 1 tablespoon of sulphur in 1 cup of warm treacle, mix well and store in a screw-top jar. Take a teaspoon of the mixture once a week until your skin clears.

SUPERFLUOUS HAIR Never shave unwanted hair on your face; shaving will only encourage the hair to regrow and will make it stronger. A treatment for a fine down of facial hair is to dab it with hydrogen peroxide diluted with an equal amount of water, which will bleach it

FACIAL STEAMING

Facial steaming is a proven aid to a clearer, more luminous skin. Boiling water can be used on its own or it can be sweetened with herbs and flowers.

1. Put some herbs and flowers into a basin and pour 5 cups of boiling water over them.

2. Cover your head with a towel and lower your face over the bowl. Close your eyes and let the steam circulate for five minutes. Rinse your face with warm water, dab on cold sage tea to close the pores, then lightly dry.

Caution: Do not steam your face if you have thread veins, serious skin disorders, breathing difficulties, or heart problems.

Herbal combinations
Use equal quantities of the ingredients to make up 2–3 handfuls of fresh herbs or 2 tablespoons of dried herbs.

For dry to normal skin Chopped spearmint, rose petals and chamomile flowers

For oily skin Chopped marigold, peppermint and lemongrass, crushed lavender flowers

To moisturise and soothe the skin Chopped orange blossoms and marigold, crushed fennel

To stimulate and firm the skin Chopped lavender, peppermint and rosemary leaves, crushed aniseed

and make it less noticeable. Wash the solution off thoroughly with plenty of warm water.

Pluck out any noticeable hairs with tweezers or use a commercially prepared wax treatment – this does not remove the hairs permanently, but it does leave the skin perfectly clear and discourages regrowth.

FRECKLES Freckles used to be known as sun kisses, and it is a matter of opinion whether they are a disfigurement or not. For those who dislike freckles, it may be worth reflecting on this charming remark: 'A face without freckles is like a garden without flowers'. However if you want to get rid of your freckles, here are some mixtures that our grandmothers used for treating them.

Mix ½ teaspoon of tincture of benzoin with 250 ml of rose-water and apply at night. Or soak fresh elder flowers in boiling water overnight, strain, and apply the liquid every evening. Alternatively, slice a green cucumber into skim milk, let it stand for an hour then use the milk liberally, rubbing it well in.

SKIN CARE TIPS There are many ways to smooth and beautify skin.
• Daily cleansing of your face and the application of a moisturiser help prevent wrinkles and protect your skin from dirt and drying air.
• Never stroke in creams or moisturisers around your eyes; instead, pat them in gently, using only the cushions of your fingertips with feather-light pressure.
• If your skin is very delicate, use a comfortably hot face washer after cleansing to gently remove any remains of the cleanser.
• One of the simplest ways to brighten up a tired face is to bathe it in cold water and then dab it with cologne-soaked cotton wool. This stimulates the circulation and is soothing.
• Make sure your hands are perfectly clean before removing or applying make-up.
• Always replace the lids of jars and bottles when not in use to stop the mixtures they contain oxidising, evaporating or being contaminated with microbes.

MAKE-UP Cleverly applied make-up can camouflage features that are out of proportion and hide many imperfections.

Foundation A touch of darker foundation beneath puffy eyes reduces their prominence, and for a too-broad nose use a darker shade of foundation on either side, taking great care with blending. And you can disguise a double chin by using foundation a tone darker. It is important to blend the different tones where they meet.

Rouge In the early 1900s, daring young ladies applied a touch of rouge to their earlobes to give their faces a younger look – a trick that was copied by actors. Rouge was also used to disguise less attractive features. Today, you can disguise a heavy jawline by shading with blusher along the edges, and a narrow face will look less sharp if you spread blusher well over your cheeks, away from your nose. To lengthen a round face, apply blusher mainly on the cheekbones and taper the colour off towards the chin.

Taking Care of the Pence

When baking with eggs, put the shells to one side until the cake is in the oven. Then, with your fingers, extract the residual egg white clinging to the egg shells and smooth it all over your face and throat. Put your feet up for ten minutes – the pack will do its work on your face while the oven does its work on your baking.

Applied correctly, make-up can create an illusion of beauty.

GILDING THE LILY

The artificial, enamelled look that characterised make-up in the 18th century was frowned upon by the outwardly straitlaced Victorians, who considered make-up vulgar and common. Women did not go completely without make-up, but they took pains to use it subtly, applying a dash of rouge to simulate an innocent blush, or a dusting of face powder to create the ethereal appearance that was in vogue.

Patent creams and cosmetics had been available commercially for most of the 19th century, but they often contained dangerous substances such as arsenic and lead, so many women made their own, following recipes and simple tips handed down by their mothers and grandmothers, such as biting their lips to make them red and using geranium juice as rouge. However, by the beginning of the 20th century cosmetics manufacturers had eliminated most of the poisons and a move towards the open use of make-up was under way.

PAN-CAKE MAKE-UP
Max Factor's Pan-Cake, which appeared in 1938, was the first water-soluble cake foundation. It took its somewhat ambiguous name from its panchromatic tones, which were used in film make-up. The foundation's chalky, mask-like qualities made it an overnight success, and the makers developed a range of colours to match women's skin tones.

PACKAGING THE PRODUCT
Cosmetics companies were quick to realise that packaging was often more important for sales than the products themselves, and highly decorative containers of metal and glass appeared. Women's magazines and beauty manuals began to highlight new trends and give space to cosmetic advertising, and by the 1920s the industry had become fiercely competitive. Sales skyrocketed in the 1930s, buoyed by the popularity of Hollywood – women wanted to look like the stars they saw regularly in films. Production fell by 75 per cent in World War II, but the effects of make-up on troop morale were widely recognised and after the war the industry quickly recovered.

VANITY, THY NAME IS WOMAN
As travel became more common, the portable make-up case, or vanity case was the ideal accessory for the well groomed woman. This one was marketed by Revlon in about 1950.

DISCRETION … THE BETTER PART

Face powder was one of the few beauty aids that the conservative Victorians considered acceptable. In 1913 the powder compact revolutionised the packaging of face powder, which ever after came with powder puff and mirror. In 1915, lipstick in a slide tube arrived, and by the 1920s women were wearing bright red lipstick to advertise their new-found freedom. Edwardian women coloured their eyelashes with cosmetic crayon, but the potential of eyeshadow was not fully explored until the 1930s.

CHECKING UP

Once make-up took off commercially, manufacturers incorporated mirrors into their powder compacts so that a discreet touch-up was possible.

MAKING UP

For a fancy-dress party, why not make up as a 1920s 'flapper'?

1. Apply a light-coloured foundation, covering your eyebrows. Rub soap over your eyebrows and apply more foundation to conceal your natural eyebrow line.

2. Draw in high-arched brows with a fine eyeliner or eyebrow pencil above the natural brows.

3. Use blue or green eyeshadow, outline your eyes with black kohl pencil and apply thick black mascara or false eyelashes. Paint your lips in a Cupid's bow.

4. Draw a black beauty spot or glue on a sequin. To complete the look, wear a straight black wig with a fringe and headband and a black velvet choker.

A pair of sparkling eyes

ACCORDING TO THE OLD SAYING, THE EYES ARE THE WINDOWS OF THE SOUL; MAKE THE MOST OF YOUR EYES, AND KEEP THEM ALWAYS SHINING BRIGHT.

If your eyes are your best feature, the best way to accentuate them is by wearing colours that flatter them. For example, strong blue tones enhance blue eyes, while deep golden tones and shades of green highlight green or hazel eyes. Bright colours, especially reds, suit dark-eyed women.

EYE CARE An excellent way to rest your eyes, and one recommended down through the years by eye experts, is a simple method known as 'palming'. To do this, close your eyes naturally, then cup your hands and place them over the closed lids. The soothing effect can be

Treat the delicate skin around your eyes with care – never rub it, and rinse it with cool fresh water.

BETTER LIGHT MEANS BETTER SIGHT

intensified by rubbing your palms together vigorously before placing them over your closed eyes.

• Do not disregard the simple rules of eye health. To read, sew or write in a bad light is not advisable. Work with the light source above and behind you, so that it shines over your shoulder.

• When drying your face, pat it dry with a soft towel rather than wiping it so that you do not stretch the delicate skin around your eyes.

• Your eyes need cleansing just as much as anything else, so give them the benefit of a good bathe with a reliable eye lotion. You can make an excellent lotion by putting 1 teaspoon each of salt and bicarbonate of soda into 600 ml of boiled water. Allow the mixture to cool then shake well and bottle. Strain through cotton wool or coffee filter paper before applying daily.

Using an eye bath An eye bath, inexpensive and available from pharmacies, is by far the most effective way to bathe your eyes. Never use the same lotion for both eyes, because if one eye has any trace of an infection the lotion will transmit it to the other. Always rinse the eye bath in hot water and dry thoroughly before putting it away.

Half-fill the eye bath with lotion, lower your head and place the eye bath gently but firmly over your eye. Tilt your head back and swill the lotion across your eyeball by moving your head slowly to each side and then backwards and forwards. Lower your head again, remove the eye bath, and dab the eye gently with a clean cloth. Discard the lotion and rinse the eye bath with hot water. Repeat for the second eye.

Eye exercises Eye exercises will keep your eye muscles strong and the eyes themselves clear and bright. For the best results, do the exercises every day, even if it is only for a few minutes.

• Look quickly from extreme to extreme of your visual field. For example, look up to the right then quickly down to the left six times, then up to the left and down to the right. Focus straight ahead at some distant object, then quickly bring your attention to something directly in front of you. Repeat six times.

• Squeeze your eyes shut three or four times.

• Blink quickly at least 50 times.

REVITALISING TREATMENTS A good, bracing treatment for the eyes is to bathe them first, and then apply the beaten white of an egg to the flesh around them, gently patting it in place until it is dry. You will feel the flesh tingling beneath the mask that the egg white forms. Leave the mask on for a few minutes then remove it with warm water, and finish up by giving the eyes a cold douche.

Drinking eight glasses of water a day will help to brighten dull eyes and clear the complexion.

Tired eyes Make an infusion of fresh or dried borage or fennel leaves, strain through coffee filter paper or cotton wool, then splash the warm liquid over your eyes.

Freshly grated apple also makes a wonderfully refreshing compress for tired eyes. Place 1 heaped teaspoon of the apple between two pieces

Used for centuries by women in the Middle East to beautify the eyes, kohl became newly popular in Australia and other Western countries in the 1950s.

Fennel has many beauty applications. It has feathery leaves and in summer produces clusters of small yellow flowers.

of gauze and place the pads over your closed eyes while you lie back and relax for at least 20 minutes.

Puffy eyes If your eyes look puffy, it may be because you are lacking sleep. Try to make it a habit to get good, regular hours of sleep in a well-ventilated room.

Revitalise puffy eyes with the juice of a grated raw potato strained through fine muslin. Soak two wads of cotton wool in the fluid and place them over your eyelids. Rest with your feet up for 20 minutes then rinse the potato fluid off with warm water.

Another way to reduce puffiness is to pat your skin with cotton wool soaked in cooled parsley or mint tea.

Sore eyes To soothe sore eyes, use cotton wool pads soaked in a cold tea made from crushed fennel seeds. Place them on your closed eyelids when using a face mask.

EYELASHES Lightly massaging the edges of your eyelids with almond oil is a sure way to make the eyelashes grow; if you do this every day, the lashes will be glossy as well as long. Brush your eyelashes gently upwards to encourage them to curl. Use a stiff toothbrush to separate lashes after applying mascara.

EYEBROWS In the late 1800s, women darkened their eyebrows with burnt cork, burnt cloves, black frankincense, gall or walnut juice. One mid-Victorian recipe suggested using lampblack mixed with cream – not something you would want to do today, even if you could get hold of lampblack. A later recipe suggested rubbing the eyebrows with a little brilliantine or coconut oil to darken them, and applying an infusion of wine and mint leaves to thicken them.

Here are some other ways to groom your eyebrows so they show off your eyes to best advantage.

Shaping your eyebrows You can shape your eyebrows by plucking unwanted hairs with a good pair of tweezers – the best kind have rounded, not pointed, ends. First dab a little vaseline on the eyebrows and wait a few minutes for it to work in; this makes the process much less painful. Use short, sharp movements in plucking the hairs. Always remove the hairs from the lower edge of the brow, as the more width there is between the eyelids and the brows, the better.

Thick eyebrows If your eyebrows are very thick, it is best to visit a beauty specialist to have them shaped for the first time. After that, you can keep them shaped yourself.

Sparse eyebrows To encourage thicker growth, gently massage your eyebrows with a little vaseline each night. Castor oil is also good, as it darkens the eyebrows as well as making them grow.

Eyebrow make-up Use two eyebrow pencils – brown and black – to achieve a natural look. Draw the line slightly above your brow line, and brush the hairs up to meet the pencilling. Use a black eyebrow pencil only if your hair is really dark.

To give your eyebrows a fine-pencilled look, dip an eyebrow brush in a clear oil, then colour the brows lightly with an eyebrow pencil.

MAKING THE MOST OF YOUR EYES
Clever eye make-up and eyebrow shaping can bring out the beauty of your eyes and minimise the less attractive aspects.

1. Create width between close-set eyes by plucking your eyebrows away from the bridge of your nose and applying heavier shadow to the outer corners of your eyelids.

2. To disguise narrow eyes, pluck your brows in a high arch and apply heavier eye shadow close to your nose.

3. If you have deep-set eyes, apply eye shadow evenly over your eyelids just above your eyelashes and use mascara on the outer edge of your top lashes.

Smiling through

MODERN RESEARCH HAS DEMONSTRATED THE
SINCERITY OF THE OLD ADAGE THAT LAUGHTER
IS THE BEST MEDICINE.

A happy and relaxed frame of mind will show in fresh, smooth lips
and a readiness to smile, but tiredness, tension and anger will
manifest themselves in pursed lips and a tight jaw. When you feel out
of sorts, try smiling; after a while you will feel better and smiling will
become a habit.

LIPS The only 'respectable' lip colouring in the 1800s was a discreet
application of rouge, but women had various tricks at their disposal to
make their lips look especially bright and alluring, though the effects
were strictly temporary.

To brighten the lips Rub your lips with eau de Cologne and then
with a little cold cream to prevent them from feeling cold and hard.
Another old trick was to suck the lips to stimulate the circulation and
brighten the colour: Scarlett O'Hara, on her way to charm Rhett
Butler in *Gone with the Wind*, 'bit her lips until they stung to make
them red'.

For cracking lips Purified fat scented with rosewater was once used
to soothe sore or chapped lips. If your lips tend to crack in cold or dry
weather, use a white lipsalve under your usual lipstick. At night,
smear vaseline or skin food on your lips before retiring. Avoid licking
your lips in windy weather as this will cause chapping very quickly.

MOUTH An age-old treatment to ensure healthy gums, white teeth
and fresh breath is to massage the teeth and gums with a fresh sage
leaf or use warm sage tea as a mouthwash. If your gums are sensitive
and bleed when you brush your teeth you should see a dentist, but
massaging with ice water or lemon peel will give temporary relief.

Breath sweeteners To sweeten your breath, wipe your tongue
several times with small pads of gauze soaked in lemon juice, or
chew on a few caraway or anise seeds. Gargling with mint tea or a
little rose-water will also freshen your breath.

TEETH This is one field where modern methods are definitely
preferable to the 'good old ways'; our forebears did not have a
particularly good record for dental health. Still, some of their recipes
for tooth cleaners and mouthwashes are cheap, safe and effective, and
can come in handy if you have forgotten to buy toothpaste and need
to freshen your mouth.

Brushing Brush your teeth from the gums downwards for the upper
teeth and from the gums upwards for the lower teeth, so that the
bristles go between your teeth as well as cleaning the front and back

A WORD OF CAUTION
Laugh, and the world laughs with you,
Weep, and you weep alone.
– 'SOLITUDE', ELLA WHEELER WILCOX
(1850–1919)

*Gleaming white teeth and a
lovely smile are the legacies of
regular brushing.*

surfaces. Always use dental floss and an orange-wood toothpick after brushing to remove any tiny particles of food that may be lodged between the teeth. To keep your teeth in perfect condition, clean them after each meal. Replace your toothbrush as soon as the bristles start to lose their springiness.

To clean and whiten teeth Mix together equal parts of salt and bicarbonate of soda and brush this on just as you would an ordinary tooth powder. To remove all stains and make your teeth sparkling white, dip a damp toothbrush in bicarbonate of soda and brush gently. Rinse your mouth thoroughly and repeat if necessary.

Alternatively, crush a few strawberries and rub the pulp across your teeth, or use 1 teaspoon of lemon juice in a cup of water as a toothwash – this treatment helps to remove tartar.

CHIN AND NECK The skin of your neck needs just as much care as your face. For correcting wrinkles of the neck, massage it daily with a good moisturiser or skin food. Warm the cream slightly to soften it, and massage briskly upwards with firm strokes. (For further massage techniques, see pages 292–3.)

If your neck is inclined to be flabby, pat it with a mixture of astringent and tonic to stimulate the circulation and firm the skin, then massage it with skin food.

Treatments for the chin and neck Combine some crushed strawberries with a little almond oil and strain the mixture through cheesecloth. Rub this lotion into the skin on the neck and chin to take away that crepy look. To bleach and refresh the skin, pound a handful of blanched almonds in a little hot water until the water is milky. Stroke the mixture gently all over your neck and leave on for at least 10 minutes. Rinse off with warm water.

A cream made from almond oil, beeswax, rose-water and oil of geranium can be used to good effect on the chin and neck. Melt 30 grams of beeswax in 90 ml of almond oil in the top of a double boiler. Very slowly add 3 tablespoons of rose-water, beating all the time. Remove from heat and continue beating until cool, then beat in two drops of the geranium oil. Another treatment is to apply a beaten egg to your neck, rinsing it off after a few minutes with warm water.

Appearing first in tins, and then in metal tubes, toothpaste heralded vast improvements in dental health.

The Way We Were

'... the young girl had regular and delicate lineaments; eyes shaped and coloured as we see them in lovely pictures, large, and dark, and full; the long and shadowy eyelash which encircles a fine eye with so soft a fascination; the pencilled brow which gives such clearness; the white, smooth forehead, which adds such repose to the livelier beauties of tint and ray; the cheek oval, fresh, and smooth; the lips too, ruddy, healthy, sweetly formed; the even and gleaming teeth without flaw; the small dimpled chin; the ornament of rich, plenteous tresses – all advantages, in short, which, combined, realized the ideal of beauty, were fully hers.'

– *JANE EYRE*, CHARLOTTE BRONTË (1847)

The crowning glory

EVERY WOMAN CAN HAVE BEAUTIFUL HAIR,
WHETHER IT BE STRAIGHT OR CURLY, LONG OR
SHORT, DARK OR FAIR.

It should crown her like a halo, grace her like a silken cap and
shine like a star. Like the skin, the hair must be in good
condition if it is to be beautiful. A prerequisite for well-
conditioned hair is the body's general health, so the right diet,
absolute cleanliness and regular grooming are important.

BRUSHING Brushing stimulates the blood flow to the scalp and
distributes the rich oil from the sebaceous glands through your
hair to make it glossy and lustrous. Regular brushing can also
do a great deal to prevent dandruff. To keep your scalp and hair
in top condition, combine your daily brushing routine with
scalp massage (see page 292).

For lively, glowing hair, brush regularly with long, even strokes that
do not tear or jerk the hair. Brushing removes worn-out hairs, and if
you brush faithfully every night, new hairs will soon replace the ones
you have lost.

Brushing techniques In the good old days virtually all women wore
their hair long, and folk wisdom prescribed a hundred brush strokes
morning and night. In the late 1990s, long hair is back in favour and a
systematic brushing routine is still recommended, but a hundred
strokes is thought excessive: too much brushing can cause damage to
the hair roots.
• Tilt your head forwards and brush from the scalp outwards, lifting
the hair so that it pulls away from the skin.
• With your head still tilted forwards, brush from just above the nape
of your neck up and over the crown of your head to your forehead and
down the length of the hair.
• Tilt your head back and brush back from your forehead over your
crown and down to the base of your scalp.
• Brush all the hair from the right side of your head over to the left
and then from the left side to the right.

SHAMPOOS AND CONDITIONERS Today's range of commercial
shampoos, conditioners and hair treatments is bewilderingly wide, and
many of these products are extremely expensive. Save money by
making your own shampoos and conditioners from traditional recipes,
and experiment to produce exactly the right mixtures for your hair
type, perfumed with your favourite scent or essential oil.

Before shampooing, part your hair in different places and brush
briskly along the partings with a good, stiff-bristled brush. If you have
dry hair, rub a little warm olive oil into your scalp about an hour
before you shampoo it.

*Traditional shampoos, which can
be made at home, are just as
effective as commercial brands.*

*A silver-backed brush and comb
set, complete with tray, was a
common sight on the dressing
tables of yesteryear .*

These days many people wash their hair every day, but this practice would have surprised our grandmothers, for whom hair-washing was  not simply a matter of standing under a warm shower and then turning on the electric hair dryer. It is difficult to make set rules about how often hair should be washed – it really depends on your hair style and hair length, and the type of life you lead, as well as on whether your hair is dry or oily, fine or coarse.

Rosemary and rose shampoo First melt 125 grams of transparent soap in 1½ cups of water and stir in 60 grams of glycerine. Stir until cool, then add 30 grams of tincture of green soap (can be ordered from pharmacists), 45 drops of oil of rosemary and 30 drops of oil of roses. Mix the whites of 3 eggs with 1 cup of water and stir into the soap mixture. Shake well and let stand for 24 hours. Strain and store in a screw-top bottle.

It's little wonder grandmother recommended a nightly brushing. The act of gently brushing your hair not only stimulates new growth, it also calms and relaxes – an ideal way to end any day.

Egg and rosemary shampoo Beat the yolk of an egg with ½ teaspoon of rosemary oil, then add 600 ml of warm water. Use the mixture warm, rubbing well into your scalp. Rinse several times with warm water to make sure all traces are removed. Do not use hot water – it will cook the egg, making it difficult to remove.

Egg conditioner Egg yolk is very rich and makes an excellent conditioner for your hair. At bedtime, rub a lightly beaten egg into your scalp with the tips of your fingers, then rinse with warm water.

Avocado and egg conditioner Beat up half an avocado with 2 eggs until the mixture is frothy, and massage the mixture well into your scalp. Leave on for ten minutes, and then use a little warm water to work up a lather before rinsing thoroughly.

RINSES Rinses incorporating herbs or vegetables can bring out the gloss and beauty of your hair after shampooing and conditioning. Some rinses darken or lighten the hair, and some – for example, the water that potatoes have been boiled in – are even reputed to prevent greyness. Whatever your hair colour, sprinkle a few drops of your preferred scent into the final rinsing water.

Dark hair One of the best rinses for enhancing the warm tones and highlights of dark hair is cider vinegar. Add 3 tablespoons of this vinegar to a glass of cool water, rinse your hair in the ordinary way, and then pour the mixture over your head and leave it on for about ten minutes. Rinse in tepid water.

Rosemary also makes an effective rinse for dark hair. Make a decoction of rosemary (see p. 265), using 30 grams of rosemary and 4 cups of water, allow to cool, and use as a final rinse.

Fair hair A final rinse with an infusion of chamomile or the juice of a lemon diluted with 600 ml of water makes blonde hair shiny and lightens the colour.

To darken blonde hair Infuse 30 grams of tea in 300 ml of boiling water. Let the mixture stand until it is cool, and then strain it and add 60 grams of glycerine. Mix well and use a soft sponge to apply the mixture to the roots of your hair.

Another darkening rinse for fair hair can be made by boiling 30 grams of sage leaves in 5 cups of water for half an hour. The longer the sage is steeped, the darker the rinse will be. This rinse also disguises white hair.

Red hair Place 30 grams of henna leaves in 5 cups of water and boil until the mixture is reduced by half. Apply the stain to the roots of your hair with a small brush – a clean toothbrush is ideal – and then distribute the henna evenly through your hair with a hairbrush. Wash off and dry thoroughly afterwards. *Caution*: The quantity of leaves suggested should be enough to give your hair a gentle tint, but always follow the advice given on the packet of henna, as the strength of different products varies.

Invigorating rinse Rinse your hair daily with warm, strong sage tea. Used regularly over time, this simple treatment will make your hair thick and strong.

LOCKS AND TRESSES
When I lie tangled in her hair,
And fettered to her eye,
The gods that wanton in the air
Know no such liberty.

– *Lucasta*, Richard Lovelace (1618–1658)

Shampooing too frequently can destroy the hair's lustre. Herbal rinses improve the hair's condition and enhance its natural beauty.

The Magical
MARCEL METHOD
of permanent Hair waving
+
STRAIGTH HAIR IS A NUISANCE
+

MARCEL'S PERMANENT LTD
353, Oxford Street :: LONDON W.1.

STYLING The development of the cold permanent wave process in the 1920s amounted to a revolution in hairstyling technique, but before that time women used common household substances to hold a style. Once or twice a week they would dampen their hair with one of these preparations and leave it in pins or curlers overnight.

• Beat 60 grams of gum arabic (from craft shops) into a mixture of 1 teaspoon of pink orange flower water and 850 ml of rose-water.
• Pour 600 ml of hot water over 3 teaspoons of quince seed and let it stand for several hours. Thin down the resulting mucilage with water or cologne and add a few drops of lavender oil.
• Rinse fine hair with beer: this will give it more body and help it to hold its style.

HAIR PROBLEMS Some of the old-fashioned remedies can help with common hair problems such as dandruff, dry or damaged hair, dull hair, oily hair and thinning hair.

Dandruff Mix 1 tablespoon of castor oil with 2 tablespoons of cider vinegar. Rub your scalp thoroughly with the mixture, leave on for 30 minutes, then shampoo as usual. Add 2 tablespoons of cider vinegar to the final rinse.

Nettles were thought to be effective in the treatment of dandruff and a good tonic for the scalp and hair. Steep a handful of nettles in 4 cups of boiling water. When cool, strain and rub some of the liquid into your scalp before washing your hair. Use the remainder as a rinse.

Dry or damaged hair Use a burdock decoction as a final rinse and make a mixture of 50 drops of oil of rosemary and 3 tablespoons of almond oil and massage a little of this into your scalp daily. For dry hair, massage a little olive oil into your scalp and hair, wrap your head in a hot towel for 30 minutes or leave overnight before shampooing.

Give yourself a weekly hot oil treatment. Stand a mug of olive or almond oil in a saucepan of hot water, dip your fingertips into the warm oil and rub vigorously into your scalp, parting the hair and working directly on the scalp. Massage for five minutes, then wrap your head in a hot towel. Leave for another five minutes, then shampoo.

Dull hair Soak some cotton wool in cologne and rub down the parting in your hair. Rub around your hairline and behind your ears. Sprinkle a little more cologne onto your scalp and comb well in. Rub your head thoroughly and briskly with a hot towel, picking up separate pieces of hair

Du Pont Combs

Combs were the preferred method of grooming permed hair, because hair brushes made permed hair uncontrollably frizzy.

Taking Care of the Pence

You can make an economical setting lotion by dissolving a teaspoon of gelatine in half a cup of hot water. Add a teaspoon of glycerine and two cups of hot water and mix well. Pour the mixture over your hair after shampooing and rinsing, and then dry and style in the usual way.

and rubbing them between the two surfaces of the towel. Sprinkle a little more cologne on the brush before the final grooming.

Oily hair Oily hair quickly becomes lank, but a little salt rubbed into your scalp before washing will help.

Another between-shampoos trick is to shake on some cornflour at night and brush out thoroughly in the morning.

Thinning hair Boil a handful of rosemary leaves and box leaves in a quart of water until it is reduced to one pint, strain and cool the mixture, and add a wineglass each of rum and glycerine. Keep in well corked bottles and use occasionally.

Another old remedy, said to leave the hair light and fluffy, was to dissolve 60 grams of tincture of green soap (can be ordered from pharmacists) in water perfumed with oil of bergamot, wet the hair, rub in a few drops of the solution and rinse.

TIPS FOR HAIR CARE These hair care hints were formulated in 1915, but they are still valid today.
• Do not shampoo with very hot water; for oily hair, use tepid water.
• For the final rinse, use water as cold as you can bear; this stimulates the circulation in the scalp.
• Towel your hair gently – rough towelling makes your hair brittle and damages dry hair.
• Use a comb with wide-set teeth for just-washed hair.
• Hair that is unmanageable after washing can be brought under control with several vigorous brushings.
• Do not brush oily hair too much – brushing distributes oil from the roots to the ends of the hair. To keep oil in check, brush hair thoroughly with a brush sprinkled with lavender or rose-water.
• Keep flyaway hair in place by combing it with a comb dipped in a little almond or olive oil.
• Wash brushes and combs in 1 litre of water with 2 teaspoons of ammonia, rinse well and dry in the sun. Alternatively, scrub between the teeth of the comb and the bristles of the brush with a nailbrush and pure soap, and rinse thoroughly.

COLOURS TO COMPLEMENT YOUR HAIR In earlier times, advice about style and grooming was more prescriptive than it is now, and there were rules even about hair colour. Women were encouraged very strongly to consider the colour of their hair when they are choosing their clothes. While this advice seems obvious today, you may be pleasantly surprised by some of the suggestions on this list from yesteryear.
• Ash blonde – charcoal grey, mauve, dusty pink, lilac, indigo, olive and moss green
• Honey blonde – leaf green, royal blue, amber, yellow, black, white
• Red – black, terracotta, golden brown, mahogany, powder blue, white, lime green
• Brunette – red, peacock blue, emerald green, shell pink, violet, black, cream
• Grey or white – pastel pinks, ice-blue, sapphire blue, black, mauve, lilac, fuchia, emerald green

The Way We Were

Hair loss has always been a cause for concern, and over the years many remedies have been suggested. Some treatments were bizarre, but this one is harmless and might work. If you are in lawful possession of a still, it may be just the remedy you have been waiting for:

'An excellent water to prevent hair from falling off and to thicken it. Put four pounds of unadulterated honey into a still with twelve handfuls of the tendrils of vines and the same quantity of rosemary tops. Distil and cool as slowly as possible. The liquor may be allowed to drop until it begins to taste sour.'

A New System of Domestic Cookery Formed upon Principles of Economy (1837)

HAIRSTYLES IN HISTORY

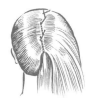

Hair is a unique accessory, provided by nature but arranged according to fashion. Hairstyles accompany fashions in clothing and hats, and always veer from long to short and back again: When Victorian frills and feathered hats were the rage, woman's hair cascaded and trilled; 1920s fashions, with their lack of curves and rising hemlines, were accompanied by sleek cropped hair, and the forced austerity of the World War II years saw smoother styles.

In the mid 19th century, hairstyles were still influenced by Queen Victoria's simple style, parted in the middle and coiled low over her ears. Later her influence declined and hairstyles became more elaborate, but the Queen banned showy coloured plumes and then short hair, so those wearing the fashionable tightly curled hair used false curls or ringlets for court appearances.

THE HAIR HARVEST

In the late 19th century, fashion favoured smooth rolls, plaits or a chignon, a style that promoted a thriving trade in human hairpieces. The hair to make them came mainly from poor girls, some of whom regrew their hair year after year to make a little money.

FASHIONING A FRENCH ROLL

The French roll is a classic way of dressing long hair that will never go out of fashion. These easy instructions are designed for medium-length hair: for really long hair, simply work with more sections of the free hank of hair.

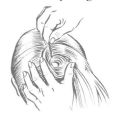

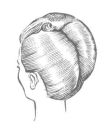

1. Give your hair a good brushing, sweep it to one side at the back and secure it at the centre back with bobby pins.

2. Bring up half of the free hank of hair from your nape, roll it around your finger and secure it with a long bobby pin.

3. Take back the front hank of hair, roll it over the first roll and secure it with bobby pins.

4. *Et voilà!* You have created the classic French roll.

WAVE OF THE FUTURE

The earliest permanent waving process, developed in 1905, involved applying borax paste to the hair, rolling it on solid brass electrically heated curlers and leaving it on for twelve hours. It was expensive and dangerous – no wonder women welcomed the advent in 1949 of the 'home perm'.

Which Twin has the Toni?

(and which has the $15 beauty shop wave? See answer below)

van Bosch
BOYER Succr

35, BOULd DES CAPUCINES
PARIS

PRETTY AS A PICTURE

Towards the end of the 19th century, hairstyles became ever more extravagant. These long, romantic tresses illustrate the powerful influence of the pre-Raphaelite painters.

UNDER THE DRYER

The first true hair dryer was invented around 1890 by Alexandre F. Godefroy and consisted of a bonnet attached to an outlet in the chimney pipe of a gas stove. Electric hair dryers were available by 1906, and the first hand-held hair dryer suitable for home use became available in 1920.

The body beautiful

BEAUTY IS MORE THAN AN ENCHANTING FACE;
IT ALSO DEPENDS ON A GRACEFUL BODY AND
SUPPLE ARMS AND LEGS.

Few are born with all the elements of beauty, but any woman can make her body more beautiful through healthy eating, exercise, skin care and plenty of rest and relaxation. Good grooming is important too, and a few minutes spent every day on tending the nails and applying moisturisers all contribute to the overall impression of a beautifully cared for body.

FEET Your feet should be comfortable at all times – painful or uncomfortable feet show plainly on the face in the form of lines and a drawn look. Badly fitting shoes or unsuitable heel height are often to blame for foot discomfort, so choose your footwear with care. Wear different shoes every day, so that the pressure comes on different parts of your feet; this is better for your shoes as well, and also helps to prevent smelly feet.

Our forebears bathed tender feet in Cologne water and shook talcum powder into their shoes for coolness and comfort in hot weather. A popular remedy for swollen feet was to bathe them in hot sea water, and one authority claimed that a 10-minute soaking every night in hot Epsom salts water (30 grams to each litre of water) would do more to cure soreness and rest the feet than any proprietary preparation.

Aching feet Shave half a cake of ivory soap as finely as possible, dissolve it in 600 ml of hot water, and add 60 grams of Epsom salts. Bottle the mixture and use it to bathe sore feet for five or ten minutes.

Corns and calluses Marigold leaves were recommended for treating corns – rub them on night and morning.

Calluses can sometimes be even more uncomfortable than corns. A simple old-time remedy is to dissolve a handful of soapsuds and some bicarbonate of soda in a basin of hot water and soak your feet for five minutes. Rub the calluses briskly with a scrubbing brush and then dry your feet on a rough towel. Using a rotary movement, rub your feet firmly with pumice stone, then apply antiseptic lotion. It may take several treatments to wear away the damaged skin.

Resting your feet Try this simple trick when your feet are very tired, particularly the insteps – you will be surprised how effective it is: Lie on the bed face down and place a pillow under the insteps of both feet

The arms, legs, and the body, as well as the face, require attention if they too are to look beautiful.

Until the emergence of the flapper in the 1920s, long skirts kept a woman's legs well hidden.

so that the whole width of both feet is supported and slightly elevated. In this position your feet are at ease and the arch of the instep relaxed.

Weak arches can cause great discomfort, but you can strengthen them with a simple daily exercise. Stand with your bare feet flat on the floor and spread them out as far as possible, then slowly curl your toes under, drawing them in as far under your foot as you can.

LEGS Remove normal hair growth with an emery disc, a wax treatment or a pumice stone. Shaving is a good preliminary treatment for dense hair – use a rich soapy lather to soften the hairs – but after that first shave, treat the regrowth by rubbing with a pumice stone or emery disc. To banish goose flesh, rub your legs daily with a stiff, dry brush or with coarse friction gloves moistened with eau de Cologne.

For legs that gleam like silk, massage them with almond or olive oil, particularly after a hair-removal treatment.

Varicose veins Varicose veins are caused by pooling in the blood vessels of the legs, brought about by standing for too long. The best preventative is a daily brisk walk, which helps to keep the blood moving. Never sit with your legs crossed; this position can shorten the calf muscles and inhibit circulation.

HANDS It has been said that nothing reveals a woman's character more clearly than her hands and nails. Wash your hands in lukewarm water (not hot) and rinse them in cold water. Dry your hands properly every time you wash or rinse them, gently pushing down the cuticles, and

Nourish your hands with the surplus cream after massaging your face. Stroke it in gently as though you were putting on gloves, starting at the fingertips. And before discarding a squeezed lemon, rub the flesh into your elbows and the backs of your hands for whiter, softer skin.

287

apply a good hand lotion. For dirty tasks, wear comfortable gloves; rub a little glycerine and rose-water into your hands before putting them on.

Cleaning your hands To remove stains from preparing vegetables, rinse your hands with a little cider vinegar. After gardening, cover your hands with a rich hand lotion and, with the lotion still on, scrub them in warm soapy water. Then dip a small muslin bag filled with oatmeal into fresh warm water and rub your hands with it. This treatment softens and whitens as well as cleans your hands.

Fragrant hand lotion Mix 60 grams of glycerine and ⅓ cup of elderflower water (from craft shops) together. Stir in 12 drops of lavender, rose or bergamot oil and 8 drops of lemon juice.

Chapped hands Melt 10 grams of paraffin wax and add 100 grams of petroleum jelly and 30 grams of lanolin. Stir constantly, beating in 2 tablespoons of water as you do so. Stir in 4 drops of oil of roses and ¼ teaspoon of alcohol when nearly cold.

To make a soothing hand lotion, mix together 30 grams each of honey and almond oil, the juice of a lemon and an egg yolk.

To whiten the hands This recipe makes an excellent soap for whitening hands. Take a wineglass of eau de Cologne and one of lemon juice; then scrape two cakes of toilet soap into a powder, and mix well. Pour the mixture into a mould and allow to harden for a few days before use.

Cosmetic gloves If you have neglected your hands, make yourself a pair of cosmetic gloves. Unpick a pair of soft leather gloves, three or four sizes too large for you, and spread the insides with a glove paste. Sew up the seams again and wear the gloves at night.

To make a home-made glove paste, heat 1 tablespoon of honey until runny and then beat in 2 tablespoons of ground barley, an egg white and 1 teaspoon of glycerine. Cool and add 150 ml of brandy and a few drops of oil of lavender. Another old glove paste recipe is to beat the yolks of 2 eggs briskly and, while still mixing, very gradually add 2 teaspoons of sweet almond oil and 2 soup spoons of rose-water.

Exercising your hands Press your fingers together, and slowly and gently try to force your fingers back towards your wrist. Do this simple exercise night and morning to stretch the muscles and tendons and keep your hands supple and strong.

NAILS Manicure your nails regularly — well tended and well shaped nails are a prerequisite for beautiful hands. When you file your nails, aim for an almond shape. At one time, a little white half-moon at the base of each nail was considered a sign of great beauty. Some women possess these half-moons naturally; in others they can be encouraged to

MAKING A FRICTION GLOVE

A friction glove is very handy for rubbing your face, neck and upper arms, as well as your legs. You can your own in half an hour from the good bits of an old, rough towel.

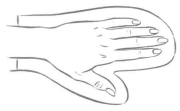

1. Trace the outline of your hand to make a pattern in the shape of a mitt with a thumb compartment.

2. Use the pattern to cut a 'glove' from doubled rough towelling, allowing 2 cm for the seam and 4 cm for the wrist hem. Stitch around the seam and turn up the wrist hem, leaving an opening.

3. Thread a piece of elastic or ribbon into the opening and through the hem. Sew the elastic together at the ends so that the glove fits your wrist snugly, or tie the ribbon in a bow.

appear if the cuticles, the ridges of skin where the nails emerge from the flesh, are pushed back gently and regularly at the base with an orange stick.

Manicure routine Shape each nail with an emery board, first with the coarser side and then with the fine side. Do not use a steel file – they can damage your nails. Soak your fingertips for five minutes in warm olive oil and then for five minutes in warm, soapy water to soften the cuticles and cleanse the nails; the olive oil nourishes the nails and helps to prevent brittleness.

Dry your hands thoroughly, then rub a little cuticle cream or vaseline around the base of each nail. Carefully push back each cuticle with the rounded end of an orange stick – never cut the cuticle. Clean under the nails gently with the pointed end of the orange stick moistened in diluted lemon juice to remove any stains. Dab a little nail paste or powder onto each nail and polish with a chamois buffer, available from pharmacies, or apply a commercial liquid varnish but make sure you remove all traces of old varnish first.

Nail powders Make a simple nail powder with zinc oxide (from pharmacists) perfumed with a few drops of oil of roses. Or follow an old French recipe: mix together 15 grams of violet talcum powder and an equal amount of powdered starch, and colour with a couple of drops of cochineal.

Brittle nails If your fingernails tend to break and split, soak them in warm water before trimming them with sharp scissors. To strengthen brittle nails, massage almond oil into your nails each night and drink 2 teaspoons of gelatine dissolved in half a glass of fruit juice daily for six weeks. A daily dose of dill seed tea is also said to be effective.

ARMS A weekly massage with moisturising cream will keep your arms and elbows smooth. When applying hand cream, remember to use some on your arms and elbows as well.

Goose flesh Upper arms are prone to goose flesh: each time you bathe, give them a good, brisk rub with a well soaped pumice stone, a friction glove or a loofah, and apply skin food after drying.

You can make a simple, old-fashioned lotion to soothe goose flesh. Pour equal parts of strained lemon juice and glycerine into a clean bottle and shake thoroughly. At bedtime, shake the bottle again and rub the lotion in thoroughly to stimulate the circulation.

BACK We often neglect our backs, perhaps because they are not only hard to reach, we rarely ever see them. You should, however, use a back brush as part of your daily bath or shower routine.

An orange stick has a rounded end that is useful for forcing back the skin surrounding the cuticles.

The Way We Were

'Who has not felt the beauty of a woman's arm? – the unspeakable suggestions of tenderness that lie in the dimpled elbow, and all the varied gently-lessening curves, down to the delicate wrist, with its tiniest, almost imperceptible nicks in the firm softness. A woman's arm touched the soul of a great sculptor two thousand years ago, so that he wrought an image of it for the Parthenon which moves us still as it clasps lovingly the time-worn marble of a headless trunk.'

– *THE MILL ON THE FLOSS*, GEORGE ELIOT (1860)

Give your back a beauty treatment once a fortnight. After drying yourself, rub your back briskly with a towel and then smooth moisturising cream onto your back and shoulders with a thick pad of cotton wool tied to the back brush.

If the skin on your back is oily, treat it with a mild astringent after the back scrub, particularly during the winter. Witch hazel mixed with an equal quantity of water makes a good astringent for the back. Pour onto a cotton wool pad and apply with the back brush. Another treatment is to scrub your back with a well soaped loofah. Rinse off all traces of soap with cool water and dry with a rough towel. This will make your skin tingle and keep it young by stimulating the circulation.

SHOULDERS You can improve the shape of your shoulders by exercising, and a weekly massage with moisturiser will soften the skin. For supple shoulders, there is no better exercise than skipping morning and evening – the action of turning the rope loosens up the muscles.

BATHS A quick shower is a good way to get started in the morning, but a long warm bath is a tonic that thoroughly relaxes the muscles and the nervous system. The best time for your daily bath is either immediately before your evening meal or at bedtime. Add a few drops of your favourite perfumed oil to the bath.

Refreshing baths A good, pure soap is essential; apply it with a fairly stiff loofah glove – the friction will do wonders for your skin. After soaping, lie back and relax for ten minutes. When you have finished, soak the loofah in cold water and give yourself a good hard rub down before drying your body with a fairly coarse towel.

Epsom salts in a hot bath with an icy face washer placed on your forehead can be very invigorating in hot weather, and a cup of cider vinegar added to a hot bath takes away stiffness after exercise and relieves aching and swollen feet. Bergamot leaf tea poured into a hot bath is also revitalising and gives the water a pleasant aroma.

For an almost instant refresher, a warm bath followed by a brief cold shower cleans and stimulates.

A luxury bath This elaborate bath routine used to be recommended for keeping the skin healthy and renewing its vitality.

Fill the bathtub with warm, soapy water. Before you step into the bath, lather yourself all over with a fine sponge. Stay in the soapy bath for five minutes, then empty the tub and fill it again with tepid water, into which you pour 100 ml of concentrated vinegar and 5 drops of oil of geranium. Stay in this second bath for 10 minutes, then dry yourself with soft, warm towels.

When your body is dry, use a friction glove to rub your skin with a mixture of 10 grams of alum, 200 ml of lavender water and 300 ml of Cologne water. This mixture is astringent and tonic in its action and helps to strengthen the skin. Rub it in gently for no more than five minutes.

Soap substitutes Oatmeal and bran are soothing substitutes for soap, particularly if your skin is delicate. Put 1 cup of each into a stocking,

A GOOD SHOULDER EXERCISE
Repeat regularly to maintain suppleness and a pleasing shape.

Clench your hands, raise your elbows to chest height and bring your knuckles together in front of your chest. Then pull your elbows down hard to touch the sides of your body so that your fists are pointing upwards.

Words of Wisdom

'When one feels very much fatigued, fill a pint cup with pine needles and add enough boiling water to make about 2 quarts of tea. After drinking a wine-glassful, pour the rest into a hot bath. After bathing, go to bed; you will awaken thoroughly refreshed.'

– HOW TO BE BEAUTIFUL,
T. DEAN (1890)

tie the top and place it where the hot tap water will run through it. Alternatively, put 500 grams of barley meal and 1 kg of bran in a cheesecloth bag and submerge in the bath.

Bath vinegar for oily skin Place 2 cups of fresh flowers or herbs in a wide-mouthed glass jar; bergamot and lemon balm are good additions to any others you may choose. Pour 5 cups of wine or cider vinegar over the flowers or herbs. Keep the mixture tightly covered, stirring it with a wooden spoon every second day. If the aroma is not strong enough after ten days, strain the mixture and repeat the process with a fresh batch of herbs. When the vinegar is ready, strain it into a bottle and cap tightly. Use a cupful each time you bathe.

Effervescent bath salts Mix together 250 grams of bicarbonate of soda, 200 grams of pulverised tartaric acid, 100 grams of cornflour and a few drops of perfumed oil (mixtures of lemon, bergamot, lavender and bay leaves are especially recommended) in a blender for a minute or two. Add 1–2 tablespoons of the mixture to bath water. The minute bubbles of gas released by the mixture have a soothing and refreshing effect on the skin.

Bath bags Give yourself a fragrant and rejuvenating bath with a bath bag. The luxury of a bath softened and delicately perfumed in this manner is particularly pleasant in hot weather.

Cut a piece of muslin about 20 cm square and place a handful of herbs or flowers in the centre; bay leaves, chamomile flowers, rosemary leaves and rose petals are a delightful combination. Gather the corners of the cloth together and tie tightly with a ribbon. Make several bags and use one each day instead of a sponge, or tie a bag to the tap so that the hot water runs through it as the bath fills. The bags can be emptied and refilled as required.

A bath for sensitive skins Dissolve 100 grams of cornflour in a little hot water and mix together well in a blender. Stir in ½ cup of milk and add to the bath water. This recipe is reputed to be a great beautifier of the skin.

Home-made bath oils Chop a handful of fresh flowers or herbs and place in a bowl or a glass jar. Cover the flowers or herbs with sulphated castor oil (from craft shops), stir the mixture and leave it in a warm place to settle for a week. Repeat this process until the oil imparts a strong fragrance. Finally, strain the oil and store in a tightly corked or capped bottle in a cool cupboard. Use the oil sparingly: too much will make the surface of the bath dangerously slippery. In a full bath, 1–2 tablespoons is sufficient.

After the bath If you have not used bath oil, apply a moisturising cream or lotion after your bath. A mixture of two parts of rose-water to one part of glycerine is an excellent light skin moisturiser. For a richer treatment, you should warm 2 tablespoons of olive oil with 5 drops of oil of lavender. Mix well, and then beat in 1 cup of lavender water.

A steaming hot bath after the rigours of the day soothes, comforts and relaxes.

Soap and a back brush are essential toiletries; bath crystals and salts invigorate.

Rubbed the right way

THE VIRTUES OF MASSAGE HAVE BEEN CELEBRATED
FOR CENTURIES; SOME SAY IT IS THE OLDEST KNOWN
OF THE HEALING ARTS.

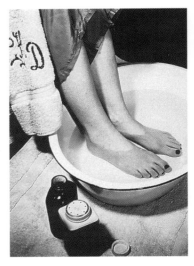

Loosen up your feet before a massage by soaking them in an infusion of lime or marigold flowers or lavender leaves, combined with a little salt.

At one time the term 'massage parlour' carried improper overtones, but today massage is enjoying a renaissance. Its importance is being rediscovered, not just for treating health conditions but for relaxing stressed and tired bodies, untying knotted muscles, calming jangled nerves, and generally promoting physical and mental wellbeing. It is impossible to look beautiful if your body and mind are tense. Taut nerves, as well as affecting your health, act directly on your face, tightening it up and causing lines and wrinkles. And massage can give you a positive feeling of being beautiful – the mere fact that you are pampering yourself is a marvellous boost to your wellbeing.

SELF-MASSAGE A complete body massage by a trained practitioner is one of the most luxurious and effective beauty treatments you can have, and it is certainly worth finding the time and money to treat yourself to one every now and then. In between times you can apply self-massage techniques that are wonderfully effective, smoothing tired muscles, stimulating the circulation to the skin's surface and rejuvenating your complexion.

Foot massage Massaging with a good moisturising cream or oil keeps your feet and ankles supple and eases sore, tired feet. It also helps to prevent the development of a rough, hard carapace of skin on the soles of your feet.

First soak your feet in a warm foot bath for five minutes and dry them thoroughly. Smooth the moisturising cream or massage oil over the top of your feet, working with long, firm strokes from your toes to your ankles. Massage the balls of your feet with your thumbs on top and your fingers underneath, working firmly with a rotary movement across the foot, starting at the base of the big toe and moving out to the little one. Take each toe in turn in your hand and rotate it ten times, first to the right and then to the left.

Scalp massage A tight scalp constricts the blood vessels and diminishes the supply of blood to the scalp, causing the roots of the hair to atrophy. To remedy this, give your head a regular, thorough, vigorous massage, using a circular movement. This is one of the finest treatments for hair that has lost condition, and it will even prevent your hair from thinning, as it brings needed nourishment to the scalp. It will also have a beneficial and strengthening effect on your face, lifting sagging muscles and taking

A regular facial massage will take but a few minutes each day – and will reward you with many years of looking good.

Massaging your face

You can massage your face at any time, but it is usually best done at night after applying a moisturiser. Be sure to remove all traces of make-up before applying the skin food or massage oil, and take care not to stretch the skin, especially in the delicate area around the eyes. Repeat each step ten times.

4. To discourage horizontal lines, massage from the middle of your forehead to your temples, again with a circular action.

1. Smooth a generous application of moisturising cream or slightly warmed oil firmly and gently up to your cheekbones and then out to your ears.

5. Starting at the inside corners of your eyebrows, lightly stroke the skin above and below your eyes. Then gently smooth your eyelids from the top to the lashes.

2. Starting at the corners of your mouth, massage your upper lip with a circular movement.

6. Pinch firmly from your chin along your jawline on each side towards your ears – about eight pinches will cover the distance.

3. To smoothe out frown lines, massage in a circular movement from the bridge of your nose to your hairline.

7. Place your hands at the top of your neck just underneath the chin and smooth down to the base of your neck and out towards your collarbones.

away that tired, drooping look.

Work first from the hairline at the nape of your neck over your crown and down to your forehead. Press firmly, moving the scalp as you do so. Then massage in the reverse direction. Finally, work from just in front of your ears to your crown.

Facial massage Regular massage to release facial tension is one of the best guarantees against a prematurely aged appearance. The diagrams above show you how to carry out a facial massage. Regularity is the secret. Do not expect to give yourself this treat once a week and get results – the daily routine is vital, and it takes only a few minutes.

Words of Wisdom

'Do not make the mistake of thinking that, when it comes to massage, one direction is as good as another. Sometimes when friends say to me with an air of virtue, "Oh yes, I massage my face well every day," I find myself thinking, "Well I wish you wouldn't." For I know that they know little about the way to massage, and care less. That the cream is rubbed in is all that concerns them. How it is rubbed in is of no consequence. Yet between rubbing in the right direction and rubbing in the wrong one lies all the difference between correcting wrinkles and making them. If you iron a piece of material the wrong way, you stretch it and get it out of shape. Much the same thing happens with your face.'

– *Be Beautiful*, J. Cleland (1947)

Perfect presentation

LOTIONS, CREAMS AND MAKE-UP CAN
HELP IMPROVE YOUR PHYSICAL SELF, BUT
TRUE BEAUTY RELIES ON MANY FACTORS.

Women once endured great physical and social restrictions, but the basic principles of deportment are still valid.

Just as important as a clear skin, shining eyes and glossy, well groomed hair are the way you sit, stand and move, and the way you speak and interact with other people. Our grandmothers and great-grandmothers placed great emphasis on these aspects of behaviour; young women were trained to sit up straight, to move elegantly and to speak and listen respectfully. These constraints on behaviour were in some ways as repressive as the whalebone corsets that women once wore, but the principles of graceful deportment and well modulated speech were sound and healthy, and are as valid today as they ever were.

POISE Poise comes with self-confidence, and self-confidence begins with being happy with the way you look. Careful grooming is the first step: your skin, nails and hair must be scrupulously clean and well tended. The amount you spend on clothes depends on your personal budget, but it pays to buy the best you can afford. Take the time to discover the styles and colours that suit you and that you feel comfortable in – and be thankful that 'fashion' is no longer the tyrant that it once was.

Attention to detail is the key to successful dressing. Your accessories and jewellery can be as flamboyant or as understated as you like, but they should not quarrel with your clothes or with each other.

DEPORTMENT One dictionary definition of deportment is 'the manner in which a person behaves, especially in physical bearing'. Good deportment – the art of sitting, standing and moving gracefully – adds that final gloss to beauty and careful grooming. It is good for your health too: it is one way of protecting yourself against back problems and varicose veins. Practise sitting, standing and walking in front of a mirror.

Sitting As a rule, sit quietly with your hands resting in your lap, and train yourself not to fidget with your hair or clothing. A lively gesture or two can invigorate a conversation, but do not fling your arms around as though you are practising semaphore.

Many working men and women have to spend hours of every day sitting down, and the way you sit is important. Practise sitting down: do not bend at the waist, collapsing the upper part of your body, but keep your body erect while you bend your knees and lower yourself gently onto your chair. Sit well back in your chair, so that your spine

A BEAUTIFUL WOMAN
She walks in beauty, like the night
Of cloudless climes and starry skies;
And all that's best of dark and bright
Meet in her aspect and her eyes …
– LORD BYRON (1788–1824)

is properly supported. Never twist your feet around the legs of your chair or cross your legs at the knees – these are ugly habits, and can create circulation problems. Legs slightly angled to one side and crossed just above the ankles can look elegant, especially if you are lucky enough to have long, slender legs.

Standing Correct posture is important to your self-image as well as to your health; standing upright and yet relaxed can make you look kilograms lighter than you are. Visualise a straight line running up from the floor, through your body and head, to the ceiling. Keep your head erect and your shoulders back, but do not brace them – let them sit easily and naturally. Your weight should be evenly balanced and your jaw and facial muscles relaxed. And if no seat is available, resist the temptation to lean against walls or tables; walk around a little to stimulate your circulation and prevent aching legs.

Walking Take moderate-sized steps, swinging your legs from your hips in a length of stride that feels comfortable. Let your feet glide across the floor in smooth, even paces, your body following naturally, your arms and hands loose and relaxed. Imagine that you are moving in slow motion when you enter a room, especially if you are nervous about confronting a roomful of strangers: it is far better to look and feel at ease than to charge through an entranceway like a mighty rushing wind.

VOICE The most expressive and persuasive language loses much of its beauty if the voice that utters it is unattractive. Sounds from an external source are transmitted by airwaves, but we hear our own voices mainly through skullbone resonances, and they can sound disconcertingly unlike what other people are hearing. For some feedback on the sound of your voice, cup the two parts of an empty chocolate box around your ears so that the ends meet in front of your mouth and recite a poem or a short sentence.

The good news is that most vocal problems are not difficult to fix. Correct breathing is the first thing: do not gasp and gabble, but take your time and breathe deeply so that your voice is supported on a column of air. Talk or read aloud, slowly and carefully, pronouncing each word with care. Using your chocolate box, try pitching your voice low and then a little higher – you will easily hear how much pleasanter the low tone sounds. Make a conscious effort to speak slowly: it is easier on your listeners and less stressful for you.

The rules of good posture have changed remarkably little over the years. A late 19th century health manual cautioned against slouching and urged young ladies to sit with a straight back.

The Way We Were

Lola Montez (1818–1861) was an Irishwoman, born Marie Dolores Eliza Rosanna Gilbert. She passed herself off as a Spanish dancer and conducted a notorious affair with Ludwig I of Bavaria until her influence over him made her unpopular with his subjects. She fled to America, and even made a brief tour of Australia. By all accounts she was not a very good dancer, but she was exceptionally beautiful. When her dancing career ended, she became a proselytiser on the art of beauty: 'Every woman owes it not only to herself, but society, to be as beautiful and charming as she possibly can', she said.

Child's

play

**GAMES FROM EARLIER DAYS TO
DEVELOP LIFE SKILLS THROUGH PLAY**

BC – before computers

FROM ABOUT 1850 THERE WAS A GRADUAL BUT MARKED IMPROVEMENT IN THE QUALITY OF LIFE OF WORKERS IN THE WESTERN WORLD.

Merchants and factory owners became wealthier, the wages of workers rose, and the working day became shorter. Annual bank holidays and the Saturday half-day holiday were instituted, and everyone, including children, benefited from an increase in leisure time.

GOING TO THE SHOW Once or twice a year, travelling shows and circuses visited local areas. Children could try their luck at the coconut shy and the shooting gallery, ride on the swings and roundabouts, and watch jugglers and acrobats performing in bright, spangled costumes. They could pay a penny to slip into a darkened tent and marvel at the bearded lady or the thinnest man in the world, or watch troupes of performing fleas. There were hot pies, sweets and cakes to sample, and some evenings there was dancing. And then there were the animals ... horses and ponies galore, often an elephant or two, and almost always at least one cranky looking camel snarling and snapping at anyone who came near.

VISITING THE THEATRE As special treats, children were taken to pantomimes and equestrian shows, and the children of the better-off were sometimes taken to the ballet or a popular light opera.

A TRIP TO THE BEACH Parents took their children on day trips or holidays to the country and to the coast. At the beach, children built sandcastles, paddled in rock pools and splashed about in the surf. They enjoyed team races and sometimes listened to concerts on the sands.

A holiday at the beach was considered so beneficial that charitable institutions persuaded wealthy philanthropists to pay for organised excursions for the children of the poor, while on half-days and holidays, city children sometimes made short trips to the country for picnics. Often it was the only time the city dwellers ever saw a real live cow or a sheep.

OUTDOOR GAMES Organised sports such as football and cricket became increasingly popular. By the end of the 19th century many schools had begun to arrange sports competitions and coaching for their pupils, and some form of compulsory recreation soon became a feature of school life.

'TRUNDLING THE HOOP is a pastime of uncertain origin, but it has long contributed to the health and amusement of the youth of Great Britain ... On a cold frosty morning, the hoop is an invaluable companion to a boy, as he is enabled by its aid to defy the weather, and dispense with overcoats, comforters, and all such devices for keeping out the wintry wind. Often have we envied our juvenile friends, as they have rushed past us with their hoops, and lamented that custom should prevent grown-up people indulging in the same healthful recreation.'
– *EVERY LITTLE BOY'S BOOK*
(ABOUT 1870)

A portable performance of Punch and Judy, in which the hunchback Punch defeats his antagonists one by one, was an indispensable feature of British seaside entertainment in Victorian times.

The Way We Were

In some ways, the old days were not quite as good as we should like to think. While the wealthy could afford to give their children the best, until well into the 19th century many working people in the industrialised nations were either living in poverty in city slums or eking out a tough living in the country.

Necessity often forced poor people to see their children as potential wage earners or as props for their old age. Many children worked long days helping to support their families, or spent their childhoods minding their younger brothers and sisters. They were often hungry or sick, and had no time for play and no money for toys.

Conditions improved as influential people became concerned about children's welfare. Laws were passed to limit or ban child labour, and education to a certain level became compulsory. By 1900, nearly all children had the health and leisure to enjoy a carefree childhood.

But although there were so many organised leisure activities, children did not abandon their traditional pursuits. They roamed the streets and countryside, playing the games that generations of children before them had played – marbles, cat's cradle, hopscotch and skipping. They played with tops and hoops, went fishing, swimming and boating, tottered around on stilts, kicked balls and flew kites.

INDOOR ENTERTAINMENTS There was no shortage of things to do in bad weather or after dark. Children read magazines and books, often reading aloud to other family members. They played card games, gave concerts and performed plays. Popular songs were sold in sheet music form, and families would gather around the piano to sing them. When visitors came, everyone joined in playing party games such as charades and consequences. Children wrote stories, plays and poetry, kept scrapbooks, and drew, embroidered and made things.

THE INDUSTRIAL REVOLUTION New inventions and manufacturing techniques made it possible to mass-produce toys, games, dolls and books, and businesses were quick to take advantage of the booming children's market. The well-to-do parents fitted out their children's nurseries with elaborate clockwork toys, dolls' houses, toy theatres, model shops and villages, toy soldiers, steam trains and boats. Colourful jigsaw puzzles and board games became popular with both children and adults.

More children learned to read at school and books became cheaper, so children's writers such as Louisa M. Alcott, Lewis Carroll, May Gibbs and Mark Twain became beloved and famous.

A French doll of 1880 and a German model locomotive of 1902 demonstrate the level of sophistication that toymaking had achieved by the latter half of the 19th century. The doll's clothes are originals by Jumeau.

Come out to play

MANY CHILDREN'S OUTDOOR GAMES ARE HUNDREDS, OR EVEN THOUSANDS OF YEARS OLD, AND MOST HAVE BEEN HANDED DOWN DIRECTLY FROM OLDER CHILDREN TO YOUNGER ONES.

Children spend less time nowadays playing together, and sometimes we fear that we will lose our traditional games. The following pages describe a few that were popular in the good old days Before Computers. Some involve a bit of rough and tumble and may need to be discreetly supervised, but these sorts of games can develop social skills as well as strength, speed, physical control and nimble reflexes.

CHASING GAMES There are countless versions of chasings, which is sometimes called 'tig' or 'tag'. Basically, one person is the chaser, or 'It', and everyone else tries to avoid being touched, or tagged, by 'It'.

Hand chasings The chaser runs after the other players until someone is caught. The two players then join hands and set off together to capture someone else. Each child who is caught after this joins hands with the others, with the chaser leading the line and tagging players. The game finishes when the last child is captured.

Shadow tag This chasing game appeals mightily to young children. Instead of tagging someone's body, the chaser has to step on another player's shadow. When players step out of the sun into the shade, their shadows disappear and they are safe.

POWER GAMES The fun in these games comes from pitting your strength against that of others, as an individual or as part of a team.

Tug-o'-war For this game you need an open space, a strong rope and an even number of players. Mark a central line and position an equal number of players on each side, with each team holding one end of the rope. The first team to pull the other team over the line is the winner.

Statues Players choose a puller, who seizes one player after another by the hand, flings each around in a circle, and then lets go. The players must stay in whatever positions they land, however awkward, and they must not move, or even blink. The puller inspects the 'statues' and eliminates anyone who moves by tapping that player on the shoulder. Any 'statues' who fall over are also disqualified. If no one is caught moving, the puller eliminates the most boring 'statues'. The last 'statue' left standing becomes the next puller.

These 1890s schoolboys are playing Tournament, in which the 'knights' perch on the shoulders of the 'horses' and try to pull each other off their mounts. Play on a surface that is soft to fall on, such as grass.

RUNNING, JUMPING AND STANDING STILL You need plenty of open space for these games – ideally a large open garden, a park if you live in a city, or a paddock if you live in the country. In today's traffic conditions, it's best to avoid streets and roads.

Leapfrog One player bends over with arms resting above the knees and another player vaults over the first player's back. When there are a number of players, the game is played with everyone bending over in a line. The last player in line runs forward and vaults over all the other players until the end of the line is reached. This player then bends over, and the player who is now last in line leapfrogs over the others. The game lasts until everyone is too exhausted to carry on.

Novelty races All races have the same object – to be the first across a finishing line – but there are many ways of making the journey. In a three-legged race, pairs of competitors stand side by side and tie their two closest legs together before racing the other pairs to the finishing line. In a wheelbarrow race, half the competitors walk on their hands while their partners hold up their legs and drive them along as if they were pushing wheelbarrows. For a chariot race, two people cross their arms and link them to form a seat for a third person.

A mixture of sunshine, fresh air and exercise is a good prescription for a strong, healthy body when you grow up.

Leapfrog is a game that needs no equipment and develops physical strength and coordination.

BALL GAMES There are hundreds of traditional games to play with a ball, or a bat and a ball. The simple ball games that children still play were probably the forerunners of highly competitive formalised sports such as tennis, golf and cricket.

Handball is a fast, energetic game for two players. Use chalk to mark out a flat, hard surface about half the size of a tennis court, with a wall at one end. Play with a small, soft ball, such as a tennis ball or a rubber ball, which you hit with the palms of your hands. The game starts with one player throwing the ball against the wall. The other player lets it bounce once on the ground before hitting it back against the wall. The first player returns the ball in the same way, and play continues until one player misses the ball. This earns the other player a point. Nobody scores if the ball bounces out of the boundary. The first player to score 25 points wins the game.

Square ball is played on a court about 3 metres square, divided into four smaller squares numbered 1 to 4. One player stands in each square, with the player in square 4 acting as the server, and the remaining players line up outside the court. The server begins the game by bouncing the ball to a player in one of the other squares. Players must let the ball bounce once in their squares before they hit it into another square. When a large ball is used, players bounce the ball with both hands, but a small ball is bounced with only one hand.

Players are 'out' if they fail to return a ball, or if the ball they return bounces in their own squares, on a line, or outside the court. A player who is 'out' must line up behind the others watching the game from outside the court area; the rest of the players then move up a number to fill the empty square. The player at the front of the line outside the court area goes into square 1. The object is to work up to square 4, to be the server, and to stay in this position.

Fungo can be played with any kind of bat and ball, but it should be played in an open area away from windows and passersby. One player is the batter and the rest are fielders. The fielders spread out in front of the batter, who tosses a ball into the air and hits it with a bat. The fielders must try to catch it. The winner is the first fielder to catch the ball an agreed number of times.

HOPSCOTCH Children have been playing hopscotch for hundreds of years. There are many variations of the game, but all involve marking out a court with several numbered compartments on the ground, throwing a small flat object called a puck — it can be a stone, a piece of tile or an oyster shell — into each compartment in numerical sequence, and then hopping up and down the court from compartment to compartment.

Classic hopscotch Players form a queue, with the first player at the starting line throwing the puck into the first compartment of the court. The

Urchins in the United States in the 1920s choose sides for a baseball game by 'hand-over-handing' the bat.

WHERE GO THE BOATS?

Dark brown is the river,
Golden is the sand.
It flows along for ever,
With trees on either hand.

Green leaves a-floating,
Castles of the foam,
Boats of mine a-boating –
Where will all come home?

On goes the river
And out past the mill,
Away down the valley
Away down the hill.

Away down the river,
A hundred miles or more,
Other little children
Shall bring my boats ashore.

– A CHILD'S GARDEN OF VERSES,
ROBERT LOUIS STEVENSON (1885)

player then hops into the compartment, turns around, kicks the puck out of the court, and hops back to the starting line. Next the player throws the puck into the second compartment and hops once into compartment 1 and then into 2. The player then turns and kicks the stone into compartment 1 and then out of the court.

The player throws the stone one compartment further each time, working up and back down the compartments to the starting line. A player is 'out' if the stone is thrown onto a line; if the player fails to throw or kick the stone into the right compartment; or if the player hops on a line, rests the raised foot on the ground, or falls over before getting back to the starting line. The player must then go to the back of the line and the next person in the queue gets a turn. On their next turn, players start from where they left off.

KICK THE CAN This is a version of hide and seek. Find a spot with a good choice of hiding places, and set boundaries before the game starts so that players do not wander too far away to hide.

One player – the seeker – puts a can in the centre of a circle and another kicks it out. This is the signal for everyone except the seeker to hide. The seeker must retrieve the can and put it back in the circle before looking for the other players. When a player is spotted, the seeker must run back to the circle, bang on the can and call out that player's name. The named player must come out of hiding and stay in the circle as a 'prisoner'. Other players can free 'prisoners' by creeping up and kicking the can out of the circle while the seeker is not looking. No one can be captured while the can is outside the circle.

MESSING ABOUT IN BOATS During World War II, with so many resources devoted to the 'war effort', few families had money to spare for luxuries, including toys – even if they were available. *Unk White's Boat Book*, published in Sydney in 1943 on the cheapest, roughest newsprint, combined nutrition, economy and inventiveness by showing children how to make toy boats out of fruit peelings.

To make 'the orange peel racer', eat an orange quarter, carefully keeping the peel intact. Stick a dead match into the white inner surface of the peel for the mast, and add a stiff piece of paper for a sail. To make 'the passion fruit tub boat', cut a passion fruit in half, scoop out the contents and eat them. Use a toothpick for a mast and draw bright stripes on a piece of paper for a sail.

CLAPPING GAMES These are a great way to develop coordination and a sense of rhythm, as they are played by repeating a set of hand movements, gradually increasing the speed each time. The player who loses the rhythm or claps in the wrong order loses the game.

'My Mother Said' In some clapping games, players keep the rhythm by chanting a rhyme. This one used to be a traditional favourite:

> My mother said I never should
> Play with the Gypsies in the wood.
> If I did, she would say,
> 'Naughty little girl to disobey.'

HOPSCOTCH COURTS
Many generations of children in virtually every country of Europe have played hopscotch; scholars excavating a Roman site in Britain found a hopscotch court scratched on a pavement.

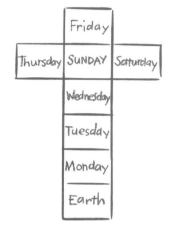

The Monday–Tuesday hopscotch court is one of the simplest designs.

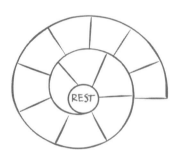

Snail hopscotch is one of the few hopscotch games played without a puck.

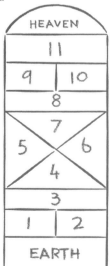

Like many hopscotch courts, this one is marked out to symbolise the human journey from Earth to Heaven.

303

The clapping order is: clap hands, slap partner's hands, clap hands, slap right hand against partner's right hand, clap hands, slap left hand against partner's left hand. Each word of the chant is met with a slap or clap, and as the chanting gets faster, so does the clapping.

SKIPPING In some skipping games the skipper jumps alone with a short rope; others are group games in which players skip over a long rope turned by two other players. Still others use two ropes, which are turned in different directions while skippers jump between the two. The names of skipping games tend to reflect the skipping actions.

Rock the cradle The two turners swing the rope backwards and forwards like a cradle three times and then full-circle three times, repeating these actions alternately until the skipper misses a jump and must change places with one of the turners.

Fox and goose Players line up behind each other on one side of the rope, usually with the oldest at the front of the line. While the rope is turned, the players run under the rope in turn and line up again on the other side. On the way back, they jump over the rope and line up again. The game continues with the leader jumping the rope in a different way each time and the others copying. The leader may jump the rope twice, or turn around while jumping – the variations depend on the skill and imagination of the leader. A skipper who touches the rope takes the place of one of the turners.

MARBLES In the past, children organised marbles tournaments that involved an entire district, and many players had a favourite shooter marble – a taw – that they treasured above all their other marbles.

Ringer A circle about 3 metres in diameter is drawn on the ground and 13 marbles are arranged in a cross in the centre. Shooting from outside the circle with slightly larger marbles, players try to knock the 13 marbles out of the circle. All players must shoot in the same way, by balancing the marble on the underside of the forefinger and flicking it into the circle with the thumbnail. They must keep the knuckles of the shooting hand on the ground to prevent them from using the wrist to increase the power of the shot. Players are allowed one turn at a time, and retrieve their taws at the end of the turn. Any marble knocked out of the ring becomes the property of the shooter; the player with the most marbles at the end of the game is the winner.

Traditionally, marbles were hardly ever bought; they simply passed from hand to hand as different players captured them by winning the game. 'Alleys' – large glass marbles enclosing vivid threads of colour – were highly valued, and to lose one was a minor tragedy.

A SKIPPING RHYME
Andy SPANdy SUGARdy CANdy,
FRENCH Almond ROCK!
Breadandbutterforyoursupper's
allyourmother's GOT!

– Elsie Piddock Skips in Her Sleep,
Eleanor Farjeon (1937)

Knucklebones

THIS ANCIENT GAME IS ALSO KNOWN AS JACKS, FIVESTONES, DIBS AND CHUCKS. OVER THE CENTURIES IT HAS BEEN PLAYED WITH SHEEP KNUCKLEBONES, STICKS, STONES AND SEA SHELLS.

The game is usually called knucklebones in Australia and New Zealand, although the individual pieces are referred to as jacks. Until the 1930s, butchers sold sheep knuckles to young customers in packets of five, and in the early 1900s toy manufacturers came up with 'knucklebones' made of wood, metal or plastic. In America, children played jacks with metal or plastic double tripods and a small rubber ball for the taw. English children sometimes played with five wooden cubes.

BASICS OF THE GAME There are four basic knucklebone tricks – ones, twos, threes and fours – but the variations and complications of this simple sequence are almost infinite. When you can perform the whole sequence with one hand, repeat it with the other hand.

Players must complete a fixed number of tricks in a certain order. Each trick is harder than the previous one, and if you drop a jack or make more than one attempt to pick it up, you are out. You are also out if a jack strikes you or if you move after tossing the jacks. On your next turn, you must repeat the last trick you attempted.

Ones, twos, threes and fours To play ones, toss all five jacks into the air and catch one on the back of your hand. If you catch more than one, shake the others off until only one remains – this is called the taw. Leave the other jacks exactly where they fall, then toss the taw up and catch it in your palm. Toss the taw again and pick up one jack while the taw is in the air, then catch the taw before it reaches the ground. Put the captured jack aside, toss the taw again and pick up another jack. Carry on until you have captured all the jacks.

Twos is like ones, except that with each toss you must pick up two jacks at once. For threes, pick up three jacks together and then the remaining jack. For fours, pick up all four jacks at once.

Scatters Start each trick in the sequence by holding all five jacks in your hand and scattering them over the floor. Choose one jack to be the taw, toss it up and pick up the correct number of jacks.

Clicks and No clicks To play clicks, scatter the jacks, choose a taw, throw it up, pick up one jack and then catch the taw, clicking the two pieces together as you do so. Keeping the jack in your hand, toss the taw again and pick up another jack. Click the taw against the two jacks. Continue until you have picked up all the jacks. You are out if the other players cannot hear the jacks clicking.

No clicks is a good deal more difficult: you are out if the other players hear the click of the jacks.

Scottish writer Robert Louis Stevenson noted the antiquity of the game of knucklebones: 'The harmless art of knucklebones, he wrote, 'has seen the fall of the Roman empire and the rise of the United States.'

You can make your own set of genuine knucklebones. Ask a friendly butcher to save them for you when he bones out legs of lamb, and then boil them clean.

BLOWING IN THE WIND

The first kites were flown in China well over 2000 years ago, and were made of wood or cloth. A tale about the Chinese general Han Hsin, who lived about two centuries before Christ, tells of a kite being flown over a palace to measure the distance between the general's army and the palace walls so that the invading forces could dig a tunnel the correct length to allow them to storm the fortress.

At first kites were used only for military purposes – for signalling, to measure distances and to carry messages – but in the Sung dynasty (AD 960–1126) they began to be flown for fun. 'Kites Day', held on the ninth day of the ninth Chinese month, evolved during this period. On this day, people would assemble to fly kites on the hills surrounding their towns. With the introduction of Kites Day, Chinese kites became more varied and attractive. Figure kites, kites in the shape of birds and flying insects, and vivid dragon and centipede kites appeared. Kite fighting also became popular.

EARLY EUROPEAN KITES

The windsock, flown as an army standard during the Roman period and later in the Middle Ages, was the only type of kite known in the West until the 16th century. A small fire could be lit in the mouth of this dragon, from a 9th century painting, and the banner used as a signal at night.

THE DIAMOND DESIGN

The familiar diamond kite with its long tail was developed in Europe during the Renaissance. It is just one of many kite designs. The long tail acts as a keel to stabilise the kite while it is flying.

THE JOURNEY OF THE KITE

From China, the kite spread to other countries in South-east Asia and to the Pacific region, India and Arabia. In many countries it had spiritual significance. For the Polynesians, kites represented heroes and gods and were links to the heavens. In Indonesia, kites took on the souls of their fliers and were also seen as messengers of the gods.

Buddhist monks are thought to have brought the kite to Korea and Japan. Japanese kites were often decorated with lucky symbols such as the crane or the tortoise, representing long life, or the dragon, which was a symbol of prosperity. On the fifth day of the fifth Japanese month, windsocks in the shapes of fishes were flown to celebrate the birth of boy babies.

MAKING A TAIL-LESS KITE
Will a tail-less kite fly? Make a bow kite yourself and see.

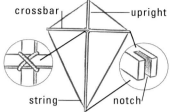

1. Notch the ends of two pieces of light, strong wood, one piece $2/3$ the length of the other. Bind the pieces together as shown and thread string from notch to notch.

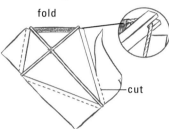

2. Place the frame on a piece of paper and cut around it, leaving 25 mm all round. Snip the corners, fold the edges over the string and tape or glue down.

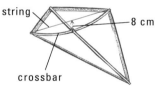

3. At the back, stretch string from one end of the crossbar to the other until the bar bows.

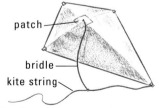

4. Glue a strong patch to the front at the intersection of the crossbar and the upright and thread one end of a piece of string through the patch. Tie the end to the joint and tie the other end to the bottom notch to form a bridle. Attach the kite string $2/3$ of the way down the bridle.

THE EVER-POPULAR KITE
Once introduced to the West, the kite's progress was rapid. By the 18th century, kite flying had become a very popular sport. The practical applications of the kite also attracted interest. In 1752, Benjamin Franklin hung a metal key from a kite line and demonstrated the existence of electricity in lightning. In the 19th century, William Eddy and Lawrence Hargrave developed two new tail-less kites – the bow kite and the box kite.

PAPER KITES
Light-weight paper, invented in first-century China, proved the perfect material for kites.

For a rainy day

THE COMBINATION OF WET WEATHER AND KIDS
BURSTING WITH ENERGY IS A CHALLENGE, BUT IT
CAN BE MET WITH A LITTLE ADULT SUPERVISION.

Yesterday's children did not have television and video games to keep
them quiet when they could not play outside, but they were not
deprived without them because they had dozens of indoor pastimes
that kept them busy and at the same time developed their creative and
thinking skills. They sometimes got bored and squabbled, just as
children do today, but they also forged strong relationships and laid
the foundations for a lifetime of happy memories.

1. Draw an animal's head and neck.

2. Fold the paper back and draw an
animal's body below the fold.

3. Fold the paper back again and draw
an animal's legs.

4. Unfold the
paper to see the
whole animal.

ANIMAL CONSEQUENCES This is a
variation of the word game known as
consequences, but it can be played
by youngsters as well as older people
because it involves drawing instead
of writing. Don't forget that birds,
frogs, snakes, fishes, insects, beetles
and butterflies all count as animals.

At the top of a piece of paper, draw
an animal's head and neck. Then fold
back the paper halfway down the
neck and pass it to the person on
your left.

On the paper that your neighbour
gives you, sketch an animal's body,
joining it to the neck drawn by the
previous player. Then fold the paper
just above where the body ends and
pass it on again to your left.

On the next paper you get, draw
an animal's legs onto the end of the
body that is showing at the fold.
Pass the paper to your left again.

Unfold the paper you now have
and show everyone your strange
animal. As an extra step, make up
a comical name for your animal.

COIN DRAWINGS It is surprising how many things you can draw using
circles. To start, find several coins of different sizes. Trace around
them, joining some of the circles together and leaving others separate.
Then add some details to make funny faces, animals or anything you
can think of, such as the pennyfarthing bicycle on the right. Younger
children may find it easier to work with jam jar lids.

The children of the past used imagination and simple everyday materials like scissors and paper to fill the long hours until the sun came out and they could play outside once again.

DOTS Start with a square of about six dots; with practice you will be able to play it with a larger square, and you will also learn how to place the lines strategically so that you can complete squares yourself and at the same time prevent your opponent from doing so. Playing instructions are in the right-hand column.

TELEGRAMS Before faxes and e-mail, if you wanted to send someone an urgent message you sent a telegram. Each word cost money to send, so people left out words like *a* and *the*. To play telegrams, write down a phrase, leaving plenty of space between the letters. Now write a 'telegram' made up of words beginning with the letters of the original phrase. The words must be in the same order as the original letters. To make this a scoring game, vote for the funniest message.

NOTHING TO DO

Need Over Two Hundred Iron Nails. Great Timber Opportunity Dawning - Oswald.

DOTS: A PAPER AND PENCIL GAME FOR TWO PLAYERS
This is one of the easiest pencil and paper games yet invented.

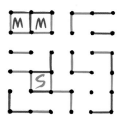

1. Make a square of dots.

2. Take turns to join the dots, drawing only one line at a time.

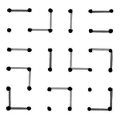

3. When you fill in the fourth side of a square, write the initial of your name inside the square.

M	M	M	M	S
S	S	M	M	N
M	S	S	S	S
M	S	M	M	S
M	M	M	S	S

4. The winner is 'M', with a total of 14 squares completed.

TRACING You do not need to be good at drawing to create beautiful pictures. Tracing is an easy way to make a basic shape, and you can then add detail and colour. Trace around objects such as coins, tins or glass tumblers to make circles, or around boxes to make squares or rectangles. You can also trace around your own hands or feet, or spread a large sheet of paper on the floor and trace around someone else's body.

A traditional way to trace a picture or photograph is to lay tissue paper or tracing paper over it and carefully mark the outline with a soft pencil. Another technique is to trace directly onto drawing paper by sticky-taping the picture to a windowpane and sticky-taping the drawing paper over it. The light shining through the glass will illuminate the picture, making it easy for you to trace its outline.

You can also create very interesting effects by rubbing over textured objects such as coins or leaves. Place the object under a piece of drawing paper and lightly shade over it with a soft pencil or a crayon.

Tracing an illusion Try tracing around your reflection, or the reflection of a friend, in a mirror with unwanted lipstick or a crayon – you may find this easier to do with one eye closed. You'll be surprised how small the traced outline is: that's because you are at arm's length from the mirror, so your reflection is slightly smaller than your face.

SILHOUETTES It is easy to make an attractive silhouette picture. Fasten a sheet of drawing paper to a wall and get a friend to stand between the paper and a light source so that his or her shadow falls on the paper. The most effective silhouettes show the person's head and neck in profile, so that you see the shape of the brow, nose, mouth and chin.

The light source can be a desk lamp or strong sunlight shining through a window – just as long as it casts a crisp shadow on the paper. Get your friend to move about until the shadow you want fits on the paper, then trace around the shadow. Cut out the outline and paste the silhouette onto a contrasting background. To make a traditional black and white silhouette, paint the cut-out silhouette black or transfer the outline onto black paper and then cut it out. Mount the silhouette on a white background.

You can make a silhouette of your favourite singer or film star by tracing around a magazine or poster photograph. Cut out the traced outline and mount it on a contrasting background.

THOUSANDS OF YEARS AGO, the ancient Greeks and Romans learned how to carve the small silhouettes that we call cameos from glass, semiprecious stones, and even shells. In the 19th century, cameos were used to decorate goblets, vases, tableware and jewellery. Later, fairground and street artists cut customers' profiles from black paper and pasted them onto white backgrounds to create inexpensive portraits in silhouette.

Silhouette art appeared in many popular formats, such as this Victorian birthday card. The artist has added interest to the figures with a colour wash over the children's clothes.

Birthday Greetings

The Way We Were

'I saw not long ago what was to me an original amusement for children for a stormy day. Two children, each with paper and pencil, seated themselves in a front window of a house and counted passersby. Lucy counted persons going in one direction and Mary those going the other way. A group of school children would send Mary ten or twenty ahead, and then, at the last minute, just as the half-hour time limit was expiring, Lucy would win the game with a band of labourers moving in the other direction. If a closed carriage went by, the excitement ran high trying to decide how many were the occupants. Sometimes the game was varied by counting animals only.'

– *The New Idea* (1905)

FLYING MACHINES In 1903 the American brothers Wilbur and Orville Wright built an aeroplane that could take people into the air, and the first descent by parachute from an aircraft took place in 1912. But children were making paper planes and parachutes long before these momentous events occurred; a book published in 1881 described how to make a paper parachute.

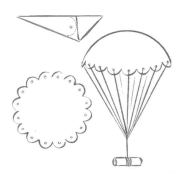

Paper parachute Take a piece of tissue paper or other light paper about 25 cm square. Fold the paper from corner to corner to make a triangle, fold it again so that the corners closest to you meet, and fold it twice more from the top left and the bottom right corners. Cut a semicircle through all the layers of paper, at the opposite end to the apex, and pierce a hole through the middle of the semicircle, as shown in the diagram. Unfolded, you will find you have a scalloped circle.

Cut 16 pieces of strong thread about 40 cm long. Tie a knot in one end of each thread and pass one thread through each of the holes in the scallops. Gather the threads about two-thirds of the way down their length and tie them together with another piece of thread, making sure they are all the same length above the tie. Attach a small piece of cardboard or rolled-up paper to the loose ends to act as a weight. Take the parachute outside on a breezy day, hold it up until the wind catches it underneath, then let it go. A good breeze will lift it quite high into the air.

MAKING A WINDMILL The instructions in the right-hand column show you how to make a windmill from paper. For a longer-lasting, faster-spinning windmill, use thin, flexible cardboard and a short, fine nail instead of paper and a drawing pin. Threading a bead onto the nail on either side of the folded card will allow the windmill to turn more easily.

MAKING A WINDMILL
All you need is some paper, a drawing pin and a stick.

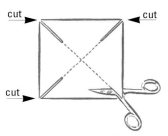

1. Fold a 12 cm square of paper in half, corner to corner. Unfold it and fold it again so that the other corners meet. Cut along the fold lines from the outside to about two-thirds of the way to the centre point.

2. Bring one point of each triangular piece into the centre so that all the points overlap.

3. Push a drawing pin through the central points and into a straight stick, leaving space between the head of the pin and the windmill so it can spin.

JACK-IN-THE-BOX Most children from wealthy families in the 19th century would have owner a jack-in-the-box. These timeless toys can be quite elaborate, with the jack jumping out to the accompaniment of music, but you can make a simple jack-in-the-box yourself with a matchbox: just follow the instructions in the right-hand column.

MUSICAL MYSTERY TASK If you are tired of sitting quietly, try playing this game with a group of friends. Send a volunteer out of the room while the rest of the group thinks up a simple task, such as taking a book from the bookshelf and putting it on the windowsill. Then call the volunteer back into the room with 'music', which the group can make by humming, buzzing, banging pots and pans, or any other means you can think of. The volunteer has to guess what the task is and perform it to the group's satisfaction.

Your group must not talk or make any noise except the music to direct the volunteer – for instance, make the music louder when the volunteer moves towards the bookshelf, and softer when he or she moves away. Once the volunteer realises that the task is to do with the bookshelf, use the music to point out the next part of the task: taking the book off the shelf. Carry on until the person completes the task or gives up in frustration.

CUT-OUT DOLLS If you have a spare hour or two, dressing a paper doll can be lots of fun. Draw the doll yourself and colour it in, or find a suitable magazine picture. The face, arms and legs are the most important parts – the body will be covered with clothes. The doll should be no more than about 15 cm high and should be standing and facing forwards. Paste the finished doll onto thin cardboard and cut it out.

Making the doll's clothes Trace lightly around the doll's body with a pencil to get a basic shape you can use as a guide. Make sure the clothes you design fit snugly against the doll's body at the shoulders, waist and hips. At these places, add small tags that can be folded to attach the outfit to the doll. You could colour the clothes with crayons or felt-tipped pens and stick on scraps of fabric, feathers or beads. When you have finished designing an outfit, cut it out, fold the tags over and hang the clothes on your doll.

MAKING A JACK-IN-THE-BOX
Make this in minutes for hours of fun.

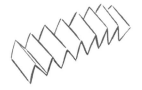

1. Cut a strip of stiff paper, about 30 cm long and half as wide as the matchbox. Fold the paper concertina-style – over, and then over again in the opposite direction – until you have completely folded the strip.

2. Cut out and decorate a small round paper face and paste this to one end of the strip.

3. Paste the other end of the strip to the bottom of the box and hold down the folded strip as you close the box.

4. When you open the lid, the jack-in-the-box will spring out.

Words of Wisdom

'There is a book of Mrs Nesbit's called *The Magic City*, which is all about a boy building a town, not only with ordinary bricks, but with everything the grown-ups allow him to use: candlesticks for pillars, books for walls, waste paper baskets for towers, brass finger bowls for cupolas, and chessmen for statues. This is one of the best of wet day games, but it needs room, the whole floor as a rule, and the grown-up should state very clearly what is, and what is not, to be used by the architects.'

– *THE HAPPY HOUSEWIFE* (1934)

PAPER BEADS Before machinery made it possible to mass-produce jewellery, people often made their own. The steps on the right show you how to make some beads from paper. String them together to make an attractive necklace or belt. You will need some plain or patterned paper, such as wrapping paper, wallpaper or pages from magazines; paper glue; a knitting needle; some string, ribbon or fishing line; and a clasp for fastening the ends together.

SKITTLES This game is a home version of ten-pin bowling. In the good old days, it was played with glass bottles, or sometimes with specially made wooden skittle sets, but modern plastic bottles are better – and safer.

You can play skittles indoors without causing any damage if you use a soft ball and bowl it along the floor. At one end of a room or a hallway, line up nine bottles in a triangular pattern – four in the back row, three in the middle row and two in the front row – leaving a little space between bottles. Stand behind a line four or five paces from the bottles and roll the ball along the floor. Score one point for each skittle you knock over.

TWENTY WAYS OF GETTING THERE If it is still raining and you and your friends are getting a bit fidgetty, this game will use up some energy. It is best played in a long, clear space such as a hallway, but it can be played in a room provided you can move anything breakable out of the way and make enough space.

Each player must travel from one end of the hallway or room to the other in a different manner. If the first person walks, the second might hop and the third might crawl, and so on. No one is permitted to use the same mode of travel twice. Players are out of the game when they cannot think of a new way of getting to the other end. The winner is the player who manages to invent a new way of getting there after all the other players have run out of ideas.

MAKING PAPER BEADS
Scraps of colourful paper can be transformed into special jewellery.

1. Cut triangles of paper 30 cm long and 2 cm wide at the thick end.

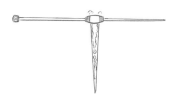

2. Run the glue along the wrong side of the strip, except for 2 cm at the thick end. Starting at that end, wind the strip around the knitting needle. As soon as the paper is stuck down, take the bead off the needle and set it aside.

3. Keep going until you have made enough beads to form a necklace. Create different effects by making wider or narrower beads, or by placing glass or wooden beads between the paper ones.

313

Hanky panky

WHAT COULD BE MORE MAGICAL THAN A MOUSE
GROWING OUT OF THE FOLDS OF AN ORDINARY
HANDKERCHIEF AND THEN SPRINGING INTO LIFE,
SCUTTLING UP ITS CREATOR'S ARM AND JUMPING
INTO THE LAP OF THE FASCINATED OBSERVER?

The handkerchief mouse is not the only clever handkerchief fold, but
it is the most spectacular and the best loved. Follow the illustrations
and instructions on the opposite page to make the mouse.

MANIPULATING THE MOUSE Hold the handkerchief mouse in the palm
of your hand with your fingers curled under slightly at the tail end,
then snap your fingers up towards your palm (see diagram, below left).
As the mouse jumps, place your right hand over its tail to stop it
'escaping', timing it so that you grab the tail while the mouse is still
moving to create the illusion that the mouse is trying to run away.
With practice you will be able to make the mouse jump right out of
your hand into a friend's lap. Take the mouse back into your left hand,

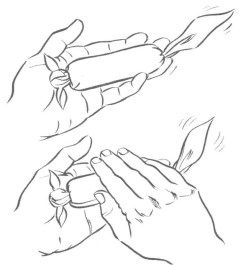

talking to it and stroking it gently
(see diagram, bottom left); as your
stroking hand reaches the back of the
mouse and covers your other hand,
snap your fingers towards your palm
and pretend to be surprised to see
the mouse jump again. The secret is
to distract attention from your left
hand by masking it with your right
hand and chatting as you work.

To end the game, untie the mouse's
ears and ask two children to pull the
ends as for a Christmas cracker, so
that the mouse magically unravels
into a handkerchief.

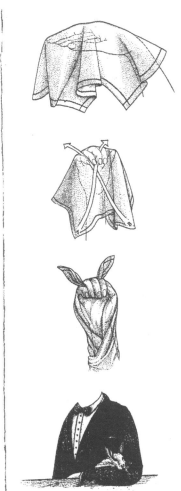

*Handkerchief illusions to
entertain small children have been
around for a long time. These
illustrations for making a
handkerchief rabbit appeared in a
book of children's games and
pastimes by the children's writer
Lewis Carroll (1832–98).*

Words of Wisdom

'Idleness is the parent of a host of evils, so it is
of infinite importance to train the young in
habits of industry. Hands were made to work
with, so teach the children the use of their
hands in some occupation suited to their years. If you do not help the
development of the constructive faculties in your children, you are doing the
reverse, because the busiest thing on earth is a healthy child; its hands must
be employed either in constructive or else in destructive occupation.'

– *THE NEW IDEA* (1904)

Making a handkerchief mouse

The instructions for making the handkerchief mouse look fairly complicated, but it is well worth the effort to master them. Start with a man's large handkerchief or a linen table napkin, and after a little practice try it with a woman's handkerchief, which will make a smaller mouse that will be easier to manipulate.

1. Spread the handkerchief out flat on the table and bring corners a and b together to form a triangle.

2. Fold the two side points so that they overlap in the centre and align with the bottom edge.

3. Starting from the bottom, roll up the handkerchief, making at least four or five turns, until the sides you folded in have disappeared.

4. Turn the handkerchief over and fold the rolled ends towards the middle so that they overlap.

5. Bring up points a and b and tuck them into the opening.

6. Tuck your left thumb into the lower pocket and with your right hand keep turning the rolled handkerchief inside out until you have a firmly packed roll of fabric with a thinner loop tucked into both ends.

7. Pull gently at the loop of fabric until two corners of the handkerchief come free. These two points form the head and the tail of the mouse; the rolled up section is the body.

8. Open out the larger point. Hold the corners with your thumbs and forefingers and twirl the body around the head a few times.

9. Knot the ends together neatly to form the mouse's head and ears.

315

Deal them out

CARD GAMES ARE A GREAT WAY TO HAVE FUN WITH FRIENDS, AND THE PLAY CAN BECOME FAST AND FURIOUS. ALL YOU NEED IS A PACK OF PLAYING CARDS – KNOWN AS A 'DECK' – AND, FOR SOME TYPES OF CARD GAMES, A SCORE SHEET.

All group card games have a dealer, who shuffles the cards to get them into random order, and deals them out to the players. Players choose the dealer by 'cutting' the cards: each player takes a card from the deck, and the one with the highest card becomes dealer. The group of cards each player receives is called a 'deal' or a 'hand'.

SNAP Deal out all the cards face down in piles in front of each player. The player on the left of the dealer starts the game by placing a card face up in the middle of the table. In clockwise turns, each player places a card on top of the centre pile. When two cards directly following each other make a pair, players 'snap' it by putting their hands on top of the pile and calling out *Snap!* The player whose hand touches the cards first takes all the cards in the pile, putting them underneath his or her original pile, and then restarts the game. When one player holds all the cards, the game is over.

DONKEY Go through the pack and take out as many sets of cards – four of the same court card or of the same number – as there are players. (The rest of the pack is not used.) You will also need some small, unbreakable objects such as matchboxes, and paper for scoring.

Players sit in a circle with one fewer matchbox in the centre than there are players: five players would play with 20 cards (five sets of four) and four matchboxes. The dealer shuffles and deals four cards to each player. The object of the game is to acquire all four cards in a set – for example, four threes or four Jacks. When the dealer calls *Pass*, everyone takes an unwanted card from their hand and passes it to the player on their left. They then pick up the new card, keeping it if it will help to make a set or passing it on. Players go on picking up and passing on cards until one player holds all four cards in a set. That player *quietly* puts down the cards and takes one of the matchboxes. As soon as the other players notice this, they make a grab for

'**"WHO CARES FOR YOU?"** said Alice (she had grown to her full size by this time). "You're nothing but a pack of cards!" At this the whole pack rose up into the air, and came flying down upon her …'
– *ALICE'S ADVENTURES IN WONDERLAND*, LEWIS CARROLL (1865)

The Way We Were

Building card houses was once considered a suitably genteel amusement for children:

'Tom could build perfect pyramids of houses; but Maggie's would never bear the laying on of the roof ... and Tom had deduced the conclusion that no girls could ever make anything. But it happened that Lucy proved wonderfully clever at building: she handled the cards so lightly and moved so gently that Tom condescended to admire her houses as well as his own.'

– *THE MILL ON THE FLOSS*, GEORGE ELIOT (1860)

the other objects. The slowest player scores *D* on the score sheet. The game begins again, and at the end of each round a letter is written beside the loser's name until one player has lost enough times to score the whole word *DONKEY*.

TWIST, OR SWITCH The aim is to get rid of all your cards before anyone else, discarding high cards – court cards, tens and nines – first.

The dealer removes the Jokers, deals seven cards to each player, and then places the rest of the pack face down in the centre of the table, turning the top card face up and putting it beside the pack. The player on the dealer's left places a card on top of the one lying face up. This card must either have the same value as the card in the centre or be of the same suit: for instance, if the card in the centre is a three of clubs, the next card played must be a three of another suit or a club.

In this game, Aces do not belong to any suit and can be used to switch suits to a player's advantage: for example, a player who has mainly diamonds can place any Ace on the three of clubs and call out *Diamonds* to change the suit from clubs to diamonds. Tactics are important: there are only four Aces, so use an Ace only when you cannot follow with any other card. On the other hand, do not keep an Ace for too long, because a player caught with an Ace at the end of the game scores 15 points, and the aim is to score low, not high.

A player who cannot play a suitable card must pick up from the pile in the centre. When one player has no cards left, the others tot up the values of the cards left in their hands. Jacks, Kings and Queens score 10 points and an Ace 15; a player left with a four, a six, a ten and an Ace would score 35 (4 + 6 + 10 + 15). After an agreed number of games, the player with the lowest total score is the winner.

A standard pack of cards has four suits – hearts, diamonds, spades and clubs – each made up of cards numbered from one (the Ace) to ten and a Jack, a Queen and a King. In most card games, the Ace is the highest scoring card. Two Jokers, often used as wild cards, complete the pack.

Along with building card houses, constructing a tower of cards was a favourite rainy-day pastime for Edwardian children.

String and things

ALL PARENTS HAVE HEARD THAT PLAINTIVE CRY:
'WHAT CAN I DO NOW?' INSTEAD OF SWITCHING
ON THE TELEVISION, TEACH THE CHILDREN SOME
USEFUL OLD CRAFTS.

The humblest of household scraps can be used to make simple
artefacts, decorations and playthings. Here are just a few of the
hundreds of things that children can learn to create with leftover bits
of string, wool and paper, as well as instructions for using food tins
and string to make a toy telephone that really works.

POMPOMS Pompoms are fun and easy to make, and have a variety of
decorative uses. In the old days, children's scarves and beanies often
sported pompoms. You can stitch these fluffy balls to the corners of
cushions, or make them with metallic thread or wool as inexpensive
home made Christmas decorations. And making multi-coloured
pompoms is a good way of using up bits of leftover knitting wool.

  You need some wool or thread, a compass, a sheet of thin card, a
pencil and scissors. Fold the card in half and draw a circle with the
compass; a circle 9 cm in diameter will make a good-sized pompom.
Then draw another circle about a third of the size in the centre. Cut
around the edge of the larger circle to create two round pieces of card.
Place the pieces together and cut out the inner circle to make two
identical cardboard rings.

  Place the two rings together and wind the wool around them as
shown in the right-hand column. To complete the pompom, carefully
cut through the wool around the edges of the card and then ease the
two pieces of card gently apart. Wind some wool tightly around the
middle of the pompom between the cards and tie it in a firm knot.
Pull off the cardboard rings and fluff up the pompom.

PAPER WEAVING You can create some very pretty effects by weaving
together strips of paper of different colours. The technique used is the
same as for weaving thread; centuries ago, in China and Japan, bags,
mats, and sometimes even clothes were produced by weaving
together narrow strips of twisted paper. You won't be able to
make clothes from your paper weaving creations, but they make
wonderful wall hangings and gift cards.

  Cut two squares of the same size from pieces of differently
coloured paper. Draw a series of evenly spaced vertical parallel
lines on one piece of paper. Starting a little way in from the
edge, cut along each line with a craft knife or a pair of scissors,
stopping before you reach the bottom edge.

  Cut the second square into horizontal strips and place
the first of these strips over the first vertical strip in the
other square, then under the second vertical strip and over

The Way We Were
Learning to make things from
everyday objects is one of the
joys of childhood:

'There were so many other raw
materials, too, with which to
make things, and I mastered
them slowly, one by one,
always with a feeling of pride.
It was a wonderful thing to
create, with your fingers your
eyes, your hands.'

– ON SUNDAYS WE WORE WHITE,
EILEEN ELIAS (1978)

WINDING THE POMPOM
Patience is the key to creating a
good pompom. The more wool you
wind around the card, the fuller
and fluffier your pompom will be.
Cut long pieces of wool and wind
them into balls small enough to fit
through the centre hole in the
pieces of card.

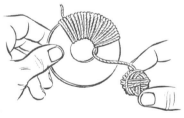

Drop the end of one ball of wool
into the ring and wind the wool
around the pieces of card. When
you have finished one ball, begin
another. Keep winding wool
around the cardboard rings until
they are completely covered and
the hole has almost disappeared.

the third and so on until you reach the end of the row. Begin the second row by placing the horizontal strip under the first vertical strip, and the third row by placing it over the first vertical strip again. By keeping to this sequence, you will create a checkerboard pattern.

Experiment with different sequences: for example place a horizontal strip under one vertical square and over the next two, with paper strips of different widths, and with curved instead of straight strips, and see what other patterns you can create.

FRENCH KNITTING Pieces of cord knitted the 'French' way make great belts, bracelets and ropes, and can even be sewn in a spiral to make a decorative mat or a beret. The cord is knitted on a small wooden spool. In the good old days, wooden cotton reels made ideal spools, but they are difficult to find nowadays. Instead, use a scrap of plywood about 4 cm square and 1 cm thick, and ask an adult to drill a 1 cm hole through the centre. Then hammer four small nails or four stout pins around the hole in the positions shown in the diagram in the right-hand column.

To begin 'knitting', thread one end of a long piece of wool through the hole and wind the piece of wool anti-clockwise twice around the posts on the spool so that there are two loops around each post. With a nail or the straightened end of a paper clip, pick up the bottom loop on each post and lift it over the top loop and over the head of the post. Then make another loop around each post and lift the lower loops over the heads of the posts again.

Follow this sequence until you have knitted enough cord, pulling down the thread hanging through the hole every so often to prevent the cord from bunching up. To tie off the cord, thread the end of the wool through the loop on each post, then lift the loops off the posts, draw the wool tight and knot the end.

TINPOT TECHNOLOGY Have fun with a friend by making this toy telephone: one tin acts as a transmitter, capturing the sound waves from your voice and sending them along the string to the receiver tin at the other end.

You will need two clean, empty tin cans and a long piece of string. Ask an adult to help you punch a small hole in the centre of each of the closed ends of the cans with a hammer and nail over an old piece of wood. Then join the cans by threading the ends of the string through the holes in the cans. Knot the ends of the string inside the cans to hold them in place.

Ask a friend to take one of the cans and go as far away from you as possible, and then to whisper a question into the open end of the can. Cup your own can over one of your ears and see if you can hear your friend's question.

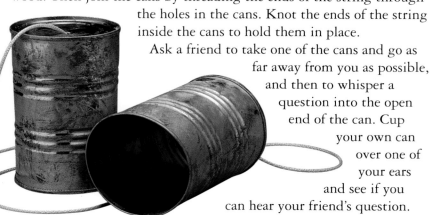

STARTING THE CORD

The French knitting method illustrated here is not difficult – it requires only a wooden spool and some perseverance.

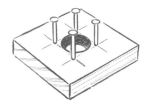

1. File the edges and corners of the spool smooth and position four nails to form a square around the hole in the middle.

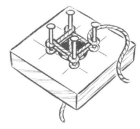

2. Loop the wool loosely around each nail twice, moving in an anticlockwise direction.

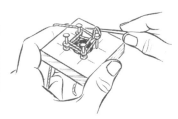

3. Lift the bottom loop over the top loop and over the head of the nail.

A GOOD READ

One of today's most optimistic truisms is 'You can't curl up in bed with a computer.' Ever since the mass production of children's books made leisure reading a possibility for ordinary girls and boys, children have been snuggling up with a good book. Those of us who cherish the time spent reading in our youth hope that generations of children to come will experience the same joy.

With the end of child labour in the English-speaking world, children had time for more pleasurable pursuits. The expansion of education equipped them with reading skills, and publishers were happy to expand into children's literature. By the middle of the 19th century moral tales for children had given way to new forms such as fairy tales, fantasy and adventure stories. Animals began to talk, a little girl became lost in a fantastic world and men travelled beneath the sea long before submarines were invented. Many of the children's books written in our grandparents' time remain favourites with children today.

RUDYARD KIPLING
Born in India in 1865, Kipling wrote many books for both adults and children, and won the Nobel Prize for Literature in 1907 for his writing for adults. Among his best loved books for children are *Kim*, *Just So Stories* and the two *Jungle Books*.

MESSING ABOUT IN BOATS

Published in 1908, *The Wind in the Willows* was written by Englishman Kenneth Grahame for his four-year-old son, 'Mouse'. Grahame spent his childhood playing on the banks of the Thames, and *The Wind in the Willows* is the story of the Rat and the Mole, who live on the riverbank and have a large circle of unforgettable animal friends such as the vain Toad, the brave Otter and the wise Badger. Together the Rat, the Mole, the Badger and the Otter save Toad from his own folly and restore him to his ancestral home, Toad Hall, which the rascally weasels have stolen from him.

GONE FISHING

Written by Mark Twain and published in 1876, *The Adventures of Tom Sawyer* is the tale of a young boy growing up in a small rural town on the Mississippi River. Tom plays hooky from school to go fishing, falls in love with the fetching Becky, runs away from home and has the satisfaction of interrupting his own funeral. He helps to solve a murder and eventually finds real buried treasure. Like many classic children's tales, *The Adventures of Tom Sawyer* found its way into comic books.

PUDDIN THIEVERY

The charms of Norman Lindsay's *The Magic Pudding*, published in 1918, are many. With its strong black and white illustrations, Australian speech and slang (not to mention insults) and its rollicking verse, it has been a favourite with generations of Australian children. Sailor Barnacle Bill, penguin Sam Sawnoff and koala Bunyip Bluegum join forces to foil the Puddin Thieves who are set on stealing Albert, an irascible pudding that can magically change its flavour.

ANIMAL RIGHTS

The young Dot gets lost in the bush and is befriended by a kangaroo who gives her the 'berries of understanding' so that she can understand what the animals are saying. She meets a succession of native animals and realises that humans hunt and kill these animals for sport and for their skins. Written by Ethel Pedley, *Dot and the Kangaroo* was published in 1895.

TO THE
CHILDREN OF AUSTRALIA,
IN THE HOPE OF
ENLISTING THEIR SYMPATHIES FOR THE MANY
BEAUTIFUL, AMIABLE, AND FROLICSOME
CREATURES OF THEIR LAND;
WHOSE EXTINCTION, THROUGH RUTHLESS
DESTRUCTION, IS BEING SURELY
ACCOMPLISHED

COVERING A BOOK

Make a fabric cover to preserve a well loved book for the young readers of the future.

1. Measure the height of the book and the width from the edge of the front cover to the edge of the back. To the longest side add the width of the front cover and add 1 cm all around for the seams.

2. Cut out the outside cover from a sturdy fabric and the lining from a fine fabric. With right sides together, sew around the edge, leaving room to turn the cover inside out.

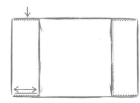

3. Turn right side out and press. Stitch up the opening, fold over the flaps and oversew the top and bottom edges as shown.

4. Embroider the title on the cover or write it with fabric paint. With the book open, slip the covers into the fabric flaps.

Tricks of the trade

TRICKS — FROM THE SOPHISTICATED TO THE SILLY —
WERE FAVOURITE FORMS OF ENTERTAINMENT IN THE
DAYS WHEN PEOPLE HAD TO AMUSE THEMSELVES.

Professional magicians and conjurers achieved spectacular effects with
the aid of chemicals, expensive equipment, elaborate props and years
of practice. But even amateurs could fill an hour with fun using
nothing more than a few household items. They relied on simple
tricks, an audience that was eager to join in, and a clever line of talk.

Practise the tricks to perfect your technique, and practise your
magician's patter as well, as an essential ingredient for success is to
build up your audience's expectations beforehand. And don't forget
the magic formula known to every performer: always leave your
audience wanting more.

THE AMAZING MAGIC WATER GLASS On a table place a glass, a jug of
water and a square piece of paper somewhat larger than the rim of the
glass. Do this with great ceremony and deliberation, telling your
audience that you are about to perform an extraordinary feat in which
you will actually defy the law of gravity! Ask a volunteer to take the
jug of water and fill the glass to the brim. Insist that the audience
check that you are using an ordinary glass, ordinary water and an
ordinary piece of paper. When they are agog with expectation, hold
the bottom of the glass and place the paper over the top, pressing it
down firmly with the palm of your other hand. Turn the glass upside
down and hold the paper in place for a minute or two, and then
remove your hand. Behold – the water stays in the upturned glass!

The explanation is simple: the pressure of the air against the paper is
greater than the pressure of the water on the other side, so that the
water stays in the glass. But if you play your part properly, no one will
remember the laws of physics.

THE NEXT TIME your hair crackles
with static electricity when you comb
it, try this trick. Tear up small scraps of
paper, comb your hair until it crackles
and then hold the comb close to the
pieces of paper. They will jump around
as though they are attracted to a
magnet. You can make it more
interesting by cutting the paper into
the shape of tiny people or animals.
The figures will jump and dance, often
standing on their heads or twirling
around, and sometimes several figures
will join together as though they are
holding hands.

THE OBEDIENT MATCHBOX Take a matchbox
out of your pocket and toss it into the air,
asking your audience to note which way up it
lands. Show them that both sides of the box
are different and then tell them that you can
make it land with the same side facing up as
many times as they wish you to. When they
have nominated a number, begin tossing the
matchbox and, sure enough, it will land the
same way up every time!

The trick is to prepare the box beforehand
by taping a heavy coin inside the bottom of
the box before sliding on the lid. Make sure
no one handles the box or looks inside it.

'THE GREAT HOUDINI' The American contortionist Harry Houdini (1874–1926) was famous for his ability to escape from apparently impossible constraints, such as locked boxes under water. There was no trickery involved; Houdini's secret was extraordinary flexibility and strength.

The handcuff trick Tie loops in each end of two long pieces of string. Slip the loops of one piece over the wrists of a volunteer, and pass the second string under the first and loop it over the wrists of a second volunteer, so that your victims are connected. Now challenge them to free themselves without untying the string or slipping the loops off their wrists. When they have tried all sorts of contortions, climbing over each other and twisting around, show them the secret: tie yourself to another person, then loop your own string, pass the loop through the loop on one of your fellow prisoner's wrists and slip it over their hands to free yourself.

Tying the knot Spread a large scarf on a table and challenge one of the audience to tie a knot in the scarf without letting go of the ends. It is quite simple – cross your arms, with one hand tucked under your forearm and the other over it, then pick up the scarf ends and pull.

EXTRA-SENSORY PERCEPTION For this trick you need to secretly enlist an assistant, with whom you work out an unobtrusive signal – scratching the nose, rubbing the hands, or pulling an earlobe.

Tell your audience that everyone gives out vibrations that are retained by objects for a short time after they are touched. With your sixth sense, you can detect these and tell which of three coins has been touched. First, polish the coins ostentatiously with a cloth 'to clean off any old vibrations', and use the cloth to place the coins on the table without touching them. Ask someone to touch one of the coins while your back is turned, and to tell you when they have done so. Turn around and put on an expression of concentration. Run your hand over the coins a few times, telling your audience you can feel the vibrations, they are getting clearer, you've just about got it. Then place your forefinger over one coin at a time, and when your finger is over the coin that was touched, your assistant will give the signal. Run your finger over the coins twice to make sure you have understood the signal and that your audience didn't try to trick you by touching two, three or none of the coins. Now pick out the coin that your assistant indicated and watch your audience's amazement.

NOT AS EASY AS ALL THAT Challenge your friends to perform these seemingly easy tasks and watch their faces when they can't do them.

Elusive cash Standing with the heels against a wall, squat down and pick up a coin in front of you without moving your heels from the wall. Tell your victims they can keep the money if they can perform the task – your money will be perfectly safe.

Instant paralysis Stand sideways against a wall with your left cheek, heel and leg touching it. Now bend your right leg and raise it.

As well as performing death-defying escapes, such as from a locked canister, shown at the top of the page, Houdini practised more traditional magic; the poster advertises a card act.

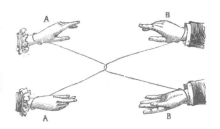

The handcuff trick was bound to have its participants tied up in knots – a surefire way to break the ice at a party.

VERBAL TRICKERY The key to success with these tricks is the wording – if you get it right, your friends will laugh at how easily they were fooled when you reveal the solution. Warm your audience up by getting them to attempt the genuinely impossible feats described on the previous page, and then boast that the next task is difficult for the majority of people but you, with your superhuman abilities, have no trouble performing it.

The migrating coin With a coin in each hand, stretch your arms as far apart as you can. Ask your audience whether they think you can put both coins into the same hand while keeping both arms outstretched. When they assure you it is impossible, ask which hand they would like you to put both coins in. (It makes no difference which hand they say, but it helps to create a feeling of anticipation.) When everyone is curious, place one coin on the table, keeping your arms outstretched, turn right around, and pick up the coin with the hand holding the other coin.

The long jump Say to someone in the audience, 'Can you put four chairs in a row, then take off your shoes and jump over them without touching them?' When the victim refuses the challenge, show your audience how it's done: line up four chairs, take off your shoes – and jump over the shoes.

CONFIDENCE TRICKS These tricks work by making a fool of one individual, so select your 'victim' carefully – do not choose someone who dislikes attention or who is likely to be irritated or embarrassed by the experience.

An unfair bargain Produce a coin and ask one of the audience to lend you another. Strike a bargain that if you can make this person say 'No' before you finish the trick, you will keep both coins, but if you cannot do so, the other person will keep them both. Then begin the performance. Holding both coins in one hand, start some dramatic magic 'business'; for example, flourish a coloured scarf over your palm, and at the same time solemnly intone some impressive-sounding 'magic words', such as *ABRACADABRA, HOCUS POCUS, ALPHA SUM ET OMEGA*. Once your victim is totally absorbed in what you are doing, break off and say, very innocently, 'Oh, have you seen this trick before?' Ten to one, the victim will be so distracted by all your magic 'business' as to have forgotten the bargain, and will say 'No' – and you can pocket both coins.

Holding the baby Ask for an adventurous person from the audience to help you to perform a 'very difficult' magic trick. Get the person to stand with arms extended in front and palms facing the floor. Place a full glass of water on the fingers of each of your volunteer's hands and order him or her to sing a nursery rhyme, such as 'Jack and Jill'. Then say, 'Thank you, that will be all, you can sit down now'.

Faced with the dilemma of how to get rid of the glasses of water, some victims will beg someone to remove them, while others will simply walk away, letting the glasses fall to the floor – so do not undertake this trick on a good carpet or with the best crystal glasses in the house.

The more polished your magic performance, the more certain you will be to enthral your audience.

Party time!

CELEBRATIONS OF OCCASIONS THAT ARE IMPORTANT
TO CHILDREN, SUCH AS A BIRTHDAY OR THE END OF
THE SCHOOL YEAR, ARE A TIME-HONOURED
TRADITION OF FAMILY AND SOCIAL LIFE.

In the 1990s there are lots of ways of marking such occasions – taking
the children and their friends out to a meal in a family restaurant, to
the beach or to the pictures – but an old-fashioned party at home can
be an exciting and inexpensive alternative. Use paper plates and cups,
and provide simple traditional food such as sausage rolls, jellies and
fairy bread and, of course, a special cake.

Party games are another essential ingredient. They need to be
organised and supervised by an adult or an older sibling, but six- to
ten-year-olds will enjoy learning to play these simple games, most of
which require no equipment at all, or can be played with chairs,
handkerchiefs or slippers. Most party games have a winner, and little
prizes add to the fun, as long as you can ensure a fair distribution!

*The traditional way to celebrate
a child's birthday is with a party,
complete with cake and candles.*

325

ONE AGAINST ALL Many children's games are based on the principle of pitting one player against the group, the object being for the odd one out to displace another player and become part of the group.

Fox Players stand in a circle while one of their number – the 'fox' – walks around the outside of the ring. The fox touches someone lightly on the shoulder, and that player must then race around the circle in the opposite direction to the fox, trying to beat the fox back to his 'den' – the empty place in the circle where the race began. The loser is the fox in the next round of the game.

Blind man's buff A player wearing a blindfold is led into the midst of the other players and turned around three times. With arms outstretched, the blindfolded player must try to catch one of the other players, who move about making noises and trying to stay just beyond reach. The first player caught becomes the 'blind man', and the game begins again.

Blind man's buff must be supervised to make sure the blindfolded player is not placed in danger. If you play the game indoors, you should make sure there are no objects that could be tripped over. If you play it outside, set boundaries, otherwise the 'blind man' will never catch anyone.

Teasing the 'blind man' is part of the fun of blind man's buff.

A HUNTING GAME This game is a great way to use up energy and work up an appetite for the party spread.

Scavenger hunt Players must find everything on a list of about 15 items, some easy to find and others more difficult. Younger players should probably be prohibited from leaving the house, but older children may be allowed to search the neighbourhood. A typical list of items could contain a feather, a bus ticket, leaves from six different trees (not bushes), something black and green, a 1982 coin, something beginning with Z, the first name of a local personality, the number of windows in a particular building, the names of two plumbers in the neighbourhood and an article of clothing.

Players hunt in pairs or groups, and are given a time limit – say 45 minutes. The winning team is the one that gets back first with all the items, or else the team that has found the most items at the conclusion of the time limit.

When the weather is fine, the garden is the perfect location for the birthday tea.

A KISSING GAME In the first few decades of the 20th century, this game was popular with young teenagers and was considered very daring. These days it would not raise so much as an eyebrow, but it will still delight young children.

Postman's knock One player stands at the door. The player elected to be the 'postman' leaves the room and closes the door, then after a few moments knocks twice. The door is opened and the postman announces that there is a letter for _____ (naming someone

in the room), and that to receive it the owner will have to pay _____ cents (naming any number, but not too many). The recipient of the 'letter' must leave the room and pay for the 'letter' – not in cents but in kisses. That player then becomes the postman.

PLAY IT WITH MUSIC Music – which can be singing, chanting or some form of recording – is an essential accompaniment to many traditional party games.

Oranges and lemons This game is sometimes known as French and English. Two tall players secretly decide who will be a 'lemon' and who an 'orange', and then stand facing each other with their hands joined above their heads to form an arch. The other players join hands and skip through the arch, singing the traditional rhyme that appears at the top right of the side column.

At the word *head*, the two players forming the arch bring down their arms to trap the player passing underneath. The trapped player must choose to be either an orange or a lemon, and then stands behind whoever of the two represents the chosen fruit. This must all be done very quietly so that no one else can hear. The trapped player stands with arms around the waist of the lemon or the orange, and the game continues until all players have been caught and are standing behind either the orange or the lemon.

Regardless of how many or how few players are on each side, the game ends with a tug-o'-war between the oranges and the lemons.

Pass the parcel Before the party, a small gift is wrapped in coloured paper and then in as many layers of scrap paper as there are players. An older person acts as a master of ceremonies, playing some music while all the participants sit in a circle and pass the parcel from hand to hand. At the precise moment the music stops, the player holding the parcel must take off one layer of wrapping paper, then pass the parcel to the next player when the music begins again. One layer of wrapping is removed each time the music stops, until the last layer comes off and the gift is revealed. The player who unwraps the final layer keeps the prize.

HOW DID PEOPLE make music for games such as pass the parcel before cassette and CD players? There was plenty of choice: some played tunes on the piano, others on the fiddle, and some even played the mouth organ. Later there were gramophone records and the pianola for those who could not play music themselves.

The gramophone was invented in the 1870s, although it wasn't until the 1920s that gramophone players were being mass-produced and sold at a price families could afford. In 1913 a portable player came onto the market, giving some children the opportunity to play musical games outdoors to the sounds of popular gramophone recordings of the day.

The pianola – a self-playing piano – was more popular than the gramophone from the late 1900s until the 1930s, when the quality of gramophone recordings improved.

Fun and games

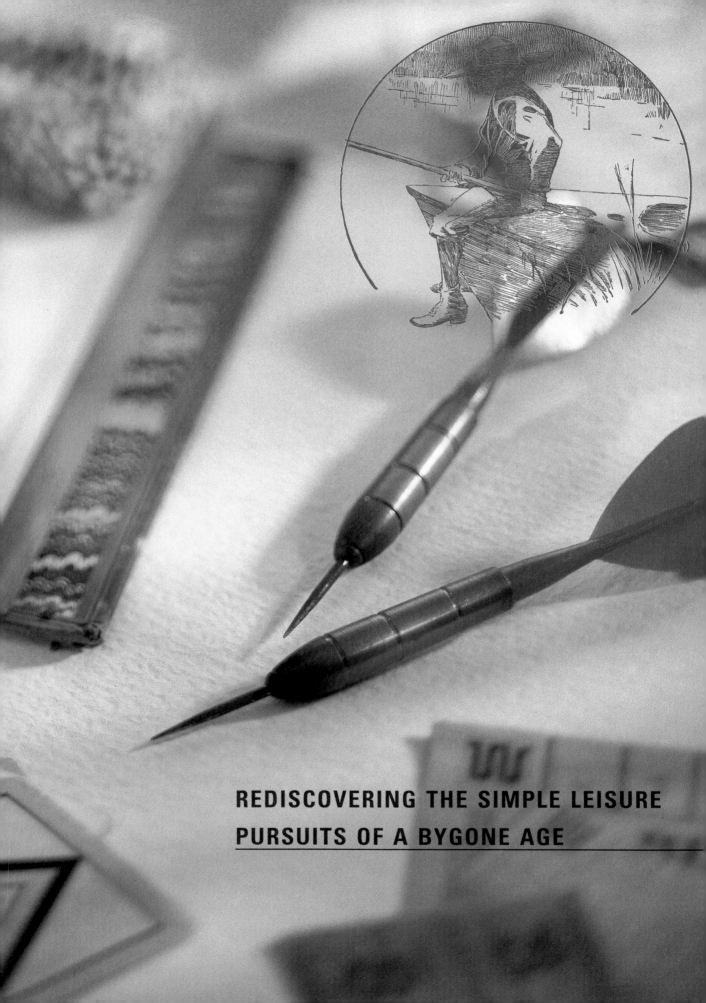

**REDISCOVERING THE SIMPLE LEISURE
PURSUITS OF A BYGONE AGE**

Stepping out

WALKING, FROM A GENTLE STROLL TO A
LONG HIKE, HAS LONG BEEN RECOGNISED AS
HEALTHY, ENJOYABLE AND EDUCATIONAL.

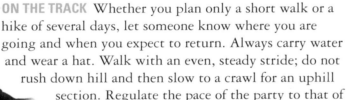

The benefits of walking – from a gentle post-meal
promenade to more adventurous rambles further afield –
have long been well appreciated as healthy, enjoyable
and educational. For the children of the better-off, the
afternoon stroll with nanny was part of the daily
routine; for the less privileged, walking or 'shank's
pony', was the natural – and usually pleasant – means
of getting from one place to another.

The late 19th century saw the beginning of walking as
popular recreation, although walkers were often looked
upon as objects of curiosity, or as cranks.

ON THE TRACK Whether you plan only a short walk or a
hike of several days, let someone know where you are
going and when you expect to return. Always carry water
and wear a hat. Walk with an even, steady stride; do not
rush down hill and then slow to a crawl for an uphill
section. Regulate the pace of the party to that of
the slowest member, not the fastest.

Walking party Have a leader at the head and a person
at the end to ensure that stragglers do not fall behind. It is a good idea
for each member of the party to carry a whistle: if someone does go
astray, a quick blast will alert the others, and an answering blast will
guide the lost sheep back to the group.

Emergency rations The best planned excursion can encounter
problems that mean the party arrives home much later than was
expected. Emergency rations – a block of chocolate, some dates or a
piece of fruit – can be very useful: the last bit of a long walk is much
tougher if you are hungry as well as tired.

BUSHWALKING ETIQUETTE There are a few sensible rules to follow:
• When walking in file, keep your place; do not push to the front.
• Walk several paces behind the person in front. It is the
responsibility of the person following to avoid springing branches,
not of the first one to hold the branches back.
• Always leave gates as you find them. Get through fences, not over
them; if it is impossible to get through, climb over at a post.
• When walking near cliff faces, take great care not to dislodge stones
or rocks. Others may be walking below.
• Do your utmost to make as little negative impact on the
environment as you possibly can.

CHOC-FULL OF GOODNESS !

*Take some high-energy food, such
as chocolate, in your pack when
you go hiking: it will pick you up
when your reserves are low.*

*A growing number of people were
taking up hiking and
mountaineering by the early
1900s. This woman is equipped
for a day's climbing.*

FEET FIRST If you are planning some hard walking, toughen soft skin by soaking your feet in a solution of alum every night for two weeks, or by dabbing methylated spirits daily onto clean, dry feet. Some old bushcraft books advised urinating on the feet at the first sign of tenderness to harden the skin. Make sure your toenails are well trimmed before setting off.

Well fitting boots and socks are essential. A lubricant between the foot and sock is useful – rub petroleum jelly or moistened soap around your heels, toes and any other likely pressure points. Make sure there is nothing in your footwear that might cause a blister (a small piece of grit, for instance).

Even so, the sustained hammering of your feet against the ground during a long walk can produce a hot spot that can quickly develop into a blister. And if a blister is allowed to rub raw, your progress will be both painful and slow.

If a blister threatens, cover the area with strong, smooth sticking plaster to prevent further development. Treat a blister that has already formed by carefully pricking it with a needle that has been sterilised in a flame, such as a match. Press on the blister gently to drain the fluid, but leave the blistered skin in place (making sure it is not creased) and then cover it with sticking plaster.

Water-rounded stones can be very tiring to the feet, so always keep your boots on when walking along a rocky riverbed. Do not dry your boots by the fire, as they may stiffen and become uncomfortable; it is better to put the boots back on still wet, for you will probably be walking in water again.

MAKING TRACKS If a number of people are walking, groups can become widely separated. There are internationally recognised signs that you can make to show which way you have gone – see the examples in the right-hand column. These signs are also invaluable if a walker is lost or injured and a search has to be mounted.

Following arrow trails The arrowhead of each sign should point in exactly the direction that the next sign is to be found. Sight an object along the line from this arrow before heading for the next one. If you suspect you have missed an arrow, go back to the last one and make your way slowly in the indicated direction. Look up and down as well as from side to side for the next sign.

LOST! Before setting off, get directions, and do not rely on your memory: write everything down. Ask also for any information that will alert you if you take a wrong turning. Remember that things look quite different when viewed from another direction, so the landmarks you remember passing on your outward journey are not what you will see on the way back; make a habit of looking behind you every few hundred metres.

If you do get lost, sit down, rest, and take stock. Often calm study of the map and your surroundings is enough to get you back on track. If not, try retracing your steps to a known feature and reorientating yourself from there. Do not push on into unknown territory. If all else fails, stay put. Look for shelter from wind, rain and sun.

BLAZING A TRAIL

Hikers often leave marks along a track to indicate their route. Make the signs with sticks, stones and other natural materials.

An arrow means 'walk in this direction'.

Sticks forming an X across a path mean 'do not follow this track'.

A pile of stones with one stone placed to the right (or left) means 'turn right' (or 'turn left').

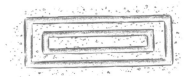

A rectangle inside a larger rectangle means 'wait here'.

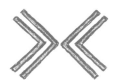

Two arrowheads pointing to each other means 'danger!'.

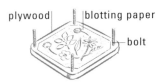

Distress signals Three of any kind of signal – three cooees, whistle blasts, smoke puffs or torch flashes – is a recognised distress signal. A smoky fire (use damp green vegetation) will also attract attention.

NATURE STUDY In the days before cameras were widely available, drawings and paintings were the equivalent of snapshots. The Victorians often kept the most detailed records of their nature observations, as well as amassing vast collections of natural objects. Less environmentally unsound was the gentle art of watercolour painting.

Keeping a record Making notes about the plants and animals you see is a simple, inexpensive and personal way to record your walks. Note the date and location, the weather, the vegetation type and the names of any plants and wildlife you encounter.

Sketching Sketching hones your observation skills by forcing you to notice details. Make a small, rough drawing of the general habitat in one corner (a stream or a grove of trees in a grassy plain, for example), and then sketch your subjects, both wildlife and plants. If you cannot identify an animal, record the time of day it was active, any distinctive markings, size, diet, and anything else that might help you identify the creature at a later time. For an unknown plant, note details such as colour, the number of petals, and leaf shape and size for identification later. Use a pencil and a small notebook. Colour can be added at home.

Pressing flowers and leaves A favourite with our Victorian forebears, this method of preservation removes moisture by enveloping the specimens in absorbent material and then flattening them under pressure. Collect specimens when the weather is dry. The less succulent the bloom, the more colour it will retain when pressed, and the brighter the fresh flower, the better the result. Autumn leaves are particularly suitable for this treatment. Flowers with thick centres should be flattened with your thumb before pressing. Specimens can take up to five weeks to dry. They can become part of the record of your walks, or can be used to decorate stationery and cards.

LASTING IMPRESSIONS
Make a flower press with two sheets of plywood with a long bolt and a wing nut in each corner, and sheets of blotting paper and card slightly smaller than the plywood.

1. Spread flowers of the same thickness on the blotting paper and cover them with more blotting paper and a sheet of card.

2. Layer more flowers in the same way, covering each layer with a blotting paper and card.

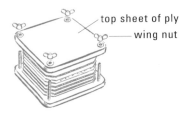

3. Fit the top sheet of ply onto the bolts and tighten the wing nuts. Replace the cardboard every day for the first week, then leave until the flowers are paper-thin and dry.

Words of Wisdom

'It must not be imagined that a walking tour, as some would have us fancy, is merely a better or worse way of seeing the country. There are many ways of seeing landscape quite as good … But landscape on a walking tour is quite accessory. He who is indeed of the brotherhood does not voyage out in quest of the picturesque, but of certain jolly humours – of the hope and spirit with which the march begins in the morning, and the peace and spiritual repletion of the evening's rest. He cannot tell whether he puts his knapsack on, or takes it off, with more delight. The excitement of departure puts him in key for that of the arrival. Whatever he does is not only a reward in itself, but will be further rewarded in the sequel; and so pleasure leads on to pleasure in an endless chain.'

– *WALKING TOURS*, ROBERT LOUIS STEVENSON (1876)

Picnic frolics

LUNCH IN THE OPEN AIR WITH FAMILY AND FRIENDS
DOES NOT HAVE TO INVOLVE BARBECUEING — TRY AN
OLD-FASHIONED PICNIC INSTEAD.

The picnic is said to have originated with Charles, Prince of Wales, who became Charles I of England in 1625. He gave such a party and invited lords, knights and squires to 'bring every man his dish of meat'. In premotoring days, the gentry travelled in a cavalcade of elegant carriages (one piled high with hampers and portable furniture), while ordinary folk made their way by dray, train or ferry.

Outfits may have been more formal than today and the spread more lavish, but the central pleasures are still the enjoyment of food, the company of friends, and perhaps a stroll or an outdoor game.

PLANNING AND PACKING A picnic involving several households should be organised a week or so in advance and arrangements confirmed the day before, when weather conditions are known. Each group can bring their own food, or an overall menu can be worked

Part of the delight of a day in the country or at the beach is planning the picnic menu to suit the tastes of all the participants.

out, and items assigned to each person or household taking part. As well as deciding on the menu, consider the packing and transport of the repast. Cars give a greater choice of destinations off the beaten track and provide shelter in bad weather. Arrange a meeting point and a time.

The basket A deep, solid wicker hamper, with divisions for utensils and food and drink containers evokes the luxury of the past and keeps your provisions in good shape.

Food and drink In earlier times, the day before a picnic was spent cooking and preparing food and packing hampers, but with today's pre-cooked foods you can put together a feast in a fraction of the time.

Simple foods are best suited to outdoor eating – good cheese, olives, cold meats, salad vegetables and crusty bread are doubly delicious when eaten by a river bank, in a leafy park or by the sea. Finger foods do away with the need to provide every member of the party with cutlery. Sandwiches travel well and are easy to eat. Small cakes wrapped separately in greaseproof paper or plastic wrap keep better than large ones and are much easier to pack.

The cuppa In Australia, tea infused in a billy can is the time-honoured way of providing the picnic cuppa. A more refined version of billy tea was to tie up the tea leaves in a square of muslin, then toss the tiny parcel into boiling water and leave it for a few minutes to infuse – the forerunner of modern teabags.

THE PICNIC SPOT Many parks in the past were equipped with tables and benches for picnickers, as they are now. If you need to spread a rug, choose a spot bare of bushes so there is no chance of snakes.

PASSING THE TIME For the large office and group picnics that were so popular in times past, an entertainment program was usually worked out in advance. Often there was a band, and events such as a single ladies' race, an old buffers' race (for men over 45!) and a tug-of-war were obligatory.

In these more relaxed times we would not force everybody to take part in picnic games, but they can be lots of fun. Games such as drop the handkerchief and treasure hunts transfer well to the picnic setting, as does a game of cricket.

The after-lunch stroll is a traditional part of a picnic. If some people want to explore the countryside, set a time for them to return. A whistle is useful for signalling the departure time to strays. Give the signal in good time, for they may be some distance away.

The invention of the motor car opened up remote picnic spots to many more people.

A VACUUM FLASK can usually be relied upon to produce a steaming cuppa instantly, whatever the weather. It will also keep things cool: to save space in the cool box, rather than trying to keep whole bottles cold, fill a vacuum flask with ice to add to drinks as needed.

The modern vacuum flask was developed in the late 19th century by the Scottish physicist Sir James Dewar. The inner of the double glass walls of the flask are coated with mercury to hinder loss of heat by radiation, and the vacuum between the two walls prevents heat loss by conduction. The fragile glass was at first protected in a metal case; plastic-covered flasks date from the 1920s. Stoppers were initially of cork.

Used properly, a flask will keep a liquid near its original temperature for many hours. For best results, keep the flask upright.

Tell me a story

THE ART OF STORY TELLING IS AS OLD AS LANGUAGE ITSELF AND IS STILL PRACTISED BY MANY TRADITIONAL CULTURES.

Not many of us have the gift of creating original stories but you can recycle other people's. The Brothers Grimm and many other writers of distinction collected and retold folk tales, which are not only works of art but are also an entertaining way of passing on community wisdom and the precepts of social behaviour.

HOW TO TELL STORIES There are some rules for effective story telling.

Conviction Know the story really well and enjoy telling it. Choose your words carefully – simplicity is the keynote. If you are adapting an existing story, make the new version your own so that you can really share it with your audience.

Pausing This is a most effective way of riveting a listener's attention. Try reading this extract from Hans Andersen's *The Princess and the Pea*, first with and then without the pause, and note the heightening effect of the pause:

  'In the midst of this horrible storm, someone knocked on the city gate; and the king himself went down to open it. On the other side of the gate there stood – (*pause*) – a princess.'

Mimicry Young listeners are captivated by imitation of voices and sounds. But do not try imitation unless you can do it well. Successful story tellers do not have to be clever mimics.

Description Weave description into the action: 'And so brave Roderick crossed the moat again over the rickety, wooden drawbridge, which swayed alarmingly and, when a foot fell upon it, creaked a hundred times louder than an unoiled hinge.' Give characters descriptive names, such as Yellow-Dog Dingo and Old Man Kangaroo.

Beginnings and endings Story beginnings should grab the child's attention. Hans Andersen's *The Steadfast Tin Soldier* begins: 'Once there were five and twenty tin soldiers. They were all brothers because they had been made from the same old tin spoon.'

  Stories should come to a satisfying and dramatic end, like Rudyard Kipling's *The Cat that Walked by Himself*: 'Then he goes out to the Wet Wild Woods or up the Wet Wild Trees or on the Wet Wild Roofs, waving his tail and walking by his wild lone.'

FAMILY HISTORY Children love to hear true stories about members of their family. The stories do not have to be particularly exciting – the point is that they are accounts of real people and children love them. All you have to do is to recount events as you remember them, or as they have been told to you. Such tales as 'The day we left the hen house door open' can be retold again and again.

Atmosphere is an important element in story telling: a scary story is much more frightening when told in the dark.

The Way We Were

'… we loved Dad's and Mother's stories, particularly Mother's stories about life on the cattle station in the Kimberleys where she had lived with her brother and their cousins for some years before marrying Dad. Because she was in those stories, they were real and there was living drama in them … There was action and excitement and fear, when she had handled a bolting four-in-hand and lived through an earthquake in Wyndham.'

– *BREAD & DRIPPING DAYS: AN AUSTRALIAN GROWING UP IN THE 20s*, KATHLEEN MCARTHUR (1981)

Your move

Games played on a marked surface with counters and dice are almost as old as human civilisation, and many of the board games played around the world today are surprisingly similar to those played by people of ancient times. In the 19th century, many of these games were played using a teetotum rather than dice, which were considered potentially sinful. Teetotums have six sides marked with numbers and a spinning handle to turn them. Some board games rely on chance and the luck of the throw, others on skill and strategy.

China has bequeathed us a rich heritage of board games, such as Mah Jong, which took on its present form in the 1800s and is believed to be based on games played in China since about 500 BC. America has been another fruitful source of board games: Scrabble – probably the most popular word game of all time – was invented by an American architect, Alfred Butts, who was unemployed during the Depression; Monopoly, another top favourite, is based on one of the games painted on oilcloth by the Religious Society of Friends in Atlantic City.

A UNIVERSAL OCCUPATION
A watercolour painting from the 1840s of the interior of a hut in New Zealand shows three Maoris absorbed in playing a board game with pebbles while the life of the village continues around them. The two male players are tattooed in traditional Maori style.

EQUIPMENT
Most board games require few tools – something to move around the playing surface and something to record a score are all that is needed. In the 19th century, board games were drawn by hand or printed and pasted onto cardboard.

AN ANCIENT TRADITION
Clay counters and dice from the Roman Empire 50 years before the birth of Christ illustrate the antiquity of games involving casting for a turn or a score.

CHINESE CHECKERS

Chinese checkers was first marketed in the US in the 1880s as Hop Ching Checkers. It is played on a six-pointed star grid, dimpled where the lines intersect to hold the marbles. The object is to transfer all ten marbles into the point of the star directly opposite.

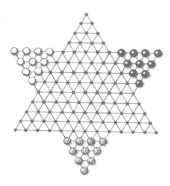

1. A checkers board set up ready for play to begin.

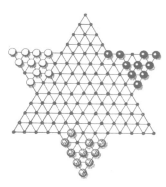

2. Example of each player's opening move.

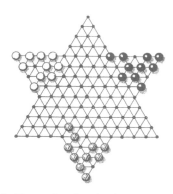

3. Example of each player's second move.

TILES AND TALLY STICKS

Mah Jong means 'the sparrows'. It is played with 144 small, rectangular tiles originally made out of ivory or bone dovetailed into a backing of bamboo. Some sets have been made out of mother of pearl, jade or semi-precious stones, and housed in richly carved or lacquered caskets.

MONEY MAKING GAMES

Monopoly is a perennially popular board game, based on making money. Below, British officers in 1942 enjoy a welcome break from warfare with a game of monopoly.

Let's party!

HOME ENTERTAINING, BOTH FORMAL AND INFORMAL, USED TO BE A MORE FREQUENT LEISURE ACTIVITY THAN IT IS THESE DAYS.

Hosts were adjured to think carefully about selecting people for dinner parties, and strongly advised against inviting 'two fine talkers with different interests' on the same evening. Many pre-1950 manuals of hospitality describe how to run large parties, where the guests play various sorts of games. Instructions exist for dozens of these diversions – there is room to repeat only a few here. But if you become serious about reviving this sort of old-fashioned entertainment, you will find plenty of help in old-time library books.

Conversation was considered an art in our grandparents' time: dinner guests were expected to be both entertaining and attentive.

PARTY TIPS It is worth taking some trouble beforehand to make your party run smoothly.

• Let your neighbours know that you are having a party. Better still, invite them along.

• Allocate a couple of bedrooms to be used as cloakrooms, one for women and one for men. If the weather is wet, set aside a place for dripping umbrellas.

• Prepare small but clear notices indicating the whereabouts of cloakrooms and bathrooms. Put labels on the actual doors, as well.

• Serve drinks from one central point to minimise mess and keep the guests circulating.

• If you have the space, keep one room or a separate outdoor area as a supper room. Invite your guests to help themselves when the food is served. For supper in the garden, burn lots of citronella candles to discourage mosquitoes.

• Fewer people smoke these days, and many nonsmokers are particular about not inhaling cigarette smoke. Let people know where they can smoke and provide plenty of ashtrays.

• Some hospitality manuals, such as *The Book of Good Housekeeping* (1944), suggest that you 'plan your parties to the minutest detail in advance and carry out your plans to the letter'. Others urge party-givers to plan a rough program, but not to make it too long or stick to it like a timetable. Alternate lively games with more peaceful ones. If people are chatting and enjoying each other's company, leave them to it for a while; there is no need to break up the friendly atmosphere with a structured game.

• When your guests leave, ask them to say their goodbyes indoors. Raised voices outside have a penetrative quality at night.

MUSIC ON A ROLL
In 1897, E.S. Votey, an American engineer, patented the pianola. This was a cabinet called a 'player piano' that stood in front of an ordinary piano, and had a row of wooden 'fingers' or 'hammers' positioned over the keyboard. Air passing through perforations on a moving paper roll inside the cabinet activated the wooden fingers to strike the keyboard. Levers and pedals allowed the operator to vary the tempo, volume and other aspects of the performance. Some player-piano rolls reproduced performances by musicians playing their own works, among them Debussy, Grieg, Rachmaninoff and Gershwin.

The radio and gramophone ousted the player piano in the 1930s, but in the 1990s the Japanese Yamaha Corporation introduced the 'Disklavier', a player piano that stores data on computer disk and activates the key-striking and pedalling mechanisms electromagnetically to record and play.

FORFEITS At parties in bygone days, it was often more common to make the losers pay forfeits than to reward the winners with prizes. Forfeits, which generally accentuate the ridiculous and add to the hilarity, fall into two main groups: those that require some purely physical action and those that depend on word play and action for an interpretation of what to do. If you decide to include forfeits in your revels, be tactful about it: give the outrageously silly ones to the natural clowns and make gentler demands on the shyer guests.

Popular forfeits of the 1880s These were many and varied:
• The statue. The unfortunate individual is placed in one position after another by different members of the company, and must remain stationary until permission is given to alter it.
• Put one hand where the other cannot touch it. (This is done by merely holding the right elbow with the left hand or vice versa.)
• Kiss the lady you love best without anyone knowing it. (The gentleman must kiss all the ladies present, his favourite among them.)

For an evening of home-made entertainment, invite friends over for refreshments and party games.

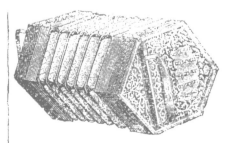

A concertina was a handy instrument to take to a party — easy to carry and a pleasant accompaniment to dances.

• Sit upon the fire. (To do this, write the words 'The fire' on a piece of paper, and then sit on them.)
• Put yourself through the keyhole. (To do this, write the word 'Yourself' on a piece of paper, then roll up the paper and pass it through the keyhole.)
• Ask a question, the answer to which cannot possibly be in the negative. (The question is: 'What do the letters y-e-s spell?')
• Spelling backwards. Spell some long word, such as hydrostatics, backwards.

MIXING GAMES The first requirement of a good party is to make the guests feel at ease with each other and with the idea of playing games. Mixing games are 'ice-breakers', designed to encourage people to talk to strangers.

Encourage your guests to mingle by playing mixing games.

What am I? One way to get your party started is to ask people to come with clues pinned to their clothes suggesting well known titles of books, films, TV programs or songs. Upon arrival, each guest is given a piece of blank paper or card and a pencil, and asked to list people's names and what they represent. Great subtlety is not required – for example, two postcards, one showing London and the other Paris, might depict Charles Dickens's *A Tale of Two Cities*.

Advertisements This game requires familiarity with current advertising material in newspapers or magazines. Cut out 20 to 30 advertisements from newspapers or magazines and black out or cut out all reference to the goods they advertise. Stick the advertisements on cards, number them, and display them around the party area. As guests arrive, give each of them blank pieces of card and a pencil and ask them to wander round identifying the products advertised. After a specified time, ask guests to swap cards with the nearest person for the cards to be marked as the answers are called out. The person with the most correct answers is the winner and may receive a small prize on the spot or bonus points to carry through the evening. The person with the fewest correct answers may be asked to pay a 'forfeit' later when everyone is more relaxed.

PROGRESSIVE GAMES Progressive games are arranged in various rooms or parts of the garden and the guests participate in pairs, playing each game in turn, and noting their scores on a card. Draw for pairs (ideally one of each sex) – this is another way of mixing your guests. Each game should take roughly the same time to complete. You will need to position an umpire or timekeeper at each station. A 'pentathlon' – a course of five games – might include:
• Darts: Each person throws six darts and the pair's total is noted.
• Quoits: Each person throws nine rings and the pair's total of rings on the pin is noted.
• Balls in the bucket: Each person throws ten balls from a set point and the number ending up in the bucket for each pair is noted.
• Tiddlywinks: Each pair plays for one to two minutes and adds the number of discs they manage to put in the cup to their score.

The Way We Were

'In summer 1938 Lady Mendl gave a huge circus party, on Gatsby proportions. The hostess, in aquamarines, diamonds and a white organdie Mainbocher, was the ringmaster in the tan-bark ring, with acrobats in satin and paillettes, ponies and clowns. Guests danced on a special composition dance floor under which there were millions of tiny springs so that it gently heaved up and down with the rhythm. Constance Spry sent three aeroplanes of roses from London to Paris for the party, and in different parts of the garden three orchestras played jazz, Cuban rumbas and Hungarian waltzes. Concealed lighting turned the garden into a dream landscape with marble statues, fountains and urns of cut flowers …

For most of the people there, it was the last party.'

– *In Vogue: 75 Years of Style*, Georgina Howell (1991)

• Marbles through the hoop: Each person rolls ten marbles from a certain distance and the pair's total of marbles through the hoop are added to their score.

Award a small prize for the highest overall score and penalise the pair with the lowest score points with a forfeit each at forfeit time.

ESTIMATION GAMES Scatter estimation games around the party area for guests to complete as the evening wears on. Let everyone know how many you have set up so they can find them all, and announce the results well before the end of the party. Reward the winner of each competition with a small prize. Examples of estimation games are:
• How many pins are there in this pincushion?
• How many dried peas are there in this glass jar?
• How much does this bucket of apples weigh?
• How long is this coiled piece of rope?

ROUND GAMES In round games there need be no winners or losers – forfeits are optional – but everyone sits in a circle and joins in the fun. Explain the rules of each game clearly and keep the pace brisk.

Twenty questions One player leaves the room while the rest choose a person, animal, place or object for him or her to guess. The player returns and is allowed 20 questions to find the answer. All questions must be answered Yes or No by one person or by the assembled company. Players should begin with general questions such as:

>Is it a person? Yes.
>Is that person a man? Yes.
>Is that person alive? No.

And so on. A player who fails to identify the subject after 20 questions may be asked to pay a forfeit.

The traveller's alphabet The first player in the circle says *I'm going to Athens* (or Amsterdam, or any other place beginning with A). The player to the left of the first player inquires *What will you do there?* All verbs, adjectives and nouns in the reply must begin with A. The second player takes the letter B, the third player C, and so on through the alphabet and round the circle. Some examples:

>First player: *I'm going to Athens.*
>Second player: *What will you do there?*
>First player: *Acquire ancient antiques.*
>Second player: *I'm going to Budapest.*
>Third player: *What will you do there?*
>Second player: *Bath beautiful babies.*

And so on. A player who gets stuck may have to pay a forfeit.

CHARADES The traditional charade probably originated in France during the 18th century. It consisted of splitting a word into syllables and hiding them in a riddle; for example, if the word is *Turkey*:

>My first is a Tartar (*Turk*)
>My second a letter (*e*)
>My all is a country (*Turkey*)
>No Christmas dish better (*turkey*)

PLAYING CARD TABLECLOTH
Recreate a 1930s bridge afternoon tea cloth. Bind the edges of a plain cream cloth with deep scarlet fabric and make napkin pockets for the corners.

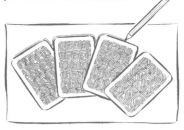

1. Make a paper pattern by drawing around the shape formed by four overlapping playing cards.

2. Use the pattern to cut out the shape four times, leaving a good seam allowance. Nick the seam allowance here and there for a less bulky fold-over.

3. Embroider satin stitch spades, diamonds, clubs and hearts as shown, and outline the edges of the card shapes with red stitching. Turn down and oversew the edges and stitch the sides and bottoms to the corners of the cloth to make the napkin pockets.

4. Make matching napkins with an embroidered motif in each corner and a contrasting border like that on the cloth.

Later, charades were played in teams with each group acting brief scenes, in which the syllables in turn and then the whole word was concealed in the dialogue.

'The Game' In the United States, a form of charades called 'The Game' became immensely popular in the 1930s, and again after World War II. The Game requires two teams. Each team member mimes to his or her colleagues the proverb, the book, song, play or film title, the familiar quotation, and so on, set by the other team. No talking is permitted, and there is a time limit on the period for identifying the correct answer. Players use conventional signs, such as hands together with palms flat to indicate a book title and fingers raised to indicate the number of words.

Sheet music was much in demand at parties, with guests gathering around the piano to give enthusiastic performances of the popular songs of the day.

CARD GAMES Card games were enormously popular between 1850 and 1950, in particular whist and bridge. Originating as a game for the lower classes, whist became a favourite with gentlemen in London's coffeehouses early in the 18th century. Bridge whist supplanted it in the 1890s, and this game developed into auction bridge around 1900. Between 1925 and 1926, New Yorker Harold S. Vanderbilt further refined auction bridge into contract bridge; it quickly spread all over the world. Playing bridge was a social skill that brought many people together in their leisure time.

Bridge parties So passionately devoted to bridge did some people become that bridge parties became all the rage. Refreshments could be lavish and always included 'bridge rolls', which were small rolls of soft white bread with various savoury fillings – an early form of finger food. On 1 December 1930 the *Australian Home Budget* ran a piece encouraging bridge hostesses to have a 'bridge room' tricked out with playing card motifs on cushions, lampshades, tablecloths and napkins.

Always put playing cards away carefully in their box or packet: once one card is bent or damaged in any way the whole pack is ruined, because keen-eyed players can identify individual cards from the damage. The surfaces of playing cards become sticky with frequent use and they are hard to play with if they do not slide over one another easily. To clean playing cards, rub them gently with chunks of white bread, discarding the bread as soon as it becomes grimy. Sprinkle the cards with French chalk on both sides when they are clean.

SINGING AND DANCING Many autobiographical accounts of the period mention dancing, music and singsongs as an integral part of home entertainment. People who played instruments gathered together for impromptu concerts. Everybody sang. Those with 'a voice' performed tuneful solos; others joined in unison round the piano or pianola. Their repertoire included hymns; popular songs and music hall ditties issued on sheet music, such as 'Take a pair of sparkling eyes', 'Just a song at twilight', 'My old man said follow the van' and 'Ta-ra-ra-boom-de-ay'; airs from Sir W. S. Gilbert (1836–1911) and Sir Arthur Sullivan's (1842–1911) operettas and other ballad operas; or the patriotic numbers of World War I, which included 'Roses of Picardy' and 'There's a Long Long Trail A-winding'. Wireless spread familiar tunes. Children were also encouraged to play, sing or recite at parties, and spent hours perfecting their 'party pieces'.

Cross the gypsy's palm

BETWEEN 1850 AND 1950, PEOPLE WERE NO
LESS CURIOUS ABOUT THEIR FUTURES THAN
THEY ARE NOW.

Count Louis Hamon (1886–1936), known as 'Cheiro', was
perhaps the most influential and popular seer of the 20th century:
European royalty, presidents and leaders of commerce consulted
him. Humbler practitioners operated more light-heartedly in
private homes and at fetes and bazaars. Fortunes were predicted
from symbolic objects such as playing cards or tea leaves, and
palmistry was a means of analysing character.

*Two of the best known cards from
the tarot deck, The Fool and
Death – the Death card is not
always as sinister as it appears.*

THE TAROT In their fortune telling form, tarot cards first appeared
in Italy in the late 14th century. Today's standard tarot deck has
78 cards, divided into two groups, which are shuffled and laid out in
'spreads' to be read. The major arcana has 22 picture cards, numbered
from I to XXI (the Fool bears no number), and representing forces,
characters, virtues and vices. Major arcana cards reveal spiritual
matters and important trends in the questioner's life. The 56-card
minor arcana is the forerunner of our modern deck of playing cards.
Each suit has four court cards and ten numbered cards. Swords (spades)
tell of power and conflict; cups (hearts) of love and emotions; coins,
pentacles or disks (diamonds) of material matters; and wands, batons
or rods (clubs) of business matters and career ambitions.

IN YOUR CUPS Fortune telling from tea leaves is quite easy to learn.
Use plain cups; patterned ones make it difficult to see how the leaves
lie. The fortune seeker drinks the tea to the last teaspoonful, holds the
cup in the right hand and swirls the dregs three times (men clockwise,
women anti-clockwise), pours the liquid away gently and upends the
cup in the saucer. The fortune teller reads from the top of the cup.

Books such as *Joan's Dream Book and Tea Cup Reader,* published in
Melbourne in 1912, give full lists of how to interpret the various
symbols – acorn, altar, and so on through the alphabet. Long straight
lines are for good fortune, curved and wavy ones suggest the opposite.
Rings foretell engagements and marriages. Triangles, horseshoes,
animals, crowns and the figure seven are signs of good luck.

HANDS UP According to *Helen's Weekly* on 20 October 1927, 'The lines
of your hands, combined with the conformation and characteristics of
your fingers ... will give an indication of your outstanding qualities –
your failings and virtues'. Whether the hands can reveal the future is
debatable, but they can reveal much about character. Open hands
suggest a frank, generous spirit; closed fists mark the opposite.
Fidgety hands denote undisciplined emotions. Hands clasped behind
the back show caution and fair-mindedness.

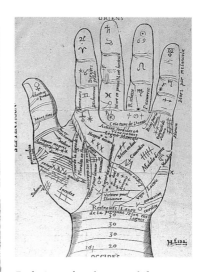

*Palmistry has been used for
centuries to reveal character and
predict fortune. This scheme was
drawn by Jean Belot, a French
chiromancer, in 1611.*

343

Beside the seaside

THE VAST PLAYGROUND BY THE SEA
HAS BEEN APPRECIATED BY DIFFERENT
GENERATIONS IN DIFFERENT WAYS.

For our Victorian forebears, constrained by questions of
modesty in regard to beachwear, it was a fine place to stroll,
take the air and perhaps collect shells. Many had faith in the
supposed curative powers of sea water, and so took to the sea
clad in neck-to-knee costumes. Later generations insisted on
more freedom, and sun, sand and saltwater became the stuff of
countless summer days. As well as enjoying the pleasures of
swimming and surfing, follow some of the good old ways of
recreating the simple joys of an era when beaches were far less
crowded but no less inviting.

*Drawn in 1918, this cartoon
contrasts an up-to-the-minute
bathing suit with more modest
prewar beachwear.*

SAND BUILDING Sand sculptures and sand modelling were popular in
the 1920s, with highly skilled sand artists plying their craft on
beaches for the appreciation of summer crowds. Using only sand and
seawater, they created life-sized sea nymphs and fantastic castles.

Sand mountains and castles Build a tall mountain encircled
by a steep winding track that travels around and around the
mountainside until it reaches
ground level. The mountain
should be made of well dampened
sand; pat thoroughly with the flat
of a spade as you build. A small,
light rubber ball set at the top of
the spiralling track should travel
downwards to the bottom of the
mountain.

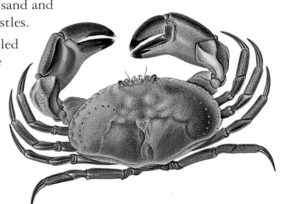

Buckets of slightly damp sand, upended
on a foundation mound of sand, will form
the towers and turrets of a castle.
Surround with a wall of sand and dig a
moat. Decorate the castle grounds with
treasures gathered along the shore. Use
pieces of broken shell to pave paths and
border miniature ponds, and make a garden of
coloured seaweed and driftwood.

Sculptures Using only damp sand, you can build up a relief
sculpture on the beach. Remove the dry top sand and smooth flat the
slightly damp sand beneath. Using damp sand, form the basic shape
of your subject – a turtle, for example, might start as an oval mound
20–30 cm high. Add features such as legs and head, then use your
hands or an ice block stick to sculpt other details and markings onto

the surface. Moisten sand as necessary. Use shells, seaweed and sticks to add texture and colour.

Dams and canals There is much fun to be had creating 'irrigation works' that are filled, and eventually swamped, by the incoming tide. Choose a time when the tide is low but coming in. Dig a shallow basin with a canal running down to the water's edge. Soon this will surge with water running into your dam. Boats of bark or large leaves can be floated on the pool and walls of sand built up on the land side to retain the waters as long as possible.

SUN SENSE Although knowledge of the dangers of the sun to the skin were not as well recognised in times past, as early as 1917 *The Australian Woman's Weekly* cautioned against overexposure and warned of the harm resulting from sunburn. It advised readers to use 'liquid powder' and hats with gauze scarves to protect the skin, 'just as armour will protect the body.' Young children should always wear shady hats as well as sunscreen when on the sands during the day.

Simple beach tent With a sheet or blanket and a pole (a discarded broom handle is ideal) you can make a sun-screening tent that the younger members of your party will take to like a cubbyhouse. Mark out a circle up to 2 metres in diameter and dig into the sands to a depth of 60–80 cm. Build up the excavated sand all around the hole like a wall, except in one part, which will act as the doorway of the tent. Next, push the pole down into the centre of the dug out area. Toss the sheet over the pole and spread the edges all around the top of the sand wall. Pile the sand on all along the border to hold the sheet well in place. You will find there is a surprising amount of room in the tent. On a quiet beach you may be able to use the same hole for several days, provided you position it beyond the reach of the tide.

ROCK POOLS A clear plastic bowl or container placed carefully on the surface of the water will remove ripples, reflections and distortions and allow you to look directly into the magical underwater world of the rock pool. Do not interfere with any living creatures in the pool.

SEASIDE SOUVENIRS Collecting shells has always been a favourite seaside activity, but these days is discouraged as it removes a part of the natural environment. You should never take a shell that is still being used, whether by its maker or by some other creature. However, for the sharp-eyed, there are many other treasures to be had. The attraction of sun-bleached driftwood has long been recognised. Even items discarded or lost from boats and piers can take on added charm when smoothed by the sea. Dried seaweed can be used in the same way as pressed flowers. Many seaside plants can be treated as everlastings. Gather a small bunch and dry them slowly out of the sun.
Caution: Do not remove vegetation from dunes and remember that all flora and fauna are protected in national parks.

A VERSATILE BEACH TOWEL
This simple way of using your beach towel to carry belongings for a day at the seaside was suggested in a 1930s magazine.

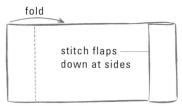

1. Turn in the ends of a large beach towel, and sew at the sides to form two large pockets.

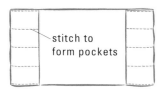

2. Stitch the flaps down at intervals to form a number of smaller pockets to hold beach needs such as sandals, bathing cap and sunscreen.

3. Wear the towel over your shoulders as a wrap, or carry it over your arm.

Going to the fair

IN OUR GRANDPARENTS' DAY, LOCAL COMMUNITIES
OFTEN ORGANISED SPECIAL EVENTS TO RAISE MONEY
FOR DESERVING LOCAL GROUPS.

These days, despite government grants and welfare payments, there
are always worthwhile projects that will founder without a little help
from the public. A fete or jumble sale can raise a bit of cash and unite
a community in a common cause, and the hours of hard work can
promote enduring friendships. Local businesses will often contribute
by donating small items as prizes.
Caution: Check with local authorities before embarking on a
community fundraising activity; you must comply with health and
safety requirements and the regulations governing games of chance.

PLANNING The great thing when putting on a full-scale community
event is to persuade enough helpers to run the attractions, including
serving refreshments. Position sideshows so that they have maximum
appeal and are safe. Signpost toilet and first aid facilities, and provide
plenty of litter bins and parking space (if possible!). Make sure you
have an adequate 'float' – a supply of small change.

FETES These old-fashioned fundraisers still have plenty of appeal.
People will pay to shy at coconuts, guess the weight of a
cake and enter their animals in a Cute Pets competition.

Fishy business A fish pond is quite simple to prepare,
and will delight young and old alike. From tin cans, cut
about 50 fish shapes and some 'useless' things – boots,
crabs, starfish and so on. Sink the tin 'catch' in a large tub
filled with water made opaque with washing blue and
make fishing lines from rods with magnets suspended
from cords. Allow each competitor three minutes to fish.
Useless things do not count and must be thrown back.
Securing a crab means forfeiting two fish. The best catch
in each round wins a prize.

GARDEN GYMKHANAS These are easier to organise than
fetes and are still a fun way to raise modest amounts of
money. Charge a small entry fee for each event. Each race
must have a supervisor, and the winners receive prizes.

Obstacle race This is a race for couples and needs plenty
of space. Set up a course of chairs or skittles. Blindfold the
men and tie strings to their arms to act as reins. The
women then 'drive' the men round the course through the
obstacles. Contestants who touch a chair or knock over a
skittle must go back to the start.

Think about how your customers will
take their purchases away: you can
save money, minimise mess and
contribute to the recycling movement
by using newspaper and preloved
plastic bags for wrapping.

*Fetes have long been used to raise
money for charitable causes and
are an enjoyable way for
community members to get together.*

The Way We Were

The Bathurst people are wild about bazaars just now. The Roman Catholics had one last week to help pay for the building of their new chapel, a lofty red-brick building faced with white, which quite overtops the church. One of Amy's servants went to the bazaar, and came back in a state of great delight and excitement, carrying an enormous doll which she had won in a raffle for 2s. 6d.; the price of the doll was £3. She was dressed as a bride, in white tarlatan, hooped petticoat, veil and wreath of orange flowers, and was so large that she would require to be kept in a good-sized box all to herself.

– *THE LETTERS OF RACHEL HENNING* (1853–1882)

Bun race Stretch a wire or a string between two poles, about 2.5 metres above the ground. Hang a row of buns along it on strings about 75 cm long. The first person to consume a bun is the winner.

Tortoise race This race is suitable for the elderly as well as the young and fit. Mark out a large circle on the lawn and place a chair at one point. A marker stands in the centre of the circle, wearing a blindfold and holding a flag. The contestants walk slowly round the circle, touching the chair as they pass. When the marker raises the flag, all must stop. The contestant who is touching the chair at that moment receives the prize.

JUMBLE SALES Jumble sales can be excellent fundraisers and they are also a good way to 'recycle' various household objects, but their success depends on efficient organisation. Encourage people to deliver clean merchandise in reasonable condition to collection points well in advance of the sale date, and then sort it into categories and mark each item with a price and a size (if applicable), and with other details, such as 'one of a pair' or 'no matching saucer'. Throw out anything that is broken or very worn.

Displaying your wares Each display table or rack should have a theme; for example, *KITCHENWARE, BABY CLOTHES, GARDEN BARGAINS*. Do not heap too many items in a restricted space; it is better to display one or two of the better items prominently at each stall, replacing each as it is sold with another such item.

Is the price right? Do not be too strict about pricing. Bargain-hunters enjoy beating the price down, and a slight price reduction or the offer of 'two for the price of one' may move stock. Towards closing time, offer the goods at a stated price and gradually lower the price until you have a buyer.

LIKE MOTHER USED TO MAKE A trestle stall offering home-made sweets, cakes and jams outside your local church or school is a sure-fire way of raising a small but steady supply of funds. Set out your wares attractively and aim to sell everything. Produce should be hygienically wrapped and clearly labelled, and preserves should show the date bottled.

Games of strength and skill, such as the 'striker' machine, have been a feature of country fairs and shows for decades, and cooking competitions have always provided a showcase for home cooks.

347

Most sincerely yours

LETTER WRITING HAS A PERSONAL WARMTH THAT
NO ELECTRONIC COMMUNICATION CAN MATCH.

In 1840, British tax reformer Rowland Hill introduced the
revolutionary pre-paid postal system (a penny for each half ounce) into
Britain. The famous 'penny post' boosted mail circulation, and by the
end of the 19th century there were 12 postal deliveries a day in
London! It was Hill's vision 'that every house might be
provided with a box into which the carrier would drop
the letters'. The system quickly caught on in other
countries; Switzerland and Brazil adopted it in 1843,
and France in 1849.

SHOWING YOU CARE Letters proliferated as literacy
increased. Travellers and emigrants described their new
lives, and soldiers and medical personnel wrote from war
fronts. Two innovations threatened letter writing: in 1869,
Austria introduced the postcard, an inexpensive and
undemanding form of correspondence that soon became
immensely popular; and in 1878, the world's first telephone exchange
opened in New Haven, Connecticut, with 50 subscribers. By 1880,
there were 61 000 telephones in the United States, and by 1900 there
were 1.4 million.

Why write a letter? In 1920, *The Australian Woman's Weekly*
commented that 'there are many occasions where nothing can take the
place of a letter' and that 'after any special mark of hospitality … a
short letter of appreciation should always be sent.' Letters of thanks
should be handwritten. They need not be long, but they should
highlight some aspect of the occasion, the gift or the favour.

INVITATIONS Telephoned invitations have largely replaced the note
inviting you for a meal or a visit. But if you do receive a written
invitation, reply in the same way, and in handwriting. Whether you
are accepting or declining, repeat the day, date and time of the
invitation to avoid confusion. If you cannot accept, it is good manners
to give the reason; for example, 'I am so sorry that I cannot come, but
I have promised to attend my sister's party that evening'.

Weddings A formal wedding is one occasion that requires a formal
answer to an invitation. Traditionally, the bride's parents send out the
invitations, including those to the bridegroom's family and friends.
Invitations used to be engraved on quality paper, but nowadays many
people use computers to produce their own. Invitations are usually
sent out four weeks before the wedding. Reply as soon as you can in
handwriting, using the third person and copying the wording and
setting out of the invitation.

Now a collector's item, the Penny Black was the first postal stamp to grace a letter.

AN AUSTRALIAN LETTER
I had written him a letter
   which I had, for want of better
Knowledge, sent to where I met him
   down the Lachlan, years ago,
He was shearing when I knew him,
   so I sent the letter to him,
Just 'on spec', addressed as follows:
   'Clancy, of the Overflow'.
And the answer came directed
   in a writing unexpected,
(And I think the same was written
   with a thumbnail dipped in tar).
'Twas his shearing mate who wrote it,
   and *verbatim* I will quote it:
'Clancy's gone to Queensland droving,
   and we don't know where he are.'
– *CLANCY OF THE OVERFLOW*,
'BANJO' PATERSON (1864–1941)

LOVE LETTERS The Victorians were a sentimental lot, and among their favourite occupations were writing love letters, affectionate inscriptions in autograph albums and St Valentine's Day cards. Young men contributed love messages coded in riddles for girls to transcribe into treasured keepsake albums. St Valentine's day cards were often hand-painted or decorated with pressed flowers; because they were traditionally unsigned, they provided a chance to express devotion without violating the strict Victorian code of etiquette.

OTHER PEOPLE'S LETTERS Even if you seldom write personal letters yourself, sample some of the published collections of correspondence written between 1850 and 1950; they provide intimate portraits of the writers and fascinating accounts of the times.

Letters Home 1939–45, collected and edited by Lurline Stuart and Josie Arnold, consists of extracts from the correspondence of Australians who served in World War II. This collection offers a broad social history of Australian experiences in the various theatres of war.

Much of the most interesting and memorable correspondence is exchanged between close relatives who are separated. *The Letters of Rachel Henning* is a collection of evocative letters about the minutiae of daily life written by Rachel in Australia to her family in England between 1853 and 1882.

The art of letter writing suffered a blow with the invention of the telephone. This early Ericsson model with switchboard was made for Lord Rothschild.

A letter handwritten with a fountain pen is a pleasure to receive – and to write.

On the air

Radio was the first mass medium that had the power to reach people instantaneously, and it had an enormous effect on the world in our grandparents' time. Radio was pioneered in the 1890s by Italian Guglielmo Marconi and Englishman Sir Oliver Lodge. The Marconi Wireless Telegraph Company was set up in 1900, but speech could not be transmitted until 1914. World War I gave an impetus to the development of the technology, as powerful transmitters and receivers emerged for field headquarters and trenches, and planes were equipped with radio sets.

In the United States radio was fully commercial, in the Soviet Union it was fully state regulated, and in other places it was a mixture of both. At first in England there was resistance from the press to the broadcasting of news, and news was broadcast only after 7 pm.

Radio became a friend to many, and in Britain the BBC might be asked the test score, to find a lost dog, or to help someone in distress.

A FIRST FOR RADIO
At 6.30 am on 20 November 1947, thousands of Americans – including the milkman – tuned into the radio to listen avidly to the broadcast from London of the wedding of Princess Elizabeth and Prince Philip.

YOUR ATTENTION, PLEASE
During the Depression, and then in World War II, radio became a powerful political force; before then, newspapers were the only source of news. From 1933, President Roosevelt spoke directly to the people in his 'fireside chats'; Prime Minister Winston Churchill used radio for his famous rallying speeches in the war; and radio was vital in coordinating the invasion of D-Day. In the London Blitz, when a bomb fell on Broadcasting House during the news, the reader paused but did not react on air for security reasons.

A FAMOUS HOAX

In 1938, Orson Welles (right) broadcast a play, *The War of the Worlds*, as a series of news reports claiming that the Martians were invading the world. Thousands panicked; some even left home, taking their furniture.

NOISES OFF

For many radio programs, sound effects were made in the studio. The BBC had an effects studio with a big bath, electric motors, a huge thunder sheet made of a sheet of iron, and a big drum with a pound of potatoes inside it to simulate the sound of an avalanche. Train noises were made by a large roller skate on a tin bath with rivets in it.

Have fun writing a simple script and recording your own radio play on a cassette tape, incorporating the sound effects demonstrated below.

A bash on the head: Whack a cabbage with a wooden stick and make appropriate noises.

Thunder: Vibrate a sheet of flexible tin.

Fire: Crumple cellophane paper with your fist.

Pistol shot: Thwack the seat of a chair with a cane.

WILL HE WIN?

By 1929 it was possible for wife of boxer Phil Scott to listen to a radio commentary on her husband's performance in a fight broadcast on UK Radio 2LO.

LISTENING IN

After World War I there was a huge popular interest in amateur radio. These New York boys are pictured in 1921 tuning in to a crystal set, which needed earphones and worked without batteries or other power sources.

Playing the game

I N Y E A R S G O N E B Y , F A M I L Y A N D C O M M U N I T Y
G A T H E R I N G S V E R Y O F T E N F E A T U R E D
A M A T E U R S P O R T S .

The point was not to win but to have fun, and participants
often collapsed on the sidelines with laughter. Hopping,
skipping or running backwards were common race
variations, and many events could be run as either a race for
individuals or a relay. Comical races and team games can
still be a feature of social gatherings such as picnics and
money-making efforts such as fetes.

ORGANISING THE GAMES For maximum enjoyment you
need some simple equipment – a pile of sacks for the sack
race, spoons and hardboiled eggs for the egg and spoon race,
and scarves for the three-legged race. Provide amusing but
inexpensive prizes for the winners and wooden spoons for
those who come in last.

*In the past, potato sacks, wool
bales and sugar bags were used
for the sack race.*

Egg and spoon races Competitors must run the course
carrying hardboiled eggs in soup spoons. If this race is run as a relay,
each runner must transfer the egg to the next runner in the team's
spoon without touching it.

Three-legged races Pairs of competitors stand side by side with
their inside legs tied together. Thus handicapped, they can compete in
running, hopping and jumping races.

Sack races Competitors line up with folded sacks at their feet. At the
starting signal, contestants clamber into their sacks and jump or
shuffle towards the finishing line.

Stepping stones Each participant has two pieces of cardboard about
30 cm square. The object is to complete the course with one foot or
the other always on one of the pieces of cardboard. Anyone who
touches anything apart from the two 'stepping stones' must go back to
the start. A variation is to have pairs of contestants, one moving the
cardboard for the other – played this way, the game was known as the
Walter Raleigh race, because the males were usually detailed to
provide stepping stones for their female partners.

'Tipped you last' One player touches another, then runs away,
shouting *Tipped you last!* The tipped player must catch and tip
another, who then takes on the role of pursuer.

Lucky spot contest At the beginning of the proceedings, announce
that there is a lucky spot in the playing area. Show competitors where
the spot is, and explain that later, on a given signal, the player on, or
closest to the spot will win a prize. Timing is important: delay the
signal until near the end of the gathering in order to sustain interest.

Save money and time by using small
potatoes instead of hard-boiled eggs in
the egg and spoon race.

Happy travelling

BETWEEN 1850 AND 1950 THE WORLD WITNESSED A
TRANSPORT REVOLUTION THAT GREATLY AFFECTED
THE WAY PEOPLE SPENT THEIR LEISURE TIME.

Popular names for the newer forms of transport, such as the iron horse
(the steam engine) and the horseless carriage (the motor car), reflected
the dominant means of travel in previous eras. Automated travel
began in 1830, when passenger trains burst upon the world, and by
1950 cars had shaped a new way of living.

TRAIN TRAVEL The wealthy could afford to make exotic train journeys
through many lands: the famous Orient Express, which ran between
Paris and Constantinople (Istanbul) from 1883 to 1977, except during
the two World Wars, was the ultimate in luxury travel.

But trains also enabled the less privileged to experience the pleasures
of an annual summer break at the beach or in the country for the first
time. The first 'packaged' rail excursion took place in 1841, when
Thomas Cook persuaded one of the British railway companies to
schedule a special train for a temperance meeting. The return trip of
24 miles (38.5 km) included tea, ham sandwiches, dancing and games.
By 1855, Cook was organising excursions to the Paris Exposition, and
the following year he conducted his first Grand Tour of Europe.

Train travel with baby Travelling with an infant is no less difficult
now than it was all those years ago. Whenever possible, advised the
old-time experts, time a journey to fit in with the baby's routine so
that the child can be fed and put to sleep just as the journey starts –
preferably on the seat, wrapped in familiar bedding, and not in your
arms. Small children suffer more from excitement, lack of rest and
overeating than they do from travelling itself: do not dance the child
about and point out the sights or offer extra food.

OCEAN TRAVEL By the 1930s, sea cruises were no longer
a holiday option confined to the wealthy. Books and
magazines of the time were crammed with advice on
packing, dressing, shipboard entertainment,
shipboard social life, travel insurance and tipping.

A sea cruise is still a popular holiday choice.
Now, as then, games such as deck quoits and
golf occupy the daylight hours and evening
entertainment consists of dances and cabarets.

Tips for passengers Some tips from the early 20th
century on sea travel now seem quaint; others are still
valid, and most apply to any method of travel.
• Take a small torch with you – it can be handy for finding
anything that rolls away under a seat or a bunk.
• Cabin luggage, or hand luggage for train and plane travel, should

*The ocean-going liner was once
the last word in transcontinental
travel, with luxurious living
quarters and public rooms – at
least for passengers who could
afford the first-class fares.*

*Duryea's 1893 Motor Wagon,
with its huge, narrow-rimmed
wheels and sleek, sporty look, was
a fine example of the 'horseless
carriage' that was soon to bring
about a transport revolution.*

contain only what you will be needing during the journey. And take a strong plastic bag for soiled linen.

- Put distinctive stickers on all pieces of luggage so that you can easily pick them out from a pile of suitcases on a wharf, a railway platform or an airport carousel.
- All forms of transport are subject to unpredictable turbulence; do not leave anything on a shelf or ledge.

MOTORING The invention of the motor car was one of the greatest agents for change in the 20th century. Two German pioneers, Karl Benz and Gottlieb Daimler, launched the first two working cars in 1885–86. To quote W. Howard Lewis, who co-founded the Australian Tarrant Motor Company in 1897, motors and motorists became 'the topical butts of every stage comedian's witticisms, when only the daring rode as passengers in the horseless buggies and only – in the public mind – the suicidally impelled drove them.'

But progress towards more efficient and inexpensive machines was swift. In 1907 *The Red Funnel* opined: 'Up to the present time the motor car has practically remained the toy of the wealthy. This, however, will probably not long remain the case. Like the bicycle, which not so long ago was a luxury, but which is now an everyday necessity of many working men ... the motor car is destined to serve the needs of the masses at no distant date.'

'I will build a motor car for the great multitude,' declared Henry Ford (1863–1947), and in 1908 the first mass-produced car, the Model T Ford, rolled off the assembly line (itself a manufacturing innovation). At that time the Model T cost $US950.

After 1910, motorists the world over were asked to pay taxes – registration, insurance, sales tax, petrol tax and licence fees – to finance the building and maintainence of new roads, and also as a general source of government revenue. The age of motoring was upon us, and the Sunday drive became a favourite leisure pursuit.

Motor touring Bertha Benz made the first motor tour in Germany in 1888, when she took her children to visit relatives in a car built by her husband, Karl. The patrons of an inn where the party stopped had an argument about whether the automobile was powered by clockwork or by some supernatural force.

'With a decent car and an ample supply of petrol, distance is eaten up and the holiday maker may get as far as he wishes from the Madding Crowd,' declared *Helen's Weekly* in 1927. In those days the roads were not congested and cars moved very slowly by modern standards. Most touring tips from the good old days do not apply to today's frenetic pace, but there is one that does: don't keep children in the car for too long – it tires them out and makes them fractious.

Trains made excursions to the seaside more affordable.

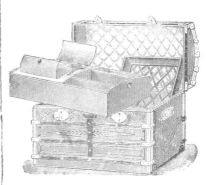

Packing for an extended sea journey once meant filling a cabin trunk, which was larger and more durable than a suitcase.

Before buffet cars and fast-food outlets, people would often take a picnic-style meal to stay the pangs of hunger on train and motor trips. Take a leaf out of their book and do the same: you will save money and ensure sensible nutrition.

Under canvas

GENERATIONS HAVE DISCOVERED THE
SIMPLE JOYS OF SLEEPING UNDER CANVAS
AND COOKING OVER AN OPEN FIRE.

Camping is still one of the least expensive alternatives for a family holiday.

There are many reasons for the enduring appeal of the camping holiday: the satisfaction of living with nature; the conversation, songs and laughter around the campfire; and, after a well earned sleep, the thrill of rising at dawn to another day of freedom.

GETTING THERE In earlier times campers hiked to their destinations, but by the 1920s the motor car had made bush camping grounds more accessible. The basic equipment remains the same – a tent, sleeping bags and cooking gear – but having a car to cart your paraphernalia allows you the luxury of at least a few fold-up chairs. Nonetheless, cut down what you take to the bare bone. Making do is part of the fun!

Some essentials No matter where you plan to pitch your tent, these will come in very handy:

- Matches in a watertight container
- Torch and a spare globe and battery
- Whistle on a cord
- First aid kit – always carry one, even if you are only taking a short stroll from the main camp

HITTING THE TRACK Plan to camp at existing campsites. Tell someone of your route and your expected time of return, and let them know when you get back.

CHOOSING THE CAMPSITE Select a campsite early, so that everything is organised before nightfall. Today most national parks have campsites with water and fireplaces; otherwise, camp at a previously used site to limit environmental damage, or on sandy or hard soil, rather than grass.

Shelter In cold weather a few bushes sheltering the site from the wind can make several degrees difference in the temperature – find the place where the bushes are least disturbed by the breeze.

Where not to camp Do not camp close to bushes, where insects are likely to be more plentiful. Do not camp under dead trees; they may shed branches. Do not camp in a place that will become a watercourse if it rains, or on a hilltop where the tent will take the full brunt of the wind – a hillock in a hollow is the ideal. Pitch the tent on level ground with its back to the wind and upwind from the campfire.

SLEEPING OUT You can camp without a tent, even in winter, provided the weather conditions are dry – all you need is a waterproof ground sheet, a sleeping bag and a little expertise.

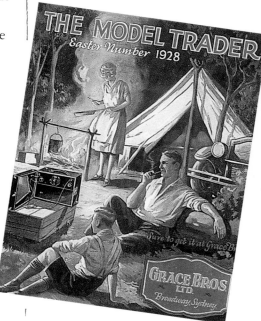

Choose your campsite carefully – it can have a profound effect upon your enjoyment of your holiday.

Make sure there are no sticks, roots or pebbles where you plan to lie. Make a base of grass and leaves to insulate you against cold from the ground, or use layers of newspaper. Place the ground sheet over the 'bush mattress'. Boots placed toe to toe or a smooth flat rock padded with clothing will suffice as a pillow.

Shake your sleeping bag well to fluff up the filling. Draw your bag together at the top to stop warm air escaping; hooded bags will also keep your head warm. If you do not have a hooded bag, wear a woolly hat or wrap a towel or some spare clothing around your head. Eat a little just before sleeping to give extra warmth. Sleep with your back to the fire. Air your bag in the sun every morning.

THE CAMPFIRE Campfires are now prohibited in many areas, for good reasons: a moment of carelessness can endanger life and property and have a devastating effect on the environment. On the positive side, cooking with a fuel stove is quicker and easier.

Campfire rules If an open fire is permitted, there are a few simple rules. Never light a fire on a hot windy day. Keep the fire small. A site on slightly sloping ground has the advantage that the air is always in motion, so that smoke does not cling to the ground around the fire. Do not build a fire surround with rocks from a watercourse; they are

Part of the fun of camping is cooking over an open fire. A forked stick with sharp prongs can be used to grill meat.

Keep an eye open for small containers to use for food, matches, spare batteries and the like. Film canisters, plastic-lidded coffee tins, lightweight cylinders and lidded tubes that were originally home to effervescent vitamin pills or fruit pastilles can all be happily recycled. Label them clearly. As the years go by, many of these will also come to hold memories.

likely to explode. Clear the ground of loose leaves and twigs in a 2-metre radius before you light up.

Use only dead fallen wood. To set the fire, push three small sticks about 25 cm long into the ground around a small pile of dry leaves or crumpled paper and twigs so they form a small pyramid, then lean more sticks and twigs over this.

Camp cooking Take particular care with food and cooking. Burns and scalds from cooking accidents are among the most common of camping injuries and attention to cleanliness will minimise the likelihood of stomach ailments. When planning what to take, think about your likely daily kilojoule needs. Your body needs lots of energy in cold weather, so take extra carbohydrates.

Carrying food Remove foods from paper, cellophane, cardboard and glass packaging and repackage before you leave home. In the days before plastic containers, food was usually carried in small tucker bags, made of the same waterproof fabric as tents, and tied with tapes or string. Such packaging was both lightweight and reusable – an easy option today is sturdy plastic bags.

Stow all your food containers together in a larger sack, like the dilly bag carried by oldtime swaggies, so that all food is accessible in one go. Foods such as butter, jam and honey require screw-top containers. Wrap eggs individually and pack them in the billy; pack soft fruits in a billy or in drinking mugs.

Cooking gear Basic requirements are two billycans, one fitting inside the other, and a frying pan with a short handle (or saw off the handle and in camp use push a stick into the stump) for ease of packing. A cake tin can serve as both plate and cooking utensil. A deep aluminium plate (or a cake tin) placed over the frying pan makes a simple but effective camp oven – place in, and cover with, hot ashes. Scour cooking and eating equipment thoroughly to avoid risk of food poisoning. Keep the inside of your billycan shiny and the exterior black, but touch-clean – any buildup of charcoal makes it slower to boil. Put in a cloth bag before packing.

Boiling the billy A billycan suspended over the fire will boil far more quickly than one resting on a bed of coals. The simplest method is to place a long, stout stick over a rock or pile of stones with the end from which the billycan is to hang positioned over the flames, and hold down the other end of the stick with a heavy rock.

STRIKING CAMP When you depart, leave as little evidence as possible of your presence. If you have used a fire, be absolutely certain that it is out; there should be no steam at all after you have emptied at least two buckets of water on the ashes. Stack any unused wood against a tree. Carry out all rubbish. Allow no pollution to get into the water.

Sometimes camp must be struck in poor weather. Remember that any fabric packed away while still wet is liable to mildew and rot. Air it well as soon as you can before stowing it away for the next trip.

BUSH BED
Emulate the pioneering spirit: build a bush bed like those that Australian stockmen used in the old days if they needed to camp in the same spot for several days.

1. Drive four sturdy forked branches firmly into the ground, forks uppermost. These will be the corner posts.

2. Two long poles form the side supports of the bed. Slide them into either edge of sturdy wheat or chaff bags (you will probably need two), then suspend the poles, with the bags hanging between them, from the forks. Stuff the bags with grass or leaves for warmth and comfort.

Merry Christmas!

IN MANY PARTS OF THE WORLD, CHRISTMAS
IS THE TIME WHEN FAMILIES GATHER TO
REVIEW THE PASSING YEAR.

When we dress a Christmas tree, decorate our homes
with evergreens and exchange gifts, we are keeping
alive traditions that go back thousands of years and are
a glorious mix of pagan and Christian festivities. In
the long northern European winters, the evergreen
was a potent promise that the green of springtime
would return. The Druids of ancient Britain and
France decorated oak trees with fruits and candles
to honour their harvest gods. The custom of
exchanging presents symbolises the gifts of
the three Wise Men to the Christ child.

*A kiss beneath a sprig of mistletoe
is a Christmas tradition.*

CHRISTMAS CARDS Sending Christmas cards is a comparatively recent
innovation, but it has become very much part of Christmas good cheer
and is a simple way to keep in touch with loved ones far away.

Stencilling You can make a number of similar cards in a
simple design of your own with a stencil – the equipment is
not expensive and will serve you year after year. You will need
a few small paintbrushes, a stencil knife, a cutting board,
some oil paints and some thin, tough paper for the stencil
plate: purpose-made stencil paper is available from craft
shops, or use thick tracing paper.

Use the stencil knife to cut holes in the plate in the shape
of the desired design, remembering that blocks of colour are
easier to work with than fine lines. Place the plate over the
blank card and apply colour to the holes, then remove the
plate carefully and allow the design to dry.

DECK THE HALLS Christmas is twice as much fun when some creative
effort goes into the preparations. Even small children can help to make
an Advent calendar, a Christmas wreath and coloured streamers.

Advent calendar In the Christian year, Advent begins on the fourth
Sunday before Christmas, and an Advent calendar is basically a series
of small visual surprises. Paint a Christmas tree on a large sheet of
cardboard and make little decorations of tinsel and coloured paper. As
each day of Advent dawns, stick a new decoration onto the painted
tree, culminating on Christmas Eve with a star or an angel at the top.

Christmas wreath Make a Christmas wreath fragrant with pine, fir
and spices. Inexpensive bases are available from craft shops, or you can
make your own from wire or cane: shape a sheaf of long stems into a
circle and bind it at regular intervals with thin wire, string or ribbon.

*The commercial Christmas
card was the brainchild of Sir
Henry Cole; in 1843 he had
1000 cards printed.*

Decorating materials can include evergreen cuttings, a spray or two from your Christmas tree, or stems from a florist – fir, pine, and eucalypts such as the grey-leafed Argyle apple. Fragrant dried flowers, spices such as cinnamon sticks, dried moss, dried berries and ribbons can also be used. To make the wreath, attach decorating materials of your choice all the way round, using thin wire and floral pins (both from craft shops) and glue.

THE TREE No artificial tree can replace a living pine, which will permeate your whole home with its subtle perfume. Stand the tree as straight as possible in a green-painted tub weighted down with bricks and stones and spread sand or soil over the weights to conceal them.

Trimming the tree In the good old days real candles were placed on the tree, often with drastic consequences; as one 1919 magazine sagely advised: 'Small coloured candles make a dazzling glory, but even if they could be made to stand erect and firm they would still drop wax, and would smoke or even singe the green "needles" on the branches above. Besides, all fir and pine trees readily take fire when dry, because of the resin they contain.' No wonder the magazine suggested safer alternatives such as shiny rosettes, silvery bells and tinselled balls, lacquered spangles and coloured beads.

Traditional decorations Fruits, especially gleaming oranges and frosted apples, are a traditional decoration. To frost an apple, dip it in warm sugar syrup and roll it in coarse sugar. Other traditional trimmings include bundles of cinnamon sticks tied with festive ribbon; pine cones frosted with white paint or highlighted with silver or gold paint and tied with red ribbon; flags; and bags of sweets.

THE CHRISTMAS TABLE Fill a central vase with white or golden flowers in season and place sprays of small-leaved golden variegated holly around the base. A wreath with a candle set in the middle also makes an attractive centrepiece for the Christmas table. Decorate place cards and menu cards with festive motifs, such as a Christmas tree or bells.

Christmas crackers Making your own crackers is very easy, and you can use them to enclose little trinkets, either home made or bought. Silly riddles inside Christmas crackers are an established tradition: if you make your own crackers, why not include some old riddles like these from 1887:

Q *Why is a race-horse like a hotel waiter?*
A Because he runs for cups, plates and steaks.

Q *Why is a plum tart like a bad sovereign?*
A Because it's not currant.

Q *What grows bigger the more you contract it?*
A Debt.

Q *What's worse than raining cats and dogs?*
A Hailing trams.

Q *What's the difference between forms and ceremonies?*
A You sit upon the one, and stand upon the other.

A CHRISTMAS RHYME
Christmas comes but once a year,
And when it comes it brings
good cheer,
A pocket full of money
and a cellar full of beer.
– TRADITIONAL

CHRISTMAS STREAMERS
Old-fashioned Christmas streamers are easy and fun for children to make.

1. Cut a 5-cm strip from the ends of two rolls of crepe paper, one red and one green.

▨ green ☐ red

2. Unroll the strips and join their ends at right angles with a staple or a piece of sticky tape. Fold the green strip down over the red, then the red over the green.

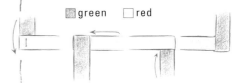

3. Carry on to the ends of the strips. Fasten the ends together and open out your streamer.

Index

A

aches and pains 246
acne and pimples 270
Adam Bede 67
Adamson, Helen Lyion 32
Advent calendars 358
Adventures of Tom Sawyer, The 320
advertisements (game) 340
airing clothes 170
Airy, Anna 99
alcoholic drinks 73
Alcott, Louisa May 183
Alford, Henry 209
Alice's Adventures in Wonderland 316
almond skin cleansers 266
altering garments 175–9
alum 151
aluminium cookware 18
amateur sports 352
American Woman's Home, The 32
anaesthesia 248, 249
Andersen, Hans Christian 335
Anderson, Hugh 117
angels on horseback 5
animal consequences 308
annual house inspection 117
antiseptics 248
ants 30–1
Anzac biscuits 53
apothecary 240
apple crumble 70
apples 70
  harvesting 209
apple sauce 43
aprons 25
arches, garden 220
arms 289
Armstrong, Lawrence 229
arum lilies 203
arnica ointment 237
Arnold, Josie 349
Aronson, Mrs F.B. 163
arrowroot 238
arthritis 234
Art Deco 84–85
Art Nouveau 84–85
Arts and Crafts Movement 84
aspirin 247, 249
astringents and toners 267–8, 270
athelbrose 73
attics and roof spaces 141
Auden, W.H. 65
Australasian cuisine 52–3, 64–5
Australian Baby Book, The 256
Australian Garden Fair, The 206

Australian Home Beautiful, The 86, 104
Australian Home Budget 88, 342
Australian Woman's Mirror, The 22
Australian Woman's Weekly, The 345, 348
Australian Women's Weekly, The 185
Autoviello, Signor Guglielmo 98
avocado and egg hair conditioner 281
awnings, canvas 95–6, 144

B

baby and child care 256–9
baby clothes, washing 157
backache 235–6
back care 289–90
bacon 45
  fat 44
bacteria 248, 249
bad breath 236, 277
baked apples 70
baked eggs 56
baked fish 48–9
baking 59–63
baking soda 107
ball games 302
bamboo 103
bamboo glue brush, making 131
banana peel 29
bands (sewing) 175
barley water 230
bath bags 291
bath mats from bedspreads 178
bath oils 291
bathrooms, cleaning 105, 109
baths 247, 290–1
  bed baths 253
  pain relieving 232–3, 235
bath salts, effervescent 291
bathtubs 122
  and basins 105
batik 174
batter 60
Baudelaire, Charles 90
Bauer, Hermann 164
Bauhaus 84–85
BBC 350-351
beach outings 298, 344–5
beach tent, making 345
beach towel, making 345
beauty care 264–95
Be Beautiful 293
bedbugs 138
bedrooms, cleaning 109
beds 102
  bush, making 357
  invalid 253
bed wetting 256–7
bees 204
Beeton, Mrs Isabella 12, 14, 39, 42, 64–5, 155

Behring, Emil Von 249
Belot, Jean 343
Bennett, H. 16
Benz, Bertha 354
Benz, Karl 354
berets 185
berry fruits 208
beverages 71–3
billy boiling 357
billy tea 334
birdbaths 224
  making 214
bird feeder, making 215
birds 204
  attracting 214–15
biscuits and cakes 61–3
black (colour) 90
blackheads 270
black-out material 166
blankets 158
  edging 152
bleaching 159, 160
blind man's buff 326
blinds 95–6
  veranda 113
blisters 238
blood stains 155
blood transfusion 249
blue (colour) 90
blueing 159
board games 336–7
  equipment 336
  Maori 336
  money making 337
  word 336
Boelter, W.R. 30
boiled beef and carrots 45
boils and carbuncles 236
Bombers and Mash: The Domestic Front 1939–45 178
Book of Cookery and Household Management, Mrs Beeton's 14, 42, 64–5, 155
Book of Good Housekeeping, The 79, 338
Book of Kings, The 46
books
  children's 320–1
  cookery 64–5
  covering 321
borax 156, 285
borders, herbaceous 202
botanical insecticides 199
bran dry-cleaner 168
bran water 166
brass 100, 137
brass bedsteads 104
brass furniture fittings 133
bread 59
bread and butter pudding 58
Bread and Dripping Days: An Australian Growing up in the '20s 335
bread knives 16 bread sauce 43
breakfast 228
breath sweeteners 236, 277
Brett's Gardening Guide 201

Breuer, Marcel 85
brick fireplaces 140
bricklaying 145
bricks 145
Bridge 342
bridge cloth, making 341
bridge rolls 342
Brillat-Savarin, Jean-Anthelme 38, 51, 64
brittle nails 289
Brontë, Charlotte 278
Brontë, Emily 144
brooms and brushes 107
bruises 236–7
brushing hair 279
Budding, Edwin 222
bulbs, garden 196
bunions 238–9
bun race 347
burns and scalds 34, 260
burns on furniture 135
burnt pots and dishes 22
bushwalking 331–2
Busman's Honeymoon 29
butter and cheese 55
buttered rum punch 73
butterflies 204
button keepers 152
buttons 152
button shanks, making 152
Butts, Alfred 336
Byron, Lord 294

C

cabbage 238
cakes and biscuits 61–3
cake stalls 347
calluses and corns 286
cameos 310
Campbell, Ross 16
campfires 356–7
camping 355–7
campsites, choosing 355
candle grease 135
candles, herb 33
cane and bamboo 103
cane furniture 136
canvas 144
carbuncles and boils 236
cardboard and paper, recycling 28, 29
card games 316–17, 342
carpetbag steak 51
carpet sweepers 107
carpets
  cleaning 89
  colour 92
  patching 127
  stair 127
Carroll, Lewis 314, 316
carrot ferns 217–18
carved wood 103, 135
carving knives 17
carving, ornamental 103, 135
cast-iron cookware 18, 22
cats 204, 215
Cat that Walked by Himself, The 335

cauliflower cheese 67
ceilings
  cleaning 110
  plaster 129
cement 131
Chain, Ernst 249
chairs, repairing 132–3
Chandeliers and Billy Tea 13
chapped hands 288
charades 341–2
Chardonnet, Hilaire 151
84 Charing Cross Road 61
Charles I of England 333
chasing games 300
checkers, playing 337
cheese and butter 55
cheese soufflé 57
'Cheiro' *see* fortune telling
chicken 41, 43
chicken broth 250–1
chickenpox 257
chilblains 239
childbirth 248, 249
children, travelling with 353
children's books 320–1
children's clothes, making
  over 177
child's garden 213
chimneys 140–1
china and glassware 15
  broken 34
  storing 23
  washing 21
china glue 131
chin and neck 278
chisels 118
  sharpening 119
chloroform 248, 249
chocolate/cocoa stains 155
cholera 248, 249
chooks *see* poultry
chopping boards 19
Christmas 358–9
Christmas cards 358
Christmas crackers 359
Christmas decorations 358–9
Christmas trees 359
chucks *see* knucklebones
Churchill, Winston 350
Cider with Rosie 159
cistern repairs 122
'Clancy of the Overflow' 348
clapping games 303–4
cleaning
  blinds and awnings 96
  daily and weekly 108–9,
    110
  floors 88–9
  kitchens 13, 15
  lampshades 86–7
  paint and woodwork 76–7
  paintbrushes 79
  wallpaper 81
  windows 95, 96
cleaning agents 107–8
cleaning equipment 106–7
cleansers, facial 266–7
Cleland, J. 293

Cliff, Clarice 85
climbers 196–7
clocks 137
clothes, storage and packing
  170–1
clotheslines 160–1
clothes pegs 161
clothes props 160–1
cloudy ammonia 107
coal fires (for cooking) 24
coat hangers 170
cockroach control 30, 31
cocoa 72
coffee 71–2, 73
coffee pots and teapots 15, 22
coffee stains 155
coin drawings 308
cold frames 206
colds and flu 246–7, 248
cold showers 233
cold sores 237
Cole, E.W. 218
Cole, Sir Henry 358
Coleridge, Samuel Taylor 221
Coles Childland 128
colic 258
Colonial Ballads 117
colour combinations 92
colourfast dyes 151
colours
  to complement hair 283
  in decorating 90–2
  dyeing 172, 174
colour schemes, kitchen 13
companion planting 200
Complete Home Encyclopedia
  121
composting 29
compresses and poultices
  235, 236
concrete, repairing 147
condensation 13, 141
condiments 47
conditioners and shampoos
  279–81
confidence tricks 324
constipation 237
cookery books, past 64–5
cooking 38–73
  camp 357
  for invalids 250–1
cooking utensils 18
cook's knives 16
cool drinks 72–3
Coolgardie safe 25
  improvising 25
copper 100, 137
copper (for washing clothes)
  164
cordons (gardening) 207–8
cork floors 89
corkscrew, emergency 17
corned silverside 45
corns and calluses 286
corrugated iron roofs 146
cosmetic crayons 273
cosmetic gloves 288
cosmetic recipes 264–5

cosmetics industry 272–3
cottage gardens 212–13
cotton 150
  ironing 163
  washing 157
cotton fabric 103
coughing 246
cough mixture 246
counters (board games) 336
*Countrywoman in New South
  Wales, The* 157
Cowper, William 12, 205
crackers, Christmas 359
cracks in furniture 136
cracks in plaster 128–9
cramp 237
crayon marks 76–7
crazy patchwork 180
cream and cucumber skin
  cleanser 266
creamy lavender skin
  moisturiser 268
creosote 141
cretonne and chintz, washing
  166
Crile, George Washington
  249
crop rotation 200
croup 258
cruets 47
crystal 101
cucumber and mint skin toner
  268
Cuffley, Peter 13
cupboard doors 23
cups and mugs, cleaning 21
currants 208
curtains 94–5
  making 94
  recycling 179
  renovating 166–7
  washing 166–7
cushions, cylindrical 179
custards 58
cutlery 16
  fish 48
  storage 23
  washing 20, 22
cut-out dolls 312
cuttings, propagation 192–3

D
Daimler, Gottlieb 354
dairy foods 54–8
daisy chain, making 99
damask 150
damping down ironing
  162–3
dams and canals, sand 345
dandelion leaf tonic 230
dandruff 282
Daniel, Hawthorne 130
dark hair 281
darning 152
Dean, T. 290
decanters
  removing stoppers 137
  washing 21

decoctions, making 265
decor, kitchen 13
delphiniums 209
dents in wooden furniture 134
deportment 294–5
desserts 63, 70
detoxification 234
devilled herrings 50–1
devil's food cake 62–3
De Vries, Leonard 145
Dewar, Sir James 334
diarrhoea 237–8
dibs *see* knucklebones
dice 336–337
diet
  invalid 250–1
  and nutrition 228–9
digging the garden 191
'Dinner, The' 40
diphtheria 249
Diplomate au Kirsch 65
dishcloths, mops and sponges
  20
dishwashers 21
disinfectant, room 252
disklavier 338
distress signals 332
dividing plants 193
dogs 204
dolls clothes, paper 312
dolly mop 22
donkey 316–17
doors
  draught-proofing 141
  repairing 125
Dot and the Kangaroo 321
dots (game) 309
doves and dovecotes 214
drainage 116
  garden 198
  paths and steps 223
drains, blocked 122
draught excluders 141
draught-proofing 141
drawers, repairing 134
*Dr Chase's Recipes; or
  Information for Everybody* 261
*Dr Chase's Third Last and
  Complete Receipt Book and
  Household Physician* 255
drilling ceilings 129
drills 118
drinks 71–3
drunkard's path quilts 181
dry-cleaning 168–9
dry hair 282
dry ingredients, measuring
  26–7
drying washing 160–1
dry skin 267, 269, 271
Duryea's Motor Wagon 353
dusting and vacuuming
  108–9
dyeing curtains 167
dyeing fabrics 172–4
dyes
  fixing 151
  natural 173–4

E

earache 238, 258
eating habits 228–9, 242
Eddy, William 307
efflorescence 145
egg and rosemary shampoo 281
egg and spoon race 352
egg cartons as seed trays 28
egg hair conditioner 281
eggnog 73, 251
eggs 54–8
  for invalids 251
  steamed 251
eggshells 29
  bleaching with 159
  cleaning decanters with 21
eiderdowns 158
elbow patches 176
electrical leads 124
electricity 24, 25, 116, 124, 164
Elias, Eileen 318
Eliot, George 67, 289, 316
Elsie Piddock Skips in her Sleep 304
enamelware 18
  cleaning 22
English and Australian Cookbook, The 64
Enquire Within 34
entertaining, home 338–42
entertainment 298–327
Escoffier, Auguste 53
espaliers 207
estimation games 341
Every Little Boy's Book 298
ether, sulphuric 248, 249
exercise
  and fitness 230, 235–6
  hands 288
  and relaxation 264
  shoulder 290
extra-sensory perception 323
eye baths 275
eyebrows 276
eyelashes 276
eyes
  care of 274–6
  exercises 275
  puffy 276
  sore 276
  tired 275–6

F

fabrics
  curtain 95
  fireproofing 35
  furnishing 103–4
  scraps 178
fabric softener 151
face care 266–71
face cloths from towels 178
face massage 293
face packs 269–70
face powders 272, 273
fair hair 281
family histories 335

Faraday, Michael 124
Farjeon, Eleanor 304
feet 286–7
felt hats 184
Fein, Wilhelm 118
Fence Around the Cuckoo, A 160
fences 147, 219
fetes 346
fig trees 207
file wallets 121
fingernails 288–9
fire extinguishers 35
fireplaces 140–1
fires *see* safety
first aid 260–1
fish 48–51
  baked 251
  canned 50–1
  smoked 49
fish and chips 48
fish cakes 49
Fisher, Alva 165
Fisher, M.F.K. 43, 65, 67
fishy business (game) 346
fitness and exercise 230, 235–6
fivestones *see* knucklebones
flapper, making up as a 273
flashing (roofs) 146
flatulence 242
fleas 139
Fleming, Alexander 248, 249
flies, control of 31, 138
floorboards, repairing 126–7
  staining 89, 127
floor coverings
  kitchen 13
  kitchen safety 35
floors, cleaning 88–9, 109
Florey, Howard 249
flower arranging 97–9
flower press, making 332
flower pyramid, making 98
flowers, picking 209
Flowers of Delight 145
fluorescent lights 124
flyscreens, mending and replacing 144
Food 64
food safes 24, 25
food shopping 39–40
foot care for bushwalkers 331
foot massage 292
foot problems 238–9
Ford, Henry 354
forfeits 339–40
Forgotten Household Crafts 63
forks 16
Fortunes of Richard Mahoney, The 229
fortune telling 343
foundation make-up 271, 272
fox and goose (skipping game) 304
fox (game) 326
Franklin, Benjamin 307

freckles 271
Frederick, C. 39
French knitting 319
French omelette 56
French roll (hair style), making 284
fresh air 229–30
fresheners, herbal 93
friction glove, making 288
frost, bleaching with 160
Frost, Robert 147
frosting glass 137
frothy omelette 56
frozen pipes 123
fruit 207–8
  harvesting 209
fruit face masks 269
fruit fools 70
fruit juice stains 155
frying meats 43
fuller's earth 168
fundraising events 346–7
fungo (game) 302
fungus disease of plants 200
fur, cleaning 168
furniture 102–4
  refinishing 135–6
  restoration 132–6
  veranda 113
fuses 124

G

gadgets, kitchen 15
'Game, The' 342
games
  board 336–7
  children's 300–17
  fundraising 346–7
  outdoor 352
  party *see* party games
  picnic 334
garage sales *see* jumble sales
Garden, The 221
Garden and the Home, The 212
garden arches 220
garden bed edgings 223
gardeners, landscape 202–3
garden frames 196
garden gymkhanas 346–7
gardenias 203
garden paths 223
gardens 188–225
  indoor 216–18
  kitchen 32–3, 212
  knot 211
  natural 202
  ornaments 224–5
  planning 188–9, 202–3
  rock 210
  seating 224–5
  tools 190
  vegetable 32, 204, 312
garden sheds 190
Gardens in Australia 189
garlic 241
gas (power) 24, 116
gates 219, 220
Geissler, Hermann 164

ginger beer 72–3
ginger snaps 62
Girl's Own Book 300
glass
  cleaning 101, 137
  cutting 143
  recycling 29
glass glue 130–1
glassware 15
  broken 34, 130–1
  storing 34
  washing 21
glove paste 288
gloves
  cosmetic 288
  leather 183
  surgical 249
glues and gluing 130–1
Godefroy, Alexandre F. 285
Gone With the Wind 152, 278
Good Housekeeping 21
gooseberries 208
goose flesh 289
grafting 193
Grahame, Kenneth 320
gramophones 327
Grandmother's Household Hints 32
grape vines 208
grass stains 155
grass tree 203
graters 14–15
  nutmeg 47
grease and crayon marks 76–7
grease and oil stains 89
green (colour) 90
greenhouses 205
Gropius, Walter 84
gruel 250
gum arabic 131
gum leaves 209
gum water 157

H

hair
  facial 270–1
  problem 282–3
  thinning 283
hair care 279–83
  for invalids 253
hair dryers 285
hairpieces 284
hairstyles 284–5
halitosis *see* bad breath
Halstead, William 249
Hamon, Count Louis 343
handball 302
hand care 287–9
hand chasings 300
handcuff trick 323
handerchief tricks 314–15
hand lotion, fragrant 288
hand towels 15
Hanff, Helene 61
Han Hsin 306
Happifying Gardening Hobby, The 218

Happy Homes 231
Happy Housewife, The 308, 313
Hargrave, Lawrence 307
Harp in the South, The 142
harvesting 209
hats 184–5
hat trimmings 184, 185
headaches 242, 245
Health 109
health spas 232
health tonics 230
healthy living 228–31
heat marks on furniture 134
heat treatments 243
hedges 219, 220–1
Helen's Weekly 168, 182, 343, 354
hemlines, altering and removing 175
herbaceous borders 202
herbal fresheners 93
herbal medicine 240–1
herbal teas 231, 242
  making 265
herb candles 33
herb lawns 223
herbs
  drying 32–3
  for facial steaming 270
  growing 32–3, 211–12
  and spices 46–7
  storage 47
Herodotus 46
Hestercombe 202
hiker's signs 331
Hill, Rowland 348
Hill's hoist 161
Hippocrates 239
History of Food 64
Home and Garden 21
Home and Garden Beautiful 82, 112, 113, 199
Home and Garden Lovers 90
Home and Health 230
Home Front Family Album, The 177
home maintenance 116–47
honey 240
honey skin moisturiser 268
hoops 298
Hope, A.D. 40
Hope Vase 98
hopscotch 302–3
horseradish 47
hot baths 232–3, 247
Houdini, Harry 323
house exteriors 147
  maintenance 117
Householder's Complete Handbook, The 130
Household Guide or Domestic Cyclopedia, The 110
Household Manual, The 250
Household Pests and Household Remedies 30
Housewife, The 229
housework 106–11

Howell, Georgina 340
How to be Beautiful 290
How to Cook a Wolf 43
How to Repair Furniture 135
How We Lived Then 166
hydrangeas 28
hydrotherapy 232
hygiene 248–9

I
ice chests 24
ice cream, making 65
iced tea and coffee 73
ikebana 97
ills, common 234–9, 242–5
imperial measurements 26
impossible tasks (tricks) 323
indigestion 244
indoor gardens 216–18
'In Flanders Fields' 97
ingrowing toenails 239
ink stains 135, 155
insecticides 30
insect pests 30–1, 138–9, 170, 171
  garden 199–201
insects, beneficial 201
insomnia 230–1
insulation 141
interior decoration 76–113
interior decorating 84–5
interior house maintenance 117
invalid food 250–1
invalid nursing 252–5
invitations, formal 348
In Vogue: 75 Years of Style 340
irises 203
Irish stew 44–5
ironing 162–3
  curtains 167
  pleats 165
ironing board covers 163
irons 164
  cleaning 163
ironware 22

J
jack-in-the-box, making 312
jacks *see* knucklebones
jam roly poly 63
jams and jellies, cooking 69
Jane Eyre 278
Jekyll, Gertrude 202, 203
jellies, fruit 70
jelly bag 69
Jenner, Edward 249
Joan's Dream Book and Tea Cup Reader 343
juice skin toners 268
Jungle Books 320
jumble sales 347
juniper 46
Just So Stories 320

K
Keats, John 73
kedgeree 50

kerosene 108
kick the can (game) 303
Kiddie Songs 259
Kim 320
King Solomon's temple 46
Kipling, Rudyard 320, 335
kitchen gardens 32–3, 212
kitchens 12–35
kitchen scales, improvising 26
kitchen scraps 29
kitchen shears 17
kites 306–7
  bow kite, making 307
Kiwi bread 59
knitting wool, recycling 177
knives 16–17
knot gardens 211
knucklebones 305
Koch, Robert 249
kookaburras 215
Kooka stove 24
'Kubla Khan' 221

L
La Physiologie du Goût 64
Labour-Saving House, The 15
lace, heirloom 157
lace trimming 177
lacquered metal 137
lacquering 135, 136
ladders 147
Ladies' Journal 255
lagging 123
lamb 41, 42, 43
lamb's fry 43
lamingtons 52
lamps 86–7
lampshade making 87
landscape gardeners 202–3
Larousse Encyclopedia 212
Larousse Gastronomique 64
laryngitis 243
lavender and rosemary potpourri 93
lavender wand, making 93
lavender wool wash 157
lawns 222–3
Lawrence, D.H. 44
layering plants 193
leadlighting, repairing 143
leapfrog 301
leather, dry-cleaning 168
leather gloves 183
leather patches 176
leather shoes 182–3
leather upholstery 104
Le Corbusier 84
Lee, Laurie 159
leek and potato soup 66
legs, care of 287
leisure 298–327
lemonade 72, 250
lemon pancakes 60
lemons, harvesting 209
Letters Home 1939–45 349
Letters of Rachel Henning, The 347, 349

Letters to the Rev. J. Newton 12
letter writing 348–9
Lewis, W. Howard 354
'Ligeia' 129
life expectancy 248
light bulbs, changing 124
lighting 86–7
  and colour 92
  for indoor plants 216
  kitchen 13, 35
  workbench 121
Lindsay, Norman 321
linen 150
  ironing 163
  washing 157
lips 277
lipstick 273
lipstick stains 155
liquid ingredients 26–7
Lister, Joseph 248
Little Women 183
locks, stiff 125
  cylinder 125
Lodge, Oliver 350
loganberries 208
Longmate, Norman 166
loose covers 103–4
lotions, wrinkle 269
Lovelace, Richard 281
love letters 349
Lower, Lennie 185
Lucasta 281
lucky spot contest 352
Lutyens, Edwin 202

M
Macbeth 254
Mackintosh, Charles Rennie 84
Maclurcan, Charles 65
Maclurcan, Mrs Hannah 65
Magical Mysteries 324
Magic City, The 313
Magic Pudding, The 321
magic water glass trick 322
magnets 121
magpies 214
Mah Jong 336–7
mahogany 102–3
make-up 271–3
  eye 276
make-up cases 272
mangles 158
manicures 289
manuring 191
marble 101, 304
marking ink (recipe) 150
Marconi, Guglielmo 350
Marconi Wireless Telegraph Company 350
marmalade 69
martini 73
masks, face 269
massage 234, 235, 242–3, 292–3
Maurice, Furnley 259
Mawarra 202
mayonnaise 57–8

McAdoo, Martin 170
McArthur, Kathleen 335
McCrae, John 97
McCullough, Colleen 77
measles 248
measurements
  for cosmetic recipes 265
  recipe 26–7
measuring devices, kitchen
  14, 26
meat 41–5
  cured 45
  grilling meats 43
  scraps 29
  roast 41–3
  stewed 44–5
  stock 45
meat safes 25
medical breakthoughs 248–9
Melba, Dame Nellie 53
mending 152–3
'Mending Wall' 147
menu planning 39
meringues 58
metal fireplaces 140
metal roofs 146
metals
  cleaning 100–1, 137
  lacquering 137
  recycling 28
methylated spirits 108
mildew
  on canvas 144
  on clothes 154–5
  on furniture 135
milk and cream 54
milk jugs, washing 21
Mill on the Floss, The 289,
  316
mincers 43
mint sauce 43
mirrors 83, 101, 137
Mitchell, Margaret 152, 278
mixed drinks 73
mixing games 340
moisturisers 268
money making board game
  337
Monopoly 337
Montez, Lola 295
mops 107
mordants 173
More for Your Money 16
morning sickness 245
Morris, William 85
mortar (bricklaying) 145
mortar and pestle 46
Morton, William 249
moths, clothes 170–1
  repellents 170, 171
motoring 354
mouth care 277–8
mowing 222
Mrs Maclurcan's Cookery Book
  65
mud stains 89
mulled wine 73
mumps 257–8

Murray, Mary 173
musical mystery task 312
muslin curtains, washing
  166–7
mustard poultice 234
My Lady's Journal 268
'My Mother Said' 303
My Mother's Ways 173
My Son, My Son 62
My Summer in a Garden 193

N
nail care 288–9
nail powder 289
nails (fastening devices) 118
nappy rash 259
nasal congestion 244, 246
Nash, Ogden 126
native plants 189
  combining with exotics 203
nature study 332
nausea and vomiting 244–5
neck and chin 278
neck ties 157
Nesbit, Mrs 313
net curtains 166–7
neuralgia 243
New Furniture From Old 136
New Idea, The 311, 314
New System of Domestic Cookery
  Formed Upon Principles of
  Economy, A 283
nosebleeds 261
novelty races 301
Nown, Graham 39
nursing, home 252–5
Nutrition and Health 229, 239
nuts and bolts, removing 133

O
oatmeal 250
  porridge 63
oatmeal cleansers 267
oatmeal water 250
obedient matchbox trick 322
obstacle race 346
ocean cruises 353–4
'Ode to a Nightingale' 73
oil-based fires see fires
oil finishing furniture 136
oil stains on concrete 147
oily hair 283
oily skin 267, 269, 271, 291
ointments, making 238
old fashioned (drink) 73
Old Testament 46
olive oil and honey cleanser
  266
omelettes 56
onions, pickled 68–9
onion soup 66
On Sundays We Wore White 318
orange (colour) 90
orange jelly 251
oranges and lemons (game)
  327
ornamental carving 103, 135
oven temperatures 40

Oxford sausages 44
oysters 51
oyster steak 51

P
Pace, Dorothy 121
packing clothes 171
paintbrushes 78–9
  storage 121
painted walls and woodwork
  cleaning 76–7
painting 77–9
paints, storage 121
paint stains 135
palette knives 17
palmistry 343
panama hats 184
Pan-Cake (make-up) 272
pancakes, lemon 60
paper and cardboard,
  recycling 28, 29
paper beads, making 313
paper glues 131
paper templates for quilts
  180, 181
paper weaving 318–19
parachute, making a paper
  311
parchment lampshades 87
paring knives 16
Park, Ruth 142, 160
parquetry 88
parsley lotion 268
parsley sauce 49
party games
  adult 339–42
  children's 325–7
passionfruit vines 208
pass the parcel 327
paste cleaner 76
Pasteur, Louis 248, 249
pastimes 298–327
pasting wallpaper 80–1
pastry 61
pastry boards 19
patches, leather 176
patch pockets 176
patchwork 180–1
  hexagonal patchwork,
  making 181
Paterson, A.B. ('Banjo') 348
paths, garden 223
patinas on furniture 135
paving patterns 223
pavlova 52–3
peach Melba 53
pears, harvesting 209
Pedley, Ethel 321
Peel, Mrs C.S. 15
Penrose Annual 183
penicillin and antibiotics
  248, 249
peppermint poultice 234
perfume marks 135
permanent waves 285
pergolas 221
period pain 243–4
perspiration stains 155

pests 30–1, 138–9, 170–1,
  199–201
pewter 100
'Philosopher in the Kitchen,
  The' 64
Physiology of Taste, The 51
pharmaceutics 240
piano keys 136
pianolas 327, 338
pianos 104
picket fences 219
pickled onions 68–9
pickles and preserves 68–9
picnics 333–4
picture backing, replacing 83
picture frames 83
picture hooks in plaster walls
  128
picture rails 82–3
pictures 82–3
pimples and acne 270
pine, raw 103
pipes, water 123
plain cake 61
planes (woodwork) 119
plant propagation 192–3
plant repotting 217
plaster walls and ceilings
  128–9
plastic, reducing use of 28
plates and dishes, cleaning 21
plates and plaques 83
playing cards 316–17
playing card tablecloth,
  making 341
pliers 118
Pliny 46
plumbing 122–3
plush, dry-cleaning 169
pneumonia 248
pockets, repairing 176
Poe, Edgar Allan 129
poise 294
poisoning 261
polished wooden furniture
  102–3
polishing cloths from socks
  178
pomanders 93
pompoms, making 318
ponds 225
pork 41, 43
porridge 63
postcards 348
postman's knock 326–7
posture 294–5
potatoes, jacket 67
potato starch 159
potato starch glue 131
potpourri 93
pot roast 45
pots and pans, cleaning 22
Potts, Mrs 164
poultices 234
  and compresses 235, 236
poultry 204
powder compacts (make-up)
  273

power tools 119
pressed flowers and leaves 332
pressure sores, preventing 255
prickly heat 259
progressive games 340–1
puerperal fever 249
Punch and Judy 298
punch (drink) 73
putty 142
pyrethrum 31
pyrethrum spray, making 138

Q

quassia spray 199
quilts 180–1
quince jelly 69

R

radio 350–1
  sound effects, making 351
raindrop spots, removing 169
rainy day activities 308–13
raspberry fool 70
raspberry leaf tea 238
reblocking hats 184
recipes, using 38–9, 264
recycling 28–9
  curtains and linen 178–9
  knitting wool 177
red (colour) 90
Red Funnel, The 354
red hair 281
refrigerators 24–5
relaxation techniques 241
  and exercise 264
repointing (brickwork) 145
repotting plants 217
rice, ground, as cleaner 169
rice pudding, old-fashioned 63
rice starch 159
rice starch glue 131
Richardson, Henry Handel 229
rich moisturiser 268
ringer (marbles) 304
rinses, hair 281
rinsing 158
Riva-Rocci, Scipione 249
Robinson, William 202
rock gardens 210
rock pools 345
rock the cradle 304
rodents 139
rolling pins 19, 63
roofs 117, 146
Rooseveldt, Franklin D. 350
Root, Waverley 64
rose hat trim 185
rosellas and parrots 215
rosemary and rose shampoo 280
roses 197
rose-water and witch hazel toner 268
Röntgen, Wilhelm 248, 249

rouge 271, 272
round games 341
rubber floors 88
rubber gloves 20
rugs, floor 89, 127
  curling, to correct 127
rusty iron and steel 137
rusty knives 17

S

sachets, fragrant 171
Sachse, Bert 52
sack race 352
Sackville-West, Vita 202
safety
  fires 35, 141
  kitchen 34–5
  with sharp objects 34–5
salmon mousse 50
salt
  as cleaner 169
  as condiment 46-47
  for fixing dyes 151
sand building 344–5
sarsaparilla 241
sash windows, repairing 142
saucepans, burnt 18, 22
saunas 233
sausage rolls 61
sausages, Oxford 44
saws 118
Sayers, Dorothy L. 29
scalds and burns 34, 260
scalp massage 292–3
scavenger hunt 326
Scientific American, The 122
Scientific Management in the Home 39
scorch marks 163
Scotch broth 66–7
Scott, Phil 351
Scrabble 336
scrambled eggs 56
scratches
  on glass 101, 137
  on wood 134
screen frame mending 144
screwdriver 118
screws 118
  removing 133–4
sculptures, sand 344–5
sea bathing 233
seed beds, making 195
seeds 192
  propagation 194–6
Semmelweis, Ignaz 249
semolina pudding 251
Serve it Forth 67
setting lotions 282
setting the table 40
sewing 152–3
  alterations 175–9
Seymour, John 63
shadehouses 205–6
shadow tag 300
Shakespeare, William 254
shampoos and conditioners 279–81

sheds, garden 190
sheet changing for invalids 254
shell collecting 345
shelving, temporary 23
shepherd's pie 42, 43–4
Shibasabura Kitasato 249
shingle roofs 146
shirts, folding 162
shock 260
shoes 182–3
shopping 39–40
short pastry 61
shoulder exercise 290
showers 122
  cleaning 105
  cold 233
shows and circuses 298
sieves 15
silhouettes 310
silk 150
  ironing 163
  washing 157
silver 100–1
  cutlery 22
silverfish 171
Simple Household Remedies 244
Simpson, James Young 248
Singer, Isaac Merrit 176
singing and dancing 342
sinks 122
sinusitis 244
Sissinghurst 202
sitting 294–5
sitz baths 232
sketching 332
skin care 266–71
skin problems 270
skipping 304
skirting boards 141
skittles 313
sleep 230–1
sleep-outs 113
sleeves 176
slippery elm 238
smallpox 248, 249
snail defender 200
snake bite 261
snap 316
soap 156
soap powder 164
soap substitutes 290
soft covers (furniture) 103–4
soft soap 156
soils 190
solid fats, measuring 27
'Solitude' 277
solvents 154
Sons and Lovers 44
sore throat 247soufflé collar 57
soufflés 57
sound effects, creating 350–1
soup 66–7
Spanish omelette 56
spas 232
sphygmomanometer 249
spice rack, making 47

spices and herbs 46–7
sports 298–9
Spring, Howard 62, 103
spring cleaning 109–11
spring tonics 241
square ball 302
stained glass 142
staining floorboards 89, 127
stain removal 154–5
stains
  furniture 135
  knives 17
stair carpets 127
stairs, squeaky 127
standing 295
star anise 46
starch glue 131
starching 159
starch spray 199
static electricity 322
statues (game) 300
Steadfast Tin Soldier, The 335
steam baths 233
steaming, facial 270
steam inhalation 244, 246
steel wool recycling 28
stencils, making 85
stepping stones race 352
steps, garden 223
Stevenson, Robert Louis 305, 332
St John's wort 240
stone fruit trees 207
storage
  clothes 170–1
  dairy products 54, 55
  eggs 54
  fish 48
  kitchen 12, 23
  meat 41
  tools 120–1
story telling 335
stoves 24–5
Stowe, Harriet E. Beecher 32
strawberries 208
straw hats 184
streamers, making 359
Stuart, Lurline 349
stucco 147
styling hair 282
suede, restoring 168
suede reviver 183
summerhouses 221
sunbathing 229, 345
sunburn 245
sundials 224
sunshine for bleaching 160
'Surf and Turf' 51
surgical gloves 249
swaddling 258
sweating 232, 246–7
Swift, Jonathan 51
switch (game) 317
synthetic fibres 150

T

table napkins from tablecloths 178

tables, repairing 132–3
tableware see china
talcum 255
tapestries 83
tapestry upholstery 104
taps, repacking 123
tarot cards 343
'Task, The' 205
tea 71, 73
tea leaf fortune telling 343
teapots and coffee pots 15, 22
tears, L-shaped 152
tea stains 155
tea towels 15
   softening 151
teeth cleaning 277–8
teething 259
teetotum 336
telegrams (game) 309
telephones 348, 349
   tin can 319
terrariums 218
tetanus 249
theatre 298
thermos flasks see vacuum
   flasks
These Lovers Fled Away 103
Thornbirds, The 77
threads, pulled 152–3
three-legged race 352
thumb sucking 259
tidiness 106
tie-dyeing 174
tiled floors 89
tiled roofs 146
tiles
   bathroom 105
   fireplace 140
tin cans, recycling 28
tin can telephone 319
tinctures, making 243
tinware 22
tipped you last (game) 352
tiredness 245
toastwater 251
toilets, repairing 122
tomato sauce, Italian 69
toners and astringents (skin)
   267–8, 270
tools 118–19
   care of 118
   garden 190
   storage 118, 120–1
tortoise race 347
tournament (game) 300
Toussaint-Samat, Maguelonne
   64
toy boats 302
toys and books 299
tracing 310
track signs (bushwalking) 331
tradespeople 116–17
train travel 353
traveller's alphabet (game)
   341
travelling 353–4
travel sickness 245
tray drawer, making 23

treacle tart 61
trees and bushes 197, 207
trellises 219
trenching 191
tricks 322–4
tuberculosis 229, 230, 248,
   249
tucks (sewing) 175
tug-o'-war 300
tumblers, washing 21
tuna mornay 50
turkey 43
turpentine 108
Twain, Mark 320
Twentieth Century Cooking and
   Home Decoration 163
twenty questions 341
twenty ways of travelling
   (game) 313
twist (game) 317
tying the knot trick 323
typhoid 248

U

Unk White's Boat Book 303
upholstery 103–4
   mending 135
   renewing 136
urine stains 89, 155
urns, garden 225

V

vaccines 249
vacuum cleaners and carpet
   sweepers 107
vacuum flasks 334
vacuuming and dusting
   108–9
Vanderbilt, Harold S. 342
vanilla soufflé 57
varicose veins 287
varnish 77, 78
Vaughan, Les 200
Vegemite 53
vegetable gardens 32, 212
vegetable pie 67
vegetables 66–7
   harvesting 209
velvet 104
   dry-cleaning 169
velvet collars, rejuvenating
   169
velvet curtains 167
velvet hats 185
veneer
   gluing 130
   repairing 135
ventilation
   kitchen 13
   sick-room 252
veranda plants 218
verandas 112–13
verbal tricks 324
Victoria, Queen of Great
   Britain 284
vinegar
   bath 291
   for fixing dyes 151

white 108
white wine 151
vinyl floors
   cleaning 88–9
   laying 127
   patching 127
vinyl upholstery 104
violet (colour) 90
violets, native Australian 203
visiting invalids 255
Vogue's Book of Beauty 265
voice 295
vomit stains 89
Votey, E.S. 338

W

'waggas' 180
Walker, Fred 53
walking 295, 330–2
Walking Tours 332
wall hangings 82–3
wall hooks 23
wallaby, cooking 65
Walling, Edna 189, 202–3
wallpaper
   cleaning 110
   repairing 128–9
wallpapering 79–81
walls
   cleaning 110
   plaster 128–9
Walter Raleigh race 352
Walton, Isaak 48
War of the Worlds, The 351
Warner, Charles Dudley 193
warped boards, straightening
   133
warts 245
wash dolly 164
washing (laundry) 150–1,
   156–61, 164–5
   curtains 166–7
   sorting 151
   stain removal 154–5
washing machines 164–5
washing soap and powder
   164
washing up 20–2
water 232–3
   drinking 233
   plants 198
   washing 156
   washing up 20
watering
   greenhouses 205–6
   indoor plants 216
water leaks, window 142
water lilies, native Australian
   203
water marks on furniture 135
water pipes, repairing 123
waterproof cement (glue) 131
waterproofing
   bricks 145
   footwear 182
water softeners 156
water system 116
wax stains 155

wedding invitations 348
weeds 201
weekly cleaning 108–9, 110
weighing beam 26
Welles, Orson 351
Welsh rarebit 38
what am I? (game) 340
When Grandma Was Just a Girl
   170
white (colour) 90
whitebait fritters 53
white bread 59
whitening 159
white oil 199
whitewashing 79
Wilcox, Ella Wheeler 277
windmill, making a paper
   311
Wind in the Willows,
   The 320
window boxes 144, 218
windows
   cleaning 95, 96
   decorating 94–6
   draught-proofing 141
   repairing 142–4
wind sock 306
wine glasses, washing 21
wine stains 89, 155
wireless 350–1
wire netting fences 219
Within the Home 12
wood fires (for cooking) 24
wood, gluing 130
wooden floors 126–7
   cleaning 88
   staining 89
wooden furniture 102–3
   restoring 132–6
wooden kitchenware,
   care of 19
wooden spoons 19
woodwork, cleaning 77
wool 150
   recycling for knitting 177
woollens
   dry-cleaning 169
   ironing 163
   washing 157
   whitening 159
worms 28
Worths Australian Fashion
   Journal 264
wreath, Christmas 358
wrens 215
wrinkles 268–9
wrought iron fences 219
Wuthering Heights 144

X, Y

X-ray 248, 249
yarrow 240
Yates, Frank 135
Yates, Raymond F. 136
150 Years of Cookery and
   Household Management 39
yellow (colour) 90
Yorkshire pudding 61

Acknowledgments

The photographs reproduced in *Good Old Days, Good Old Ways* came from the sources listed below.
Abbreviations: APL= Australian Picture Library; Bridgeman = Bridgeman Art Library, London/NewYork; MEPL = Mary Evans Picture Library; PLA = The Photographic Library of Australia. Positions on page: *l* = left; *r* = right; *c* = centre; *t* = top; *b* = bottom.

Cover background Corbis-Bettmann/APL. 10 *l* Hulton-Getty/PLA. 12 *t* AKG London. 13 The Advertising Archives. 14 *r* AKG London & MEPL. 15 *tl* Archive Photos/APL; *tr* MEPL; *bl* Corbis-Bettmann/APL. 16 Robin Smith/PLA. 18 *both* MEPL. 19 *tl* Robin Smith/PLA; *tr* Hulton-Getty/PLA; *b* Powerhouse Museum, Sydney. 20 *t* MEPL; *bl* AKG London. 21 *t* MEPL; *b* Hulton-Getty/PLA. 22 *b* MEPL. 23 *br* MEPL. 24 *tl & br* The Advertising Archives; *tr* Hulton-Getty/PLA; *bl* MEPL. 25 *tl* John Carnemolla/APL; *tr* Powerhouse Museum, Sydney; *b* Wood River Gallery/PLA. 26 *b* The Advertising Archives. 28 *t both* Hulton-Getty/PLA; *tr background* Courtesy of Arthur Baker; *b* Corbis-Bettmann/APL. 29 *b* Hulton-Getty/PLA. 30 *tl* Archive Photos/APL; *tr* The Advertising Archives; *b* Culver Pictures. 31 *tl & b* Corbis-Bettmann/APL; *tr* MEPL. 32 *tr* Archive Photos/APL. 33 *t* MEPL. 34 MEPL. 37 *tr* Corbis-Bettmann/APL. 38 *t* The Advertising Archives; *br* MEPL. 41 *t* Culver Pictures; *b* The Advertising Archives. 43 *t* The Advertising Archives; *c* Culver Pictures. 44 Mitchell Library/State Library of New South Wales. 45 *both* MEPL. 46 *cl* AKG London; *cr* Colin Hawkins/PLA. 47 *cr & b* Powerhouse Museum, Sydney. 48 *b* Culver Pictures. 50 *t* Corbis-Bettmann/APL; *b* Mitchell Library/State Library of New South Wales. 51 *t* Archive Photos/APL; *b* Corbis-Bettmann/APL. 52 *b* Australian Archives of the Dance. 53 *tl & bl* Peter Luck Productions; *br* Performing Arts Museum, Victoria. 54 Robin Smith/PLA. 55 *t* The Advertising Archives. 56 *both* Robin Smith/PLA. 57 *t* Culver Pictures. 58 *b* Powerhouse Museum, Sydney. 59 Corbis-Bettmann/APL. 60 *b* Corbis-Bettmann/APL. 61 *b* Powerhouse Museum, Sydney. 62 *t* AKG London; *c* The Advertising Archives. 63 *b* Hulton-Getty/PLA; *br* Powerhouse Museum, Sydney. 65 *t* Mitchell Library/State Library of New South Wales; *c* Queensland Museum; *b* Private Collection/Bridgeman, London/NY. 66 *t* Hulton-Getty/PLA; *b* Culver Pictures. 67 *b* Robin Smith/PLA. 68 *t* Corbis-Bettmann/APL. 70 *t* The Advertising Archives. 71 *tl* Robin Smith/PLA; *tr* Hulton-Getty/PLA; *b* AKG London. 72 *t & bl* The Advertising Archives; *br* Archive Photos/Welgos/APL. 73 *b* The Advertising Archives. 74 *tl* Culver Pictures. 76 *t* The Advertising Archives; *b* Archive Photos/APL. 78 MEPL. 80 Hulton-Getty/PLA. 82 *t* MEPL. 83 *tl both* Guy Marche/ APL. 84 *tl* Water-lily lamp, 1902, by Louis Majorelle (1859-1926), Musée d'Orsay, Paris/Giraudon/Bridgeman; *tr* Tiffany Studios 'Dragonfly' table lamp, Bonhams, London/Bridgeman; *cl* Hulton-Getty/PLA; *bl* Chair designed for the White Dining Room, Ingram Street Tearooms by Charles Rennie Mackintosh (1868-1928)/ The Fine Art Society, London/Bridgeman. 84-85 Isokon Long Chair, designed for the Isokon Furniture Company by Marcel Breuer (1902-81) 1935-6/Private Collection/Bonhams, London/Bridgeman. 85 *tl* Clarice Cliff 'Bizarre' series ceramics, Newport Pottery/Private Collection/ Bridgeman; *tr* Victoria & Albert Museum, London/Bridgeman. 86 *tl* Culver Pictures; *b* The Advertising Archives. 87 *t* Archive Photos/APL. 88 The Advertising Archives. 89 *bl* Archive Photos/APL. 91 *b* MEPL. 92 *b* MEPL. 93 *t* Angus McNeil Collection/APL. 94 *t* Culver Pictures. 95 Corbis-Bettmann/APL. 96 *t* Archive Photos/APL. 97 *t* MEPL. 98 *tl* MEPL; *bl* Mitchell Library/State Library of New South Wales; *br* Victoria & Albert Museum/E.T. Archive. 99 *tl* August Keepsake by Anna Airy (1882-1964)/Bonhams, London/Bridgeman; *tr & bl* MEPL. 100 *b* MEPL. 102 *t* AKG London; *b* The Advertising Archives. 103 *t* AKG London; *b* Culver Pictures. 104 *b* The Advertising Archives. 105 *t* Corbis-Bettmann/APL; *c* Culver Pictures; *b* Archive Photos/APL. 106 *t* The Advertising Archives. 107 *t* Robin Smith/PLA; *b* The Advertising Archives. 108 *b* Culver Pictures. 109 *t* The Advertising

Archives. 110 *b* MEPL. 112 *t* Robin Smith/PLA; *c & b* Culver Pictures. 116 *t* The Advertising Archives; *b* MEPL. 117 *t* MEPL; *b* Corbis-Bettmann/APL. 118 *lt* MEPL; *lc* Corbis-Bettmann/APL; *all others* Culver Pictures. 119 *t* Robin Smith/PLA; *b* The Advertising Archives. 120 *t* The Advertising Archives. 123 *t* MEPL; *b* The Advertising Archives. 124 *t* MEPL; *b* Robin Smith/PLA. 125 *t* Robin Smith/PLA. 126 *b* Culver Pictures. 128 *b* AKG London. 129 *all* MEPL. 130 *t* Culver Pictures. 132 The Advertising Archives. 134 *b* The Advertising Archives. 135 *t* AKG London. 136 *t* Culver Pictures. 137 *b* Oliver Strewe/APL. 138 *tl* Corbis-Bettmann/APL; *cr* AKG London; *br* MEPL. 139 *t* Arthur Rackham Collection/MEPL; *bl* MEPL; *br* Corbis-Bettmann/APL. 140 *tl & b* MEPL; *tr* The Advertising Archives. 141 *t* Jean-Loup Charmet/Science Photo Library/PLA; *bl* Robin Smith/PLA. 142 *t* Douglass Baglin/APL; *b* Hulton-Getty/PLA. 144 *t* Hulton-Getty/PLA. 145 *t* The Advertising Archives. 147 *t* Archive Photos/APL; *b* Corbis-Bettmann/APL. 150 *t* The Advertising Archives; *bl* MEPL; *br* Corbis-Bettmann/APL. 151 *t* Corbis-Bettmann/APL; *c* Robin Smith/PLA; *b* The Advertising Archives. 153 *b* Robin Smith/PLA. 154 The Advertising Archives. 155 *b* The Advertising Archives. 156 *tl* Corbis-Bettmann/APL; *cr* Powerhouse Museum, Sydney; *b* Robin Smith/PLA. 157 *t* Corbis-Bettmann/APL. 158 *b* Powerhouse Museum, Sydney. 159 *b* Corbis-Bettmann/APL. 160 *tl* Courtesy of Hills Industries; *tr* Powerhouse Museum, Sydney; *b* Powerhouse Museum, Sydney. 161 *t* Courtesy of Hills Industries; *b* Powerhouse Museum, Sydney. 162 *bl* MEPL. 163 Powerhouse Museum, Sydney. 164 *cl* MEPL; *cr* Culver Pictures; *bl* The Advertising Archives; *br* Powerhouse Museum, Sydney. 165 *l & rb* Corbis-Bettmann/APL; *rt* AKG London. 166 Culver Pictures. 169 Corbis-Bettmann/APL. 170 *t* AKG London. 171 *t* Corbis-Bettmann/APL; *b* Zefa/APL. 172 *both* MEPL. 174 *b* MEPL. 175 *t* The Advertising Archives. 176 *t* Corbis-Bettmann/APL. 177 *b* Angus McNeil Collection/APL. 179 Noeline Kelly/APL. 180 *tl* E.T. Archive; *bl* Hulton-Getty/PLA; *br/t* Crazy patchwork quilt, c.1875/ Smithsonian Institution/Bridgeman; *br/b* Powerhouse Museum, Sydney. 180-81 Nearly Done, published 1898 (aquatint) by Walter Dendy Sadler (1854-1923) (after)/Stapleton Collection/Bridgeman. 181 *t* E.T. Archive; *br* American quilt, 19th century (cotton patchwork)/Private Collection/ Bridgeman. 182 Corbis-Bettmann/APL. 183 *t* Corbis-Bettmann/APL; *b* MEPL. 184 *bl* MEPL. 187 *tr* Corbis-Bettmann/APL. 188 *t* AKG London; *b* MEPL. 189 *t* Corbis-Bettmann/APL. 190 *all* AKG London. 191 *b* AKG London. 192 *t* AKG London; *b* Archive Photos/APL. 194 *t* MEPL; *b* The Advertising Archives. 196 *tl* MEPL; *cr* Archive Photos/ APL. 197 *l* MEPL; *r* Culver Pictures. 198 *both* MEPL. 199 *br* Culver Pictures; *all others* MEPL. 200 *b* Culver Pictures. 201 *tr* Culver Pictures; *cl* MEPL; *b* Archive Photos/APL. 202 *tl & bl* MEPL; *all others* Trisha Dixon. 203 *t both* Trisha Dixon. 204 *t* MEPL. 205 *t* MEPL. 207 *t* MEPL; *b* Archive Photos/APL. 208 *t* Archive Photos/APL; *all others* MEPL. 209 MEPL. 210 *b* MEPL. 211 *b* MEPL. 212 *t* MEPL; *b* Archive Photos/ APL. 213 *t* Archive Photos/APL; *bl* MEPL; *br* AKG London. 214 *tr* MEPL; *br* Mitchell Library/State Library of New South Wales. 215 *t & bl* Mitchell Library/State Library of New South Wales. 216 *t* MEPL. 218 *bl* The Advertising Archives; *br* Archive Photos/APL. 219 *b* MEPL. 220 *b* MEPL. 222 *t* Archive Photos/APL; *bl* The Advertising Archives. 224 *tr & b* The Advertising Archives. 225 *bl* MEPL. 228 *t* MEPL; *b* Index Stock/PLA. 229 *l* AKG London; *r* MEPL. 231 *t & bl* MEPL; *br* Culver Pictures. 232 *t* The Advertising Archives. 233 *t* AKG London; *c* MEPL. 234 *tl* Archive Photos/APL; *b* Corbis-Bettmann/APL. 235 *b* Culver Pictures. 236 *tl* AKG London; *b* MEPL. 237 The Advertising Archives. 239 *t* MEPL; *b* Index Stock/George Marks/PLA. 240 *tr* Archive Photos/ APL; *cl* Hulton-Getty/PLA; *b both* MEPL. 241 *t both* MEPL; *bl* Wood River Gallery/PLA. 242 *tl* MEPL; *tr & b* The Advertising Archives. 244 *b* Index Stock/George Marks/PLA. 245 *t* Hulton-Getty/PLA; *b* MEPL. 246 *t* Corbis-Bettmann/APL; *b* The Advertising Archives. 247 *t* AKG London. 248 *l* Corbis-Bettmann/APL; *c* MEPL. *r both* Science Photo Library/PLA. 249 *t* MEPL; *c* AKG London; *b* Culver Pictures. 250 MEPL. 251 *t* MEPL. 252 *tl* Archive Photos/APL; *tr* MEPL. 255 *t* The

Acknowledgments

Advertising Archives; *b* Culver Pictures. 256 *b* Culver Pictures.
257 *tl* & *b* Archive Photos/APL; *tr* Culver Pictures. 259 *b* Culver Pictures.
260 *tl* & *b* Corbis-Bettmann/APL; *tr* Hulton-Getty/PLA. 261 *t* Corbis-
Bettmann/APL. 262 *bl* MEPL. 264 *t* The Advertising Archives;
bl Wood River Gallery/PLA; *br* Corbis-Bettmann/APL. 265 *tr* MEPL.
266 *t* MEPL; *b* Archive Photos/APL. 268 *t* Culver Pictures; *b* The
Advertising Archives. 269 *t* Archive Photos/APL; *b* Hulton-Getty/PLA.
270 *tl* Culver Pictures. 271 Index Stock/George Marks/PLA. 272 *tl* & *bl*
The Advertising Archives; *tr* MEPL; *br* Archive Photos/APL. 273 *tl* Index
Stock/PLA; *tc* Hulton-Getty/PLA; *tr* Culver Pictures; *b* MEPL. 275 *tl*
Mitchell Library/State Library of New South Wales; *tr* Hulton-Getty/
PLA. 277 *b* MEPL. 278 *t* The Advertising Archives; *b* Archive Photos/
APL. 279 *t* MEPL. 280 *b* The Advertising Archives. 281 *t* The
Advertising Archives; *b* Index Stock/George Marks/PLA. 282 *tl* MEPL;
cr The Advertising Archives; *b* Archive Photos/APL. 283 Culver Pictures.
284 *t both* MEPL; *c* Hulton-Getty/PLA. 285 *tl* Corbis-Bettman/APL;
tr Culver Pictures; *b both* Hulton-Getty/PLA. 286 *bl* MEPL; *br* Archive
Photos/APL. 288 *tl* MEPL. 289 *t* Culver Pictures; *b* Archive Photos/APL.
291 *t* MEPL; *b* Culver Pictures. 292 *t* Archive Photos/APL; *b* Culver
Pictures. 294 *t both* MEPL; *b* Hulton-Getty/PLA. 295 *b* AKG London.
296 *bl* Brian Shuel/ Collections. 298 *t* MEPL; *bl* Wood River Gallery/
PLA; *br* Culver Pictures. 299 *tl* Hulton-Getty/PLA; *tr* AKG London;
bl Michael Teller/ AKG London; *br* E.T. Archive. 300 Brian Shuel/
Collections. 301 *b* Brian Shuel/Collections. 302 *t* Culver Pictures;
bl Bradman Collection/ State Library of South Australia, Adelaide. 304 *bl*
The Advertising Archives; *br* Corbis-Bettmann/APL. 305 *t* Culver
Pictures. 306 *tl* & *cl* Corbis-Bettmann/APL; *cr* MEPL. 310 *b* MEPL. 311 *t*
Hulton-Getty/PLA. 312 The Advertising Archives. 316 *b* MEPL.
317 *b* MEPL. 319 *b* Corbis-Westlight/APL. 320 *tr* Corbis-Bettmann/
APL; *cl both* Arthur Rackham Collection. 321 *t* Suzie Ireland/APL. 322 *b*
MEPL. 323 *t both* Harry Price Collection, University of London/MEPL.
324 The Advertising Archives. 326 *t* MEPL; *b* Culver Pictures. 327 *t*
MEPL; *b* Culver Pictures. 330 *tl* & *b* Corbis-Bettmann/APL; *tr* MEPL.
334 *t* Corbis-Bettmann/APL. 335 *t* Arthur Rackham Collection/MEPL.
336 *cr* Watercolour c.1845 by Joseph Jenner Merrett (1816-54)/National
Library of Australia, Canberra/ Bridgeman; *br* Musée Alesia, Alise-Sainte-
Reine/Giraudon/Bridgeman. 337 *b* Hulton-Getty/PLA. 338 *t* MEPL;
b Hulton-Getty/PLA. 340 *t* Hulton-Getty/PLA; *b* Corbis-Bettmann/APL.
342 *t* Archive Photos/APL. 343 *all* MEPL. 344 *tr* & *br* MEPL; *bl* Wood
River Gallery/PLA. 345 *bl* MEPL. 346 The Advertising Archives. 347 *all*
Culver Pictures. 348 *tl* MEPL; *tr* John Carnemolla/APL. 349 *t* Zefa/APL.
350 *tl* Culver Pictures; *tr* Corbis-Bettmann/APL; *bl* Archive Photos/APL;
br AKG London. 351 *tl* Archive Photos/APL. 351 *tr* & *b* Culver Pictures;
c MEPL. 352 Culver Pictures. 353 *t* AKG London; *b* Archive Photos/
APL. 354 *t* Hulton-Getty/PLA; *b* MEPL. 355 *tr* Hulton-Getty/ PLA.
358 *t* Culver Pictures; *b both* MEPL. 359 *t* Corbis-Bettmann/APL.

Sources of quotations appearing in the text are listed below. The
publishers have made every effort to trace the copyright holders of text
quoted in this book. Any person or organisation we have failed to reach is
invited to contact the Editorial Director at Reader's Digest General
Books, 26 Waterloo Street, Surry Hills, NSW 2010.

12 *Within The Home* (1924); *Letters to the Rev. J. Newton* William Cowper
(1731-1800). 13 *Chandeliers and Billy Tea* Peter Cuffley, Five Mile Press,
Hawthorn (1984). 16 Ross Campbell in *The Australian Women's Weekly*
(1959). 21 *Good Housekeeping* (1913). 29 *Busman's Honeymoon* Dorothy L.
Sayers, Gollancz (1937). 30 *Household Pests and Household Remedies* W.R.
Boelter (1909). 34 *Enquire Within* (1880). 39 *150 Years of Cookery and
Household Management* Graham Nown (1986). 40 'The Dinner', A.D.
Hope Carcanet . 43 *How to Cook a Wolf* M.F.K. Fisher (1943). 51 *The
Physiology of Taste* Brillat-Savarin (1755-1826). 44 *Sons and Lovers* D.H.
Lawrence, Penguin, Harmonsworth (1913). 57 *Adam Bede* George Eliot
(1859). 59 *Food* Waverley Root (1980). 61 *84 Charing Cross Road* Helene
Hanff, The Viking Press, New York (1970). 62 *My Son, My Son* Howard
Spring, Collins, London (1938). 63 *Forgotten Household Crafts* John
Seymour, Dorling Kindersley (1987). 67 *Serve it Forth* M.F.K. Fisher
(1941). 68 *Food* Waverley Root (1980). 71 *Mrs Beeton's Book of Cookery and
Household Management* Ward Lock (1986). 73 'Ode to a Nightingale', John
Keats (1795-1821). 77 *The Thorn Birds* Colleen McCullough (1977). 79
The Book of Good Housekeeping (1944). 81 *Home and Garden Beautiful*
(1913). 86 *The Australian Home Beautiful* (1926). 90 *Home and Garden
Lovers* Girl's Friendly Society (1940). 97 'In Flanders Fields', John McCrae
(1872-1918). 103 *These Lovers Fled Away* Howard Spring (1955). 104 *The
Australian Home Beautiful* (1928). 109 *Health* (1932). 110 *The Household
Guide or Domestic Cyclopedia* (c. 1900). 112 *Home and Garden Beautiful*
(1913). 113 *Home and Garden Beautiful* (1913). 117 *Colonial Ballads* Hugh
Anderson (1962). 121 *Complete Home Encyclopedia* Dorothy Pace (1947).
126 'A Termite Tale', Ogden Nash (c.1930). 128 'A Mouse Caught in a
Cage', *Coles Childland* (1902). 129 'Ligera', Edgar Allan Poe (1809-1849).
130 *The Householder's Complete Handbook* Hawthorne Daniel (1936). 135
How to Repair Furniture Frank Yates (1950). 136 *New Furniture from Old*
Raymond F. Yates (1951). 142 *The Harp in the South* Ruth Park (1948).
144 *Wuthering Heights* Emily Brontë (1847). 145 *Flowers of Delight*
Leonard de Vries (1765-1830). 147 'Mending wall', Robert Frost
(1874–1963). 152 *Gone with the Wind* Margaret Mitchell, Avon Books,
USA (1936). 155 *Mrs Beeton's Book of Cookery and Household Management*
(1861). 157 *The Countrywoman in New South Wales* (1937). 159 *Cider with
Rosie* Laurie Lee (1959). 160 *A Fence around the Cuckoo* Ruth Park (1992).

166 *How We Lived Then: A history of everyday life during the Second World
War* Norman Longmate, Hutchinson & Co. (1971). 168 *Helen's Weekly*
(1927). 170 *When Grandma Was Just a Girl* Martin McAdoo (1983). 173
*My Mother's Ways: Being a book of household hints from the early 1900s in
Australia* Mary Murray, Mallon Publishing Pty Ltd (1996). 177 *The Home
Front Family Album: remembering Australia 1939-45* Weldon (1991). 178
Bombers and Mash: The Domestic Front 1939–45 Virago Ltd (1980). 183
Little Women Louisa M. Alcott (1868). 185 *Australian Women's Weekly*
(1933). 189 *Gardens in Australia* Edna Walling, Oxford University Press
(1944). 193 *My Summer in a Garden* Charles Dudley Warner (1870). 199
Home and Garden Beautiful (1913). 201 *Brett's Gardening Guide* (1919).
205 'The Task', William Cowper (1731-1800). 206 *The Australian Garden
Fair* (1923). 212 *The Garden and the Home* (1923). 218 *The Happifying
Gardening Hobby* E.W. Cole (1918). 221 'Kubla Khan', Samuel Taylor
Coleridge (1722-1834). 228 *Nutrition and Health* (1943). 229 *The Fortunes
of Richard Mahony* Henry Handel Richardson (1930). 230 *Home and
Health* (1909). 232 *The Right Way With Baby* (1914). 239 *Nutrition and
Health* (1943). 244 *Simple Household Recipes* (1899). 250 *The Household
Manual* (1899). 255 *Dr Chase's Third Last and Complete Recipe Book and
Household Physician* (1887). 261 *Dr Chase's Recipes. or Information for
Everyone* (1866). 264 *Worths Australian Fashion Journal* (1899). 265 *Vogue's
Book of Beauty* (1933). 268 *My Lady's Journal* (1906). 277 'Solitude', Ella
Wheeler Wilcox (1850-1919). 278 *Jane Eyre* Charlotte Brontë (1847).
281 *Lucasta* Richard Lovelace (1618-1658). 283 *A New System of Domestic
Cookery Formed Upon the Principles of Economy* (1837). 289 *The Mill on the
Floss* George Eliot (1860). 290 *How to be Beautiful* T. Dean (1890). 293 *Be
Beautiful* J. Cleland, The Australian Woman's Weekly Home Library
(1947). 298 *Every Little Boy's Book* (c.1870). 300 *The Girl's Own Book*
(1848). 302 'Where the Boats Go', *A Child's Garden of Verses* Robert Louis
Stevenson (1885). 304 *Elsie Piddock Skips in Her Sleep* Eleanor Farjeon
(1937). 308 *The Happy Housewife* H. Simpson (1934), reproduced by
permission of Hodder and Stoughton Limited. 311 *The New Idea* (1905).
313 *The Happy Housewife* H. Simpson (1934), reproduced by permission of
Hodder and Stoughton Limited. 314 *The New Idea* (1905). 316 *Alice's
Adventures in Wonderland* Lewis Carroll (1865); *The Mill on the Floss*
George Eliot (1860). 318 *On Sundays We Wore White* Eileen Elias (1978).
324 *Magical Mysteries* (c.1925). 332 *Walking Tours* Robert Louis Stevenson
(1876). 335 *Bread & Dripping Days: An Australian Growing up in the 20s*
Kathleen McArthur, Kangaroo Press (1981). 338 *The Book of Good
Housekeeping* (1944). 340 *In Vogue: 75 Years of Style* Georgina Howell,
Random Century (1991). 347 *The Letters of Rachel Henning* (1853-1882).
348 *Clancy of the Overflow* A.B. 'Banjo' Paterson (1864–1941)